OTHER NATURE BOOKS BY THE SAME AUTHOR:

**Birding Northern California**
1999, Falcon Press

**Discovering Yolo County Wildlife**
1996, Yolo Audubon Society and Yolo Basin Foundation

# Southern Oregon's Bird Life

## Including: Klamath Basin, Rogue River Valley, Southern Cascades, and Siskiyou Range

by John Kemper

**Drawings and Photographs by the Author**

Outdoor Press
Medford, Oregon

## ACKNOWLEDGMENTS

I would like to express my thanks to John Beckstrand, Thomas Cottingham, Ray Ekstrom, David Menke, Kit Novick, Kevin Spencer, and Steven Summers for the assistance they gave me in preparing the material in this book. I would also like to express gratitude for Don Roberson's website, from which I was able to obtain useful information on topics such as gulls and titmice. Dennis Vroman was also very helpful, regarding certain birds in the Rogue Valley.

Information gained from the Oregon Bird Records Committee, the Oregon Birds Forum, and the Oregon Breeding Bird Atlas was vital to the species accounts. The two publications, *Birds of Jackson County, Oregon - Distribution and Abundance*, and *A Birder's Guide to the Klamath Basin,* by Steven D. Summers, were especially important as sources of information.

My most special thanks go to the members of the Jackson County Checklist Committee, with whom I was privileged to serve, and who taught me more than they probably realize, about the birds of Jackson County. They are: Stewart Janes, Norman Barrett, Richard Cronberg, James Livaudais, Marjorie Moore, Thomas Phillips, Howard Sands, Gary Shaffer, Joseph Shelton, and Pepper Trail. Stewart Janes, especially, has been a remarkable source of information.

Even though the usefulness and correctness of the material was immeasurably enhanced by the contributions of the folks above, I suspect that some errors may still remain, and for those the blame is all mine.

Copyright 2002 by John Kemper

**ISBN 0-9722509-0-5**

# CONTENTS

|  | Page |
|---|---|
| **Acknowledgments** | *ii* |
| 1. **What This book Is All About** | 1 |
| 2. **Birding** | 5 |
| 3. **The Lay of the Land** | 16 |
| 4. **Places To Go Birding** | 21 |
| 5. **How To Use This Book** | 39 |
| 6. **Species Accounts** | 45 |
| **Appendix A:** Definitions, Names, and Abbreviations | 307 |
| **Appendix B:** Organizations | 314 |
| **Appendix C:** References | 316 |
| **Index** | 322 |

# MAPS

| | |
|---|---|
| **Josephine County, Oregon** | 23 |
| **Jackson County, Oregon** (including part of Siskiyou County, California) | 27 |
| **Klamath Basin** (including the southern part of Klamath County, Oregon and parts of Siskiyou and Modoc Counties, California) | 31 |

# COLOR PLATES

| | | |
|---|---|---|
| Plates I, II | following | 42 |
| Plates III, IV | " | 90 |
| Plates V, VI | " | 138 |
| Plates VII, VIII | " | 186 |
| Plates IX, X | " | 234 |
| Plates XI, XII | " | 282 |

# Chapter 1 - WHAT THIS BOOK IS ALL ABOUT

This book is about birds and birdwatching, primarily in a Southern Oregon setting, including adjacent areas in Northern California. It covers Jackson and Josephine Counties, and the southern part of Klamath County, in Oregon. It also includes the northern part of Siskiyou County in California, and a piece of Modoc County. It is a marvelous area, full of scenic beauty, and has some of the best birding in the country.

The book emphasizes the birds themselves, and where they might be found. The major purpose is to give a *feel* for what has been called the joy of birding. In fact, it might have been called exactly that -- *The Joy of Birding* -- except the title is already taken.

A part of the "joy," of course, is the simple pleasure of being in the out of doors, and of exploring new places. Most of the birders of my acquaintance cite this as one of the major benefits of the hobby of birding. However, the birds themselves form the core of this hobby.

Birders like to be able to put names on the species they see, so identification is important. Also, birders like to know something about how birds behave, and about their natural history. I have included a fair amount of information on behavior, simply because I find such things interesting, and hope that others will, too. We live in a world where we are surrounded by birds. We are enchanted by them because of their beauty, their energy, and their competence at what they do to survive.

This is not an identification manual. There are numerous wonderful field guides on the market that do a fine job in this respect. A list of some recommended ones is given at the end of this section. However, ID tips are included in the text for certain species, especially in cases where pairs of species strongly resemble each other, as with Western and Clark's Grebes. Since this book does not provide identification information of the type that appears in field guides, I assume the reader will have a field guide at hand, and can use the pictures to see exactly what a bird looks like.

Note that some species of birds may call for much more material on the details of identification than is possible here. Shorebirds are a good example. A great book, *Shorebirds of the Pacific Northwest,* by Dennis Paulson, makes the point. Paulson's book gives everything you would ever want or need to know about the identification of shorebirds, which sometimes requires attention to many subtle details, but it requires 406 pages to carry out its job. If I tried to give similar depth to all the species included herein, my calculations say the book would be over 2000 pages long.

I have used many references in putting together this book. Among them is a marvelous series of 20 books written in the early part of the last century by Arthur Cleveland Bent, called *Life Histories of North American Birds*. The thing I love the most about Bent's books, besides the incredible store of good information in them, is his anecdotal style, as he records the experiences of himself and other field ornithologists as they watched birds. Bent not only was willing to fasten human emotions and actions on his birds (this is called "anthropomorphism," a practice that horrifies modern biologists), but he also didn't hesitate to include the personal experiences of himself and his contributors.

Modern biologists avoid anthropomorphism, and tend to confine their writings to crisp statements of fact. This is laudable science, but it isn't much fun to read. I prefer Bent, and in writing this book I have followed him as my guiding spirit. In fact, I quote him a lot, partly because he has fascinating insights to bird behavior, and because I enjoy the personal intensity he brought to his writing.

Bent, in his books, quotes a great deal from the writings of Major Charles Emil Bendire (1836 to 1897), and his writings are so enlightening and useful that I have often quoted him directly, taking the quotes from Bent's *Life Histories*. In fact, Bendire was the originator of *Life Histories of North American Birds*, which Bent later enlarged and carried to completion. Bendire was an officer in the Army, and was posted to many remote locations in the west, where he diligently pursued his ornithological work. Because so many of his writings refer to Fort Klamath, I assume that must have been one of his posts.

As did my heroes, Arthur Cleveland Bent and Major Charles Bendire, I have not hesitated to include personal experiences, because I think this helps to communicate the atmosphere of birding, and enhances the personal nature of this enchanting hobby. I also have not avoided attributing emotions to birds, if I thought it was appropriate.

In my following of Bent, there is one exception, I hope. The exception is that writers in the 19th and early 20th centuries tended to fill their descriptions with exceedingly purple prose. I have tried to avoid doing that. Sometimes purple prose is fun to read, and I have even quoted some examples. But it does get tiresome after a while.

**Oregon Breeding Bird Atlas.**

A major resource for this book is the Oregon Breeding Bird Atlas, researched in the period 1995-1999, and published in 2001. The various levels of breeding detection are "possible," "probable," and "confirmed." In broad terms, the definitions are as follows

"Possible" breeding: an adult has been seen during breeding season.

"Probable" breeding is any of the following: pair has been seen during breeding season; singing; holding territory; courtship behavior; probable nest site, but nest not seen.

"Confirmed" breeding is any of the following: nest building, except for wrens, woodpeckers, and some raptors, who often build dummy or roosting nests; distraction display; female with egg in oviduct; used nest found; recently fledged young with adult in attendance; adult carrying food; bird entering or leaving probable nest site; adult carrying fecal sac; nest with eggs; nest with young.

**Oregon Birds Forum**

This is the web site for the information being developed for a new edition of *Birds of Oregon*. This is an incredible resource for anyone interested in Oregon's birds, and has been invaluable in the preparation of this manuscript.

***Birds of Jackson County*, and *A Birder's Guide to the Klamath Basin***

These two booklets were my principal sources for the construction of the bar charts in this book. However, I have altered the charts wherever I had information that made me feel it was necessary, whether it was from information gleaned from *The Oregon Birds Forum*, the *Oregon Breeding Bird Atlas*, or from my own experiences or from the experiences of others.

**To the reader:**

The principal readers of this book, I presume, will be those who have a developing interest in birds, but feel uncertain of their skills. Even though such folks often describe themselves as "beginners," I prefer to think of them as situated at one of the most magical times in birdwatching, when everything is new and brings with it a sense of discovery.

If experienced birders want to read it, well, that's great with me. Who knows, they might even discover something they didn't know before. If so, then my day is complete.

## Some Recommended Field Guides

***Field Guide to the Birds of North America*** (Third Edition), Jon L. Dunn, Chief Consultant. National Geographic Society, Washington, DC, 1999. To me, this is the best all-round guide. However, beginners sometimes find the book to be somewhat intimidating, because many illustrations of regional subspecies are shown, and so are many sub-adult plumages. However, in the long run, it is the very inclusion of these things that makes birders come to love this book.

***The Sibley Guide to Birds,*** by David Allen Sibley. Alfred A. Knopf, NY, 2000. The publication of this book was a landmark in birding. It is huge, with 544 pages, and 6,600 illustrations painted by Sibley. It is so comprehensive in coverage of subspecies and sub-adults that it can be even more intimidating to beginners than the "National Geo" guide. Yet this comprehensiveness is what makes it so valuable. Most people consider it to be too large and heavy to carry in the field, but generally have it available in the car for reference.

***Birding in the American West,*** by Kevin J. Zimmer. Cornell University Press, Ithaca, NY, 2000. This is not a field guide in the usual sense, but provides details on the identification of some of the more difficult species. Also, it concentrates on western species, thus reducing the "eastern bias" sometimes demonstrated by other guides. Many species of birds show a certain amount of variation between east and west, and in the past some field guides have been accused of neglecting western variations. It is not the best choice for beginners, but as a person becomes more and more experienced, it becomes invaluable and without equal, in my opinion.

***Birds of North America,*** by Kenn Kaufman. Houghton Mifflin Company, NY, 2000. This is probably the best book today for beginners. Kaufman has deliberately oriented his book in that direction. It is more compact than the others, and thus is preferred by many for carrying into the field.

***A Field Guide to Western Birds*** (Third Edition), by Roger Tory Peterson. Houghton Mifflin Co., Boston, 1990. Roger Peterson's field guides have long been the gold standard for birders. Two disadvantages to his guides are (1) to cover the entire country you need two guides -- East and West, and (2) the range maps are in the back of the book, rather than on the same pages with the illustrations. Also, since Peterson's book is now the oldest (1990) of the five books listed here (a new edition of his eastern guide was published in 2002), it doesn't show many of the name changes that have occurred in recent years. Nevertheless, it is a fine book, and loved by many. After all, it is Peterson's guides, more than any other, that have lighted the way for hundreds of thousands, maybe millions, of people as they entered into birding.

# Chapter 2 - BIRDING

## BIRDING AND BIRDWATCHING

The terms **birding** and **birdwatching** have both been used to describe what we do. I tend to regard the two terms as interchangeable, although some people make distinctions. "Birdwatching" means, well, watching birds. "Birding" includes watching birds, but it also includes keeping lists -- world lists, North American lists, state lists, county lists, and backyard lists. Probably, it is *listing*, more than any other thing, that separates birdwatchers from birders.

Now, I don't mean any disrespect to the activity of listing. I'm a lister myself. I have even been known to engage in that ultimate act of an over-the-edge birder -- jump on the next plane to go see a rare bird that just showed up in Texas. But I get my greatest joy from *watching* birds, seeing them go about their daily lives, and simply in being in the out of doors.

The **American Birding Association (ABA)** was originally organized principally around the activity of listing. Today, listing is still an important aspect of the ABA, but it has broadened beyond that. More and more, it has taken over the whole range of birds and their conservation, partly because the National Audubon Society, which originally meant *birds* to most people, has gravitated in the direction of general conservation.

Birds are still important to the Audubon Society, but when Audubon dropped the publication of *American Birds,* ABA picked it up, changing its name to ***North American Birds.*** The purpose of *North American Birds* is to document the changing panorama of North American bird life, including changes in populations, ranges, and seasonal occurrences. It carries this mission out through an extensive organization of volunteers, who collect the information on observations, and publish it quarterly, by region. On the Pacific Coast south of Canada there are three regions: Oregon-Washington, Middle Pacific Coast, and Southern Pacific Coast. This publication, in one form or another, for 50-plus years has documented most of what we know about bird distribution.

ABA also publishes ***Birding,*** issued six times a year, which contains articles about birds and birding, especially articles involving identification, birding locations, and bird behavior. Today, the ABA stands as the principal organization in North America representing birds and birders.

In Oregon, the Oregon Field Ornithologists publishes ***Oregon Birds***, a quarterly journal that documents range expansions (or contractions) of the state's bird species, and includes other articles of interest.

## SOME BIRDING TIPS

It doesn't take much to get started in birding. A good field guide, such as the *National Geographic Field Guide to the Birds of North America* (familiarly called "National Geo") is essential, plus a pair of binoculars. Many people have gotten started with rather inexpensive binoculars, and these can serve quite well, but most people eventually upgrade to something better. (See section on "Binoculars.")

When a person is getting started in birding, there is a natural tendency to look at the bird, and then start thumbing through the field guide until a match is found. This is probably not the best way to proceed, but we've all been there and done it exactly that way, at one time or another. No doubt it's a step that we all have to go through, and it does have the advantage that you eventually get pretty familiar with the field guide. But there is no substitution for going into the field, as often as you can, and keep looking at the birds. Eventually, the birds will become more and more familiar, especially after you have a good idea of what to look for.

The book you are now holding tries to give you a feel for that -- what to look for. It tells you where the various species are likely to be found in our area, and provides a little "bar chart" for each species, that gives you an idea of *when* they are likely to be found, and how common (or how rare) they are.

One of the troubles with a field guide is that it has to cover the entire continent. The National Geo guide, for example, has more than 800 birds in it. However, in Southern Oregon, less than half of these (373) have ever shown up, and about 120 of those are either accidental or irregular, and are unlikely to be encountered. Thus, we wind up with about 253 birds in our area that are more or less "regular." That's still a lot of birds, but is easier to deal with than the 800+ in the field guide.

The most basic rule of all is: **get to know the common birds.** Once you become familiar with them, where they live, and how they behave, then an unusual bird will stick out like a sore thumb. A mistake that is often made, when one is getting started, is to zero on in a picture in your field guide that seems to match the bird you are looking at, but is of a bird that has never shown up locally. Your first assumption should be that the bird is a common one, before you start thinking about rarities. An old saying among birders is, "If you're in North America, and hear hoofbeats, your first thought should be of *horses,* not *zebras*."

**Watch the bird's behavior,** and try to narrow your bird down to a particular group. That way, you have fewer pages to search through. If it's sitting on a branch out in the open, flying out periodically to catch an insect, and then returning to the same perch, then it's probably a good idea to start your search among the flycatchers. If it's scratching around on the ground, then it's probably a waste of time to look through the flycatchers, vireos, or warblers, which tend to forage in the air or in the trees, and it will probably be most productive if you look through the ground-feeding birds like the thrushes, thrashers, and sparrows.

**Get a good look at the bill.** If it's thin and sharp, then it's probably an insect-eater, and the kinglets and warblers would be a good place to start looking. If the bill is stout, and looks like it's strong enough to crack a seed open, then start by checking out the sparrows, finches, and grosbeaks.

Get familiar with the **family groupings.** These groupings place closely related birds together in your field guide, and help to focus your search. Once you learn where the family groups are located in your field guide, you can go to them quickly, without having to start your search each time from the beginning of the book. A corollary of this is to spend lots of time at home **becoming familiar with your field guide**, so that when you go into the field, you don't have to start from scratch.

**Hold still** as much as you can. Obviously, you will have to be moving at least part of the time, but birds often freeze in the presence of motion or noise, but will soon start becoming active again if you hold still and remain quiet for a few minutes. Try to **conceal yourself** as much as possible, by looking over the top of a bush, or standing partly behind a tree.

Try a little bit of **pishing,** or **spishing,** as it is sometimes called. This is a sound made with your lips: *sshh sshh sshh.* Sometimes this makes birds curious, and they will pop up to see what's going in. However, it doesn't always work, and sometimes just seems to scare them and make them hide. Nevertheless, it's worth trying.

An alternative is to make a sound like a Northern Pygmy-Owl, which is easy to produce by making short little whistled hoots. (Get yourself one of those wonderful tapes or CDs with birds' songs, if you want to know exactly what a pygmy-owl sounds like.) Sometimes this brings little birds like chickadees, titmice, warblers, and kinglets swarming around you, trying to locate the owl. Obviously such things should not be overdone, because it would not be fair to the birds to overstress them, by dragging them away for too long from the important job of getting enough to eat.

**BINOCULARS**

Binoculars come in two basic types -- **"Porro prism"** and **"roof prism."** The Porro prism type has two offset barrels, in the traditional binocular configuration. The roof prism type has two straight barrels. In both types, the prisms are arranged in such a way that your eye receives an upright image. Roof prism binoculars have more optical elements in them, and require greater precision in manufacturing than the Porro type. Thus, they are more expensive. The quality of the image can be high with either type. The principal advantages of the roof prism type is that it tends to be lighter, and has greater resistance to internal fogging.

**Red-tailed Hawk**

Binoculars are generally marked with numbers, such as **8 x 40.** The first number is the magnification, or "power," and the second number is the diameter of the objective lens in millimeters. (The objective lens is the large lens, farthest from the eye.) Typical **magnifications** used in birding range from 7-power to 10-power. When I first began birding, I was told I should not use

8-power binoculars, because the magnification was so high that I couldn't hold the binoculars steady enough. Today, I use 8-power routinely, and have friends who swear by 10-power. My belief is that holding binoculars steady is essentially something that develops with practice. The only downside that I see to 10-power is that the field of view decreases as the magnification increases, so 10-power glasses have smaller fields of view than 8-power.

The second number ("40" in the example given above), is more important than many people realize. First of all, larger lenses let in more light, and the image tends to be brighter. Secondly, the objective lens controls something called **exit pupil,** which is very important. The exit pupil on a pair of binoculars is easy to calculate: just divide the first number into the second. In the example above, dividing 8 into 40 gives 5, which is the diameter of the exit pupil in millimeters. Five mm is about right for a good exit pupil, and exit pupils smaller than 4 mm can give trouble. The downside of a large objective lens, of course, is that it makes the binoculars heavy.

You can actually *see* the exit pupils, by holding the binoculars up against a bright surface, such as the sky. Hold them at arm's length with the objective lens away from you, and look at the little bright circles that appear in the eyepieces. These are the exit pupils.

The exit pupil of a binocular has been compared to looking through a drinking straw. If the straw is too small, it's hard to get it lined up with your eye, and look through it. A larger straw is obviously better. This is why so many people, especially kids, when they look through binoculars may say, "I can't see anything." They usually are having trouble lining up the exit pupils with the pupils of their own eyes, often because the exit pupils are too small. This is the main problem with many compact binoculars. A typical compact might be an 8 x 20, in which case the exit pupil is only 2.5 mm, and is too small.

The next thing to be concerned about is **field of view.** The most typical way of expressing a field of view is by the diameter, in feet, of the circular area at 1000 yards that you can see. The binoculars I currently use are 8 x 42 (5.25 mm exit pupil), and the field of view is 365 feet at 1000 yards. If I were to go to a power of 10, in the same line of binoculars, my field of view would drop to 294 feet at 1000 yards. Some people don't seem to mind this, and are willing to trade a smaller field of view for the higher power, but I happen to like as much field of view as I can get. It means I can see a larger area when I'm searching for a bird, and am more likely to spot it quickly if the field of view is reasonably large.

Some manufacturers mark the field of view in terms of degrees, instead of so many feet at 1000 yards. The conversion is that 1 degree equals 52.5 feet. So my binoculars, which give me 365 feet at 1000 yards, have a field of view of about 7 degrees.

The final factor to think about is **closeness of focus.** This might not seem very important, but just wait until you're following a warbler in the bushes, trying to get a good look at it, and it comes so close to you that it goes out of focus. This is the very reason I changed binoculars to the ones I now have. My old ones, which I thought were great, could only focus down to 14 feet. The ones I now have go down to 6 feet. Maybe this factor isn't as important to you as it was for me, but my advice is not to settle for anything that can't focus down to at least 15 feet.

There are other factors, such as depth of field, eye relief, transmittance, twilight factor, and focusing mechanism, but the ones I have gone over in the above, are the most basic.

Cost? You can pay anything from $50 to $1000. The quality of the image, in general, improves with price. However, the ones at the bottom of the price range give remarkably good images. My advice is to try them out in the shop, and look at various objects through them to be sure your are getting an acceptable image. Then, when you find something that seems right for you, you can make the decision regarding how much you want to pay.

## SPOTTING SCOPES

Sooner or later, you will start to think about a spotting scope. These have much higher magnifications than binoculars, and require tripods to hold them steady. Also, since the magnifications are so high, the fields of view are correspondingly small, and sometimes it's difficult to locate the bird you're looking for. The magnification is built into the eyepiece, and you can get interchangeable eyepieces.

Eyepieces typically come in 15x, 22x, 30x, and 20x-60x zoom. The zoom lens has the advantage that you can use the wide field that goes with the lower power to find your bird, and then zoom in on it to the higher magnification. The zoom lenses made by some manufacturers don't produce very good images at the higher magnifications. On the other hand, there are some zooms on the market that have incredibly fine images at the high magnifications. It's all a matter of cost. You can easily sink $1700 into a scope, eyepiece, and tripod. But, if you're going to take the step of getting a scope, you should get the best one you can afford. It's a good idea to try one out in a store before buying.

Scopes are only useful in open, distant-viewing situations. They are the most useful when you are looking at ducks or geese on a lake, or at shorebirds on the mudflats. You can also use one when scanning birds at the seashore, but the combination of narrow field of view, and finding a bird that is constantly disappearing from view in the waves, makes for a frustrating task. On a pelagic trip, when the boat is plunging about, a scope is totally useless. Even in a forest-birding situation, carrying a scope is generally too much of a nuisance, for the very few times you will get to use it.

## PLUMAGE

It is impossible to describe birds without using some of the technical terminology for feathers. A few of the more frequently used terms are shown in the figure on Page 11.

## SONGS AND CALLS

Birds' "songs" are thought of as long and complex, while "calls" are short, but the dividing line is sometimes not clear. Biologists regard calls as innate, whereas songs must be learned, although some people claim that calls can be learned, too. Different calls may have different functions: to signal the presence of danger, to maintain contact, or to keep the flock together. Songs, too, may have different functions. One song type may be used to attract females, while another may be intended to ward off competing males. Sometimes songs serve both purposes.

A lot of emphasis is placed in this book upon songs. This is because, when you are in the field, your first intimation there is a bird nearby is likely to be its song. Your eyes can only see what is directly in front of you, but your ears can pick up everything within a 360-degree circle. Many times, you won't see the bird at all, but only hear it, and it's nice to have some idea of the identity of the source.

It's difficult to convey a good idea of a song by just using the written word. Nevertheless, it can be useful to give some kind of English words to the song, not because it gives an accurate rendition of the song itself, but because it gives a "handle" on remembering the song. Examples are *"Quick! Three beers!"* for the song of the Olive-sided Flycatcher, and *"Tweedledee? Tweedledum"* for the song of the American Robin. Usually, the written words can convey the cadence, although they cannot give the actual melody.

The best thing of all, of course, is to listen to recordings. There are some excellent ones available on the market, and I strongly recommend those in the Peterson Field Guides series, called *Western Birding by Ear, Eastern/Central Birding by Ear, and Eastern and Central More Birding by Ear.* These are generally available in nature stores, both as cassettes and as CDs, and can be ordered by mail from the American Birding Association.

## KEEPING LISTS

Most people keep lists of one sort or another, just for their own enjoyment. In the ABA, where listing sometimes is taken very seriously, there are certain rules:

The bird must have been observed within the prescribed area, i.e., within the particular continent, country, state, province, or county to which the list applies. A particularly important area for the ABA is North America, which includes the 49 continental United States, Canada, the French islands of St. Pierre et Miquelon, and adjacent waters to a distance of 200 miles. (Never heard of St. Pierre et Miquelon? They belong to France, even though they are in North America.) This is known as the **ABA Checklist Region.** Hawaii and Bermuda are not included. Greenland was not included until 2002, when the ABA added it, following the lead of the American Ornithologists' Union (AOU). Note, also, that the region does not include Mexico, contrary to the definition of North America used by AOU in its *Check-List of North American Birds.* AOU's definition covers everything in North America from the Arctic through Panama, including the West Indies and the Hawaiian Islands.

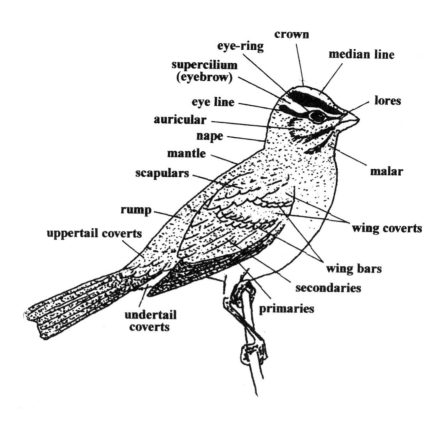

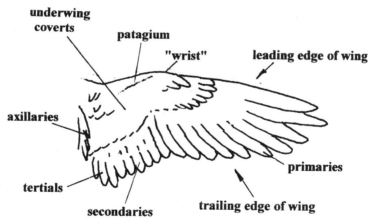

Underside of Wing

**SOME FEATHER TERMINOLOGY ON BIRDS**

An interesting consequence of the rule concerning the ABA Checklist Region is, if you're standing on the edge of the Rio Grande, and observe a bird on the Mexico side, it doesn't count for your Northern American list. Sorry. You can, however, console yourself by putting it on your Mexico list.

When members of ABA refer to their "life lists," meaning the species of birds they've seen in their lives, they're likely to be referring to their North America lists, within the ABA Checklist Region. The total number of species for this region is 906. As of 2000, 287 people had seen 700 or more of these, and 771 had seen 600 or more. (Yes, ABA publishes these numbers annually.) Six hundred life birds is considered a difficult and respectable achievement. Seven hundred was considered, not too long ago, as a remarkable goal, achievable by only a few who had the adequate time and resources to travel to all corners of the continent. But, by 2000, there were 19 people with 800 or more on their North American life lists, and the number who have done so rises each year.

Other people, when they refer to their "life lists," mean the number they have seen in the entire world. This is a different ball game, because there are believed to be between 9,000 and 10,000 species of birds in the world. The number is controversial, depending upon which authority you consult. The all-time world champion in this regard was Phoebe Snetsinger, who had accumulated 8,384 birds on her world list before she was killed in a vehicle accident while birding on Madagascar, in 1999.

To "count" on one's life list, the bird must be one that is currently accepted by the ABA Checklist Committee. This rule is especially important when it comes to introduced species, because to be "countable," the species must have established a wild, self-sustaining population. For example, the Black Francolin, a game bird introduced in Louisiana, once was considered "countable," but then the population went into collapse and the species was removed from the list. For another example, the Ring-necked Pheasant, an introduced species, is well-established and is "countable." But the cockatoo I saw in my neighbor's yard is obviously an escaped cage-bird, and is not.

Another rule is that the bird must have been alive, wild, and unrestrained, when identified This rule eliminates caged birds, and those that have been carried to an area in a cage, and then released. This rule is important because there is a major commerce in caged birds in Mexico. Sometimes a bird may have been transported in a cage to a community just south of the Mexican border, and then escape, subsequently turning up on the U.S. side. If this is a bird whose natural range is far distant from the border, and which has never turned up on the U.S. side before, it can hardly be looked upon as a natural, wild bird.

The bird can be identified either by sight or sound. This rule caused convulsions in ABA when it was first proposed. Prior to its adoption, all birds had to be *seen* and identified, in order to count. Traditionalists within ABA wanted to keep that rule, and argued that inclusion of "heard birds" would dilute the credibility of their lists. But some birds, especially night-birds, are very hard to see.

A perfect example is that of the Yellow Rail, which is practically never seen, but is often heard, making a "ticking" sound in a marsh at night in the spring. A common technique, when the rule said you had to *see* the bird, was for a group to wade into a marsh at night, locate a bird by its ticking sound, and then slowly close in on it until the bird was finally spotted, cowering in the center of the circle. The trouble is, those marshes are also the nesting grounds, and who knows how many nests got damaged by birders tromping at night through the marsh. So the rule got changed, not only to give the Yellow Rails a break, but also to spare all other birds that make clearly identifiable noises, and might be damaged by overzealous birders trying to get an identification by sight.

Finally, the bird must have been encountered under conditions that conform to the ABA Code of Birding Ethics. The code is included at the end of this chapter, and it is worthwhile to read it. The Code was adopted because some folks were raising an objection to the whole process of birding. They said that the activity of birders tromping through habitat was injurious to birds' welfare, and should be stopped. So the ABA adopted a code that would curb the more extreme aspects of what birders might do, recognizing that the birds' welfare is paramount.

The ABA also knows that the long-range welfare of birds and their habitats depends upon the existence of a large group of people who want to have a flourishing bird population that they can enjoy. The ABA reasoned that, as more and more people come into birding, they will lend political support to the maintenance and expansion of wildlife habitat.

## CHRISTMAS COUNT

This is an organized activity of the National Audubon Society which takes place each year in the two or three-week period surrounding Christmas, in which groups of people go out and count all the birds they can during a one-day period, inside a designated "count circle." A "count circle" is a area 15 miles in diameter. In Southern Oregon, including the California portion of the Klamath Basin, there are six count circles: Medford, Grants Pass, Klamath Falls, Little Applegate, Illinois Valley, and Tule Lake.

In the 2000-2001 Christmas Count, there were 1533 count circles in the United States, 297 in Canada, and 50 in the Caribbean, Latin America, and the Pacific Islands. There were 51,637 observers involved. Each year, National Audubon publishes a huge book (the 2000-2001 book contains 666 pages), that shows all the results obtained in all the count circles. A lot of the information included in the book you are holding came from these Christmas Count publications.

## RARE BIRD ALERTS

If you are on e-mail, you can have dozens of messages come to your computer every day, telling you about various birds that have shown up the day before in Oregon, some of them rare, some of them not. This is called Oregon Birders On-Line, or OBOL.

You sign up (it's free) by sending a message to the following address:
**lyris@lists.orst.edu**
The message should say:
**SUBSCRIBE obol firstname lastname**
Where it says, "firstname" and "lastname," you put in your own name.

Sadly, the addresses of lists of this sort tend to change fairly rapidly, so I hope this address will continue to be valid at least until this book is published.

You can also get recorded messages about rare birds in Oregon over the telephone by calling

Oregon statewide:   **(503) 292-0661**
Klamath Basin:     **(541) 850-3805**

These may be long distance calls for you, of course. Also, like e-mail addresses, rare bird alert telephone numbers tend to change from time to time, but these were valid as of 2002.

## ABA CODE OF ETHICS

**Fundamental principle:** Everyone who enjoys birds and birding must always respect wildlife, its environment, and the rights of others. In any conflict of interest between birds and birders, the welfare of the birds and their environment comes first.

1  **Promote the welfare of birds and their environment.**

1(a)  Support the protection of important bird habitat.

1(b)  To avoid stressing birds or exposing them to danger, exercise restraint and caution during observation, photography, sound recording, or filming.

Limit the use of recordings and other methods of attracting birds, and never use such methods in heavily birded areas, or for attracting any species that is Threatened, Endangered, or of Special Concern, or is rare in your local area.

Keep well back from nests and nesting colonies, roosts, display areas, and important feeding sites. In such sensitive areas, if there is a need for extended observation, photography, filming or recording, try to use a blind or hide, and take advantage of natural cover.

Use artificial light sparingly for filming or photography, especially for close ups.

1(c)  Before advertising the presence of a rare bird, evaluate the potential for disturbance to the bird, its surroundings, and other people in the area, and proceed only if access can be controlled, disturbance minimized, and permission has been obtained from private landowners. The sites of rare nesting birds should be divulged only to the proper conservation authorities.

1(d)  Stay on roads, trails, and paths where they exist; otherwise keep habitat disturbance to a minimum.

2  **Respect the law and rights of others.**

2(a)  Do not enter private property without the owner's explicit permission.

2(b) Follow all laws, rules, and regulations governing use of roads and public areas, both at home and abroad.

2(c) Practice common courtesy in contacts with other people. Your exemplary behavior will generate goodwill with birders and nonbirders alike.

**3 Ensure that feeders, nest structures, and other artificial bird environments are safe.**

3(a) Keep dispensers, water, and food clean and free of decay or disease. It is important to feed birds continually during harsh weather.

3(b) Maintain and clean nest structures regularly.

3(c) If you are attracting birds to an area, ensure the birds are not exposed to predation from cats and other domestic animals, or dangers posed by artificial hazards.

**4 Group birding, whether organized or impromptu, requires special care.**

*Each individual in the group, in addition to the obligations spelled out in Items #1 and #2, has responsibilities as a Group Member.*

4(a) Respect the interests, rights, and skills of fellow birders, as well as people participating in other legitimate outdoor activities. Freely share your knowledge and experience, except where code 1(c) applies. Be especially helpful to beginning birders.

4(b) If you witness unethical birding behavior, assess the situation, and intervene if you think it prudent. When interceding, inform the person(s) of the inappropriate action, and attempt, within reason, to have it stopped. If the behavior continues, document it, and notify appropriate individuals or organizations.

*Group Leader responsibilities (amateur and professional trips and tours).*

4(c) Be an exemplary ethical role model for the group. Teach through word and example.

4(d) Keep groups to a size that limits impact on the environment and does not interfere with others using the same area.

4(e) Ensure everyone in the group knows of and practices this code.

4(f) Learn and inform the group of any special circumstances applicable to the areas being visited (e.g., no tape recorders allowed).

4(g) Acknowledge that professional tour companies bear a special responsibility to place the welfare of birds and the benefits of public knowledge ahead of the company's commercial interest. Ideally, leaders should keep track of tour sightings, document unusual occurrences, and submit records to appropriate organizations.

*Reprinted through courtesy of the American Birding Association*

# Chapter 3 - THE LAY OF THE LAND

**DEFINITION OF "SOUTHERN OREGON"**

The way I use the term "Southern Oregon," I feel I must include part of Northern California. This is because the area's most outstanding birding area -- the Klamath Basin -- sits directly astride the boundary between the two states. Birds pay no attention to state boundaries, so I've decided to follow the birds' lead, and also pay no attention. Thus, my definition of "Southern Oregon" includes Josephine County, Jackson County, the southern part of Klamath County (the part that lies within the drainage basin of the Klamath River), a part of Siskiyou County in California, and a part of Modoc County, also in California. The decision of what to include is based upon what lies within the drainage basin of the Klamath River.

This region has some of the most scenic land in America. It has Oregon's only national park, Crater Lake NP, and three national monuments: Oregon Caves NM, Cascade-Siskiyou NM, and Lava Beds NM. Two great mountain peaks stand as sentinels over the area -- Mount McLoughlin (9495 feet) in the north, and Mount Shasta (14,162 feet) in the south. In between are vast interior basins: the Upper Klamath Basin in the north, extending into the great prairies of the Wood River Valley; and two basins in the south: the Lower Klamath Basin, and the Tule Lake Basin.

The region is drained by two magnificent rivers. The Rogue River rises on the slopes of Crater Lake and Mount Mcloughlin, and drains to the west, passing through the Rogue River Valley until it finally enters a narrow canyon on its way to the ocean. The Rogue has two major tributaries, each with its own valley -- the Applegate River and the Illinois River.

The other great river is the Klamath. It also rises on the slopes of Crater Lake and Mount McLoughlin, and includes tributaries coming from the eastern Cascades, such as Wood River and Williamson River. These streams join in forming the largest freshwater lake in Oregon, and one of the most scenic: Upper Klamath Lake. The level of the lake is maintained between 4137 and 4147 feet by a low dam constructed by the Bureau of Reclamation. The outflow of the lake is called Link River, and it flows only a short distance into Lake Ewauna, next to the city of Klamath Falls. Lake Ewauna is the official beginning of the Klamath River, which breaks through the Cascades, and flows through a narrow canyon to the sea.

**"WEST OF THE CREST"; "EAST OF THE CREST"**

The natural divide for this region is the Cascade crest, which acts as more or less of a dividing line for many bird species. In this book, when abundance is shown on the bar charts, it is often necessary to show different abundances for **west** and **east**, meaning west of the crest, and east of the crest. However, in our region the crest is not as sharp a dividing line as it is farther north in Oregon. Instead, it is a broad region of moderately high elevations, mostly ranging from 4000 feet to 6000 feet, more of a plateau than a sharp crest. It, too, is a region of great beauty, with extensive forests, great meadows (called "prairies"), and lovely lakes.

The Cascade crest is well defined in the region running from Crater Lake NP south to Mount McLaughlin, and over the summit of Brown Mountain. Fish Lake is to the west of the divide, and Lake of the Woods is to the east. South of Lake of the Woods, the divide takes a strong swing to the west and more or less follows the course of Dead Indian Memorial Road, first on one side, and then on the other. At the upper end of Howard Prairie Lake, the divide swings to the south again, leaving both Howard Prairie Lake and Hyatt Lake to the east of the crest. At Green Springs Summit, where OR 66 crosses over, the Cascades blend into the Siskiyous. The region contains two wilderness areas: Sky Lakes Wilderness, and Mountain Lakes Wilderness.

**Great Horned Owl**

The Siskiyou Crest runs east and west, close to the Oregon/California border. The highest peak is Mount Ashland (7532 feet). The upper parts are open subalpine habitat, and the mountains fall off on both sides into complex mountain ridges, heavy forests, and deep canyons. The Siskiyou Mountains extend from the Cascade-Siskiyou NM, on the east, to a vast expanse of mountains and forests in Josephine and Curry Counties on the west, including the Red Buttes Wilderness and Kalmiopsis Wilderness.

**WEATHER**

The climate east of the crest is somewhat drier and colder than west of the crest, reflecting its higher elevation and more interior location. The elevation at Medford is 1300 feet and at Klamath Falls is 4100 feet. The average annual precipitation at Medford is 20 inches, and at Klamath Falls is 14 inches. In the mountains, the precipitation is much greater. Crater Lake NP, for example, averages 69 inches of precipitation yearly, and the snowfall can be 50 feet per year. The average maximum July temperature at Klamath Falls is 85°F, and at Medford is 89°F. The average minimum January temperature at Klamath Falls is 21°F, and at Medford is 30°F.

**HABITATS**

As we become more and more familiar with birds, we soon learn that certain birds are more likely to be found in some habitats than in others. For example, we expect to find ducks on the water, rails in a marsh, and dippers on a stream. We would not go hunting for longspurs in a forest; instead, we would search for them in short-grass fields. Too much reliance upon habitats can be risky, of course, because birds do fly, and often turn up in the "wrong" habitats. Nevertheless, a knowledge of some typical habitats to be found in Southern Oregon can be useful, in looking for birds.

In the *Oregon Breeding Bird Atlas,* 57 different habitat types that occur in Oregon are described. We will not go that far in this book, but will give brief descriptions of 18 kinds of habitats that are typically encountered in Southern Oregon. These habitat descriptions combine and generalize on the information provided by the *Breeding Bird Atlas,* and have been supplemented by information from *Natural Vegetation of Oregon and Washington,* published by Oregon State University Press.

**True fir/mixed forest.** This type of forest is typically found at the higher elevations of the southern Cascades, and has tree species such as white fir, red fir, and mountain hemlock. Some of the bird species associated with this habitat are Pileated Woodpecker, Hammond's Flycatcher, Steller's Jay, Red-breasted Nuthatch, Hermit Thrush, Hermit Warbler, and Western Tanager.

**Mixed conifer forest.** This kind of habitat is widely distributed in Southern Oregon at mid-elevations. On the west side of the Cascades it is transitional between the deciduous foothill forests and the true fir/mixed forests of higher elevations. On the east side, it is transitional between the ponderosa forests of the lower elevations and the montane forests at upper elevations. Typical tree species are Douglas-fir, white fir, incense cedar, with some ponderosa and sugar pines. Some bird species are Mountain Quail, Pileated Woodpecker, Steller's Jay, Red-breasted Nuthatch, and Black-headed Grosbeak.

**Douglas-fir/mixed deciduous forest.** This forest is most commonly found at intermediate elevations in the Siskiyous. It is transitional between the lower-level deciduous-dominated woodlands, and the upper-level true fir forests, and has typical tree species such as Douglas-fir, tanoak, madrone, and Pacific dogwood. Some bird species are Band-tailed Pigeon, Cassin's and Hutton's Vireos, Steller's Jay, Chestnut-backed Chickadee, and Black-throated Gray Warbler.

**Siskiyou Mountains mixed deciduous forest.** This type of forest is special to southwestern Oregon, particularly in the valleys of Josephine and Jackson counties. Characteristic tree species are madrone, white oak, and black oak, with some Douglas-fir and incense cedar. It also has poison oak. Some bird species are Wild Turkey, Hutton's Vireo, Ash-throated Flycatcher, Nashville Warbler, and Purple Finch.

**Ponderosa pine-dominated forest.** This is found principally east of the crest at mid to lower elevations, and is widespread in Klamath County. It is dominated by ponderosas, but may also include some incense cedar, white fir, junipers, and sagebrush. Some bird species are Williamson's Sapsucker, Hairy and White-headed Woodpeckers, Pygmy and Red-breasted Nuthatches, Western Tanager, and Cassin's Finch.

**Lodgepole pine forest.** If you encounter a pure stand of even-aged lodgepoles, it is probably the result of a fire sometime in the past. Often, there is a grassy understory. As a stand matures, other species start to come in, such as white fir and Douglas-fir. Some bird species are Hairy and Black-backed Woodpeckers, Dusky Flycatcher, Mountain Chickadee, and Cassin's Finch.

**Subalpine.** This is the area just below timberline, with subalpine fir, whitebark pine, mountain hemlock, and red fir. Often, it is highly attractive, with open meadow-like spaces between the trees. Some bird species are Clark's Nutcracker, Olive-sided Flycatcher, Mountain Chickadee, Mountain Bluebird, and Townsend's Solitaire. Black-crowned Rosy-Finches may sometimes be found here, although they are more likely to prefer the rocky, open alpine regions above timberline.

**White oak woodland.** This is a common habitat in the Rogue Valley. The characteristic tree is Oregon white oak, but black oak, Douglas-fir, ponderosa pine, and Oregon ash may also be included, as well as poison oak. Some bird species are Wild Turkey, Acorn Woodpecker, Western Scrub-Jay, Oak Titmouse, White-breasted Nuthatch, Western Bluebird, Black-throated Gray Warbler, and Lazuli Bunting.

**Juniper woodland.** Common in the southeastern part of Klamath County. The habitat is characterized by western juniper, of course, but there may be some ponderosa pine included, with an understory of sagebrush and bunchgrasses. Some bird species are Swainson's Hawk, Golden Eagle, Long-eared Owl, Common Poorwill, Gray Flycatcher, and Pinyon Jay.

**Chaparral.** Consists of dense shrub-dominated vegetation. This is a northern extension of California chaparral and is relatively common in the Rogue Valley, and is also found to some extent in the foothills. Some representative shrubs are manzanita, buckbrush ceanothus, and poison oak, and some bird species are Common Poorwill and Blue-gray Gnatcatcher. There is also a **manzanita-dominated shrubland** that forms a mosaic with conifers at higher elevations in the Siskiyous, with birds such as Dusky Flycatcher, Nashville Warbler, Green-tailed Towhee, and Fox Sparrow.

**Sagebrush steppe.** A "steppe" is arid land, generally treeless, with plants adapted to limited water supplies. Sagebrush steppe occurs in southeast Klamath County, and is characterized by Great Basin sagebrush (*Artemisia tridentata*), rabbitbrush, and bunchgrass. Some birds are Common Poorwill, Sage Thrasher, Brewer's Sparrow, and Sage Sparrow.

**Riparian woodland.** The word "riparian" refers to vegetation along a river, stream, or lake edge. West of the crest, typical vegetation is red alder, bigleaf maple, and willows. East of the crest, typical vegetation is cottonwoods, white alder, and willows. Some of the bird species are Western Wood-Pewee, Willow Flycatcher, Tree Swallow, Western Scrub-Jay, Bewick's Wren, and Spotted Towhee.

**Lakes and ponds** are permanent bodies of fresh water, with birds such as grebes, ducks, Osprey, Bald Eagle, gulls, Belted Kingfisher, and Black Phoebe.

**Rivers and streams** are permanent streams with year-round water. Some typical birds are Common Merganser, Spotted Sandpiper, Belted Kingfisher, American Dipper, and Black Phoebe.

**Freshwater marsh.** There are large areas of such marsh in the Klamath Basin, and smaller areas in the Rogue Valley. These are characterized by moderately tall grass-like vegetation with strong stems such as cattails and bulrushes. Typical birds are Green-winged Teal, Cinnamon Teal, Sora, Virginia Rail, Black-necked Stilt, American Avocet, Marsh Wren, and Yellow-headed Blackbird.

**Farmlands.** Farmlands can be good places for certain birds, especially the brushy edges and hedgerows. The term includes pastures, croplands, and orchards. Some birds are Killdeer, Mourning Dove, Western Kingbird, swallows, Savannah Sparrow, Lark Sparrow, Western Meadowlark, and various blackbirds.

**Urban.** Built up areas can also be good for certain birds, such as Rock Dove, Mourning Dove, Anna's Hummingbird, swallows, Black-capped Chickadee, American Robin, Brewer's Blackbird, House Finch, and goldfinches.

**Rocky areas and cliffs.** Some typical areas of this sort are the Table Rocks in the Rogue Valley, Crater Lake, Sheepy Ridge near Tule Lake, and the Petroglyphs Section of Lava Beds NM. Some birds that like such places are Prairie Falcon, White-throated Swift, Rock Wren, and Canyon Wren.

# Chapter 4 - PLACES TO GO BIRDING

Directions for getting to the sites are given in the site descriptions. In some cases, a few bird species are listed that might be expected. Note that the presence of a particular species assumes you are there in the correct season. The numbers are keyed to the maps on Pages 23, 27, and 31.

## JOSEPHINE COUNTY:

**1. King Mountain Rock Garden** - From I-5, at Exit 76, turn east on Coyote Creek Road and go 11.3 miles to the parking area for King Mountain Rock Garden, almost on top of King Mountain. The road changes from paved to good gravel at 5.4 miles. At 6.1 miles, at a fork in the road, keep left; at 6.7 miles, keep right. This area has been designated by BLM as an "Area of Critical Environmental Concern." It is not especially birdy, but has mountain birds such as Red-breasted Nuthatch and Fox Sparrow. Also, it has delightful wild flowers in spring, and a rough half-mile trail to the top of a subsidiary peak of King Mountain, with splendid views

**2. Golden Coyote Wetlands** - From I-5, at Exit 76, turn east on Coyote Creek Road and go 3.5 miles to the mining ghost town of Golden. Park on the right, just opposite the old general store. The area is open to the public, and is owned by Golden Coyote Wetlands, Inc., a non-profit organization whose purpose is to maintain the old buildings, and to restore the mining areas (the wetlands) for wildlife habitat. A trail runs down into the wetlands, for riparian and wetland birds.

**3. Horse Creek Meadow** - From the center of Merlin, go west on Galice Road 8.4 miles to Taylor Creek Road, also called Forest Road 25, and turn left. The road is mostly one lane and is very twisty, but is paved. At 13.3 miles, you come to a road on the right that leads to Sam Brown Horse Camp (0.1 mile) and Sam Brown Campground (0.3 mile). To the left is a road that leads in 0.1 mile to a locked gate, which is the Taylor Creek Trail Trailhead. Park without blocking gate. Take the road beyond the gate; it is about ¼ mile to Horse Creek Meadow, and the meadow is about ½ mile long. The birding is good both along the road, and adjacent to the meadow. The area is called Horse Creek Wildlife Area, and it is managed for wildlife values, so vehicular travel on the road is not allowed. A bird-banding station is operated nearby. In 1990, a Warbling Vireo was banded here, and was recaptured in 1998. In between, it presumably made the 4500-mile round trip eight times to its wintering grounds in Mexico.[1] (At Big Pine Campground, 1.0 mile back down F.R. 25, there is a nature trail that originates at the day use area, and makes an easy loop, passing a very large ponderosa pine along the way.)

---

[1] Many thanks to Dennis Vroman, for supplying this information.

**4. Indian Mary Park** - From the center of Merlin, go 7.1 miles west on Galice Road to the entrance to the park, on the right. There is a large campground, situated on a flat near the Rogue River, and a picnic ground below, next to the river. There are lots of lawns, but there also are nice forest edges around the periphery of the picnic ground and campground that offer birding opportunities, at least in seasons when the park is not crowded with people.

**5. White Horse Park** - From the intersection of North 6th Street and G Street in downtown Grants Pass, go west for 7.6 miles on G Street. (G Street becomes Upper River Road.) The park is on your left. Drive through the campground to the parking area at the day use area, just below the campground. A nature trail begins from here, that makes a loop about one mile long. The trail gives access to the river, then to an area with brushy habitat, and finally to a cottonwood grove with large trees, that includes a small pond. The entire area has extensive blackberry tangles. This is an outstanding birding area, except in seasons when it might be crowded with people. The blackberry tangles are especially appealing to Yellow-breasted Chats and Wrentits, and the numerous nesting boxes attract Tree Swallows. The pond may have Wood and Ring-necked Ducks. This is one of the better places to find Red-shouldered Hawk.

**6. Fish Hatchery Park** - From the intersection of US 199 and OR 238 in Grants Pass, go 1.5 miles south on OR 238 to New Hope Road and turn right. It is 3.1 miles to Fish Hatchery Road, where you turn right, go 2.8 miles to Wetherbee Drive, and turn right again. It is 0.6 mile to **Fish Hatchery Park (North Unit).** The park adjoins the Applegate River, and has a nature trail. To get to **Fish Hatchery Park (South Unit),** from the intersection of Fish Hatchery Road and Wetherbee Drive, continue 0.7 mile on Fish Hatchery Road to the South Unit on the right. The gate is locked in the winter, but you can walk the short distance down to the park, which is located directly across the river from the North Unit.

**7. Tom Pearce Park** - Take Exit 55 from I-5 (intersection of I-5 and US 199), go west on US 199 for 0.2 mile and turn left on Agness Avenue, go 0.1 mile, and turn left (east) on Foothill Drive. Go 0.7 mile on Foothill, and, where Foothill veers left to go under the freeway, continue straight on Tom Pearce Road. It is 1.0 mile to Tom Pearce Park, which is located on the Rogue River. This is a largely a city-type park, with green lawns and picnic areas, but there are trails that lead to good habitat.

**8. Pearce Riffle Park** - Follow directions as above, for Tom Pearce Park, but when Foothill Drive veers left to go under the freeway, continue on Foothill Drive 2.0 miles to Averill Road, turn right and go 0.6 mile to park. The park is next to the river, and has a nature trail.

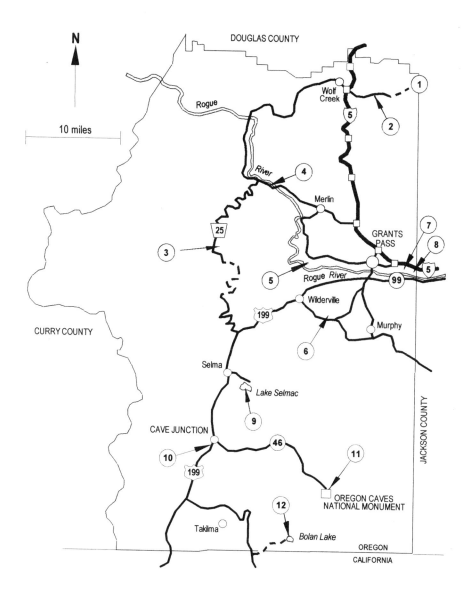

**JOSEPHINE COUNTY
OREGON**

**9. Lake Selmac** - This is probably the most popular recreational area in Josephine County, with five campgrounds, swimming areas, and two boat launches. Nevertheless, it offers some good birding opportunities. To get there, turn west on Lakeshore Drive from US 199, about 0.5 mile south of Selma. (Selma is about 20 miles south of Grants Pass on US 199.) After turning toward the lake, it is 2.0 miles to the entrance, and a "Y" intersection. The left-hand fork is the continuation of Lakeshore Drive, and leads, in about 1.7 miles to Eagle Loop Campground, a playground, boat launch, and Mallard Loop Campground. Next to Mallard Loop is a parking area labeled "Horse Staging Area," which gives access to a footbridge across the creek, and to a trail. The trail, also used by horses and bicycles, leads through mature Douglas-fir forest, and has typical forest birds. Back at the "Y" intersection, the right-hand fork is labeled "Reeves Creek Road," and leads along the lake shore, in 0.8 mile, to South Shore Drive on the left. There is parking here, and an opportunity to observe waterfowl on the lake, consisting mostly of coots, Mallards, Canada Geese, and Buffleheads. South Shore Drive ends in 0.4 mile at a boat launch parking area, which gives access to the other end of the trail that begins at Mallard Loop.

**10. Illinois River Forks State Park** - This is a delightful little park, with lawns, picnic tables, and a couple of short trails near the river that pass through good birding habitat. The entrance is 0.6 mile south of Cave Junction on US 199, on the west side of the highway.

**11. Oregon Caves National Monument** - This popular monument is 19.5 miles east of Cave Junction, on OR 46. The caves themselves constitute the main attraction, but the monument is located in a beautiful forested canyon, typical of the Siskiyous. There are some short trails that originate from the visitor center and run through the forest. The birds are those that are typical in montane forests, such as Steller's Jay, Western Wood-Pewee, and Black-headed Grosbeak. In spring, the *vroom vroom vroom* of Blue Grouse may be heard from the mountainsides. On the road to the caves, **Grayback Campground** is located 11.4 miles from Cave Junction. This is a great campground, and a bonus is the wheelchair-accessible **Grayback Interpretive Trail** that runs along the creek.

**12. Bolan Lake** - This is a lovely little lake situated at 5500 feet elevation, surrounded by mature fir forest, just beneath the Siskiyou Crest. To get there, go 6.3 miles south of Cave Junction on US 199, and turn east on Waldo Road, which ultimately leads to Happy Camp, on the Klamath River. From US 199, it is 17.0 miles on paved highway to the road to Bolan Lake, which is gravel, but can be traveled by ordinary cars in good weather. It is 5.8 miles to the lake, which has a small campground on one shore. A trail originates in the campground and travels above the lakeshore, with birds such as Varied Thrush, Hermit Thrush, Red-breasted Nuthatch, and Yellow-rumped Warbler.

# JACKSON COUNTY:

**13. Valley of the Rogue State Park** - From Exit 45B on I-5 (15 miles west of Medford) follow signs into park. Much of this popular park is in manicured green lawns, but there are lots of trees and brushy edges for birds. A broad path follows the edge of the river.

**14. Lower Table Rock** - From junction of OR 62 and Antelope Road (5.8 miles north of Medford) go west on Antelope Road 1.8 miles to Table Rock Road, turn right (north), and go 4.2 miles to Wheeler Road. Turn left, and follow Wheeler Road 0.7 mile to parking lot for Lower Table Rock Trail, on left. The trail is managed by The Nature Conservancy, Bureau of Land Management, and Rogue River Ranch. It is about 1.5 miles to the top, with an elevation gain of 800 feet. The birds here are typical of oak savanna and chaparral, including Acorn Woodpecker, Ash-throated Flycatcher, Blue-gray Gnatcatcher, Western Bluebird, and both towhees. A possibility is White-throated Swift.

**15. Upper Table Rock** - From junction of OR 62 and Antelope Road (5.8 miles north of Medford) go west on Antelope Road 1.8 miles to Table Rock Road, turn right (north), and go 1.8 miles to Modoc Road. Go right (east) on Modoc Road 1.4 miles to parking for Upper Table Rock Trail, on left. The trail is managed by the Bureau of Land Management. It is about 1.3 miles to the top, with an elevation gain of 700 feet. The habitats and birds are similar to those at Lower Table Rock.

**16. Kirtland Road Sewage Ponds** - From junction of OR 62 and Antelope Road (5.8 miles north of Medford) go west on Antelope Road 2 miles to its junction with Kirtland Road. The Vernon Thorpe Regional Water Reclamation Facility (familiar name is "Kirtland Road Sewage Ponds", or just "Kirtland Ponds") is directly across the road. A set of shallow ponds, sometimes dry, lies across Kirtland Road on the right. Apply in the office for permission to enter the facility. One of the large ponds can be viewed without entering the facility, by going west on Kirtland Road 0.3 mile to a gravel road on the right with a locked gate. The ponds are good in the winter for various raptors, gulls, and waterfowl. If there is water in the shallow ponds, they can have shorebirds during migration.

**17. Tou Velle State Park** - From junction of OR 62 and Antelope Road (5.8 miles north of Medford) go west on Antelope Road 1.8 miles to Table Rock Road, turn right (north), and go 0.8 mile to entrance to Tou Velle State Park, on right. There is another entrance 0.2 mile further north, on the left, across the river. Tou Velle State Park has a general citified appearance, with extensive lawns, parking areas, and picnic areas. (The portion of the park across the river, and on the opposite side of Table Rock Road, is less developed.) It can be crowded on weekends. However, it has many trees, and has birds such as woodpeckers, nuthatches, swallows, and sparrows, depending upon season. At the end of the parking area farthest from the entrance, there are trails leading to the Military Slough portion of the Denman Wildlife Area. Nearby, there is a large pine tree riddled with holes, that serves as a granary tree for Acorn Woodpeckers. There is a Great Blue Heron rookery visible from the west end of the park near the check booth, in the tops of the tall trees on the opposite side of the river.

**18. Lost Creek Lake** - The turnoff to this area, on the left, lies about 29 miles north of Medford on OR 62. It is just beyond Casey State Park, and is called "Takelma Drive." **McGregor Park** is on Takelma Drive 0.3 mile from the turnoff, on the right. The park has picnic tables, a visitor center that is open seasonally, and a system of trails near the river. The turnoff to **Rivers Edge Park** lies on Takelma Drive about 0.2 mile beyond McGregor Park, on the right. Turn on this road, go past the parking lot near the dam next to the fish hatchery, and turn left on a narrow paved road that comes just before crossing the dam. This road has turnouts and park benches, and extends upstream about 0.5 mile along the river. (There is another section of Rivers Edge Park on the opposite side of the river.) This section of the river, known as the **"Holy Water,"** because of its fishing, is a quiet stretch extending from the big dam that holds back Lost Creek Lake, to the fish hatchery. In the winter, waterfowl such as wigeons, Ring-necked Duck, Bufflehead, and both species of goldeneye often congregate here and in the section of the river below the fish hatchery.

**19. Denman Wildlife Area (Military Slough Unit)** - From junction of I-5 and OR 62 in Medford (Exit 30), go north on OR 62 for 5.1 miles to Agate Road and turn left and then north on Agate Road for 1.8 miles to gravel road on left (Touvelle Road) with locked gate. A key to the locked gate can be obtained from the Fish and Wildlife district office described in the next section. This area is open to hunting in season, but is probably one of the better birding areas in the Valley. Touvelle Road extends 1.2 miles to the end at the Rogue River. There is a series of small ponds on the left and an extensive marsh. At the end of the road, trails go in both directions, leading to riparian habitat and giving access to the Rogue River and its tributary, Little Butte Creek. The trail to the left leads along the river to Tou Velle State Park. About half the distance from the locked gate to the end of the road, another trail leads to the left, over a low hill and to Tou Velle State Park. There are extensive marsh areas visible from this trail.

**20. Denman Wildlife Area (Whetstone Pond)** - From junction of I-5 and OR 62 in Medford (Exit 30), go north on OR 62 for 5.1 miles to Agate Road and turn left. Go north on Agate Road and then almost immediately turn left on E. Gregory Road. Go 0.4 mile to sharp left turn in road. The district office of the Fish and Wildlife Department lies directly ahead (apply here for key to the gate described in foregoing section), and the parking area for Whetstone

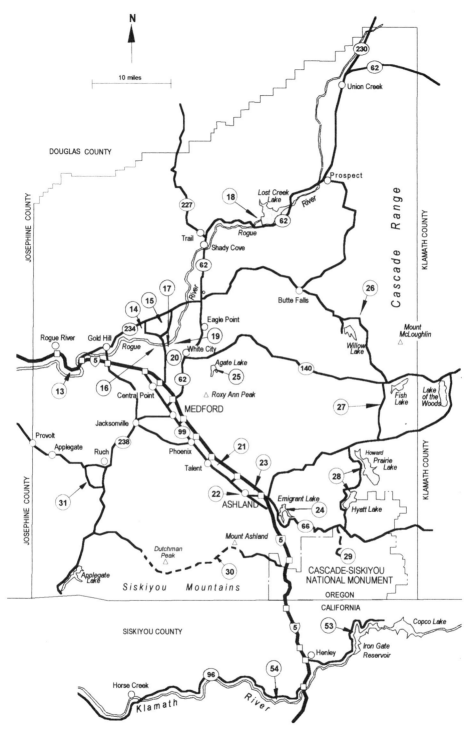

**JACKSON COUNTY, OREGON**
Including part of Siskiyou County, California

Pond is to the right. Whetstone Pond has waterfowl in the winter, including a more-or-less resident flock of Canada Geese. The pond is closed to hunting, but the rest of the area is open to hunting on Saturdays, Sundays, and Wednesdays, in season. A nesting platform on the opposite side of the pond usually has a pair of Ospreys in the spring and summer.

**21. Lynn Newbry Park (Bear Creek Greenway)** - From I-5 at Exit 21, near Talent, turn toward Talent and then turn left within 100 yards for the parking area at Lynn Newbry Park. The paved bike path extends south, remaining near Bear Creek, and passes through excellent riparian forest. There are a couple of ponds to the east of the bike path within the first half mile.

**22. Lithia Park** - From Ashland Plaza in downtown Ashland, trails lead up Ashland Creek for a mile and more through Lithia Park. Lithia Park is a great place, offering creekside birding, with birds such as American Dipper and Winter Wren. Wood Ducks are sometimes present in the duck pond along with the resident Mallards.

**23. Ashland Pond** - In north Ashland, turn west from intersection of Oak and Nevada Streets, go 0.4 mile on Nevada St. to Glendower St., and turn right. It is 0.2 mile to the end of the street, where there is a gate, and limited parking. The dirt road beyond the gate is open to the public; there is pedestrian access around the gate, on the right-hand side. This is a delightful area, with a broad, easy trail (dirt road) that leads about ¼ mile to the pond. The trail completely encircles the pond, giving access to good riparian habitat.

**24. Emigrant Lake** - From the junction of I-5 and OR 66 at Exit 14 near Ashland, go east on OR 66 3.2 miles to the main entrance to Emigrant Lake Recreation Area. The main entrance provides access to the major recreational area, including picnic grounds, campgrounds, green lawns, and a water slide. During prime season and on weekends, the numbers of people tend to reduce bird activity. The shore line of other parts of Emigrant Lake can be accessed by continuing east on OR 66 as follows, with the mileage from the main entrance shown in each case. (a) 0.6 mile, gravel road on left; (b) 0.8 mile, dirt road on left; (c) 1.0 mile, dirt road on left; (d) 1.8 miles, Old Siskiyou Highway, with limited parking on left, and a one-half mile walk down an old overgrown paved road to lake -- good for shorebirds beginning in August when the water levels drop; this old road is sometimes called "Rosebud Lane," because of the extensive fields of wild roses nearby; (e) 2.7 miles, gravel road on left, soon turning to pavement, leading in 0.6 mile to lake, with boat launch ramp; (f) 3.0 miles, Songer Wayside, on left, with parking area and access to lake. Emigrant Lake is a large reservoir, good for eagles and other raptors, waterfowl in winter, and shorebirds in migration.

**25. Agate Lake** - From the junction of OR 62 and OR 140, 5.5 miles north of Medford, go 3.5 miles east on OR 140 to E. Antelope Road and turn right. Go 0.7 mile, turn right at sign saying "Agate Lake," and go 0.7 mile to lake. To get to the opposite end of the lake, from OR 140 go 1.8 miles on E. Antelope Road and turn right on Dry Creek Road. Go 0.8 mile, turn right on Old Dry Creek Road (gravel), and go 0.3 mile to dirt road on right (passable by ordinary car in dry weather). It is 0.5 mile on this dirt road to the lake. In fall migration, when the water level drops, muddy edges are exposed that can draw shorebirds. Gulls, waterfowl, and various raptors are often present.

**26. Whiskey Spring** - From junction of I-5 and OR 62 in Medford (Exit 30), go north on OR 62 for 14.0 miles to Butte Falls Road and turn right. Go to Butte Falls (15.6 miles), and then 9.4 miles further, to turnoff on left for Whiskey Spring Campground, which lies 0.2 mile from the turnoff. In addition to the campground, there is a picnic area with a nature trail. The nature trail, sometimes on board walks, goes all around a beaver pond, a distance of about one mile. The wetlands by the campground can be quite active during spring migration with warblers. The ponderosa pine stands to the east and south of the campground provide habitat for Wild Turkey, Northern Pygmy-Owl, and Pygmy Nuthatch (rare).

**27. Forest Road 37** - From the intersection of OR 62 and OR 140, 5.5 miles north of Medford, go 28.1 miles east on OR 140 to junction with Forest Service Road 37 on right, just before coming to **Fish Lake.** This is a paved road that connects OR 140 with Dead Indian Memorial Road at Deadwood Prairie, a distance of about 8 miles. Along the way, it passes several campgrounds, and crosses some small streams. There are side roads, mostly gravel, that provide access to birding for montane species.

**28. Howard Prairie Lake and Hyatt Lake** - From the junction of I-5 and OR 66 at Exit 14 near Ashland, go east on OR 66 0.6 mile to Dead Indian Memorial Road, turn left, and go 16.7 miles to Hyatt Prairie Road. Turn right, and go 1.9 miles to entrance to **Grizzly Creek Campground,** on left. **Hyatt Lake** lies 4.4 miles further. Great Gray Owls are sometimes seen in the great meadows that occur in this region. From the junction with Hyatt Prairie Road, the upper end of **Howard Prairie Lake** is visible, which often has American White Pelicans in summer. The crest of the Cascades runs right through **Howard Prairie** here, not far from this junction. At Grizzly Creek Campground, there is a parking area and old dirt road at the northern end of the campground. From here, it is a short walk to a point where a good view of the upper part of the lake is possible. At Hyatt Lake, the main road follows the lake shore closely, with many short dirt roads that give access to the lake. Howard Prairie Lake (elevation 4527 feet) and Hyatt Lake (elevation 5016 feet) both lie to the east of the Cascade crest.

**29. Cascade-Siskiyou National Monument** - From the junction of I-5 and OR 66 at Exit 14 near Ashland, go east on OR 66 14.8 miles to Soda Mountain Road, on the right, which comes just before the summit. Go about 3.7 miles on **Soda Mountain Road,** which is a good gravel road passable in good weather in summer, to the second power line crossing, where the Pacific Crest Trail (PCT) crosses the road, and there is limited parking along the road. The PCT can be hiked in either direction, giving access to montane birds.

**30. Mt. Ashland and Siskiyou Crest** - Go south from Ashland on I-5, use Exit 6 for Mt. Ashland, go 0.6 mile to Mt. Ashland Road, turn right, and go about 9.5 miles on paved road to Mt. Ashland Ski Area. After the ski area, the road becomes gravel, and is designated as Forest Service Road 20. It goes more or less along the crest for about 12 miles to Jackson Gap. The road is steep and one-way in spots, but passable in good weather in summer by an ordinary car. From Jackson Gap, the road drops down to the north, to Beaver Creek Road and Applegate Road, and finally to Ruch and Jacksonville. Except for the 9.5 miles from I-5 to Mt. Ashland, which is plowed in winter for the skiers, this road is open only after the snow melts, usually from late June to October. It provides access to a wide variety of habitats, including the Siskiyou Crest, with subalpine meadows.

**31. Cantrall-Buckley County Park** - From Jacksonville, go west 8.9 miles on OR 238, and turn left on Hamilton Road. It is 0.9 mile to the park. Turn right and cross the Applegate River on a one-way bridge. The entrances to the park areas lie just ahead, with the campground to the left, and the day-use area to the right. In the day-use area, the road passes through several picnic areas and then goes downhill to more picnic areas next to the river. From the lower picnic area, the River Trail extends downstream next to the river. The birding in both the campground and the picnic area can be good during times when there aren't many people.

**KLAMATH BASIN (including the south part of Klamath County, Oregon, and parts of Siskiyou and Modoc counties, California):**

**32. Crater Lake National Park** - Crater Lake's fame is justified by the beauty of its lake, but the national park offers much more than that. Outside of the lake basin itself, almost the entire park is forested, with whitebark pine and mountain hemlock at the higher elevations, and pine/fir forest at middle and lower elevations. To get to a couple of especially nice spots, turn east on the Rim Drive 3.8 miles after passing through the southern entrance station. The **Castle Crest Wildflower Garden** is 0.3 mile on Rim Drive, and is a delightful spot to spend an hour, with the usual forest birds. **Cloudcap** lies 11.4 miles further up Rim Drive, and is the highest point reached by the road anywhere within the park, at 7865 feet elevation. This is a good place to look for Gray-crowned Rosy-Finch, in the sparsely vegetated meadows among the whitebark pines and mountain hemlocks. If it is Clark's Nutcrackers you are after, drive

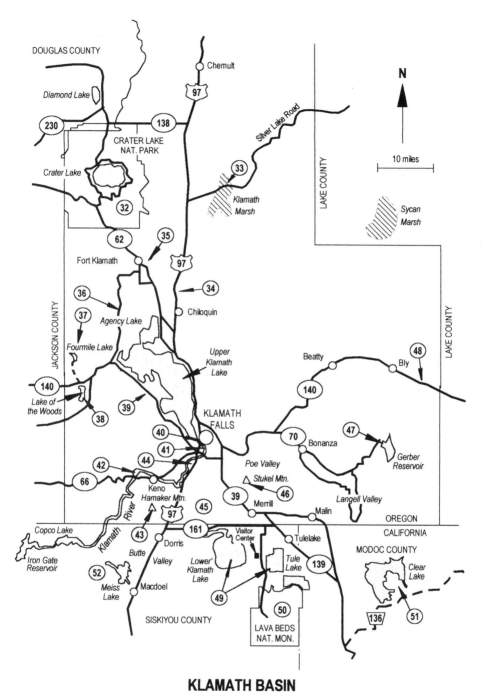

**KLAMATH BASIN**
Including the south part of Klamath County, Oregon
and parts of Siskiyou and Modoc Counties, California

an additional 3.0 miles beyond the junction with Rim Drive, to Rim Village, perched on the south rim. The nutcrackers own the territory.

**33. Klamath Marsh National Wildlife Refuge** - At first sight, it might appear that this refuge is somewhere around Upper Klamath Lake, but it's not. It's about 20 miles farther north, and formerly was called Klamath Forest National Wildlife Refuge. From Chiloquin Junction, on US 97 about 27 miles north of Klamath Falls, go 19.6 miles north on US 97 to **Silver Lake Road,** and turn east. In about a mile, the forest opens up into vast prairies, giving grand views of the mountains. The wildlife refuge begins 4.8 miles from US 97, and the road runs directly through the marsh, giving views into canals on both sides with birds such as Ring-necked Ducks, Buffleheads, and Northern Harriers. Yellow Rails have been heard along this stretch at night in May and June. At 9.2 miles from US 97, the **Wocus Bay Road** goes off to the right, which is a fair dirt road (impassable in winter) that leads in 4.6 miles to a wildlife viewing area overlooking Wocus Bay. This is a prime waterfowl breeding area, with shallow channels and marshes. Just before getting to the overlook, there is a canoe launching area on the right.

**34. Collier Memorial State Park** - This delightful state park, which has two day-use areas, a logging museum, and a campground, lies about 30 miles north of Klamath Falls, 3.4 miles north of Chiloquin Junction, on US 97. The day-use areas and campground offer forest birding in mixed ponderosa/lodgepole forests. The major day-use area, with grassy lawns under the pines, is next to the Williamson River, at the point where it is joined by Spring Creek. The second day-use area is across US 97, past the logging museum, and about 0.5 mile further, on Spring Creek. The campground is 0.3 mile north of the main day-use area, and adjoins the Williamson River.

**35. Fort Klamath and Wood River Valley** - To get to **Jackson F. Kimball State Park,** go 2.3 miles north from Fort Klamath on OR 62 to Dixon Road, and turn right (east). It is 1.6 miles to Sun Mountain Road, where you turn left 0.3 miles to Kimball Park. There is a small campground here, with typical forest birds, but the major attraction is the source of the **Wood River,** located next to the campground. The river bubbles forth in springs from the dry mountainside, and forms beautiful, clear pools, before running its short course to Agency Lake. Returning to the junction of Dixon Road and Sun Mountain Road, if you go 1.8 miles south on Sun Mountain Road, you come to the entrance to the **Wood River Day Use Area,** and turn right. It is 0.6 mile to the parking area next to the Wood River. There is a delightful set of trails and boardwalks through the aspen groves and next to the river, complete with viewing platforms and benches, all of it barrier-free. Almost anything might turn up here. It is even claimed that Yellow Rails have been heard here (at night, of course), but more typical birds are Hairy Woodpecker, Western Wood-Pewee, Willow Flycatcher, Warbling Vireo, Black-billed Magpie, and Black-headed Grosbeak. About 7.0 miles south of Fort Klamath, on OR 62, Modoc

Point Road comes in from the right. Take Modoc Point Road to the south, passing **Petric Park Boat Launch** at 1.9 miles, to **Wood River Wetlands,** on the right, 2.4 miles from OR 62. It is 0.1 mile to the parking lot (restrooms), where there is a gate. The road beyond the gate passes between rows of willows and cottonwoods, which in spring can have Willow Flycatchers, Yellow Warblers, and Brown-headed Cowbirds, plus others. **Henzel County Park** lies 3.4 miles farther along Modoc Point Road (restrooms). From the boat launch area, you can see across Agency Lake, and pick up Western, Clark's, and Eared Grebes on the lake surface. A scope is useful.

**36. Westside Road** - Westside Road intersects OR 140 about 25 miles north of Klamath Falls. The sign says, "Fort Klamath and Rocky Point." However, note that there is another turnoff to Rocky Point that comes about 0.8 mile before Westside Road, assuming you are coming from Klamath Falls. Westside Road leads through lots of good birding habitat, but two prime points are Rocky Point Boat Launch and Malone Springs. To get to **Rocky Point Boat Launch,** go 2.9 miles north on Westside Road from its junction with OR 140, and turn right 0.1 mile to the boat launch. There is parking here, and restrooms. There is also a fishing pier sticking out into the lake, from which you can see grebes, terns, and swallows in summer. To get to **Malone Springs,** go 6.2 miles north on Westside Road from its junction with OR 140, to a gravel road turnoff on the right. This leads, in 0.4 mile, to a small parking area and boat launch. There is an old abandoned road leading toward the north that gives access to good birding habitats. **Crystal Springs Rest Area** is 9.7 miles north of OR 140, and is a pleasant spot with restrooms and picnic tables. At 13.9 miles from OR 140 is **Jack Spring,** a location where Yellow Rails have been heard at night. Look for Milepost 3 (on west side of road), and then go 0.3 mile further, where there is barely enough room to park off the road on the east side. At this point, you can see out to the marsh, through a gap in the trees. At 16.1 miles is **Mares Egg Spring,** with sufficient parking for three or four cars next to the road, and a short rough footpath leading to the spring.

**37. Fourmile Lake** - The access road is about 32.5 miles from Klamath Falls, on OR 140, 0.6 mile beyond the road to Lake of the Woods (see below). It is 5.5 miles on good gravel road to the lake. At a couple of points, Mount McLoughlin can be seen to the west. Fourmile Lake is situated in a lodgepole pine forest, with a campground along one shore. A trailhead is located within the campground, that gives access to a trail to Squaw Lake and to the Pacific Crest Trail. The trail leads through open lodgepole pine forest, with birds such as Hairy Woodpecker, Mountain Chickadee, Red-breasted Nuthatch and Yellow-rumped Warbler. Be prepared for mosquitoes.

**38. Lake of the Woods** - The road to Lake of the Woods is about 32 miles from Klamath Falls, on OR 140. This road provides access to Aspen Point Campground and Lake of the Woods Resort, and in 1.2 miles comes to Dead Indian Road. Sunset Campground lies 1.2 miles to the right, on Dead Indian

Road. Lake of the Woods is very heavily used, but the adjacent areas provide good forest birding.

**39. Southwest Shore of Upper Klamath Lake** - From the intersection of OR 140 and Westside Road, go 3.5 miles south to Forest Service Road 3639 on left, which goes to **Odessa Creek Campground,** on a good gravel road. There is a small campground and a boat launch, with brushy habitat and sloughs from the lake. Returning to OR 140, go south 4.5 miles to road on left, leading to **Eagle Ridge Park.** It is 4.4 miles on good gravel road to the park, which has a small campground and a boat ramp. Beyond the campground, the road deteriorates in quality to a fair dirt road with long stretches of one lane. The road runs directly next to the lake, giving grand views across the lake to Mount McLoughlin. There are forest birds here, but the main attraction is the marshes near the road, with many species of ducks. Returning to OR 140, continue south another 5.3 miles to **Howard Bay,** where the highway runs directly on the lake shore. There is a small parking area between the road and the lake, giving views of goldeneyes, scaups, and grebes.

**40. Lakeshore Drive** - This road leaves US 97 in the north end of Klamath Falls, and more or less follows the southern shore of Upper Klamath Lake until it joins OR 62, about 6.5 miles from US 97. The northern parking lot for **Link River Nature Trail** is about 0.5 mile from US 97. The section of the river next to the parking lot is almost certain to have Western and Clark's Grebes in the spring and summer, and Hooded Merganser and Barrow's Goldeneye in winter. There is a pedestrian gate here (no horses or bicycles permitted) to a gravel road that leads next to the Link River for about 1.5 miles to its southern terminus near the Favell Museum. (See section on Lake Ewauna.) The riparian growth next to the river provides habit for many species, and the river itself forms a flyway for birds moving from Lake Ewauna to Upper Klamath Lake. At the southern end, in winter, there often are Black-crowned Night-Herons roosting in the trees on the opposite side of the river. Back on Lakeshore Drive, continue for about 0.5 mile to **Moore Park** on the left, and the **Moore Park Boat Ramp** on the right. There are two more parking lots just beyond, all of which provide views into the lake. Moore Park to a large degree is a typical city park, and can be crowded on weekends, but has roads and trails at its upper forested end with woodland birds.

**41. Lake Ewauna and Link River** - If coming from the north on US 97, exit where the sign says "Klamath Falls, City Center." The exit curves around and comes to a stop sign at Main Street. The **Favell Museum** is directly across Main Street, and there are parking lots to the left of the museum, where the southern entrance to the **Link River Nature Trail** is located. (See above section on Lakeshore Drive for more information about the nature trail.) *Do not park so that you block the turning around of the school buses in the large dirt lot at the beginning of the trail.* To get to **Lake Ewauna,** go west on Main Street from the Favell Museum, cross the bridge, and immediately turn right into the parking lot next to the lake, at **Veterans Memorial Park.** If approaching on US 97 from the south, matters are a bit more complicated. Probably the best thing to do is to follow the downtown exit road until it becomes Klamath Avenue, going east, one-way, into downtown. At the first opportunity, turn left, go one block to Main Street, and go back west toward US 97. The turn into Veterans Memorial Park comes just before the US 97 overhead, and the Favell Museum comes just after the overhead. Lake Ewauna has ducks, white pelicans at times, and gulls. This is the prime spot for gulls in the Klamath Basin.

**42. Klamath River and Boyle Reservoir** - From **Keno**, on OR 66, go west on OR 66 for 5.7 miles to a large parking area on the right, next to John C. Boyle Reservoir, which is a dammed-up section of the Klamath River. Scan the surface of the reservoir for water birds such as pelicans, cormorants, mergansers, and terns. I saw three species of terns here once, in mid-May: Forster's, Caspian, and Black. Directly across OR 66 is a gravel road that leads, in 1.1 miles to **Topsy Campground,** a delightful campground on the shore of the river.

**43. Hamaker Mountain** - From Keno, on OR 66, go 1.0 mile west on OR 66 to Hamaker Mountain Road. It is 8.2 miles to the summit on a paved, but "low maintenance" road. (A sign next to the road says "No Recreational Activity on Roadway," but this refers to wintertime activities, such as sledding or snowmobiles.) The summit is covered with antennas and a large parking area. The views are sensational. The birding is good in the open fir forest below the summit, and at many points along the road, with birds such as Olive-sided Flycatcher, Mountain Chickadee, Green-tailed Towhee, and Fox Sparrow.

**44. Miller Island (Klamath WA)** - From the intersection of US 97 and OR 140, go south on US 97 2.5 miles to the entrance to the Klamath WA (Miller Island Unit). Turn right, cross the railroad tracks, and enter the wildlife area. At 0.2 miles, there is a parking area and nature trail on the right. The road extends for 3.0 miles to its end at a boat ramp on the Klamath River. It is paved for 2.0 miles, and then becomes gravel, making several right-angle turns. There are several large ponds that provide resting places for waterfowl, and trees here and there for raptors, especially for Bald Eagles in winter.

**45. Township Road and Straits Drain** - From the junction of OR 140 and US 97, go 11.4 miles south on US 97 to Township Road, on the left. Township Road runs east and west, about 2 ½ miles north of the border with California. Most of the land south of Township Road belongs to the Lower Klamath NWR. Straits Drain lies 3.8 miles east of US 97, and is the main drain that connects Lower Klamath Lake to the Klamath River. A good gravel road runs parallel to the drain on the east side, and connects to CA 161 directly opposite the point where the tour road from Lower Klamath NWR exits. The fields are sometimes flooded in spring, and provide good shorebird habitat.

**46. Stukel Mountain** - Stukel Mountain is the prominent high point to the southeast of Klamath Falls. It is reached by going south to Dehlinger Lane, on OR 39 4.0 miles from where OR 140 goes west from OR 39. Go east 1.7 miles on Dehlinger Lane to Hill Road, turn left and go 0.7 mile to where a road goes into a rock quarry on the right side. Go up the paved road into the quarry for 0.2 mile to an orange gate, where a gravel road begins. The land, including the quarry, belongs to the Bureau of Land Management (BLM), and the public has the right to use the road, even though the sign at the entrance says, "No Trespassing." The orange gate is closed from December through April. The first half-mile is narrow and steep, but it gets better further up. The road passes through sagebrush slopes and then into ponderosa pines. At one point there is a gate marked "private," and the road crosses a corner of private land, but BLM has constructed a road around the private portion, that remains on public land, but this road may not be passable under muddy conditions. At about 4.0 miles the road levels out into a saddle, but then climbs 2.0 miles more on a steep and narrow road to the summit, where there is little room for cars. There are lots of meadowlarks and scrub-jays in the open country, and Rock Wrens and Fox Sparrows in the brushy country toward the top. Chukars have been seen occasionally along the road.

**47. Gerber Reservoir and Gerber Potholes** - Gerber Reservoir is a large reservoir in a shallow mountain basin, constructed by the Bureau of Reclamation. The surrounding land is managed by the Bureau of Land Management. There are two developed campgrounds on the shore of the lake, and three less developed campgrounds nearby, attractively situated in ponderosa pine forest. The most interesting wildlife watching is provided by ephemeral ponds in the vicinity, called "potholes," that have nesting habitat for Canada Geese, Mallards, Cinnamon Teal, Willets, and Sandhill Cranes. To get there, from the junction of OR 140 and OR 70 go east on OR 70 through **Bonanza** 25.0 miles to the reservoir, following signs. On the way, you pass through the vast, lovely, green **Langell Valley.** The two developed campgrounds, North Campground and South Campground, are close to each other on the west shore of the lake, and have the usual forest birds. There is a Bald Eagle nest on the shore of the lake directly across from North Campground. To get to the Gerber Potholes, continue past the entrance to Gerber Reservoir (the road changes to gravel) for about one mile. There are potholes on both sides of the road, marked "Wildlife Watching Area." These potholes generally dry up by July.

**48. Sprague River Picnic Area** - You probably wouldn't make a special trip to get here, but if you happen to be traveling along OR 140 between Klamath Falls and Lakeview, this makes a delightful stop, with forest and streamside birding, about 4.0 miles east of Bly. A narrow, paved road leads about 0.4 mile down into the picnic area along Sprague River. There is a narrow, rough trail that encircles the area, crossing the river on footbridges.

**49. Klamath Basin Refuges** - From the intersection of US 97 and CA 161, go east on CA 161 9.4 miles to the entrance for the auto tour route for **Lower Klamath NWR.** To get to the **Visitor Center and Refuge Headquarters**, continue east from the tour route entrance on CA 161 for 7.7 miles to Hill Road, turn right (south) and go for 2.9 miles to the Visitor Center. To get to the auto tour route for the **Tule Lake NWR,** continue south for 4.7 miles from the Visitor Center. The Klamath Basin is one of the most important bird areas in North America. More than 1 million ducks, geese, and swans may be present in the peak month of November. It is also one of the most important wintering areas in the U.S. for Bald Eagles. In spring and early summer, large numbers of waterfowl and other birds breed here, including Western and Clark's Grebes, ibises, stilts, avocets, willets, snipe, terns, and Tricolored and Yellow-headed Blackbirds. Check for breeding Wilson's Phalaropes, especially in **White Lake,** which is about 4.0 miles east of the auto tour entrance for Lower Klamath NWR. As you go south from the Visitor Center, check the cliffs along **Sheepy Ridge** for nests of hawks, falcons, and owls. After exiting from the Tule Lake Auto Tour Route onto County Road 120, go east about 1.6 miles to County Road 111, turn left (north) about 0.7 mile, cross some railroad tracks, and then turn immediately right (east) on County Road 126. In about 0.9 mile the road comes to the parking area for the **Petroglyph Section** of Lava Beds NM. Breeding Prairie Falcons may have a nest on the cliff, visible from the parking lot. (See photograph on Plate IV.)

**50. Lava Beds National Monument** - From the town of Tulelake, go west on East-West Road 4.8 miles to Hill Road and turn south. The Visitor Center for the Klamath Basin Wildlife Refuges is 0.5 mile south of East-West Road, and the entrance to Lava Beds NM is 8.4 miles beyond the Visitor Center. The national monument is known for its lava fields and lava tube caves. The habitat principally consists of junipers and sagebrush. Western Scrub-Jay is the most abundant bird, but there are Canyon Wrens in the rocks, and Violet-green Swallows and Purple Martins nest in the cliff faces. The campground has nice junipers, and Oak/Juniper Titmice are resident there.

**51. Clear Lake National Wildlife Life Refuge** - Clear Lake is a dammed reservoir and is the source of Lost River, which flows north into Oregon, back into California again, and ends in the Tule Lake Basin. Thus, the source of the river is only ten miles or so from its end, but it travels 100 miles in between. At one time, Tule Lake was a vast body of water with no outlet, but Lost River is heavily managed today, with connections to the Klamath River, and there is even a tunnel through Sheepy Ridge between Tule Lake and Lower Klamath, to regulate water levels. Clear Lake NWR provides nesting sites for American White Pelicans and other colonial nesting species, and is closed to public access except for limited hunting of waterfowl and pronghorn antelopes. Access to the fringe of the lake is via Forest Road 136, a good gravel road that leaves CA 139 about 21 miles south of Tulelake. Only distant views of the lake are possible, and the road mostly travels through sagebrush and junipers -- meadowlark and

Horned Lark country -- where you can travel for miles without seeing a house or another car. About 20 miles from CA 139, the road enters the extensive juniper/pine forests of the **Devils Garden.**

**52. Butte Valley and Meiss Lake** - From the small town of Macdoel (on US 97 about 30 miles south of Klamath Falls, go 0.4 mile south on US 97, and turn right on Meiss Lake Road. The pavement ends in 2.4 miles, and the road turns to gravel. The tour route for **Butte Valley WA** begins 4.0 miles from US 97, and extends about 5.0 miles through the wildlife area, with mostly marshes on one side, and **Meiss Lake** ("Meiss" is pronounced locally as "Meese") on the other. Many kinds of water birds breed here, including large breeding colonies of California and Ring-billed Gulls. **Juanita Lake** lies about 2 miles south of the wildlife area, on Forest Road 46N04. To take a tour through **Butte Valley,** which is famous for its raptors, go north from Macdoel about 1.0 mile on US 97 to Sheep Mountain Road on the right. Follow Sheep Mountain Road until it begins to head due east. Continue, partially on gravel, for about 5 miles to the end of the public road. Go north on Macdoel-Dorris Road to Shady Dell Road, and return to US 97. The area is mostly farm fields, and is good for eagles and hawks. After returning to US 97, go north on US 97 for 2.2 miles and turn west on Sams Neck Road. Look for Sage Thrasher and Brewer's Sparrow in the sagebrush. Meiss Lake lies in a closed basin, and has no natural outlet. Thus, some might argue that it is actually not a part of the Klamath Basin, but is its own basin. However, the lake and valley are so closely connected to the Klamath Basin proper, that it is included here.

## KLAMATH RIVER CANYON (see map of Jackson County, Page 27)

**53. Iron Gate Reservoir** - About 21 miles south of Ashland, on I-5, exit at **Henley** exit, Exit 789. Go east on Copco Road 8.0 miles to Iron Gate Fish Hatchery, where you can cross the bridge to the hatchery, park, and bird the grounds. Then go 9.5 miles further to the upper end of the lake at Fall Creek Park, passing numerous picnic areas on the way which can be birded. At Fall Creek Park, turn sharply back downhill and park. **Fall Creek Park** offers attractive birding habitat next to the lake. From there you can walk 100 yards or so down the gravel road toward the residences, and observe a small pond on the right, where I saw ten Wood Ducks when I was there last, in mid-May.

**54. Trees of Heaven** - About 25 miles south of Ashland, on I-5, take the exit for CA 96, the Klamath River Highway. At about 6.8 miles down this highway is Trees of Heaven Campground, which has attractive campsites near the river, and a paved nature trail. Birds which have occurred here are Lewis's Woodpecker, Yellow-breasted Chat, and Bullock's Oriole. Downstream within 3 or 4 miles are two more river access points, Cayuse, and Skeahan Bar, with similar birding opportunities.

# Chapter 5 - HOW TO USE THIS BOOK

**SPECIES ACCOUNTS**

The major part of this book is organized into "species accounts." Mostly, an account will give a feel for the distribution and seasonality of a particular species, and usually includes a general description, but not to the extent that it would be in a traditional identification field guide. It is assumed that a field guide is at hand, and that reference will be made to the illustrations and descriptions therein. However, some hints on identification are included in certain cases, particularly if two or more species are hard to tell apart. Bird behavior is frequently emphasized, especially if I think the material is interesting, or will help a person get to know the bird better.

In scientific literature, species accounts usually give a lot of detail about things like nests, eggs, and molts. That kind of information is largely omitted from this book, partly because of its bulk, and partly because I think it lacks interest for a general audience. If something about the nests, eggs, or molts is of special interest, then I include it.

In most cases, there is one account per species, but sometimes I have grouped two, three, or even four species into one account, usually because they resemble each other and need to be discussed together. In a few cases, I included the names of subspecies in the headings of the accounts, either because they are readily identifiable forms that are counted and listed separately in Christmas Counts ("Audubon's" and "Myrtle Warbler" are a good example), or because there are recognizable forms within the species that might become separate species in the future (the Fox Sparrow complex is an example).

**BIRDS' NAMES**

**Taxonomic order.** The names of species are consistent with the *Seventh Edition of the Check-list of North American Birds* (1998), published by the American Ornithologists' Union. Possessive forms of birds' names, as in **Lewis's Woodpecker,** are spelled in accordance with that checklist. Also, with only minor exceptions, the order in which the species are presented follow that in the checklist. This is referred to as the **taxonomic order.** The exceptions are when I place a pair of birds together for discussion, in which case the taxonomic order may not quite be followed.

Many people, who are unfamiliar with the reasons behind the taxonomic order, feel that an alphabetical order would be preferable, to make it easier to find a particular species. This is understandable, because with hundreds of species' names on a list, if the order is unfamiliar, a particular species may be hard to locate.

The rationale behind the taxonomic order is that birds are grouped together in families. From the birder's point of view, this means that, for example, all the warblers are together, so are the sparrows, and so on. If the order is alphabetical, then birds such as the Yellow Warbler, the American Redstart, and the Northern Waterthrush, all of them warblers, are widely separated in the list, instead of being grouped together.

**Scientific names.** For many things in the natural world, such as plants, insects, fish, and even mammals, there are so many different common names that they are not very useful. Thus, scientific names are preferred, because that way a particular name is the same throughout the world. However, contrary to common belief, scientific names *do change,* and more often than might be supposed. But, when this is done, there is common agreement in the scientific world, and the name is the same everywhere.

A scientific name typically consists of two parts, usually given in Latin, although terms derived from other languages are also sometimes used. The first part is the name of the *genus,* which is given to a group of closely related birds. The second name is the name of the *species.* If a subspecies is involved, then there is a third name. Thus, we can have the name *Pasarella iliaca* for the Fox Sparrow, and *Passarella iliaca unalaschcensis* for a subspecies of Fox Sparrow that breeds in Alaska and winters on the Pacific Coast. The name of the genus is always capitalized. The species and subspecies names are not capitalized, even when the names are derived from the names of persons.

**Common names.** For most biological entities, common names are variable and conflicting. For birds, however, the situation with common names is different, because there is a concerted attempt to standardize them. In the United States, the Committee on Classification and Nomenclature, of the American Ornithologists' Union, publishes "official" common names, as well as the scientific ones. Of course, this only works as far as America is concerned, because other English-speaking countries don't necessarily accept the decisions of the AOU. And, in non-English countries, each country has its own set of common names in its own language.

**Name changes.** It sometimes seems bewildering, how many times birds' names get changed. To some, it seems almost capricious. Well, it is not capricious, although it sometimes can be mystifying. The Committee on Classification and Nomenclature will change the name of a bird if it comes into possession of information that demonstrates a change is necessary.

Sometimes the change results in lumping two species together, usually based on research that shows the two former species interbreed so frequently that they ought to be considered as one. This happened to "Red-shafted Flicker" and "Yellow-shafted Flicker" a few years back, and the two were lumped into one species, which then had to have a new name. Northern Flicker was the result.

Another kind of name change occurs when, instead of two species being lumped together, a single species is split into two or more. An example of this sort is when the "Rufous-sided Towhee" was split into Eastern Towhee and Spotted Towhee. In this case, the two "new" names were actually old names, and had been in use previously to describe the two forms.

Another way in which a name can change is because of the manner in which one of "our" species interacts with a similar species at a location remote from us. The case of the Green Heron is a good example. At one time it was considered to be conspecific (the same species) with a similar heron whose range overlaps with it in Panama. At that time, the two were lumped into a single species, called Green-backed Heron. Research showed that the degree of interbreeding was minimal, so the two were split, into Striated Heron and Green Heron.

**Capitalization.** It is a policy of the AOU that, when birds' names are used in publications which focus on birds, the common names should be capitalized, as in Yellow Warbler. If just the generic part of the name is used -- warbler -- it is not capitalized. This, of course, can lead to trouble. A Wilson's Warbler is mostly yellow, so we could conceivably refer to a Wilson's Warbler as a yellow warbler (not capitalized). But Yellow Warbler (capitalized) refers to a definite species.

In this book, when a currently "official" name is being used, the name will be capitalized, in accordance with the usual AOU practice. If an alternate name is used -- one that is no longer "official" -- it will be placed in quotation marks, as in "Audubon's Warbler." Likewise, names of subspecies, or older, obsolete names, will be placed in quotation marks.

**Pronunciation.** An interesting question is how to pronounce various names. There are disagreements on this topic, but I have tried to indicate in this book which pronunciations seem to have the broadest support, by consulting dictionaries and encyclopedias.

**Plurals.** Another question is how to form plurals in certain instances. For instance, what is the plural of Killdeer? Killdeer, or Killdeers? Also, what is the plural of "titmouse?" I read an article once that insisted the proper plural of "titmouse" is "titmouses," but have never been able to bring myself to say it that way. I consulted my Webster's dictionary, and found the results given in the listings below. In some cases, two forms were given. In each such case, I have put the form that was listed first in boldface type below, and the alternate form in parentheses. In this book, I have decided to go with Webster's, and have made a practice of using the first-listed forms. I was somewhat surprised, in my investigation, to discover that "Killdeers" is listed before "Killdeer," and was pleased to discover that "titmouses" is not listed at all. If the name also happens to be the full common name, as in "Brant," I have capitalized it.

Here's the list:

| | |
|---|---|
| Brant | **Brant** (*or* Brants) |
| Dunlin | **Dunlins** (*or* Dunlin) |
| Gadwall | **Gadwalls** (*or* Gadwall) |
| grouse | **grouse** (*or* grouses) |
| ibis | **ibis** (*or* ibises) |
| junco | **juncos** (*or* juncoes) |
| Killdeer | **Killdeers** (*or* Killdeer) |
| quail | **quail** (*or* quails) |
| scaup | **scaup** (*or* scaups) |
| snipe | **snipes** (*or* snipe) |
| teal | **teal** (*or* teals) |
| titmouse | **titmice** |

**BIRD-BANDING ABBREVIATIONS.**

After the common name of each species, I have added, in parentheses, the four-letter abbreviation used by bird-banders for that species. These codes are formed from the common names of the species. The rules are as follows.

(1) If the species has just one word in its name, then the first four letters of the name form the code. Thus, for Mallard, the code is MALL.

(2) If the species has two words in its name, then the code is formed by combining the first two letters of each word. Thus, for Belted Kingfisher, the code is BEKI.

(3) If the species has three words in its name, then the code is formed by combining the first letters of the first two words with the first two letters of the third word. Thus, for Golden-crowned Sparrow, the code is GCSP.

(4) If the name doesn't fit into one of the above patterns, then some other appropriate combination of letters is used to form a unique symbol. Also, in cases where use of the rules would produce non-unique codes, then other combinations are chosen, so that the codes will be unique. For example, by the rules both Tree Swallow and Trumpeter Swan would produce identical codes. To avoid duplication, TRES is used for Tree Swallow, and TRUS is used for Trumpeter Swan.

Bird-banders find these codes useful, because it saves time as compared to writing out the full names. By the same token, us ordinary birders might find them useful -- some of them, at least -- for making notes of the day's sightings. After a while, this may become almost automatic for some of the species you see frequently. For example, when I see or hear a Belted Kingfisher, I immediately think "BEKI," and even find myself pronouncing it "Beckie." Likewise, with Ruby-crowned Kinglet (RCKI) and Golden-crowned Kinglet (GCKI), I find myself saying "Rocky" and "Gecky." Willow Flycatcher (WIFL), is "Wiffle." Sure, it sounds silly, but it's quick to write, when putting down your daily sightings.

**VAGRANTS**

Every bird species is included that has been reported within the area of coverage. Of the total 373 species in this book, 44 can be considered "irregular," which means that they don't show up every year. Seventy-six are considered "vagrant," or "accidental," meaning a bird outside its normal range that has occurred only a few times. (See section on "Bar Charts" for more precise definitions of these terms.)

A vagrant or accidental bird can arrive in our region for one of several reasons. It could be blown off course by a storm, or could be here because of food failure in its normal range. Also, the vanguards of a true range expansion will be perceived as vagrants initially. A couple of good examples of range expansions are the march of the Cattle Egret across the continent, and the current movement of Great-tailed Grackles up through California and into Oregon. But there are a couple of systematic reasons that particularly affect the long-distance migrants such as warblers.

**Great Egret**

**Cattle Egret**

**Ruddy Duck (male in breeding plumage)**

**American Wigeons (male and female)**

**Black-crowned Night-Heron**

**American White Pelican**

**PLATE I**

Redheads (female and Male)

Western Grebe

Double-crested Cormorant

Canada Goose (and chick)

Wood Duck (male)

Snow Geese

**PLATE II**

One reason is called "mirror-image" misorientation. Birds are believed to follow the correct paths during migration by a combination of sun position, light polarization, stars, and the earth's magnetic field. If a bird for some reason gets its east and west orientation switched, then it might head to the southwest instead of its intended direction, southeast, which is a "mirror-image" mistake. Thus, a bird that breeds to the north of us, and that normally migrates to the Gulf Coast, would wind up in our area instead.

Another reason is simple overshoot, where migrating birds overfly their intended destinations, sometimes by hundreds of miles. Thus, a bird that normally breeds to the south of us, in spring migration could wind up in our area because of overshoot.

Most people are excited to discover vagrants, and it goes without saying that a suspected vagrant should be inspected carefully, particularly to make sure it isn't just an odd-looking member of a species that is regular.

## OREGON BIRD RECORDS COMMITTEE

Since this is a book intended for a popular audience, rather than for a scientific one, the requirements for inclusion are less rigorous than for inclusion on the lists maintained by the Oregon Bird Records Committee (OBRC). The records of the OBRC serve an important scientific purpose, to record in a rigorous context the confirmation of rare bird species seen in Oregon. Unfortunately, many people don't submit their sightings to the OBRC, and thus many sightings go unrecorded. To be included in this present book, an observation by a competent observer was deemed to be sufficient.

To submit a sighting to the OBRC, you should include your name, address, and telephone number, plus the date and location of the sighting, including the circumstances, such as light conditions, distance to the bird, duration of observation, equipment used, time of day, and time of tide if applicable.

State the details of what you observed, including only what was actually observed, not what should have been seen or heard. Stress the field marks: bill, eye, wings, tail, legs, shape, proportions. Include behavior, such as feeding, resting, flying, and interactions with other species. Describe songs, calls, or notes that were heard.

Describe your reasons for the identification, your familiarity with the species, field guides used, similar species that were eliminated, and references that were consulted. Include the names and addresses of other observers. Above all, submit a photo or a recording, if possible.

## BAR CHARTS

Each species account in this book has one or more bar charts, unless the bird is a vagrant. Bar charts offer a graphic way to describe abundance, and at what seasons of the year those abundances are likely to occur. However, since birds are living, moving, intelligent creatures, they may not always "obey" the bar charts, and may show up at times and places where they aren't expected. Nevertheless, bar charts can be useful in giving clues to the likelihood of finding a particular species.

Since our region is broadly divided into "west of the crest" and "east of the crest," with different species showing up in different abundances on either side of the crest, the bar charts have been arranged to show these differences. In such cases, the bar charts will look like this:

If there is no appreciable difference between the abundance and seasonality on the two sides of the crest, then "west" and "east" will be omitted, and the bar chart will look like this:

The meanings to be attached to the width of the bars, and to the terms "Vagrant" and "Accidental," are given below.

| | |
|---|---|
| ▬▬▬▬▬ | Common; seen on most trips to the field |
| ▬▬▬▬ | Uncommon to fairly common; seen on less than half the trips to the field |
| ――――― | Rare, but regular |
| - - - - - - - | Rare and irregular; does not always occur annually |
| ■ ■ ■ ■ ■ ■ | Irregular; not seen every year, but may be fairly common when present |
| Vagrant | Used for a bird out of range that has only shown up a few times |
| Accidental | Used for a bird out of range that is not likely to reoccur |

## Chapter 6 - SPECIES ACCOUNTS

### Family **GAVIIDAE**: Loons

**Pacific Loon** (PALO)  
*Gavia pacifica*

J F M A M J J A S O N D
|--                    -----|

**Red-throated Loon** (RTLO)          Vagrant
*Gavia stellata*

Pacific Loons are common during migration along the coast, but are very rare inland. Look for them on open water in winter, such as at Lost Creek Lake, Upper Klamath Lake, and Lake Selmac. Red-throated Loons are even more rare inland, but occasionally show up. It pays to be alert, even though loons in winter plumage can be hard to tell apart, especially if they are juveniles.

Advanced identification guides such as *Birding in the American West* (see references) give tips to identification for the more difficult cases, but in this book, I will just point out a couple of things to look for. Both of these loons are smaller than the Common Loon, and have more slender bills. The bill on a Pacific looks straight, whereas the bill on a Red-throated looks upcurved. The "upcurved" appearance actually results from the fact that the culmen (top of upper mandible) of the Red-throated is straight, while there is a distinct upward curve to the lower mandible.

The adult winter-plumaged Pacific is usually dark around the eye, while the adult winter-plumaged Red-throated is usually white around the eye. The appearance of the back is helpful, because the Red-throated's back is covered with small white spots, which are lacking in the Pacific. In fact, the word *stellata* in the scientific name of the Red-throated means "starred," and refers to the white spots on the back.

It is sometimes said that the tendency of the Red-throated Loon to hold its bill tilted up at an angle is useful in identification, but all species of loons may do that at one time or another. Also, cormorants are often misidentified as loons, because of the slender up-tilted bill. This confusion is especially likely if the cormorant is a juvenile, because juvenile cormorants are brownish on the neck, and at a distance can look quite a bit like a loon.

**Common Loon** (COLO)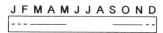
*Gavia immer*

Anyone who has seen the movie, *On Golden Pond,* knows what a loon sounds like. The weird tremolo call has often been described as a sort of maniacal laughter, and is said to have given rise to the phrase, "crazy as a loon." The call is mostly heard on the breeding grounds, but they can also sometimes be heard giving their tremolo calls during migration. Common

Loons are suspected of breeding in a couple of places in the northern Cascades, but breeding has not been confirmed.

When they come through in spring, they are in their beautiful breeding plumage, with a black and white spangled back, and a black and white necklace. In fall, when they migrate back south, some may still retain their breeding plumage, but others will have molted into winter plumage, in muted shades of brown and white.

In this plumage they somewhat resemble Red-throated and Pacific Loons, which are very rare in our area, but could occur. Here is what to look for. All of these loons in winter plumage have light-colored throats and are dark on the back of the necks. The dividing line between these colors down the side of the neck has this difference in the Common Loon: Where the black and white necklace is located in the breeding plumage, there will be a pale indentation in the line on the side of the neck. This is not the only difference in these three species, but it is easy to spot, and clinches the case.

During migration, loons should be looked for on the lakes in our area, such as Lost Creek Lake, Upper Klamath Lake, and Lake Selmac. They are strong fliers, but have great difficulties in taking off, requiring long distances. They are also strong swimmers and divers, often remaining under water as long as a minute. One reason loons are so good at swimming under water is because their legs are placed far to the rear of their bodies. This characteristic also causes them to be able to walk on land only with great difficulty. In Great Britain loons are called "divers", and our Common Loon is known as Great Northern Diver.

**Common Loon**

There is an old story, concerning whether loons are good to eat. Here is the recipe for cooking a loon: Put the loon into boiling water, together with a rock. Boil for a long time. When you can stick a fork into the rock, the loon is done.

### Yellow-billed Loon (YBLO)                                             Accidental
*Gavia adamsii*

This loon usually is found in the far north, but it occasionally strays to coastal locations in Oregon, mostly in winter. Once in while it turns up inland. There are two records for the Klamath Basin, one from the Boyle Reservoir on the Klamath River, in April 1993, and the other from Tule Lake NWR, in February 2000.

Common Loons are often mistaken for Yellow-billed Loons, even though the Yellow-billed is substantially larger. There is no problem in breeding plumage. The huge yellow bill is distinctive. But in non-breeding plumage, the differences between Common and Yellow-billed are subtle. The OBRC will not accept records for Yellow-billed Loon unless convincing documentation of details is submitted. Here are a few things to look for, to help you separate it from Common Loon.

In nonbreeding plumage, the bill on a Yellow-billed may fade to a straw color, while the bill on a Common fades to a gray color. This can make the bills on both species look light-colored. Check the culmen (the top of the upper mandible). On a Common, the top of the culmen will be black; on a Yellow-billed, the outer half of the bill will remain pale.

Both species have large bills and angular-looking heads. On a Common, the bill is usually held horizontal, whereas a Yellow-billed often holds its bill up at an angle. This is not conclusive, however. I've sometimes seen Commons hold their bills up at an angle, at least for a short time.

Bill shape can help. On a Common, the culmen has a slight convex curve on the top; on a Yellow-billed, the culmen is straight. On both species, the lower mandible curves upward. On a Common, because there is a curve to both the upper and lower mandibles, it makes the bill look dagger-shaped. Since the upper mandible of the Yellow-billed is straight, this, plus the sharp angle on the lower mandible, makes the bill look sharp and uptilted.

On a Common Loon in nonbreeding plumage, the border on the side of the neck between the dark nape and the light-colored front is diffuse and irregular, usually with one or two sharp indentations. A Yellow-billed Loon can show a similar pattern, but in the Common the top of the head will be noticeably darker than on the back of the bird. The head of the Yellow-billed will look paler than on the back of the bird, and there often is a smudgy dark spot on the auriculars.

Some of these factors tend to be subtle, but they are what you need to look for, if you think you've got a Yellow-billed Loon.

## Family **PODICIPEDIDAE**: Grebes

**Pied-billed Grebe** (PBGR)
*Podilymbus podiceps*

If there is anything approaching a guarantee in birding, it is that you can almost always find a Pied-billed Grebe, if you look in the right place. The "right place" is virtually any pond or sluggish stream. In winter, they retreat from the higher mountains and from the east side of the Cascades, but are found year-round in the valleys on the west side, at least in places where the water doesn't freeze.

There is a word that is often used to describe the Pied-gilled Grebe: cute. Some have said that they resemble the kind of "rubber ducky" that children love to play with in the bathtub. The "pied-billed" part of their name comes from the fact that, in the breeding season, they have a distinct black band around the bill. In winter, this band becomes indistinct.

The adults may be cute, but the chicks are cuter. At a young age they are heavily striped. They even may ride on the adult's back, looking like a scene staged by Walt Disney.

Only once in my life have I ever seen a Pied-billed Grebe actually fly, and then it seemed to be something of a struggle for it to make it from one small pond to another, with neck outstretched and legs dangling. Instead, when alarmed, they often sink out of sight without a ripple. They also can dive in a flash, and are called "hell-divers" by some. Once below the surface, they swim to nearby vegetation and hide there, with only the bill and eyes showing above water.

One humorist said that, since he had never seen a Pied-billed Grebe fly, he concluded they must travel from pond to pond by secret underwater tunnels. Yet, they do migrate upon occasion, although it is said that they are relatively weak fliers, and do their migration at night.

Like loons, grebes are clumsy on land, and require long running starts on water in order to get airborne. A story is told of a group of Pied-billed Grebes that were migrating at night, mistook a wet roadway for a stream, and landed. Of course, they were then unable to take off or even to maneuver properly, and were at the mercy of the auto traffic.

Mostly, Pied-billeds are silent, but they can be quite noisy in breeding season. Once, at dusk in spring, I heard a loud, dreadful sound coming from a hidden spot in nearby cattails. It sounded like *kow kow! kow! kow! kow! kow-uh! kow-uh! kow-uh!* My imagination vested the source of this voice with all sorts of menacing images, including angry coyotes, belligerent egrets, and maybe even stray alligators. Many years later, I learned that, no, it was just the lovable little Pied-billed Grebe singing his spring love song. The song is not just heard at dusk, but might be given any time of day in the breeding season.

## Horned Grebe (HOGR)
*Podiceps auritis*

## Eared Grebe (EAGR)
*Podiceps nigricolis*

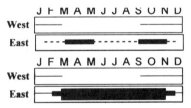

These two species are considered together, because in winter they can be difficult to tell apart. In breeding plumage there is no problem. The Eared Grebe has a black neck and wispy yellow plumes coming from the region of the "ears." The Horned Grebe has a rufous neck, and has solid yellow patches in the region of the "horns."

In winter, matters are different. Nevertheless, they can still be told apart. A mark that can be useful, especially at a distance, is the brightness of the front of the neck. Horned Grebes generally are all white on the front, whereas Eared Grebes are a dingy gray. Also, the head of an Eared Grebe usually looks as if it has a peak on top, whereas the head of a Horned Grebe is smoother and flatter. Bill shape is helpful, because the Eared Grebe has a sharper bill than the Horned, that tends to turn up slightly at the end.

Both have black caps, but the Eared Grebe is dark in the region behind and below the eye, and there is usually a white arc curling up behind the "ears". The black completely surrounds the eye. In the Horned Grebe the black extends down to the eye but not below, and it usually forms a distinct, rather straight edge across the side of the head, separating the black from the white. Between seasons, when the birds are molting, they may be so confusing that all bets are off.

In Great Britain, the Eared Grebe is called the Black-necked Grebe, because, of course, it has a black neck in breeding season. The Horned Grebe is called the Slavonian Grebe. Don't ask me why.

Like all grebes, these two are excellent underwater swimmers, and expertly pursue their prey of aquatic insects and their larvae, small fishes, and tadpoles. Horned Grebes, particularly, may be ahead of the others in their ability to stay under water, since it has been reported that they can stay down for as long as three minutes. Unlike Pied-billed Grebes, they usually don't hide in the vegetation when alarmed, but simply pop to the surface farther away from the source of the danger.

Look for both of these grebes during migration on large bodies of water, such as Lost Creek Lake and Upper Klamath Lake. East of the crest, Eared Grebes are common breeders, preferring lakes with marshy edges. Here they build their flimsy nests, which have been described as "small floating masses of rotten reeds, water mosses, and other vegetable rubbish." A typical location is the Lower Klamath Refuge. Horned Grebes are confirmed breeders in just one location in eastern Klamath County, but are considered "possible" at a couple of other locations.

### Red-necked Grebe (RNGR)
*Podiceps grisegena*

If it were not for a few pairs of breeding birds at Upper Klamath Lake, this species might be relegated to "occasional" status. However, they are known to breed near the Rocky Point area of Upper Klamath Lake. Or so I am told. It pains me to admit I have stood at Rocky Point a number of times and have yet to see one there. However, I have seen them breeding in northeast Washington state. Also, there are isolated reports of breeding at Malheur, and Klamath Marsh National Wildlife Refuge.

In migration, they are considered to be uncommon in the Klamath Basin, have been seen at Miller Island, and have shown up numerous times at the larger lakes on the west side, such as Lost Creek Lake and Howard Prairie Lake. There are even scattered winter reports. A pair is reported to have bred at Howard Prairie Lake about 30 years ago, but apparently not since, as far as anyone knows.

In breeding plumage, the slender reddish neck and white cheek patch make this species unmistakable. In fact, it could be argued that this is the most beautiful of the grebes. But in winter plumage, which they may acquire as early as September, the pattern of their plumage somewhat resembles that of the Eared Grebe, with a whitish throat, and a white crescent curling up behind the "ear." However, if you can get any kind of a size assessment, it will be apparent that they are substantially larger than any other grebe except the Western/Clark's. Also, their long sharp bills should remove any confusion with Horned or Eared Grebes.

**Western Grebe** (WEGR)
*Aechmophorus occidentalis*

**Clark's Grebe** (CLGR)
*Aechmophorus clarkii*

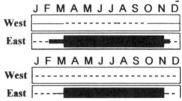

Not very many years ago, these two closely-related birds were considered to be one species. The usual criterion for separating them is the placement of the eye: If the eye is wholly contained within the black cap, it is a Western; if the eye is below the cap, and entirely surrounded by white, then it is a Clark's. Unfortunately, it is sometimes hard to tell just where the line between the black and the white lies, and sometimes it seems to go right through the eye. This may be particularly true in the non-breeding season.

A better criterion to use is bill color. In the Western, the bill is a dull, greenish-yellow. In the Clark's, it is a bright orange-yellow. This difference in bill color can be seen at surprisingly great distances. But, as always, there can be complications. In the non-breeding season, and in immature birds, these colors may be less distinct, and then there is always the possibility of hybrids. Most birders feel that, if these two criteria -- eye placement and bill color -- are uncertain, it is best to leave the bird unidentified, and call it a "Western-type."

Identification aside, I would like to say that these are among my favorite birds. Their long, slim, elegant necks and striking heads make them look like small beautiful black and white swans. In fact, they are sometimes called "swan grebes." These are also the birds who, during their mating rituals, rise up side by side and propel themselves rapidly across the surface of the water.

I love their strange call, heard often in summer but never, to my knowledge, in winter. It has been written down as *k-r-r-eek,* and one old-timer described it as sounding like the "creak of a neglected pulley block." Such a homely description aside, their calls sound to me, coming at dusk from somewhere out on a lake, like the very essence of wildness. Western Grebes tend to do it twice -- *kr-ee-k kr-ee-k* -- whereas Clark's Grebes do it more in a single prolonged note -- *kr-ee-ee-k.*

Western/Clark's Grebes differ from other grebes in the plumage of their young. In other grebes, the young generally show conspicuous stripes, but the Western/Clark's young are a light mousey gray, suggesting a loon more than a grebe.

As with other grebes, with the exception of Pied-billed Grebe, I have never seen one fly. Yet, fly they must, because they migrate long distances between their breeding and wintering grounds. They are easy to find in breeding season, when they dot the surface of Upper Klamath Lake, or sail in stately fashion down a channel at Lower Klamath Refuge. One authority claims that the Klamath Basin contains the largest breeding colonies in the country. But in winter they are scarce. Almost all go to the coast, where they dive for food in the surf. Like all grebes, they need great distances for takeoffs, and are almost helpless on land.

I once came upon a Western Grebe lying on some grass near a channel leading to the ocean. It lifted its head when I came near, and pointed its dagger-like beak threateningly in my direction. Otherwise, it was motionless. A fisherman nearby volunteered the information that the grebe had taken his bait, and that he had hauled it ashore like a fish, removed the hook, and tossed the bird on the grass. While I was considering what to do about all this, very much worried about that sharp beak, another fellow came along and asked what was going on. I explained to him what had happened, and that grebes are helpless on land. Without a word, the fellow took a jacket he was carrying, threw it over the grebe's head to nullify that sharp beak, and then picked it up and tossed it into the water, while deftly retaining his jacket. The grebe swam off, seemingly none the worse for wear.

## Family **HYDROBATIDAE**: Storm-Petrels

### **Leach's Storm-Petrel** (LHSP)  Accidental
*Oceanodroma leucorhoa*

Storm-Petrels are normally found only at sea, but one was discovered dead, in Medford, in March, 1980. However, seabirds sometimes get blown inland by storms, which must have been the case here.

## Family **PELECANIDAE**: Pelicans

### **American White Pelican** (AWPE)
*Pelecanus erythrorhynchos*

J F M A M J J A S O N D

This bird shares with the California Condor the distinction of having the longest wingspan of any American bird -- nine feet. Compared to this, the familiar Brown Pelican of the coast seems almost a piker, with a wingspan of six-and-a half feet.

Brown Pelicans are birds of the seacoast, but white pelicans are birds of inland waters. There are breeding colonies at Upper Klamath NWR and at Clear Lake NWR (Modoc County), but white pelicans are notorious for shifting their breeding colonies in response to water conditions. In 2000, they showed up in a new location, at Meiss Lake in Butte Valley, and established 15 nests there.

Non-breeding birds can be found in summer on many of the waterways and lakes of the Klamath Basin, such as Lake Euwana and the Lower Klamath NWR. On the west side, they are usually present on Howard Prairie or Hyatt Lakes in summer, in non-drought years.

One of the most thrilling sights I know is of a flock of white pelicans, circling high in the sky, alternately all flashing white simultaneously as the sun hits them just right, and then turning so they become invisible as they lose the direct sun. Wood Storks in the south do the same thing, and can be hard to tell from white pelicans. Both are big and white, with black wing tips, and both soar high in the sky.

We don't have Wood Storks in Oregon, but we do have Snow Geese, which sometimes also have been confused with white pelicans, since they, too, are white with black wing tips. It would seem that two birds of such different size would not be confused, but if you are looking at a bird high in the sky, with no frame of reference, size can be hard to judge.

In spring and summer, adult white pelicans grow strange-looking "horns," plate-like structures on their upper beaks, that drop off after the eggs are laid. Presumably, these plates play some role in breeding attractiveness, although some say they are actually defensive in nature, and provide relatively harmless targets for pelicans engaged in breeding contests, and thus protect more sensitive locations such as the all-important pouch on the lower side of the bill.

White pelicans are prodigious fliers. In a study conducted in Nevada in 1996-97, pelicans were outfitted with satellite transmitters, and tracked for a month. The results were astonishing, because it was discovered that they frequently can travel 100 to 200 miles in a single day.

Fish is the usual diet, and they have an unusual foraging method. Several pelicans will form a semicircular line in the water, and move forward together with much splashing, driving fish before them into shallow water where they can be easily scooped up. When a bird returns to the nest to feed its young, it does so by regurgitating its catch. As the young ones get older, a different method is adopted. Arthur Cleveland Bent tells the story:

> ...down the mother's throat went the head of the child till he seemed about to be swallowed, had it not been for his fluttering wings... The youngster was loath to come out and, flapping his wings, he tried in every way to hold on as she began shaking back and forth. The mother shook around over 10 or 12 feet of ground till she literally swung the young bird off his feet and sent him sprawling over on the dry tules.

**Brown Pelican** (BRPE)     Accidental
*Pelecanus occidentalis*

White Pelicans in our area are to be expected, but a Brown Pelican is outrageous. Nevertheless, they have occurred at the Lower Klamath Refuge, and on two separate occasions an observer spotted one flying up the Rogue River near Shady Cove.

## Family **PHALACROCORACIDAE**: Cormorants

**Double-crested Cormorant** (DCCO)
*Phalacrocorax auritus*

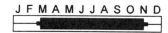

Many people, when they see a cormorant at an inland location, express surprise. They expect cormorants to be coastal birds. And so they are, for the most part. But one species, the Double-crested Cormorant, is found coast-to-coast, and seems to like inland waters as much as it does the ocean.

In Southern Oregon, there are a few inland breeding colonies, but cormorants may be found throughout the summer at places like Upper Klamath Lake and Hyatt Lake. At Hyatt Lake, particularly, there are numerous tree snags sticking up out of the surface when the water is low, and at times it seems as if every snag is occupied by a cormorant.

The other two Pacific Coast cormorants, Brandt's Cormorant and Pelagic Cormorant, do stick to the ocean. The Double-crested can be distinguished from them by two marks: (1) it has a bright yellow-orange throat pouch, and (2) when it flies, it shows a distinct kink in the neck. The "double-crested" part of the name refers to two tufts on the head that appear in breeding birds. In summer, Pelagic Cormorants give us an excellent aid to identification because the adults develop white flank patches that are highly visible in flight.

When cormorants swim on the surface, they usually swim with the bill pointed up an angle, and are often mistaken for loons. Adult Double-crested Cormorants are black, so the mistake is easily corrected. However, immature birds can cause trouble, because they look so different from the adults. The immatures are brown above, and are very pale on the breast and neck. Such a bird could easily be mistaken for a loon.

Double-crested Cormorants also are frequently mistaken for geese, because they often fly in V-formation just like geese do. Sometimes it is only when they are directly overhead, that the mistake is realized.

On the coast, Double-cresteds nest on rocky islands very much like other cormorants, and at some inland locations they do the same. A large colony in a lake in Manitoba has been described as being so dense that there were estimated to be 1500 to 2000 nests on an island only 50 yards long and 40 yards wide, extending almost to the water's edge. The whole island was reported to be slimy with excrement and reeking of dead fish, such that the odor was almost unbearable. This colony, large as it was, is dwarfed by one found on an island about one square mile in extent off the coast of Lower California. It was estimated that this colony contained almost 350,000 nests.

In some inland locations, Double-crested Cormorants often build their nests in tall trees pretty much as do Great Blue Herons and Great Egrets. I have seen colonies in Northern California where all three species were nesting in the tops of cottonwood trees in close proximity.

## Family **ARDEIDAE**: Herons, Bitterns, and Allies

**American Bittern** (AMBI)
*Botaurus lentiginosus*

One doesn't get to see bitterns very often, because they live in dense marshes and can blend with the marsh vegetation so well as to be almost invisible. Once in a while, you may get a glimpse of one in flight, in which case it can easily be confused with an immature Black-crowned Night-Heron. Both birds are brownish and striped, but the immature night-heron has wings that are more or less uniformly brown, while the bittern has dark flight feathers that contrast strongly with the rest of the wing.

Nevertheless, when you are near a marsh, it is worthwhile to check the edges of the marsh growth carefully, because there might be a bittern standing there. The extensive marshes at Lower Klamath NWR would be a good place to look. In spring, the principal evidence that one may be around is likely to be its "song," heard chiefly at dusk, and often described as loud, guttural, and "pumping."

Because of its song, the bittern has been called by some the "thunder-pumper" and the "stake driver." These names come from the song's resemblance to the sound made by an old wooden pump in action, and to portions of the song that sound like a stake being driven into soft ground. It has been rendered into English as *PUMP-er-lunk!* which hardly does it justice.

I've heard the *PUMP-er-lunk* song coming from a marsh at dusk, but have never been lucky enough to watch a bittern in action as it delivered its song. But those who have seen it say that the "song" is accompanied by violent convulsive movements, with the head thrown upward and then down, "unpleasantly suggestive of those of a person afflicted by nausea."

The reason bitterns can often remain invisible is because of their behavior when they think they are in danger. At such a time, a bittern will stand absolutely rigid, with its neck and long pointed bill sticking straight up in the air. If it is situated among the tules or cattails, its posture makes it blend in with the surrounding growth, aided by the striping on its neck, which merge with vertical lights and shadows of the plants.

One observer, while watching a bittern stand among the reeds, noticed that a breeze had sprung up, causing the plants to begin swaying. He said, "Instantly the bittern began to sway gently from side to side with an undulating motion... If your eyes were turned away for an instant it was with difficulty that we could pick up the image again, so perfectly did it blend with the surrounding flags and so accurate was the imitation of their waving motion."

But sometimes a bittern isn't quite as smart as it thinks it is. Once in a long while, if you are really lucky and catch one out in the open, it may freeze into its vertical posture, convinced it is invisible, even though it has no concealing growth around it and is the most glaringly visible thing in sight.

### Least Bittern (LEBI)
*Ixobrychus exilis*

|  | J F M A M J J A S O N D |
|---|---|
| West | vagrant |
| East |  |

I've only seen Least Bitterns twice in my life, and have to admit that I have never seen one in Oregon. But there are reports of sightings from the Rocky Point area of the Upper Klamath NWR, where they have been seen from the canoe trail, and also from the Klamath Marsh NWR. On the west side, they have only shown up twice. In the National Geographic Field Guide, their presence in Oregon is recognized by one tiny spot planted squarely on the Klamath Basin.

These birds are extremely secretive, and have been described as "masters of stealth." However, they may be present in substantial numbers even if not detected. As evidence of this, I cite the experience of a friend of mine, who was engaged in research on Tricolored Blackbirds in the Sacramento Valley. Tricoloreds often nest in large colonies in dense marshes, and the only way my friend could survey them was by walking straight into the marsh and making his way through as best he could. Least Bitterns had never been seen in those marshes, at least not under ordinary circumstances, but my friend said he surprised several during his surveys.

Least Bitterns are small birds, only about a foot long, which is less than half the size of an American Bittern. They are also more strikingly marked than their larger cousins, with light buffy plumage, contrasting with a black cap and back. Their breeding song is a soft *coo-coo-coo*, in striking contrast to the loud pumping sound of the American Bittern.

### Great Blue Heron (GBHE)
*Ardea herodias*

|  | J F M A M J J A S O N D |
|---|---|
| West | ████████████████████████ |
| East | ████████████████████████ |

The Great Blue Heron has to be one of our most familiar birds, although some folks are inclined to call them "cranes" or "storks." As a matter of fact, they were once called "blue cranes," but they are not related to cranes. Cranes do occur regularly in Southern Oregon, but not storks, at least not to date. Storks breed in the Gulf of California, and have shown up sporadically in Northern California as far north as Modoc County. There is even a record of one in British Columbia, but if it flew over Oregon nobody noticed it.

Great Blue Herons are mostly gray, somewhat like Sandhill Cranes, so there is a possibility of confusion. But in flight, Great Blue Herons fold their necks in, whereas Sandhill Cranes hold their necks out in front.

Great Blues often perch in trees, which cranes don't do. People not familiar with Great Blues are sometimes startled by this behavior, and identify them as something else. On one occasion, I had one pointed out to me as a Black-crowned Night-Heron, because it was sitting high in a tree and had its head tucked down so its long neck was not visible. In fact, it looked so much like a night-heron that I had to get out my spotting scope to be sure of its identity.

Not only do they sit in trees, they build their nests in the highest trees available, generally right in the top, or far out on the branches. Perhaps this is because they need room for their wings to maneuver, since they are too big to move about easily inside the canopy of a tree. Generally, the nests are built in communal groups called "rookeries," with many nests close together. Sometimes other species nest in close association with them. An observer once counted 69 nests in a single tree, 41 of which belonged to Great Blue Herons, and 28 to Black-crowned Night-Herons.

The sight of a Great Blue Heron standing motionless next to a pond or in a field is a familiar one. This is their hunting method, and they can stand in one spot so long, waiting for prey to appear, that researchers have sometimes have given up in trying to determine how long they can stand there. Fish are a popular food item. Usually, if a fish is caught, it will come up crosswise in the bill, whereupon the bird must toss it into the air and then swallow it head first, so it will slip down easily. If the fish is a large one, the heron may bring it to shore and beat it on the ground before swallowing.

Often, herons will hunt in dry fields, and then it is likely to be mice or gophers they are after. I once saw a Great Blue Heron catch a gopher, toss it in the air, and swallow it. The gopher was so large that the swallowing process was a difficult one, and it created a large lump in the bird's neck as it slowly went down. There have actually been a couple of deaths recorded, of Great Blues trying to swallow prey that was too large. Both cases involved lampreys that were two feet long.

**Great Egret** (GREG)
*Ardea alba*

**Snowy Egret** (SNEG)
*Egretta thula*

**Cattle Egret** (CAEG)
*Bubulcus ibis*

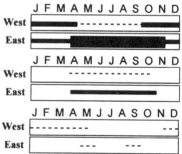

The reason these three species are considered together is that all of them are white, and are often confused. If seen side-by-side, there is no problem, because a Great Egret is about twice as large as a Snowy Egret, and a Cattle Egret, even though it is about the same size as a Snowy Egret, has a yellow bill, whereas the Snowy Egret has a black one. But a lone egret standing in a marsh can be difficult to judge as to size. A good look at the bill can help. The Great Egret has a large, yellow bill; the Snowy Egret has a thin, black bill. If you can get a look at the feet, there is another helpful mark, because the Snowy Egret has bright yellow feet.

But the fairly recent arrival of the Cattle Egret on the scene has confused things. Cattle Egrets originated in Africa, somehow made it across the Atlantic Ocean to South America, and first appeared in Florida in the 1940s. Subsequently, they expanded rapidly across the continent, showing up in Oregon in 1965. Now they are known to breed at Malheur NWR, in Harney County, and sometimes appear as vagrants in other parts of the state.

Cattle Egrets are a little smaller than Snowy Egrets, but the Cattle Egret has a yellow bill, and can look quite a bit like a Great Egret if seen alone in a field. If it is high breeding season, the Cattle Egret will have a suffused rosy color on the head and back, which sets it off from any other bird, but at other times of the year it looks like just another all-white egret, and can be confusing. The main distinguishing mark, other than size, is that the bill is shorter and stouter-looking than the Great Egret's, and the neck is shorter.

The Great Egret is one of those birds that has undergone several name changes. In the past, it was sometimes known as American Egret and sometimes as Common Egret. Both names are sometimes still used, causing some confusion as to what is meant.

Great Egrets breed on the east side, in the Klamath Basin, but are not known to breed on the west side, although they are considered "possible" breeders there. After breeding, the birds engage in what is called a "post-breeding dispersal," which is when they mostly show up on the west side.

Great Egrets often nest in tall trees, sometimes in company with Great Blue Herons, but will build their nests in small willow trees if that is what is available. They have even been known to build their nests in tule marshes, where they are placed on the bent-down tule stalks only a couple of feet above the water.

Snowy Egrets breed in the Klamath Basin, but are rarely seen on the west side. Their nesting habits are somewhat similar to those of Great Egrets, but they may be inclined to choose smaller trees for nesting, even if tall trees are available. I once entered a rookery in the Sacramento Valley that was located in a small grove of young eucalyptus trees. The grove was surrounded by flat farmland, and must have been very attractive to the birds even though the trees were only 40 or 50 feet high. It was crammed with nests, almost all containing young birds, of Snowy Egrets, Cattle Egrets, and Black-crowned Night-Herons. The birds were not unduly alarmed by my presence, because I was on a gravel road running through the grove that was used regularly by the owner of the property. In general, the birds just looked down at me with wary expressions. It was later estimated that there were 4000 to 5000 nests in that small grove. Needless to say, it stank beyond belief.

## Little Blue Heron (LBHE)   Accidental
*Egretta caerulea*

This is a bird of the southeast, but for some reason known best to themselves, individuals occasionally stray northward after breeding season. There are a few records in Oregon, and one appeared in our area at Lower Klamath NWR, in May 1996. Adults are readily recognizable in their blue plumage. However, immatures are mostly white and resemble Snowy Egrets, but have thicker bills and small black tips to the wings.

## Green Heron (GRHE)
*Butorides virescens*

|   | J F M A M J J A S O N D |
|---|---|
| West | ▬▬▬▬▬▬▬▬ |
| East |   |

The Green Heron is one of those for which the common name has flipped back and forth. First it was known as the "Green Heron," then as the "Green-backed Heron," and then back to "Green Heron." The name changes resulted from research to determine the relationship of this bird with one in Panama, called the Striated Heron. For a time it was thought that the two species were the same, and the name "Green-backed Heron" was used for the lumped species. But then further research disclosed that the two species were separate, so the name Green Heron came back.

This beautiful little heron is not easily seen. When it is, it is generally perched on a tree limb hanging low over the water at the edge of a river, or perhaps at the edge of a pond. Often, the bird is spotted only when it flies awkwardly across the water and lights on a branch. There is not very much green coloration evident on the bird, and what there is of it is on the back, mixed with blue-gray. The sides of the neck are a rich chestnut color, and the crown is black.

Some have given this little bird the name of "rubber-neck" because of the manner in which its neck is sometimes extended and other times drawn back so that it nearly disappears. In the latter posture, with its head hunched down between its shoulders, it gives the impression of being grumpy and out of sorts.

Once I was called by a neighbor, who said she had a strange-looking bird sitting on her television antenna. I asked her how big it was, and she said it was about the size of a crow, but definitely was not a crow. I was perplexed concerning what this could be, and went over to check it out. It turned out to be a Green Heron, sitting on the antenna, and yes, looking grumpy and out of sorts.

## Black-crowned Night-Heron (BCNH)
*Nycticorax nycticorax*

|   | J F M A M J J A S O N D |
|---|---|
| West |   |
| East | ▬▬▬▬▬▬▬▬▬▬▬▬ |

This is one of my favorite birds, for a very strange personal reason. For a long time, as I was first getting into birding, I wasn't sure this bird really existed. I was somewhat troubled by its name of *Night*-heron, and half feared I would have to go stumbling around in the dark in order to see one.

Then, in later years, it fell to my lot to lead field trips during the annual celebration called California Duck Days, and my assigned route took me along a dike bordering a drainage canal, with lots of willows on the opposite side. Here, every year, as dependable as the rising sun, would be an astonishing horde of Black-crowned Night-Herons, packed together in their daytime roost, containing perhaps a thousand birds.

When our field trip showed up, the birds invariably flew up in alarm, uttering cries that sounded very much like barking dogs, only to settle down again a few feet away. They were there only in the winter. In summer they would be off in their breeding colonies.

The adult is a distinguished-looking bird, larger than a crow, mostly white with a black cap and black back. Immature birds look like they belong to a different species, because they are a streaky brown color, resembling American Bitterns more than they do their own parents. It takes two and a half years for them to acquire full adult plumage.

They are rare on the west side, but on the east side a reliable place to see them is along the Link River Nature Trail in Klamath Falls. In winter, they roost in the riparian growth on the opposite side of the river from the trail, right in the back yards of the people who live there. In summer, they move elsewhere to their breeding colonies.

There is a dark side to Black-crowned Night-Herons. They are predators, of course, and have been implicated in the destruction of some Tricolored Blackbird colonies. Tricoloreds nest in dense colonies, often containing as many as 10,000 birds. In the past, such colonies were frequently in cattail marshes, which are also the natural foraging habitat of Black-crowned Night-Herons. Under such conditions, a group of night-herons has been known to essentially eliminate an entire colony in one night.

## Family **THRESKIORNITHIDAE**: Ibises and Spoonbills

**White-faced Ibis** (WFIB)
*Plegadis chihi*

When I was first getting into birding, I knew that such a bird as the White-faced Ibis existed, because it was right there in my field guide. But I didn't really believe it. Part of the reason for my disbelief is because I also knew that the White-faced Ibis was related to the sacred ibis of Egypt, and I couldn't believe that our own country could have such a weird bird. It looked like something out of prehistoric times.

Then I actually saw one. I was standing by the lower Colorado River, and this black bird with an impossibly long curved bill, all alone, came powering its way upriver, headed for someplace important. At that moment, I thought maybe I had seen the only ibis on the North American continent.

Some years later I stood by a lake in the Imperial Valley of California, and watched thousands of White-faced Ibises winging in to their nighttime roost. They lighted on an island in the middle of the lake, and eventually turned the entire island black with their numbers. I reflected ruefully on the time, not so long before, when I had convinced myself I had just seen the only such creature in the country.

Today, when I watch them flying in formation at Klamath Basin or at Malheur, they still look like something prehistoric to me. A writer of the 1920s described them in the flowery prose of the times:

> The ibis should be regarded solely as a work of art, a decorative motif in bronze, made animate by the Artist Supreme, and loaned to us for the ornamentation of wayside pools, low horizons, and interminable swamps. The Egyptians felt this decorative appeal, . . . made a god of the bird, and declared its flesh taboo.

Ibises appear almost all black, or at best a greenish bronze. In breeding season, the adults get a narrow border of white feathers at the top of the bill and around the eyes, which is where the "white-faced" part comes in. In past times, hunters referred to them as "black curlews," and shot them for market

They breed at Lower Klamath NWR, but head south in winter to places like the Imperial Valley and Mexico. In the 1970s there was a significant decline in their numbers in the Pacific Coast states, believed to be caused by loss of habitat, and by pesticides. In recent years the populations have rebounded, partly because of improvements in both habitat and in pesticide use.

**White-faced Ibis**

However, there may be another factor that confuses our ability to tell what is going on, because ibises are great travelers, and have been known to shift their nesting locations, sometimes by hundreds of miles, in response to water levels. For example, in the 1980s, they were driven from their usual nesting sites at Great Salt Lake because of high water levels. Later, they had to leave their historic breeding areas in Nevada because of the opposite problem -- not enough water. It was about that time that increased populations in the Pacific Coast states were noted, causing some to speculate that the increased numbers were partly because of population shift, and not only because of improvements in habitat and pesticides.

There are two other species of ibis in the U.S. -- Glossy Ibis, and White Ibis, both of which are residents of the southeastern part of the country. There is yet another -- Scarlet Ibis -- but there are only a few records for this one, from Florida and Texas. Glossy Ibises have not yet shown up in Oregon, but since they resemble White-faced Ibises so closely it is possible they could be overlooked. But believe it or not a White Ibis appeared near Newport, Oregon, in September 2000. Only a few people saw it, and then it moved on to the state of Washington, where it was seen by many. I tried to find it a couple of days after it first appeared near Newport, but it apparently had already moved on. Oh well. That's the way it goes, in birding.

## Family **CATHARTIDAE:** New World Vultures

**Turkey Vulture** (TUVU)
*Cathartes aura*

A large dark bird soaring in the sky most likely is a Turkey Vulture, familiarly known as a "TV". But it might not be. If it is close enough for you to see the naked red head, then all doubt disappears. At middle distances, if the underwings are clearly visible, then the two-tone pattern will provide identification: The leading part of the wing is black, and the flight feathers are silvery. But even if the bird is far away, there's a trick you can use that will usually tell you its identity, and thus astound your friends. This is because TVs soar with their wings held in a shallow V, and they frequently teeter from side to side, as if they are unstable.

Other soaring birds, such as eagles and Red-tailed Hawks, tend to hold their wings more horizontal, and they don't teeter as a usual thing, although any bird might teeter in a strong wind.

TVs are common in summer in our area, especially west of the crest, but they disappear in winter almost entirely. In fall, they begin to gather in groups, and often migrate southward in large loose flocks known as "kettles." As the birds soar within such a kettle in a circular fashion, the entire kettle drifts slowly southward. Kettles containing hundreds of birds can sometimes be seen migrating south in this fashion, often using the Bear Creek Valley leading from Medford to Ashland, and on over the crest.

Vultures, of course, eat carrion, and many people have speculated, concerning whether vultures detect their food by sight or by smell. There has been little doubt that vultures have excellent eyesight, and can readily find food that is in the open. But what about smell? Experiments have been conducted in which rotting meat has been concealed from the vultures' sight by debris, but which was nevertheless readily found by the birds. This would seem to clinch the matter, that they can use their sense of smell to detect carrion. But others have suggested that the birds actually were drawn to the carrion by the sound of buzzing flies, throwing the results of the experiments in doubt. However they do it, vultures perform a service by cleansing the earth's surface of rotting meat.

Many people refer to vultures as "buzzards," and thereby hangs a tale. In Great Britain a close relative of the Red-tailed Hawk is called the Buzzard (*Buteo buteo*). Great Britain doesn't have Red-tailed Hawks, but they do have Rough-legged Hawks, which also occur in our area in winter. Britain's Rough-legged Hawk is identically the same species as ours, but they call it the Rough-legged Buzzard. What is going on?

The explanation seems to be that northern Europe, from which most of our early settlers came, doesn't have any vultures. The common soaring hawk, *Buteo buteo,* was known to them as the Buzzard. When the early settlers came to North America and saw large soaring birds in the sky, they applied the name they knew, which was "buzzard." Many of these soaring birds, of course, were vultures, and the name of "buzzard" took hold and stuck.

## Family **ANATIDAE**: Ducks, Geese, and Swans

**Greater White-fronted Goose** (GWFG)
*Anser albifrons*

Since this bird is referred to as "greater," it implies there must be a "lesser" somewhere. And so there is, in eastern Europe and Asia. "Lessers" are about five inches shorter in length than "Greaters," and have a few other small differences, but otherwise the two species are similar. Both species have strongly barred bellies, which causes many people, especially hunters, to call them "speckle-bellies".

The "white-fronted" refers to the fact that these geese are white on the face between the bill and the eye. Confusion is possible with domesticated Greylag Geese, which originally came from Europe, but Greylag Geese don't have the barred bellies of White-fronted Geese.

Greater White-fronted Geese appear by the thousands in the Klamath Basin in the fall. By December, most have moved on to the Central Valley of California. They are primarily grazers, feeding on young grass shoots, and on waste grain. In the past, they sometimes have done so much damage to young crops that farmers have hired men to drive them away.

White-fronted Geese fly in V-formation, as do Canada Geese, and at a distance it can be difficult to tell the two apart. Highly experienced people, such as hunters, can separate the species at great distances, using such things as voice, shape, and wing-beats. Most of the rest of us have to wait until the "speckled" bellies of the White-fronts are visible, or the white chin-straps of the Canadas.

A large, dark subspecies of the White-fronted Goose, known as "Tule Goose", differs from the other White-fronts in both behavior and ecology. According to the American Ornithologists' Union, it might represent a separate species.

**Emperor Goose** (EMGO)
*Chen canagica*

**Snow Goose**
*Chen caerulescens*

**Ross's Goose** (ROGO)
*Chen rossii*

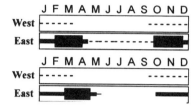

This attractive goose is a resident of the Aleutian Islands and northeastern Siberia, but occasionally strays our way, most often to coastal locations. But some of them wind up further inland. The best place to find them in our area is on the Tule Lake Refuge tour loop, usually associating with other geese.

One of the grandest spectacles in nature is the sight of an enormous flock of Snow Geese rising into the air, with their raucous alarm calls drowning all other sounds. Just what it is that sets off such an eruption often is not clear, but sometimes a Bald Eagle may be spotted powering its way through the flock, and it is a safe assumption that the eagle is the cause. But at other times no eagle can be spotted, and the cause remains mysterious.

Usually, such a flock contains both Snow Geese and their smaller cousins, Ross's Geese, often referred to collectively as "white geese." Both species are white (immature birds are grayish) except for black wingtips, but differ in size and bill shape. When flying directly overhead, a Ross's can be separated from a Snow by relative size. This only works when they are close together, so that sizes can be compared. If the flock is all Snow or all Ross's, which frequently occurs, all bets are off.

On the ground, a close look at the bills can provide identification. A Snow Goose has a large bill, and there is a conspicuous black line running the length of the bill, called a "grinning patch," or sometimes black "lips". Ross's Geese have bills that are noticeably smaller and stubbier than in Snow Geese, and they lack the grinning patch. Also, the head is more rounded.

White geese arrive in October and November in the Klamath Basin by the hundreds of thousands. By December, most have moved on to California's Central Valley, although some remain in the Klamath Basin through the winter. Most of the world's population of Ross's Geese migrates through Oregon.

There is a rarely seen morph of the Snow Goose called the "Blue Goose," once considered to be a separate species. The proportion of blue morphs to white morphs in the west is estimated to be something like 1 in 10,000. In the east, they are more common. Just why this morph should be called "blue" is not clear, because the body is dark gray-brown and the head is white. Ross's Goose has a similar morph.

Bird-banders use different codes for the various subspecies of Snow Goose: LSGO for the "Lesser Snow Goose," which occurs over most of North America, and GSGO for the "Greater Snow Goose," which occurs on the Atlantic Coast.

**Canada Goose** (CAGO)
*Branta canadensis*

**Brant**
*Branta bernicla*

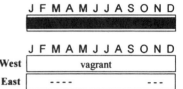

Everybody knows the Canada Goose. But what perhaps everybody doesn't know is how many different kinds of Canada Geese there are. Some authorities claim there are 10 to 11 different subspecies, ranging from 22 inches in length (the "Cackling" Canada Goose) up to 48 inches (the "Giant" Canada Goose).

The "Cackling" Goose is only slightly larger than a Mallard, and is recognizable by its short neck, rounded head, and stubby bill. This is a strictly western bird, that breeds in Alaska. Large numbers gather in November in the Klamath Basin, but most then move on to spend the winter in Central California.

Only slightly larger than the "Cackling," "Aleutian" Canada Geese breed in the Aleutian Islands, as their name implies. They almost always have a broad white band at the base of the neck, but other subspecies of Canada Geese also sometimes have white bands at this location, so this is not a completely dependable mark. The characteristic migration path is along the coast, and the annual Aleutian Goose Festival held in Crescent City each spring celebrates their passage. Aleutian Geese were classified for about 30 years as endangered, because their nesting grounds in the Aleutians were under pressure from Arctic foxes, originally imported to the islands for raising fur. Vigorous fox-control programs were established, and were so successful that Aleutians were removed from the endangered list in 2001.

In all, eight of the Canada Goose subspecies are found in Oregon. Most of these are migrants which just spend the winter in Oregon or California, but one, the "Western" Canada Goose is more or less resident. Increasingly, Canada Geese are making their homes near human developments, often on swimming beaches and on golf courses, causing some difficulties for swimmers and golfers because of their droppings. They graze on grass shoots, and golf courses must seem to them as having been specifically provided for their benefit. The increased numbers of such year-round "park geese" has been strongly influenced by releases from privately-owned captive flocks, and by relocations carried out by wildlife agencies. The geese breed widely throughout the state, wherever there is water.

The "honking" of a flying band of Canada Geese is one of those wild sounds of nature that never fails to thrill me. It makes me think of spring, and of migration to far northern breeding grounds, even when I know that the band I am hearing is probably only just moving from one local pond to another.

Brants superficially resemble Canada Geese, although a reasonably close view takes care of things. Canada Geese have white chin-straps; Brants have white "necklaces" below the chin, at the upper end of the neck, and are about the size of a small Canada Goose. Brants are primarily coastal migrants, but occasionally a few might be found inland, such as at Lower Klamath or Tule Lake refuges, during migration. There are half a dozen or so records in the Rogue Valley.

The subspecies of Brant most commonly found in the west is very dark, and formerly was considered to be a separate species, called the "Black Brant." A lighter-bellied species on the east coast, called the "Atlantic Brant," also once was considered to be a separate species. Bird-banders keep track of these separately, and use separate codes: BLBR for "Black Brant," and ATBR for "Atlantic Brant." The British call the Brant the "Brent Goose."

**Tundra Swan**
*Cygnus columbianus*

**Trumpeter Swan** (TRUS)
*Cygnus buccinator*

**Whooper Swan** (WHOS)                                   Vagrant
*Cygnus cygnus*

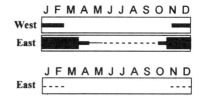

A flock of large all-white birds flying overhead is instantly recognizable as composed of swans. In our area, the chances are overwhelming that they are Tundra Swans, and flocks of thousands can be seen every fall in the Klamath Basin. By December, most of them have moved on to California's Central Valley. Even if they're not in a flock, a swan flying alone can readily be distinguished from an egret by the fact that it holds its head outstretched, whereas egrets fold their necks up when they fly.

Telling a Tundra Swan from a Trumpeter Swan can be challenging, unless they are side by side. The much larger size of the Trumpeter is apparent under such conditions. Even here there can be a problem, because a small female Trumpeter can be about the same size as a large Tundra. If all the swans you are looking at are the same size, you have to be close enough to get a good look at the heads, to tell the difference. First of all, Tundra Swans often show some yellow at the base of the bill. Trumpeter Swans never do. Also, the bill on a Trumpeter Swan is longer than on a Tundra. And, if you can see it, the line separating the black from white, that extends from the base of the gape to the eye, is almost straight in the Trumpeter. In the Tundra, there is a sharp curve in this line at the gape. If the bird is looking at you head-on, then the shape of the dividing line between black and white above the bill may be helpful. In a Trumpeter, this line is usually a pronounced "V", whereas in a Tundra, it is more of a shallow "U".

Note the fact that the above rules may not apply to juvenile birds. Juveniles are usually recognizable by the fact that they are a dusky color, instead of white like the adults.

A factor mentioned in some field guides is that there is a difference between the species regarding whether the neck is usually held straight, or slightly kinked. However, many observers have noted that members of both species may hold their necks in either of these positions, depending upon the circumstances at the moment.

Trumpeter Swans nearly became extinct in the United States in the 1930s, when there were only 66 remaining in Wyoming. A program consisting of protection from hunting, habitat preservation, and reintroductions, brought the birds back from the brink. Reintroductions in Oregon began in 1939 at Malheur NWR, and then was expanded to other locations, including Klamath Basin, beginning in 1990. Breeding has been confirmed in a couple of locations in Klamath Basin, including Upper Klamath Lake.

Trumpeter Swans are still rare in our area, and another white swan, the Whooper Swan, is even rarer. A lone Whooper Swan showed up, at White Lake in the Lower Klamath NWR, in the winter of 1991-2. This was a "first," for a bird native to Asia that is usually not seen south of Alaska. Hundreds of people (including me) traveled long distances to see it, in spite of arguments that it might be an escapee from somebody's game farm, and not a truly wild bird.

Now those arguments have subsided, because at least one Whooper Swan has shown up in the same location almost every winter since 1991. In the winter of 2000-2001 I saw three of them, an adult and two juveniles. When I first saw them they were on the Oregon side of the border (White Lake straddles the border), and a couple of weeks later I saw them on the California side. This the kind of situation that causes fits for those folks who keep state lists, and discover the bird is on the "wrong" side of the border.

A Whooper Swan is about the same size as a Trumpeter, but the mark that sets it off is the amount of yellow on the bill. It is strikingly apparent, and extends halfway and more down the bill. Tundra Swans also often have some yellow at the base of the bill, but it isn't very extensive. In Europe, a subspecies of Tundra Swan called the "Bewick's" Swan has more yellow on the bill than the Tundra, but it does not reach to the halfway point. Some years back, the "Bewick's Swan" and our North American bird, then called the "Whistling Swan," were merged to form our present-day Tundra Swan. Bird-banders keep track of the two separately, using the code WHSW for the "Whistling Swan," and BESW for the "Bewick's Swan."

When I went to see the Whooper Swan in 1991, I didn't find it the first day. I examined hundreds of Tundra Swans, most of whom were feeding with their heads under water, so you had to catch them quickly when they raised their heads. I saw lots of swans with yellow on their bills, but not enough to qualify as a Whooper.

When I returned the next morning, almost all the ponds had frozen overnight, and the swans were sitting on top of the ice, looking puzzled.

Eagles were scattered here and there, also sitting on the ice, looking uncertain concerning what to do next. People were everywhere, searching for the Whooper, and it was finally found sitting with a couple of Trumpeters, with Tundras nearby. Here were all three swans, close together, offering a perfect chance to make comparisons.

Mute Swans are also occasionally seen in our area. They can be readily recognized by the orange bill and prominent black knob at the base of the bill. The species is a native of Europe, and has been introduced in some places in North America. They are often seen in city parks, and have become more or less established as a wild population on the east coast. In the west, they have not yet been recognized as a part of the wild fauna.

## Wood Duck (WODU)
*Aix sponsa*

Wood Ducks are everybody's favorites, but seeing one can be difficult. In spite of their gaudy coloration they seem to be able to camouflage themselves well, as they lurk on still waters under overhanging branches. Usually, the first time you are aware of the presence of Wood Ducks is as they disappear rapidly flying down a watercourse, perhaps with the female uttering a characteristic loud squeal.

In the winter, they sometimes gather in flocks to roost at night on ponds. I once saw about 100 of them in a secluded wooded pond, but within a minute of the time I saw them they had also seen me, had glided under the overhanging branches, and disappeared. In our area, a pretty reliable place to find and observe them at close range, is in the upper pond at Lithia Park in Ashland. The close-up photograph in this book was taken there.

Wood Ducks breed widely throughout Oregon, and prefer to nest near water, but nests have been found as far as a mile from water. The little ones, soon after hatching, use the sharp claws they are born with to crawl up the inside of the nesting cavity and jump out of the hole. If there happens to be water below, all is fine. If there is no water, they jump anyway, and, in the words of one observer, fall "scarcely harder than a leaf or a feather." The mother then leads them to the nearest water, and they do not return to the nesting cavity.

**Wood Duck**

Typically, a Wood Duck will lay 10 to 12 eggs, but nests with up to 30 or 40 eggs have been found, presumably laid by more than one female, in a process known as "egg-dumping". One case was reported that had 31 Wood Duck eggs and 5 Hooded Merganser eggs in the same nest, with the two females actually sharing incubation duties. More often, though, the females of these two species contest each other for possession of nesting holes.

In the west, which has a scarcity of trees with proper holes in them, thousands of nest boxes have been put in place, and the regional Wood Duck population has increased as a result. However, running a nest box program is no picnic. Starlings are one of the worst enemies, and the volunteers who monitor the boxes try to discourage them. Another problem is with bees. Volunteers, checking their boxes, have often found them to be infested with bees, especially if there were eggs in the box. Experiments have confirmed that bees apparently prefer nests with eggs.

Researchers have tested various methods, in their attempts to discourage bees. One method was to try covering the lids inside the boxes with teflon tape, because teflon is so slick that bees cannot cling to it. But the bees built their nests in the teflon-lined boxes anyway, in some cases tearing off enough teflon so they could build their combs. Another method that was tried was to use insect-repelling tape inside the boxes. This worked. The tape did not appear to harm the ducks, and the bees stayed away.

### Gadwall (GADW)
*Anas strepera*

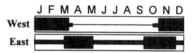

No one seems to know where the rather odd name of this duck came from, or what meaning it has, but the name apparently has been in use for several hundred years. It is one of the drabbest of ducks, since it is mostly gray all over. This has led to one of its common names: "gray duck". It has also been called "blarting duck", and "bleating duck", in apparent reference to the loud quacking calls of the female.

If you get a close look at a male Gadwall, it ceases to look drab, and begins to take on a look that has been described as "subdued elegance." The sides have an intricate black and white vermiculation, the scapulars are rust colored, and the undertail coverts are black. The bill, also, is black.

The female, like most female ducks, is harder to identify. However, there is a little trick than can be used to tell female Gadwalls and female Mallards apart. These two closely resemble each other, but there is a helpful difference in bill color. In the female Gadwall, the bill is thinner than on a Mallard, and is black on top and orange all along the sides. In the female Mallard, the bill is orange with a blotchy black area in the center.

As with almost all ducks, the males undergo a complete molt in summer, and take on a plumage that resembles the female's, called the "eclipse plumage". From about July through August, it is almost impossible to tell male from female. Then, by late September, the males are almost all back into the breeding plumage they will wear until the following summer.

Gadwalls can be readily found in our area on almost any pond, depending upon season. The Klamath Basin, where they breed regularly, is an especially good area.

## American Wigeon (AMWI)
*Anas americana*

## Eurasian Wigeon (EUWI)
*Anas penelope*

In Europe, they call the Eurasian Wigeon simply "The Wigeon", because American Wigeons are rare vagrants. In North America, it is the Eurasian Wigeon that is the vagrant, although in recent years, at least on the Pacific Coast, it has become increasingly regular in winter, on both the west and east sides of the Cascades. Whenever you spot a flock of American Wigeons, check them carefully for Eurasian Wigeons.

The male wigeons of both species have broad stripes over the tops of their heads, white or buffy in the American Wigeon, and creamy in the Eurasian. This stripe is what causes hunters to call them "baldpates." There is a broad green band sweeping back from the eye in the American, whereas in the Eurasian, the head is dark rufous. An even better recognition mark, useful from a distance, is the pinkish-brown side of the American, and the gray side of the Eurasian. When you are scanning a flock of wigeons, it is this gray side that will immediately make a Eurasian Wigeon jump out at you.

Female wigeons of the two species are hard to tell apart, although the head on the American tends to be grayish, and on the Eurasian is warmer. There is no stripe on the head in the females of either species.

American Wigeons breed in a number of places in eastern Oregon, but are only rare breeders in the Klamath Basin. One characteristic of wigeons is that they are grazers. In winter, they often take up residence in golf course ponds, and sometimes a huge flock can be seen grazing on the grass.

The call of the American Wigeon has been described as three clear whistled notes, with the middle note higher. I have a different description of it: it sounds to me very much like the noise a baby's "rubber squeaky toy" makes when it is squeezed, and I love to hear it. It is so distinctive that the moment you hear that noise coming from a pond, you know wigeons are nearby.

## American Black Duck (ABDU)                                    Accidental
*Anas rubripes*

There have been a few records of this species from eastern North America, in both Oregon and Northern California. There is some uncertainty whether these are truly wild birds, because of the possibility of escapees from private collections, and because of releases by hunting clubs.

# Mallard (MALL)
*Anas platyrhynchos*

J F M A M J J A S O N D

According to my *Encyclopedia of North American Birds,* the name "Mallard" comes from the Old French, and means "maleness." Who would want to disagree, after watching a batch of male Mallards pursue a fleeing female in spring at a city park. Also, according to my encyclopedia, Mallards have also been known as "French ducks" and "English ducks", depending, I suppose, upon the homeland of the person using the name.

I have often seen the pursuit game at city parks, but never in the wild. What I have seen in the wild, very early in the year, is pairs of Mallards setting up territory. The pairs seemed very well established, with no pursuit evident, although it may have occurred out of my sight. Whether this is a consistent difference between park Mallards and wild Mallards I am not sure, but I listened to an authority one time who seemed to think so. There is, on the other hand, a difference between park Mallards and wild ones that is inescapable. Wild Mallards are among the first to take flight when a human shows up, while park Mallards coming running to be fed.

With respect to the subject of park Mallards, the matter of hybrids comes up. At a park, a weird-looking duck may appear, usually black and white and splotchy, causing people frantically to leaf through their field guides, trying to find a match. But it's a hopeless search, because Mallards are notorious for mating with other domesticated ducks, producing weird offspring.

Most people are so familiar with Mallards that a description hardly seems necessary. They have been found breeding in every county in the state. The green head, yellow bill, white neck-ring, and pale sides of the male are instantly recognizable. It is worth noting that, if the sun is just at the right angle, the head may look purplish instead of green.

The female, as usual with ducks, is hard to identify, with her plain brown coloration that strongly resembles the female Gadwall. (See Gadwall account.) Just to make things difficult, males of most duck species undergo a molt of all the flight feathers, usually in July or August, which makes them resemble females. This is called the "eclipse plumage". As a result of the molt, they lose their ability to fly. This makes them tend to hide, prompting some to say, "Where have all the Mallards gone?" Within a month or two, they begin to molt back into their regular plumage.

Bill color is a big help. The bright yellow bill of the male remains yellowish during the eclipse plumage, although it gets duller. The female retains the orange bill, blotched in the center with black. By the way, the loud *quack! quack! quack!* that is commonly associated with Mallards is uttered by the female. The male gives a soft, raspy *kreep*.

The dull coloration of female ducks has the explanation that it is the female who broods the eggs, and her dull colors give her protection on the nest. Similarly, it is argued, the eclipse plumage of the males give them protective coloration at a time when they are flightless and vulnerable.

The usual food of the Mallard is vegetable matter, but an interesting experiment was once run, to see how effective Mallards could be in controlling mosquitoes. A pair of similar ponds was constructed, complete with mosquito larvae. One had goldfish and the other had Mallards. After a while, the Mallard pond was free of larvae, but the fish pond still swarmed with them. The Mallards were placed in the fish pond and within 48 hours had nearly cleaned out the larvae.

Mallards generally place their nests in vegetation close to the edges of ponds, but often will locate them as far as ¼ mile away from water, in agricultural fields or in brush. Occasionally, they will even place them in trees. One was once found that was 25 feet up in a tree. If the nests are in agricultural fields, this poses a problem, because harvesting the fields can result in the destruction of both the eggs and the nesting females.

In some cases, extreme measures have been taken to prevent such destruction, by deliberately flushing the females, locating the nests, and removing the eggs before harvesting so they could be hatched in incubators. If there is insufficient time to allow for such measures, then harvesting machines have sometimes been fitted with chains supported out on in front. The chain coming through the growth frightens the females and drives them from the nests. Otherwise, both eggs and females would be ground up by the harvester. By this procedure the female is saved, though the eggs are lost.

Mallards, like wigeons, shovelers, and pintails, are "dabbling ducks". These are the ones who tip their rear ends up in water a foot or two deep, and forage on the bottom. But they can dive if they need to. Stories have been related of a Mallard, to escape, swam under water to nearby vegetation and lay there with only its bill protruding. In one case a Mallard hid under a lily pad, lifting it just enough so it could breathe.

### Cinnamon Teal (CITE)
*Anas cyanoptera*

### Blue-winged Teal (BWTE)
*Anas discors*

Both of these closely-related species have blue wing panels, or *speculums,* as they are called. Aside from this, the males are easy to tell apart, unless they're in eclipse plumage, of course. (See Mallard account.) The male Cinnamon Teal in breeding plumage is a rich cinnamon color almost all over, and can't be mistaken for anything else. The male Blue-winged Teal in breeding plumage has a large vertical white crescent on the front of the face, somewhat reminiscent of a Barrow's Goldeneye.

When these two go into eclipse plumage they are not only hard to tell from each other, but also hard to tell from the females. In addition, the females of these two species resemble each other closely at all seasons, and can only be separated by characteristics that are too subtle to go into here. (See the Sibley guide, for excellent details.) Here's one little detail that can be helpful: the male Cinnamon Teal has a red eye, and it remains red in eclipse plumage.

The Cinnamon Teal is a western bird, and when one accidentally shows up on the east coast, birders will come for miles to see it. The Blue-winged Teal occurs across the continent, but is uncommon on the Pacific coast. In the east and midwest, it is much more common. Both species breed in the Klamath refuges, although the Blue-winged is considered a rare breeder. West of the crest, Cinnamon Teal is a regular though not widespread breeder, and there are "possible" breeding records for Blue-winged. Here's a hint, for finding a teal: look in the water where it has grass or other vegetation growing in it, close to the edges of the ponds.

## Northern Shoveler (NSHO)
*Anas clypeata*

I love this duck. There is absolutely no problem in identifying it, because of its huge bill. Even in silhouette, when no colors can be seen, the bill will give it away. Even the female is easily identifiable because of that bill, contrary to the case with most female ducks. The bill is so large and heavy that it looks like it ought to unbalance the bird and make it tip over in the water. Well, they do tip over, not because of their heavy bills but because they are dabblers, and this is the way dabblers generally feed.

According to one old-time observer (Arthur Cleveland Bent), the shoveler is ". . . fond of inland sloughs, marshes, streams, and ponds, where it can dabble in the shallows like a veritable mud lark." Don't know what a mud lark is? According to my trusty *Encyclopedia,* it's an old-time name for a meadowlark. Just why a shoveler should be compared to a meadowlark escapes me, but then maybe you had to be there.

There are other marks that help in the identification of shovelers, at least with the males in breeding plumage. At a distance, if a male shoveler is seen in silhouette, its rusty red side tells you what it is. From the front, the duck looks almost glaringly white, which can give you a clue concerning its identity until it turns side-on and confirms it.

Shovelers have a somewhat peculiar foraging habit, which is to lay their heads flat on the surface of the water and move slowly forward, seining whatever organisms are on the surface into their mouths. Other ducks do this, too, but not so habitually as the shoveler, in my experience. The "seining" action is facilitated by the presence of comb-like "teeth" along the edges of the mandibles.

Shovelers breed primarily in the "prairie pothole" region of the northern plains, but are also fairly common breeders in the Klamath Basin. Breeding is considered "possible" west of the crest, in Jackson County.

Old-timers called this bird the "spoonbill", and the name is not a bad one, given the shape of the bill. But "shoveler" seems to me to be just as appropriate. Besides, the name "spoonbill" is today given to the Roseate Spoonbill, a bird of the Gulf Coast that is large and pink, and has even more of a spoon-shaped bill than the shoveler. As for the "northern" part of the name, there are three other species of shovelers in the world, all of which live in the southern hemisphere.

## Northern Pintail (NOPI)
*Anas acuta*

This duck is clearly in the running for "most beautiful duck," along with the Wood Duck, Hooded Merganser, and Barrow's Goldeneye. When a male pintail glides by in stately elegance, with his long slender neck and swanlike poise, he seems to be saying, "I am the king." The female, as is usually the case with female ducks, is brown and drab, but has the same stately elegance as the male. They are shy birds, and generally are the very first to take flight when a human appears.

The long pointed tail, present in both sexes, gives the bird its name. Hunters once called them "sprigtails" (a sprig being a shoot or twig of a plant), but this has been shortened just to the colloquial name "sprig". There are two other species of pintail in the world, both of which live in South America, so ours is called "northern". The Northern Pintail, incidentally, is found around the world in the northern hemisphere. Their principal breeding-ground in North America is the "prairie pothole" region in the northern plains, but they also breed to some extent in the Klamath Basin.

Northern Pintail

The pintail is the most abundant duck in the west in winter, although its numbers seem to be declining. They are among the first ducks to arrive in the fall, and in the Klamath Basin may number in the hundreds of thousands by November.

## Garganey (GARG)                                    Vagrant
*Anas querquedula*

This teal is a vagrant from the Old World, and has shown up a couple of times on the Klamath Basin Refuges. It is small, as are all teals, and superficially resembles a Blue-winged Teal. In the male, there is a conspicuous white eyebrow extending the length of the head, rather than the vertical crescent of the male Blue-winged Teal.

## Baikal Teal (BATE)
*Anas formosa*

Accidental

The only record of this beautiful Asian bird in our area is of a male that was shot at Tule Lake NWR in 1987.

## Green-winged Teal
*Anas crecca*

This is our smallest dabbling duck. It is usually found along the edges of ponds with emergent vegetation, where it almost seems to be trying to hide. The only duck that is smaller is the Bufflehead, which is a diving duck, and boldly sits out on open water in plain view.

A male Green-winged Teal is easy to identify, because it has a vertical white line on the shoulder, contrasting with the generally gray body. Also, the head is a rich chestnut color, and there is a bold green band sweeping back from the eye. The female doesn't have these conspicuous marks, but both sexes have green speculums. Northern Pintails have green speculums, too, but we would not normally confuse a Green-winged Teal with a pintail.

But there is a problem. Once in while we may encounter a small teal that resembles the one we've just described, except the male has a horizontal white bar along the upper side below the wing, instead of a vertical white bar on the shoulder. These two were once considered to be separate species. The one with the vertical bar had the same common name we now use -- Green-winged Teal, but had the scientific name of *Anas carolinensis*. The one with the horizontal bar was called "Common Teal" *(Anas crecca)*. The "Common Teal" is an Old World bird. It is indeed common in Europe, but is a vagrant in North America. In Europe the converse is true -- it is the Green-winged Teal that is the vagrant. Thus, instead of "Common Teal", the British call their bird, simply, "the Teal."

The reason for going into all this detail is because the American Ornithologists' Union has expressed some uncertainty concerning whether these are one species or two. For the present, they have classified them as one species (and use, for the combined species, the scientific name of *Anas crecca*), although they say there has been insufficient research to settle the matter. In the meantime, many birders take careful note of whether the stripe is vertical or horizontal, anticipating the future possibility of a split. Bird-banders keep track of the two separately, using AGWT for the "American" Green-winged Teal, and EGWT for the "Eurasian" Green-winged Teal.

Green-wings are breeders in the Klamath Basin, and during the Breeding Bird Atlas program were confirmed to be nesting near the border of Jackson and Klamath counties in the southern Cascades. They are also listed as "probable" breeders at other locations in Jackson and Josephine counties.

Teals are fast fliers, perhaps the swiftest of ducks, and estimates have been made that they can fly as fast as 100 miles per hour. They frequently fly in compact flocks, wheeling and twisting as if with one mind, making one wonder how the signal to turn is given. As one observer stated, ". . . the least hesitation or mistake on the part of a single bird would result in death or a broken wing to a score."

**Canvasback** (CANV)
*Aythya valisineria*

**Redhead** (REDH)
*Aythya americana*

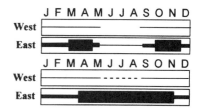

Both of these common names give clues to the identities of the birds, yet confusion is possible. The males of both species have reddish heads and canvas-colored backs, although the Canvasback has a white back that stands out like a beacon, while the Redhead's back is gray. But it is the head shapes that provide the clinchers: the Canvasback has a long black bill and a sloping profile, while the Redhead has a puffy rounded head and a bluish bill with a black tip.

Female Canvasbacks are muted versions of the males. Female Redheads are, well, brownish. But the bills and head-shapes still help to separate them: long, black, and sloping in the female Canvasback; rounded head, with a slate-colored, black-tipped bill, in the female Redhead.

Redheads, in common with many other species of ducks, frequently lay their eggs in the nests of other ducks. As many as 20 Redhead eggs have been found, for example, in a Canvasback's nest, and two Redhead females may lay their eggs in a communal nest, called a "dump nest." In one case, a nest was found that had the eggs of a Redhead, a Canvasback, and a Mallard.

Both Redheads and Canvasbacks are divers, as contrasted to birds like the Mallard, Northern Shoveler, and Northern Pintails, which are dabblers. Canvasbacks, in particular are said to be able to dive as deep as 20 feet in seek of their food, which consists partly of vegetable matter and partly of animal matter like clams and snails. Both species are more likely to be found on the east side of the crest than on the west, and are breeders in the marshes of the Klamath Basin.

**Ring-necked Duck** (RNDU)
*Aythya collaris*

A common joke among birders is that the Ringed-necked Duck might or might not have a ring around its neck, but the problem is that nobody can see it. Well, you *can* see it, but only under the right circumstances. I have a photo which shows the ring around the neck, but the light was just right, and the duck was very close.

The bird has some other characteristics that make it easy to identify, so we don't need the ring around the neck. Probably the best is the way the white side on the male is shaped. The white side is similar to that on the scaups, but there is a major difference: the white side has a conspicuous "spur" that curves up to a sharp point on the shoulder. This spur is visible from a great distance, and instantly identifies the bird. The head is peaked, instead of being round, and the dark gray bill has two conspicuous white rings, one at the base of the bill, and other out toward the tip. The female has a pattern that echoes the male, but is muted.

The rings on the bill causes many birders to say, "Why isn't it called the Ring-*billed* Duck?" As a matter of fact, it once was called exactly that, and today hunters still call it the "ringbill."

Ring-necks like small, wooded ponds. Breeding is difficult to confirm, because they prefer emergent vegetation for nesting. Nevertheless, there are breeding records from Upper Klamath Lake and from Klamath Marsh, plus a couple of "probable" breeding locations in Jackson County.

### Tufted Duck (TUDU)　　　　　　　　　　Vagrant
*Aythya fuligula*

There are a couple of records in our area, one of an adult male near Kerby, in Josephine County, in March 1989, and the other at Tule Lake NWR, in February 2000. The male in breeding plumage resembles a scaup, but has a conspicuous tuft hanging down from the back of the head, gleaming white sides, and a black back. (Scaups have gray backs.) In nonbreeding plumage, the tuft may or may not be present because of molt, and the sides become gray, although the back remains black.

Since they usually associate with scaups, it may be necessary to scope through an awful lot of scaups, to find a lone Tufted Duck in their midst.

### Greater Scaup (GRSC)
*Aythya marila*

### Lesser Scaup (LESC)
*Aythya affinis*

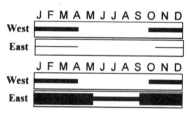

These two are classic sources of uncertainty and anguish for birders. It doesn't help that one is "greater" and one is "lesser," because you can't detect these differences reliably in the field. There is one way, however, in which these terms can be useful, and this is if the birds stretch their wings so you can see the longitudinal wing stripes on the upper sides. On the Greater, the stripe extends more than half way to the tip; on the Lesser, it extends less than half the way. Thus, the stripe is greater on the Greater, and is less on the Lesser. The fact that there is some overlap between species in this characteristic reduces its value, and only makes it helpful, rather than diagnostic.

But scaups don't stretch their wings as often as we would like, so we have to resort to other clues. Head shape is the most useful one. The head on a Greater is more rounded than on a Lesser, and the high spot on the head is the domed forehead. By contrast, the head on the Lesser is taller than on the

Greater, and is more peaked, with the peak toward the rear of the head. However, it has to be borne in mind that head shape is the result of how the feathers are held. The head on an active bird may look different than on a resting bird, and can change completely after a bird comes up from diving under water.

Head color doesn't help. Some field guides claim that one tends to be purplish and the other greenish, but in the overwhelming number of cases the heads just look black. Also, as with most such cases where the color depends upon the angle of the sun, either species could take on either color at times.

Bill shape is a good clue. The bill on the Greater is longer and heavier than on the Lesser. The longer bill on the Greater tends to de-emphasize the size of the head, and give the illusion that the head is smallish. The smaller, narrower bill on the Lesser proportionately gives more emphasis to the head, giving the illusion that it is on the large side.

The bills of both species are a light blue-gray, giving rise to the common name used by hunters: "bluebill." The black tip on the bill (called the "nail") is usually larger on the Greater than on the Lesser although, again, this feature can be variable.

Females are more subdued in color than the males, but have a feature the males don't have -- a prominent white spot on the face, next to the bill. The statements made for the males, about head shapes, apply to the females also.

The fact that I have dwelt at such length on these things shows how difficult it is to separate the two species. It is true that Lesser Scaups seem to prefer fresh water, and Greater Scaups prefer salt water, but both species can show up either place, so that is little help. In our area, Lesser Scaups outnumber Greater Scaups, but there are usually some Greaters around, mixed in with the Lessers. They usually are found anyplace there is open water, but an especially good place is the so-called "Holy Water" below the dam at Lost Creek Lake. Here, the scaups can be observed at close range and at your leisure. Another good place is Lake Ewauna, in Klamath Falls.

Greater Scaups breed mostly in Alaska, but also across the northern part of Canada. They are not known to breed in Oregon. The breeding range of Lesser Scaups overlaps that of the Greaters to some extent, but extends much further south, including parts of Oregon. It is an uncommon breeder in the Klamath Basin, and is listed as "probable" in Jackson County.

Where does a peculiar name like "scaup" come from? Well, there seems to be some confusion. It may come from an old British term derived from "scalp," in this case referring to shellfish, a favorite food item. Or maybe it's just that that is what the bird sounds like to some people as it makes one of its calls: a loud *SKAWP!*

## Harlequin Duck (HARD)                                    Vagrant
*Histrionicus histrionicus*

This beautiful duck is fairly common along the coast in winter. Breeding has been confirmed in the northern and central Cascades, but it is rare in our area, and there are no breeding records. It is estimated that there are less than 50 pairs breeding in the Cascades, and the closest probable breeding location to our area is in Douglas County, on the Umpqua River. Single birds have been reported from Lake Ewauna in Klamath Falls, and one was seen on the Rogue River upstream from Grants Pass, in December 1990. There is a specimen at the Klamath Basin Refuges Headquarters.

**Surf Scoter** (SUSC)
*Melanitta perspicillata*

**White-winged Scoter** (WWSC)
*Melanitta fusca*

West: vagrant

**Black Scoter** (BLSC)                                    Accidental
*Melanitta nigra*

Scoters are seabirds, and scarcely to be expected inland. When they do appear, they typically are on one of the large inland lakes such as Upper Klamath Lake or Lost Creek Lake. Surf Scoters, especially, have shown up perhaps a score of times. White-winged Scoters are less to be expected. There was an old report that a Black Scoter had been shot by a hunter some years ago at Tule Lake NWR, but no details are available.

**Long-tailed Duck** (LTDU)                                Vagrant
*Clangula hyemalis*

The long pointed tail of the male is what provides the name of this bird. It is a dweller of the far north, and is rare in Oregon, especially inland. Most of the birds that show up in the state are immatures or females, and lack the long tail. There are no records west of the crest in our area, but there are winter records from east-side locations such as Upper Klamath Lake and Lake Ewauna. An unusual spring record occurred in late April 2002, of a bird sighted on Upper Klamath Lake at Howard Bay.

The older name, "oldsquaw," was given because of the birds' garrulity, or "talkativeness." The name was changed because it was offensive to Native American groups, and because the name "Long-tailed Duck" has long been the name used in Britain, where the bird is fairly common.

**Bufflehead** (BUFF)
*Bucephala albeola*

This is our smallest duck. In our area in winter, small flocks of Buffleheads are to be found on almost any body of water, provided it is deep enough for them to dive. Even though the males are about half black and half white, it is the white that stands out at a distance, making them look like brilliant white spots on the water. The head has a large white patch that starts from the eye and extends all the way around the back of the head. (In the Hooded Merganser, which also has a large white head patch, the patch does not extend around the back of the head; there is a black line down the back that separates the two sides.) The female, as is usual with ducks, is brown and inconspicuous, but there is an oval white patch on the cheek which is distinctive.

Buffleheads breed in the higher elevation forested lakes in the central Cascades. They have also been confirmed as breeders in southeastern Klamath County, and are considered "possible" breeders several places in Jackson and Josephine counties. They are cavity nesters, and are small enough to have been found using abandoned flicker holes for nesting cavities.

The name Bufflehead derives from "buffalo head," a reference to the puffy appearance of the head of the male. Incidentally, that's what the genus name *Bucephala* means, too. It comes from the Greek, and means "ox-headed," or "buffalo-headed." Hunters sometimes call them "butterballs." Some other names that have been used are bumblebee duck, dapper, dipper, hell-diver, spirit-duck, and wool-head.

Just as you zero in on a Bufflehead, it is likely to dive and disappear from view. Several may dive at once, as if synchronized, but leaving one of their number on the surface, apparently to act as a guard. Their food consists of small fishes, insects, snails, and some vegetable matter. A Bufflehead's dive is so quick that some insist it can dive at the flash of a gun, and thus escape being shot.

A story is related by Arthur Cleveland Bent of a case where a Peregrine Falcon swooped on a Bufflehead, but the little bird escaped by diving. The Peregrine hovered overhead, because the Bufflehead's movements under water were clearly visible. Each time the Bufflehead came up the Peregrine swooped again, but missed each time. However, the periods under water became shorter and shorter as the little duck approached exhaustion. Finally, the Bufflehead burst from the water in full flight, but that was the end, because Peregrines often take their prey in flight as a matter of routine.

**Common Goldeneye** (COGO)
*Bucephala clangula*

**Barrow's Goldeneye** (BAGO)
*Bucephala islandica*

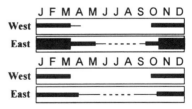

These are two of my favorites, in the contest for "most beautiful duck." If forced to make a choice, I suppose it would have to be the Barrow's Goldeneye.

The males of these two species may appear similar when one first makes their acquaintance. But, as soon as a few key marks are noted, they are easily separable. Both have black heads, but the Barrow's has a crescent shaped white spot on the cheek, whereas the Common has an oval spot.

An even better mark, because it is highly visible at a distance, is the longitudinal stripe along the upper back, with white spots that are separated by black areas. In the Common, the white spots are separated by narrow black lines; from a distance, the white spots almost seem to merge into a uniform white stripe. In the Barrow's, the spots are clearly separated by black areas that are about as large as the white spots; from a distance, the white spots stand out distinctly, instead of merging into a white line. Both species make a whistling sound with their primaries when they fly.

Field guides will tell you that the heads are not black, but that the head on a Common is greenish, and on a Barrow's is purplish. And so they are, if you happen to be standing in exactly the right place, and the sun is shining in exactly the right direction. But I have seen goldeneyes an uncounted number of times, and only twice in my life were the angles exactly right so that the green and purple showed up. When they did, they were spectacular, but most of the time the heads just look black.

The females, on the other hand, while they are beautiful birds in their own right, are almost impossible. Head shape can help, because the forehead on a female Barrow's rises at a very steep angle, giving the head a squarish appearance; in the Common, the forehead slopes up at a shallower angle The trouble is that this can be a variable matter, particularly if the bird is actively diving.

Bill color can help, especially during the winter, which is when we mostly see these birds in our area. On the female Barrow's the bill usually is yellowish for its entire length; on the Common the bill is usually black, perhaps with some yellow toward the tip. The reason the weasel-word "usually" is used, is because there is both geographic and seasonal variation in this characteristic.

These ducks are both so beautiful that we should just be able to enjoy them without worrying about details of identification. Two excellent places to observe them (in winter) are at the "Holy Water" below Lost Creek Lake, and along the Link River in Klamath Falls. In both cases the ducks will be close to you, and permit easy observation.

Common Goldeneyes nest in Canada, coast-to-coast, and there are no confirmed breeding sites in Oregon, although there are a few "possibles' designated by the Oregon Breeding Bird Survey. Barrow's Goldeneyes, on the other hand, do breed in Oregon, in lakes of the central Cascades. There are a few "possible" breeding locations in the southern Cascades.

## Hooded Merganser (HOME)
*Lophodytes cucullatus*

Here's another candidate for "most beautiful duck." The male has a fan-shaped crest with a large white patch in the center. The blackish-brown back contrasts with the rusty sides, which are separated from the white breast by two black bars. The overall impression is one of elegance. The female also has a crest, which to me seems almost like a crown. When you spot a small brownish duck with a big shaggy crest, she is instantly recognizable as a Hoodie.

Hooded Mergansers are among the smallest of ducks. In fact, when a Hooded Merganser swims near other ducks its smallness is likely to be the first thing one notices. Common Mergansers often sit right out in the open, and are frequently seen in rushing water. Not so the Hooded Merganser, which prefers shady backwaters. Often, when you find one, it is in the process of gliding across the water into the concealment of nearby foliage. In this they are very much like Wood Ducks, who also are experts at hiding. They resemble Wood Ducks, too, by preferring to nest in holes in trees. One would suppose this would produce hybrids between the two, but I have not been able to discover any confirmation of this in the literature. However, hybridizing with Common Goldeneyes and Buffleheads is apparently fairly common.

**Hooded Merganser**

Breeding of Hoodies has occurred in our area, although the birds are scarce in summer. There was one highly unusual case reported in Josephine County, in which a Hooded Merganser was nesting in a Wood Duck nesting box, but half the eggs were determined to be Wood Duck eggs. A few weeks later, a female Wood Duck was seen with a clutch of 16 young ones, three of which were Hooded Merganser chicks.

Hoodies might be found in any quiet pond, particularly ponds with trees, but good places are the "Holy Water" below Lost Creek Lake, and the Link River near Klamath Falls. However, contrary to expectations, I once saw one in a canal at Tule Lake NWR, with not a tree nearby.

This lovely little bird has collected an unusual variety of names. Here are a few: fan-crested duck, hairyhead, little fish duck, little sheldrake, mosshead, spike-bill, tadpole, tree duck, and water pheasant.

## Common Merganser (COME)
*Mergus merganser*

## Red-breasted Merganser (RBME)
*Mergus serrator*

The reason these two are put together is because the females are hard to tell apart. There is no problem with the males. Even though they are superficially similar, and both have green heads, the dark rusty breast of the Red-breasted Merganser will separate it from the Common (except for the eclipse plumage, of course).

On the females, the key is to look at the chin and throat. The female Common has a white spot on the chin that contrasts strongly with the rusty head and throat. Furthermore, where the rusty color of the throat meets the grayish body, the separating line is sharp and clean. On the female Red-breasted, the rustiness of the head blends in with the rest of the throat and body and there is no sharp contrast. The juveniles resemble the females.

In our area, Common Mergansers are, well, common. They breed here, and many remain all year. They often can be found along the Rogue River, the Link River, or on one of the lakes such as Hyatt Lake or Lake Ewauna. Red-breasted Mergansers breed in the far north. When they come south for the winter, they prefer salt water, although we may occasionally get one inland, usually on one of the larger lakes, such as Upper Klamath Lake or Lost Creek Lake.

Mergansers are fish-hunters. They have tooth-like serrations along their mandibles which help them grasp their prey. Because of this, old-timers called them "sawbills." Other names that have been used are goosander, sheldrake, and fish duck. The name "merganser" (pronouned mer-GAN-zer) comes from the Latin, meaning "diving goose."

Common Mergansers are acknowledged as the most expert divers of their tribe. The can pursue and catch the swiftest of fish, like a falcon after a pigeon. According to some observers, they can even dive into the water from full flight, swim below the surface, and suddenly emerge into full flight again.

I've never had the pleasure to see a merganser do that, but have seen another somewhat unusual foraging procedure: the bird swims very slowly on the surface with neck outstretched, the head submerged to the eyes, and the bill right at the surface. Perhaps they are capturing small organisms, as do Northern Shovelers, but it has been suggested that they are actually scouting for fish.

In the spring, it is not unusual to see a female merganser on the water, being pursued by a scrambling little batch of ducklings. On one such occasion that I observed, it seemed that the ducklings were determined to ride on their mother's back, but she didn't want them to. (With loons and grebes, the young are often seen riding on their mothers' backs.) They would hurry forward and scramble up on her back, but, as soon as two or three succeeded, the mother would sink below the surface until only her head remained above water. The ducklings were thus left afloat, but as soon as the mother returned to the surface, the whole process repeated itself: the rushing forward, the scrambling aboard, and the sinking below the surface.

Common Mergansers nest in holes in trees if they can find them, but otherwise will nest on the ground. A story is told of a mother merganser who was seen swimming round and round in the water, calling to her young ones who were emerging from a hole in a tree set back from the edge. One by one they jumped out, landing on the ground, and ran to their mother in the water. At that point the mother was frightened off, followed by her brood, leaving one duckling in the hole. By this time the mother was gone, but the duckling knew what to do, apparently guided only by instinct. It jumped from the hole to ground, ran immediately to the water, and dove out of sight.

## Ruddy Duck (RUDU)
*Oxyura jamaicensis*

This is everybody's favorite duck. In breeding plumage its body is a rich chestnut color, the head has gleaming white cheeks, and the bill turns an impossible sky-blue. Much of the time Ruddies, male and female, hold their pointed tails up at an angle, leading to their classification of one of the "stiff-tail" ducks. Although there are several "stiff-tails" on other continents, the only one that makes an appearance in North America, other than the Ruddy, is the Masked Duck of Texas, and it is rare at best.

This is one duck that has no eclipse plumage, in the sense that an eclipse plumage is held only briefly. The Ruddy goes into a drab winter plumage that is held until the following March. During the winter, the males and females resemble each other. In the male, the white cheek patch remains prominent, but the female has a streak across the center of the cheek patch at all seasons.

The courtship ritual of a Ruddy Duck is fun to watch. The male aligns himself in front of a female, stretches his neck high, puffs out his chest, and bows and nods, slapping his bill against his breast His whole demeanor is one of arrogance, as if he is proclaiming to world that he is beautiful, and knows it.

I cannot recall ever seeing a Ruddy Duck walk on land; and I understand they have great difficulty in doing so. Also, they would rather dive than fly, to escape danger. Generally, they are found on open water, often at the ponds of sewage treatment plants.

Ruddies breed in the Klamath Basin, and at times can be abundant there. Breeding on the west side has not been confirmed. They have the distinction of producing the largest eggs, relative to body size, of any of the ducks. The eggs are 2 1/2" long, larger than those of the Mallard, and almost as large as those of the Great Blue Heron. Like many of the ducks, they sometimes lay their eggs in the nests of other ducks, a trait called

**Ruddy Duck**

"brood parasitism." Usually, they choose the nests of other Ruddies for this purpose.

The Ruddy Duck has the longest list of alternate names I know of. I counted 71 in my *Encyclopedia*. Here are just a few: blatherskite, bluebill, booby, butter duck, creek coot, dicky, dinky, dumpling duck, fool duck, hard-head, paddy-whack, sleepyhead, stiff-tailed wigeon, and water partridge.

# Family **ACCIPITRIDAE:** Hawks, Kites, Eagles, and Allies

**Osprey** (OSPR)
*Pandion haliaetus*

There are two things that might give you a clue there is an Osprey around. One is the presence of a nest. These are generally highly visible, perched on the tops of dead trees, or perhaps on telephone poles. The other is a weak *yeep! yeep! yeep!* call coming from the sky. Some people claim the call reminds them of the "cheeping" note of a chicken, which seems inappropriate for such a large raptor.

Sometimes people mistake Ospreys for Bald Eagles, because of their white heads. But an eagle with a white head will also have a white tail. (But beware of immature eagles. See the eagle write-ups.) Furthermore, Ospreys have white bodies underneath, while eagles are dark.

**Osprey**

We are well supplied with Ospreys in Southern Oregon, probably because there are lots of rivers and lakes. An Osprey generally will build its nest within foraging distance of fishable water, but it does not necessarily have to be right on the water. I know of one nest that is on a power pole out in the middle of agricultural fields, with no water visible nearby. But a lake is only a half-mile away, an easy flying distance. Ospreys may occupy the same nest year after year, with birds adding material each year, making the nest ever larger. Occasionally a nest may become heavy enough to break the tree.

An old name for the Osprey is "fish hawk." An Osprey catches its fish by diving from the air, entering the water feet first. Then, as it emerges and flies off, it rotates the fish so the head is pointed forward. Apparently, Ospreys well understand the aerodynamic principle that air resistance is kept to a minimum that way.

Rarely, people have reported seeing an Osprey make its dive, disappear, and then fail to reappear. In such a case, it is assumed that the bird has caught a fish too large to be lifted, and so is dragged under and drowned. But an Osprey could easily release a fish that was too large, so something else may be going on. Perhaps the fish not only was too large, but possessed an exceedingly tough skin. Or the Osprey could have injured itself in its dive.

Osprey populations plummeted in the 1960s, because of DDT, hunting, and encroachment on breeding grounds. Several things happened that permitted their populations to recover: DDT was banned, shooting declined, and artificial nesting platforms were constructed. Ospreys readily take to artificial platforms, and may use other human-built structures, such as transmission line towers, buildings, bridges, chimneys, and channel buoys.

In one case I know of, a pair of Ospreys started to build their nest on the top of the crossbars of a power pole. This carried with it the risk of electrocution, of course. The power company came out and erected a platform on the pole which provided a nesting surface safely above the wires. The Ospreys accepted it immediately, and built their nest there.

Perhaps the most unusual case I have read about concerned an Osprey that built its nest in the top of an abandoned windmill. The vanes of the windmill had been blown off, but the rudder was still there. Thus, as the wind blew, first in one direction and the another, the nest, with the bird on it, rotated in response.

## White-tailed Kite (WTKI)
*Elanus leucurus*

Here's another bird that has gone through a couple of name changes. A few years ago it was called White-tailed Kite. Then, for a time, it was Black-shouldered Kite. Now it is White-tailed Kite again. The AOU is not just being capricious with such changes. In 1983, the AOU was convinced, on the basis of research, that our White-tailed Kite was really the same species as one in the Old World. That one bore the name Black-shouldered Kite. The name of our bird was changed accordingly, since the Old World species had received its name before ours, and thus had priority. In 1994, new research indicated the 1983 research was wrong, so the AOU changed the name back again.

Whatever its name, it's a beautiful bird. Its white tail is a major recognition mark, although other birds also have white tails. But no other North American bird has such highly visible black shoulders as far as I am aware, so to me this remains its best recognition mark.

Kites are about the size of a crow or a small gull, and are almost all white below. In fact, the resemblance of a kite to a gull may help account for the fact that we still have some around. Early in the 20th century, it appeared that the White-tailed Kite was on its way to extinction. In those days, it was common to shoot hawks on sight because they were considered to be "vermin."

Kites were especially easy to shoot, because they share with kestrels (see American Kestrel) the habit of hovering in one spot while hunting. But, they look so much like gulls, it is believed by some that many

**White-tailed Kite**

hawk-shooters overlooked them. Now that hawk-shooting is no long as fashionable as it was, White-tailed Kites have made a strong recovery.

The center of abundance of White-tailed Kites is in California, so, as the population recovered, they staged an expansion into Oregon, and have become fairly common in areas west of the crest. Breeding was first confirmed in Oregon in the 1970s, and today the highest concentration of known nests in Oregon is in the Rogue Valley. During nesting season, the birds are dispersed and may be hard to locate, but in winter they often form communal roosts in more or less permanent locations. There are winter roosts in the Willamette Valley which regularly have 20 to 30 birds.

## Bald Eagle (BAEA)
*Haliaeetus leucocephalus*

## Golden Eagle (GOEA)
*Aquila chrysaetos*

These two birds are not closely related, but are placed together for a reason: in immature plumages, they are tricky to tell apart. An adult Bald Eagles is no problem; almost everyone recognizes one on sight, with its dark body, white head and white tail. An adult Golden Eagle is recognizable by the fact that it is dark all over, has enormous slab-like wings that are held nearly horizontal, and has a golden head and nape.

**Golden Eagle (imm.)**

Immature birds of both species are dark, with varying amounts of white. Eagles take 4 or 5 years to mature, and the white portions will vary in amount and location, depending upon age. Some individuals can be very confusing, but here are some hints that will be helpful in most instances.

Let's start with the wings, as viewed from below on a soaring bird. If the white is restricted to the base of the flight feathers (primaries and secondaries), then it's a Golden Eagle. A dark bird with blotchy white all over the undersides of the wings, especially in the axillaries ("armpits") and on the underwing coverts, is a Bald Eagle. In the latter case, the underwing looks like it has diagonal white lines. There may also be some white on the primaries or secondaries, but it will not be restricted to the base of these feathers the way it is on an immature Golden Eagle. In the immature Bald Eagle, the belly may or may not have some white, depending upon the age of the bird.

The immatures of both species may have varying amounts of white in the basal part of the tail. In the Golden, the white tends to be clean and bright, with crisp edges, and includes the outer tail feathers. In the Bald, the white tends to be more diffuse, and the outer tail feathers are usually dark.

Enough? Here's another one: head projection. In the Golden, the head projects beyond the wings *less* than one-half the tail-length. In the Bald Eagle, it projects *more* than one-half the tail-length. This may sound a little murky, but can be surprisingly useful once you get the hang of it.

Golden Eagles will usually be found near foothills and mountains. Their prey tends to be things like mammals and snakes, and they are found where their prey is located. They prefer to nest on cliffs, and are widespread breeders east of the crest, but will also nest in trees. The breeding territory of a Golden Eagle may range from 10 to 40 square miles.

Bald Eagles will usually be found near water. Their nests, at least in Oregon, are almost exclusively in tall trees, usually near water. Their prey tends to be fish, waterfowl, and small mammals, although they are not above eating carrion.

It is frequently said that eagles prey primarily on sick or crippled waterfowl. Perhaps this is true, but in the literature I find references to Bald Eagles taking ducks on the wing, much like a falcon would do. I once saw a Bald Eagle flying about over a colony of nesting gulls. The gulls, of course, were in an uproar. Then the eagle dropped to the ground and disappeared from view. In a moment, it came up again, bearing a young gull in its talons, and flew off, pursued by the screaming gulls

Do eagles sometimes carry off human babies? The answer appears to be no, although there was a case of a Golden Eagle that attacked a 9-year-old girl, in which the eagle had to be beaten off. There was another case in which a Bald Eagle attacked a child while the mother worked nearby in her garden. The child screamed, and was dragged some distance by the eagle, which was gripping the child's clothing. The clothing tore loose, and the child escaped.

Both kinds of eagle breed in our area and can be found throughout the year. In the winter, many Bald Eagles move south to spend the winter in the Klamath Basin. This is certainly one of the best places to see them, but the numbers have declined since the early 1990s. It is speculated that a reason for the decline could be because one of their principal prey sources is waterfowl that have died from disease, such as avian cholera. Losses from avian cholera have been low in the latter part of the 90s, thus reducing that food source.

Nevertheless, the Basin gets lots of eagles in winter. To celebrate them, the Klamath Basin Audubon Society sponsors the Bald Eagle Conference each year in February, featuring field trips and workshops. There are now more than 230 "birding festivals" of this type each year in the U.S. and Canada, and the Bald Eagle Conference was one of the originals, dating back to 1980.

## Northern Harrier (NOHA)
*Circus cyaneus*

A fairly large brown hawk coursing low over a field or marsh, holding its wings in a shallow "V", and bearing a conspicuous white spot on its rump, is

instantly recognizable as a Northern Harrier. A somewhat smaller hawk, behaving the same way, but gray on the top and white on the bottom, with ink-black wingtips, may not be so instantly recognized, but this is the male Northern Harrier. It is the females and juveniles that are dark brown.

When I was just getting started into birding, the sight of a male harrier invariably threw me for a loop. I was familiar with the female harrier, but the male was so different that I thought it was a different species. Even the telltale white spot on the rump was not apparent to me at first, because it is set off against a gray background, instead of against dark brown.

In later years I have watched male harriers engaged in their nuptial display, which is spectacular, and decided that this was a pretty special bird. The nuptial display consists of a series of dives, each dive starting perhaps 60 feet up, and coming to within 10 feet of the ground each time. At the top, the male turns upside down, then plunges toward the ground, makes a "U" shape at the bottom, and soars up to repeat the performance. One observer claimed to have seen 71 dives in succession, although I've never seen more than five or so. The female, of course, is down below, presumably admiring the performance.

Harriers are widespread breeders east of the crest in open country, and are local breeders in the Rogue Valley. They nest on the ground, sometimes right in a marsh. I was once walking near a marsh, and apparently got close to a nest without realizing it. The female harrier came after me. I was convinced I was going to get hit, but avoided this fate by taking my spotting scope, spreading the legs of the tripod, and holding it above me like a shield. According to accounts in the literature that I have read, attacking harriers usually veer off before making contact, but there have been instances in which the birds drew blood.

The Northern Harrier was called the "Marsh Hawk" not too many years ago. Some people still call it that. But in Europe there are four members of the same genus, *Circus,* and the British use the name "harrier" for all of them. One of them is identically the same species as ours, and the British call it the "Hen Harrier." In the attempt to standardize common names among the English-speaking countries as far as possible, the name of our species was changed from Marsh Hawk to Northern Harrier. Why didn't we just adopt the British name of "Hen Harrier"? I don't really know, but I'll wager it was partly because the Americans didn't want to perpetuate the opinion held by some, that all hawks are "chicken hawks."

We get so used to seeing harriers fly low over the ground that we often fail to recognize one that is soaring overhead, where it may resemble a *Buteo*. But harriers have longer tails and narrower wings than the *Buteos*. Falcons have long tails, too, but have much more pointed wings than harriers.

About that white spot on the rump. Other hawks, especially Swainson's Hawks, sometimes also have light-colored rumps. However, the spot on a harrier is much more prominent and contrasting than on a Swainson's. A light morph Rough-legged Hawk also has a prominent white spot on the base of the tail, but the white is on the tail itself, not on the rump.

**Sharp-shinned Hawk** (SSHA)
*Accipiter striatus*

**Cooper's Hawk** (COHA)
*Accipiter cooperii*

**Northern Goshawk** (NOGO)
*Accipiter gentilis*

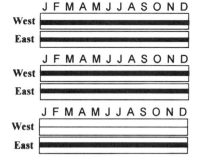

These three are known as the *"Accipiters,"* by their scientific name. The British reserve the term "hawk" for members of this genus, and don't use it for *Buteos,* as we do for Red-tailed Hawk, for example. The *Accipiters* are forest-dwelling birds with broad, relatively short wings, and long tails. Two of these, the Sharp-shinned and the Cooper's, are notoriously difficult to tell apart. There are several reasons for this, but one of the problems involves size. Cooper's Hawks in general are larger than Sharpies, but females are larger than males, in both species. For example, in the case of Sharpies, males average only about 57 percent of the weight of females. Thus, a male Cooper's Hawk is about the same size as a female Sharp-shinned.

Even the experts have trouble. The Golden Gate Raptor Observatory in San Francisco conducts hawk watches every fall, where experts count the number of hawks flying over and tabulate them by species. Since 1994 studies have been conducted to see how well their expert counters were doing on telling Sharp-shinneds from Cooper's. Hawks netted for banding were carefully identified in hand, and then released for the counters to identify. The results showed about 15 percent wrong identifications, with male Cooper's Hawks being the ones most often identified incorrectly.

**Sharp-shinned Hawk**

Without going into exhaustive detail, here are a few hints. Cooper's Hawks tend to look large-headed; Sharp-shinned Hawks by contrast look relatively small-headed. If the hawks are adults (reddish on the front), look at the black cap on the head. If it looks peaked on the rear of the crown and contrasts sharply with the back of the neck, it's a Cooper's. If the black of the crown blends into the neck, and the head looks rounded, it's a Sharpie. If it's a juvenile, and the streaking extends down through the belly, then it's probably a Sharpie; if the streaking stops short of the belly then it's probably a Cooper's. The use of the word "probably" shows that this can be a close call.

In a flying bird, if the tail the tail is strongly rounded and has a fairly wide white terminal band, then it's a Cooper's. If the tail is less rounded and has a narrow white band, then it's a Sharpie. Again, this can be a close call, depending upon such things as feather wear and stage of molt.

There are even more factors that can be considered, such as leg length, head projection, and soaring behavior, but several pages could be involved and generally are, in advanced guides. But these hints could help in most cases. In the identification of an *Accipiter,* you should look at all characteristics together, in reaching your decision. Even then, there might be some birds you can't be sure of. Remember, the experts are wrong 15 percent of the time.

As for Northern Goshawks, the first thing to remember is that they are big, about the size of a Red-tail. Both the adult and the immature have pronounced white superciliaries. Adults are light blue-gray on their bellies. Immatures resemble immature Cooper's, but are larger. Something that helps is that immature Goshawks have dark streaks on their white undertail coverts; immature Cooper's and Sharpies do not.

All of the *Accipiters* hunt primarily by sitting on concealed perches in the trees, before springing out in pursuit of their prey, which is mostly other birds. I once was standing in a clearing when three quail flew by at top speed, about four feet off the ground. Close behind them was a Cooper's Hawk. The quail dashed into the cover of thick bushes to escape the hawk; the hawk crashed into the bushes right after them, and disappeared from view. In a couple of minutes the hawk emerged on the top of the bushes, empty-handed. Where the quail went, I don't know, but I presume neither did the hawk.

On another occasion I surprised a Cooper's Hawk in the act of killing a Rock Dove on the lawn of a house. I was in my car, and remained there to watch. The hawk, probably a female, was killing the dove with her talons when I arrived, but then let go and flew up into a small tree. I stayed in my car, curious to see if the hawk could even lift the dove, let alone fly off with it. After a moment or two, the hawk flew down to the dove, picked it up, and flew off down the street with it as though it weighed nothing.

Both Cooper's and Sharp-shinned Hawks have been called "chicken hawks," although Sharpies apparently can only take small chickens. But, to old-timers, the Cooper's Hawk is *the* chicken hawk. The goshawk, too, probably deserves the name, because the literature is full of instances where they preyed on chickens.

Goshawks are principally birds of mature forests, with open understories. They often take large birds such as ducks and grouse. In fact, that's where the name comes from; it is derived from "goose hawk." But they also take mammals such as rabbits and squirrels. There's one thing on which most observers agree: it's not a good idea to be near a goshawk nest in breeding season. Female goshawks are fierce in protecting their nest sites, and have been known to inflict injury on humans. In light of their reputation for being fierce, it seems strange that the scientific name should be *gentilis,* sounding like the bird is gentle. But *gentilis* in this case means "noble," not "gentle," and is the root word for "gentleman."

Cooper's and Sharpies may be found in the forest, but also may be found right in your backyard, especially if you have a bird feeder. If the birds at your feeder suddenly disappear, and everything goes quiet, it's likely that a Cooper's or a Sharpie is hanging around.

**Ring-necked Duck (male)**

**Mallard (male)**

**Sandhill Crane**

**Lesser Scaup (male)**

**Blue-winged Teal (male)**

**Cinnamon Teal (male)**

**PLATE III**

**Rough-legged Hawk**

**Red-shouldered Hawk**

**Prairie Falcon (at nest)**

**Bald Eagles**

**Cooper's Hawk**

**Blue Grouse (female)**

**PLATE IV**

All three species breed in Southern Oregon, in forest environments. As a rule, Sharpies seem to prefer more dense woods, Goshawks more open ones, and Cooper's in between.

## Red-shouldered Hawk (RSHA)
*Buteo lineatus*

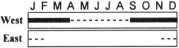

The very first record of Red-shouldered Hawk in Oregon was in 1878, and was made by that extraordinary 19th century ornithologist, Major Charles Bendire. The next record was along the coast, almost 100 years later. Since the 1970s, Red-shouldered Hawks have been on the increase in Oregon, primarily in winter, but occasionally in spring and summer. They are common in California, and apparently are expanding their range. During the 2000-2001 Christmas Count, 69 Red-shouldered Hawks were counted in Oregon. More than half were along the coast. Thirteen were in the Willamette Valley, 16 were in the Rogue Valley, and four were at Klamath Falls.

Breeding has been confirmed in Oregon only recently. Josephine County is one of the locations where breeding was confirmed, although there are "possible" sites in both Jackson and Klamath counties.

The Red-shouldered Hawk has sometimes been referred to as a *Buteo* that seems to think it is an *Accipiter*. This is because *Buteos* are generally thought of as birds of the open spaces, whereas Red-shouldered Hawks prefer wooded riparian areas, just as most *Accipiters* do. In our area, a couple of good places to see one is at the Denman Wildlife Area, near White City, and at Whitehorse Park, near Grants Pass. Both of these are near the Rogue River. However, I should mention I once saw one, during August, at Hyatt Lake, which is montane fir forest. This bird was both out-of-season and out-of-habitat, which underscores the old point that birds have wings, and can show up anywhere.

Even though they prefer to be in the woods, they are often seen sitting on telephone wires. In doing this, they adopt a somewhat unhawklike posture, sitting erect with their heads bent over, looking down. Presumably they are looking down for prey. For those who are "Peanuts" fans, and have a suitably long memory, they may remember a time when Snoopy took to sitting in small trees, pretending he was a vulture. A Red-tailed Hawk sitting on a telephone wire reminds me of Snoopy.

This bird is often referred to as our most beautiful hawk. The adult has a bright red-orange front, a black back checkered with conspicuous white "mirrors," and a tail with highly contrasting black and white stripes. Yes, there is a reddish shoulder, although it may at times be partially concealed. Overhead, the bird may be picked out by its striped tail and by the highly visible translucent crescents in the outer wings. Our western subspecies, by the way, is geographically isolated from its eastern counterpart, by a thousand-mile gap. It is much redder on the breast than the eastern subspecies, and once was called the "red-bellied hawk."

The birds are highly vocal, and this often is the best way to locate one. The characteristic call is a piercing *keeyur! keeyur! keeyur!,* sometimes repeated over and over. Be aware, however, that this call is sometimes imitated by Steller's Jays.

## Swainson's Hawk (SWHA)
*Buteo swainsoni*

In 1892, Major Bendire wrote, "On . . . the sage and bunch grass districts of Nevada, Oregon, Washington, and Idaho, Swainson's Hawk is especially abundant, outnumbering, perhaps, all the other Raptores of these regions combined. It is eminently a prairie bird, shunning the dense timbered mountain regions, and being more at home in the sparingly wooded localities found along the water courses of the lowlands."

No longer. Swainson's Hawks can still be found in eastern Oregon, but are only fairly common at best, and are rare in many apparently suitable localities. In the region covered by this book, probably the best place to find them is in Butte Valley, in Siskiyou County, California.

The reasons for the birds' decline are numerous. Shooting certainly played a part in the last century, even though the principal diet of the birds is rodents and insects, with poultry rarely being involved. But loss of foraging habitat has probably been more important. In California, where the bird is classified as "Threatened," the conversion of range land to vineyards and orchards has undoubtedly played a part. Swainson's Hawks need open fields.

During the nesting cycle they principally prey on small mammals, but after breeding, they mostly turn to grasshoppers. In fact, they are so dependent upon these insects that they were once known as "grasshopper hawks." I have watched Swainson's Hawks hopping about in fields like so many shorebirds, chasing grasshoppers. Evidently, their feet are smaller than other hawks, such as Red-tails, and they are not as capable as other hawks in catching larger mammals.

Because of their dependence upon insects, at the close of summer they migrate south, where the insects are. In the past, it was thought that the entire North American population migrated to Argentina (except a few that stuck around in Florida), involving a round trip of 11,000 to 17,000 miles. In Argentina, the hawks could find clouds of locusts on the Argentine pampas.

But Argentina, also, has been undergoing agricultural changes, and has seen an increasing use of pesticides. In 1996, researchers counted 3900 dead Swainson's Hawks in Argentina that were believed to have been killed directly as a result of pesticide spraying.

The belief that the entire population goes to Argentina each winter has been modified somewhat in recent years. By use of satellite tracking, it has been found that some of those in central California go only as far as Mexico or Colombia. It has also recently been discovered that a few remain each winter in the Delta region of California. Nine of them were counted there during the Christmas Bird Count of 2000-2001.

No one knows just why this small group chose to forego migration, but it should be noted that nineteenth-century ornithologists such as Bendire and

Ridgway recorded that a few Swainson's seemed to hang around for the winter in southeastern Oregon. Some believe that this was the result of misidentification, but Bendire and Ridgway were very familiar with Swainson's Hawks, as well as with the usual "lookalikes." Maybe they were right after all, and we just don't know as much as we think we do.

An adult light morph Swainson's Hawk is easy to identify, because it shows a pattern in the underwings which is diagnostic: The forward part of the wing is light-colored, and the rearward part (the flight feathers) is dark. No other hawk in our region shows this pattern. The belly is white, and there is a dark "bib."

But hawks can be aggravating birds, and show an incredible amount of variation. Swainson's Hawks vary all the way from light morphs to dark morphs and show all kinds of shades in between.

Swainson's Hawk

But we also have light morph and dark morph Red-tails, with everything in between. Telling a dark morph Swainson's from a dark morph Red-tail can be tricky, involving things like flight behavior and how pointed the wings are.

If the hawk turns so that you can get a glimpse of a reddish-brown tail, then you definitely know you've got a Red-tailed Hawk. But immature Red-tailed Hawks do not have red tails, and a dark morph immature red-tail can look an awful lot like a dark morph Swainson's. If the dark Swainson's is an adult, it probably will have light-colored undertail coverts, but not always. People with extensive field experience can tell which kind of hawk it is by general shape and flight behavior, but the rest of us will probably have to pass.

Like I say, hawks can be aggravating birds.

## Red-tailed Hawk (RTHA)
*Buteo jamaicensis*

J F M A M J J A S O N D

This, our most abundant and familiar hawk, can sometimes present troublesome identification problems. There are so many variations that David Sibley, in his guide, includes 39 different paintings of the Red-tailed Hawk, showing juveniles, adults, flying hawks, sitting hawks, light morphs, intermediate morphs, dark morphs, and various subspecies.

In the majority of cases, if you spot a Red-tailed Hawk sitting on a telephone pole, you will be able to identify it almost instantly. Here are some of the characteristics you would look for: a dark head, a faint white spotted "V" on the back, a belly band, and a reddish tail. This combination would probably do the job. The reddish tail, of course, is a clincher all by itself.

If it's a soaring hawk, the job is even easier, because of the dark patagial marks. These are the oblong dark marks on the leading edges of the wings, which instantly identify the bird as a Red-tailed Hawk. Some people call these marks "Hershey bars." You can identify Red-tails at fairly long distances, using the patagial marks, and your friends will be convinced you are a genius. Of course, if the reddish tail becomes briefly visible during the soaring, you don't even need the Hershey bars.

But what if it's a "Krider's Hawk," which is a rare prairie subspecies of the Red-tailed Hawk? The underparts will be very white, usually with no belly band at all, and the patagial marks may be so faint as to be invisible. Even the red tail may become a shadow of its normal self. Fortunately, we're not likely to see a "Krider's Hawk " in our area, so we won't worry about it further.

And what if it is a very dark morph? We get those occasionally in our region. If so, then the patagial marks disappear against the dark background. People are sometimes tempted to assign the name of "Harlan's Hawk" to any dark morph Red-tail they see. The "Harlan's Hawk" is a subspecies of the Red-tailed Hawk that breeds in the far north and migrates to spend the winter in the south-central part of the country, and we do get them occasionally in winter, especially in the Klamath Basin. It used to be classified as a separate species, and some people think it might become so again, so they keep records of sightings.

**Red-tailed Hawk**

Now, if you're a "lister," it's not really going to make any difference, because "Harlan's" is considered to be a subspecies of Red-tailed Hawk, and listers generally keep records of full species, not subspecies. So you would just mark it down as a Red-tail, although you might make a note that it is also a "Harlan's" in case it ever becomes a full species again.

But what if it has a red tail, even though it's so dark as to be almost black? Then it's just a dark morph Red-tail, and not a "Harlan's". "Harlan's Hawks" have whitish or grayish tails. Just to complicate things, a dark juvenile Red-tail, a dark juvenile Swainson's, and a dark juvenile "Harlan's" can look an awful lot like each other. Did I mention there is also a light morph "Harlan's" that is so light underneath that it resembles a "Krider's"?

That's the way it goes with Red-tailed Hawks. We should be grateful that some of these variants constitute only a small proportion of the population, and that perhaps 80 percent of the Red-tails you see will look like proper Red-tails.

Red-tails are outstanding hunters, and take a great variety of prey, ranging from raccoons, rabbits, squirrels, rats, mice, porcupines, skunks, ducks, grouse, quail, meadowlarks, sparrows, frogs, snakes, and lizards, to grasshoppers, beetles, centipedes, and maggots. One observer claimed that it takes about six squirrels a day to keep a pair of nestlings fed.

Red-tails nest widely in Oregon, and may re-use a nest many times. This is one bird that seems to have prospered with the expansion of agriculture, because with agriculture came an increase in open hunting territory. They have also prospered from the introduction of utility poles, for use as perches from which to hunt. However, even though such poles provide convenient perches, the electrical wires have often proved to be dangerous, and birds have been electrocuted. In many regions, a lot of attention has been given by power companies to designs which will minimize the electrocution hazard.

A friend of mine from the midwest claims that Red-tails in his region frequently hover like a kite or a kestrel, in hunting for prey. I've never seen one do that in the west, and neither has anyone I have questioned. (Rough-legged Hawks, however, do frequently hover.) One thing Red-tails certainly do, though, is to "kite." This is done in a strong steady wind, where the bird remains in one place, with the wings outspread but not flapping.

During courtship, a male may often dive on a female from a great height. As the male approaches, the female turns over in the air and presents her claws in mock combat, making an observer wonder whether this is love or war.

Red-tails are often attacked by small birds, to drive them away from their nests. Most often these are blackbirds or kingbirds, but a case has been reported of several robins driving a Red-tail to cover in a fir tree.

The characteristic call of a Red-tail is a long drawn-out rasping squeal: *kree-e-e-e-e,* dropping in pitch toward the end. It may be given while soaring, or while sitting in a tree. Steller's Jays are very adept at imitating this call, so one has to check carefully, to be sure of the source.

## Ferruginous Hawk (FEHA)
*Buteo regalis*

| | J F M A M J J A S O N D |
|---|---|
| West | ▬▬▬▬▬             ▬▬▬▬ |
| East |     ▬▬▬▬▬        ▬▬▬ |

The scientific name *regalis* means "kingly," and the name seems appropriate for one of the largest and most powerful of the *Buteos.* In fact, one of its former names was "eagle hawk." Like the other *Buteos,* it comes in color morphs -- light, dark, and in-between. Its breeding range is all through the interior west, including much of eastern Oregon. Breeding has not been confirmed in Southern Oregon, but the presence of a few adults in our area during breeding season have raised intriguing possibilities.

Mostly, it is the light morph that is seen in our region. A large white-looking hawk soaring overhead in winter is likely to be a Ferruginous. A couple of clinchers are the dark commas at the "wrists," and an almost all-white tail, sometimes with a slight cinnamon wash. If it's an adult, the dark feathering on the legs will form a distinctive "V" on the lower belly. Because of this feathering on the legs (like a Rough-legged Hawk), it sometimes has been called "Ferruginous Roughleg." It has also been called "squirrel hawk," because of its preference for small mammals.

"Ferruginous" means rust-colored, from the word "ferrous," for iron. Light morphs have varying amounts of rusty color on their wings and back. Their heads are whitish, with streaking, contributing to their regal look. When one takes off so that you can see its back, there are conspicuous light-colored areas on the outer wings.

Even if it is a dark morph, all is not lost. Viewed from underneath, which is the way you mostly see them, the leading edge of the wing will be dark, and the flight feathers will be white. The dark comma at the "wrist" will still be there, and made visible by a *white* comma that lies next to it.

Like other soaring *Buteos,* they are great hunters. Their customary habitat is open ground, so they often may perch low, even right on the ground. Occasionally, one will hover in seeking prey, as do kestrels and Rough-legged Hawks.

## Rough-legged Hawk (RLHA)
*Buteo lagopus*

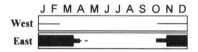

Why "rough-legged"? It's because the legs are feathered almost down to the toes. The *"lagopus"* in the scientific name refers to the same feature, although in this case it means "rabbit leg," presumably because the feathered leg looked like a rabbit's leg to the person giving it its name.

Whatever the name, this is one of our most beautiful hawks. It comes completely equipped with light morphs, intermediate morphs, and dark morphs, of course, but about 90 percent of those in the west are light morphs. A light morph, soaring overhead, is mostly white underneath, with white flight feathers, and dusky feathers on the leading portions of the wing. Usually, the belly has a dark band. Besides the whiteness, two marks stand out: (1) there are two large dark "carpal marks," one on each wrist of the wing; (2) the tail has a broad black band at the end, but the base of the tail is white.

As a Rough-leg soars and turns in the sky, the white at the base of the tail is highly visible. Care has to be taken, on a soaring bird, not to mistake the white at the base of the tail for a Northern Harrier. A harrier will be white only on top (unless it's a male, in which case it will be white everywhere underneath); a Rough-leg will be white both top and bottom (unless it's a dark morph, of course).

A light morph in sitting position usually has a head that is so light that you might wonder at first, "Is this an eagle?" But the head typically is streaked, and a look at the bill eliminates an eagle right away. In an eagle, the bill looks enormous, whereas in a Rough-legged Hawk it is comparatively tiny.

A dark morph can present a problem. Overhead, the flight feathers will be silvery, but the tail will be darkish, instead of showing the striking white in the tail that the light morph has. Dark morph Rough-legs and dark morph Harlan's strongly resemble each other. My own suggestion would be just to let them go unidentified, unless you are really into hawks.

Rough-legged Hawks are very much birds of the open country. They nest in the far north, on the treeless tundra. When they come south in winter, they still prefer open country, and the Klamath Basin is an excellent place to find them. In fact, if you have stationed yourself at the location south of Klamath

Falls where the morning eagle "fly-out" occurs in winter, you will find yourself having to sort out the Bald Eagles from the Rough-legged Hawks.

One notable thing about Rough-legs is that they regularly employ a hovering hunting technique, much like a kestrel or a kite. Ferruginous hawks often do this, too, but Red-tailed Hawks hardly ever do. Also, Rough-legs often will wait for prey on low perches such as fence posts or a hillock on the ground. Perhaps these habits represent adaptations to the treeless condition of their breeding grounds.

Some other names that have been applied to this hawk are mouse-hawk, black hawk, and squalling hawk. In Britain, it is called "Rough-legged Buzzard," because to the British, all *Buteos* are buzzards.

In the past, Rough-leg populations were in serious decline because of hunting. Here are the words of Arthur Cleveland Bent, writing more than 70 years ago, at a time when hunters shot all hawks as "vermin":

> ... this hawk is still pursued by man with his keen and cruel hunter instincts and his unreasoning prejudice against all hawks. Where a Japanese cabinet-maker would take his block and rapidly sketch the graceful poses of a hawk, the western barbarian takes his gun and kills and hardly glances at his beautiful and blood-stained victim, as he leaves it where it has fallen.

## Family **FALCONIDAE**: Caracaras and Falcons

### American Kestrel (AMKE)
*Falco sparverius*

When I was a kid, this bird was called "Sparrow Hawk," and some people still call it that. This name apparently was applied by the early settlers of our continent, who thought it resembled a bird from Europe bearing that name. What they did not know (or perhaps care) is that there are two small birds of somewhat similar size and appearance in Europe, one of which is the Sparrowhawk (an *Accipiter*), and the other of which is the Kestrel (a member of the genus *Falco,* and hence a falcon). Some years back, in the attempt to standardize the English names of birds, our "Sparrow Hawk" was changed to American Kestrel, since it, too, is a member of the genus *Falco.*

Another problem with the name is that sparrows constitute only a minor portion of the diet of our "Sparrow Hawk." If grasshoppers are plentiful, then they constitute the principal diet, although small birds may be captured from time to time. In winter, however, when grasshoppers are scarce, the diet of kestrels shifts to birds and small mammals. One person even saw a kestrel sail gently down to a Cliff Swallow's nest, support itself with one foot, insert the other foot into the nest, and extract a swallow.

Kestrels are easy to identify. First of all, they are small birds, about the size of a robin. They sit right out in the open, often on telephone wires or in the tops of trees. The markings on their cheeks is distinctive: two vertical dark bars separated by white. When they fly, their pointed wings make a boomerang shape as they glide, and when they light, they usually pump their tails a couple of times.

American Kestrel

For many raptors, the males and females look pretty much alike, but not the American Kestrel. In females, the wings and back are pretty much rufous all over, whereas in males, the wings are blue-gray. In flight, especially in the male, the tail shows a bright rufous color, reminding us that the Red-tailed Hawk is not the only raptor around with a red tail.

One of the characteristic things about a kestrel is its habit of hovering in one spot, wings fluttering, while it looks for its prey below. A small bird hovering is almost instantly recognizable as an American Kestrel. (Note, however, that even smaller birds -- namely, Mountain Bluebirds -- also habitually hover. But one is not likely to mistake a bluebird for a kestrel.)

Kestrels will lay their eggs in natural cavities or in nesting boxes, if the latter are available. They generally lay their eggs right on the bare floor, or on whatever the previous occupant may have left behind. I once watched a naturalist banding young kestrels. He would reach into the nest box with a gloved hand, while the young birds inside turned on their backs and presented their talons in defense. One of the young kestrels would be sure to grip the intruding gloved hand, whereupon the naturalist easily pulled it from the box to be banded.

## Merlin (MERL)
*Falco columbarius*

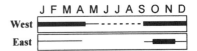

A small, dark falcon pumping past you, in a hurry to be someplace else, is almost certainly a Merlin. It formerly was known as "Pigeon Hawk." Some say this was because pigeons are a common prey item; others say it was because its flight was likened to that of a pigeon. In support of the latter view, that's what the scientific name *columbarius* means: pigeon-like. A couple of other old-time names are "bullet hawk," and "little blue corporal."

They are pretty small, only a little larger than a kestrel, but have been known to take teal, snipe, sandpipers, curlews, quail, pigeons, blackbirds, gophers, mice, bats, toads, grasshoppers, spiders, and scorpions. They are not currently known to nest in Oregon, but in 1883 Major Bendire claimed that he observed a breeding pair near Fort Klamath.

As is usually the case with hawks, there are several forms. In this case, it is not so much that there are different morphs, but that there are different regional subspecies. One of these is extremely dark, called "Pacific Merlin," or "Black Merlin" (*F. c. suckleyi*). Another one is almost as dark, called "Taiga Merlin" (*F. c. columbarius*). The third is fairly light-colored, and is called

"Prairie Merlin" (*F. c. richardsonii*). The two dark ones are the most likely in our area.

The bands in the tail may or may not be visible, depending upon the subspecies. The bands are prominent in a "Taiga," but may be faint or absent in a "Black." If a Merlin is flashing by, the tail bands may be the only thing you will see, as the bird disappears. One often may sit in the top of a tree, in which case the first thing you are likely to notice is its dark color. The next thing that generally strikes me, at least, is that the bill looks tiny, and has a peculiar "squashed-in" appearance. The smallness of the bill seems out of place for such a fierce hunter.

The speed of Merlins in flight is remarkable. They apparently have little fear of humans; I've had one of them zip by within a few feet, intent on something else, and gone before I hardly knew it was there. Few birds can escape them in direct flight; they have even been known to overtake Black Swifts. However, Rock Doves apparently can fly too fast to be captured, provided they have time to get up to speed. If the intended prey is skillful at dodging, the Merlin may come up empty-handed. Instances have been related of birds, pursued by Merlins, darting into foliage and avoiding capture. A Sharp-shinned Hawk would go straight into the foliage in pursuit, but a Merlin evidently prefers to take prey in the open.

An instance has been related, of a hunter who shot a snipe, but a Merlin appeared from nowhere, snatched the snipe from the air as it was falling, and flew off with it so fast that it was only a "blur in the air." The hunter fired at the Merlin, but the bird was out of range before the shot could be fired.

## Gyrfalcon (GYRF) *Falco rusticolus*

Vagrant

This huge falcon from the tundras is heavier than a Red-tailed Hawk. It comes in the usual color morphs from light to dark, but the gray form is the most common. It has shown up very few times in our area, but there are records from the Klamath Marsh NWR, one from the Lower Klamath NWR, and one from the Tule Lake NWR.

## Peregrine Falcon (PEFA) *Falco peregrinus*

## Prairie Falcon (PRFA) *Falco mexicanus*

These two birds are placed together because they are similar in size and shape. Overhead, both have the pointed-wing falcon shape, but the Prairie Falcon has diagnostic dark areas in the axillaries, or "armpits," clearly visible against the light-colored body. Peregrines don't have those dark areas.

In a sitting bird, if it has a conspicuous dark "helmet," then you know it's a Peregrine. Note, however, that a juvenile Peregrine may have the "helmet" reduced to a narrow moustachial streak, making it resemble a Prairie Falcon. Then you have to look at the area behind the eye. In a Peregrine this area is dark; in a Prairie it is white.

**Peregrine Falcon**

Peregrines are found worldwide. In North America, most of them breed in the far north, but the scientific name *peregrinus* means "wandering," and wander they do, in some cases as far as South America. Not too long ago, they were called "duck hawks," and ducks are on their food lists, as are coots, upland game birds, small mammals, and even other hawks such as harriers. A favorite food item is domestic pigeons, and Peregrines have been known to take up residence during winter in big cities, roosting on the tall buildings, and feasting on pigeons. They nest sparingly in our area.

Until 1999, Peregrine Falcons were on the official Endangered Species list. The move to list the species came about because in 1970 only 39 pairs were found to exist in the entire lower 48 states. After a massive captive breeding and reintroduction program, populations had recovered to the point where the species was removed from the federal list, in 1999, but remained on the state endangered list.

Peregrines are sometimes bred in captivity with other falcon species, including Prairie Falcons, for use in falconry. These hybrids sometimes escape, and can pose real identification problems.

Prairie Falcons are birds of the arid plains and hills of the American west, but generally need cliffs nearby for nesting. They may turn up anywhere, even in high alpine country after the nesting season, but the best place to look for them is near cliffs in the breeding season, preferably east of the Cascades.

One place that has been fairly reliable is in the Petroglyphs section of Lava Beds National Monument. Here, nesting Prairie Falcons can sometimes be seen right from the parking lot at the Petroglyphs. Even though cars and people are constantly coming and going from the parking area, the falcons apparently are used to them. This means you probably will not disturb the nesting birds unless you leave the lot and start walking in their direction. Look for ledges on the cliffs with lots of "whitewash" below them.

Both of these falcons are mighty hunters. I once visited a popular shorebird area, and observed that a rather large flock of American Avocets and Black-necked Stilts were huddled in a tight group, and milling about. This was rather unusual behavior, and I soon found the cause: A Peregrine was sitting nearby, eating a small shorebird. It finished off the shorebird as I watched, and then headed for the flock of avocets and stilts. It made a series of lightning-like passes at the flock, but soon gave up and flew away. I couldn't see everything that had happened, but had a mental image of the avocets and stilts all bunching together for protection, while pointing their sharp bills in the direction of the Peregrine, daunting it enough to cause it to give up.

Perhaps so. It was an appealing image, but a friend suggested to me that the thing that was really happening was the Peregrine was trying to make the avocets and stilts fly, since falcons prefer to take their prey on the wing.

At another time, I watched a Prairie Falcon attack a Mallard, which was probably half again as big as the falcon. I was taking a shorebird census at a wastewater treatment plant, and was using my car as a blind. I was on one of the rocky dikes between the ponds, and at that particular moment was seeing Mallards, lots of them. Suddenly they scattered, as a Prairie Falcon hurtled from the sky and struck one of them. The Mallard fell over and struggled weakly, while the falcon rose into the sky, turned, and hit it again.

I don't know what would have happened next, except that I interfered by slowly opening the door of my car and leaning out, trying to get a picture the next time the falcon hit the Mallard. That did it. The falcon flew off a hundred yards down the dike and sat there, waiting to see what I would do. The Mallard, for its part, slowly regained part of its senses. It couldn't stand up, but struggled on its side across the dike to the water and fell in. It then swam off, looking reasonably normal.

## Family **PHASIANIDAE**: Partridges, Grouse, Turkeys, and Old World Quail

### Chukar (CHUK)
*Alectoris chukar*

J F M A M J J A S O N D
East

Here's one of those cases where the scientific name is also the common name. (Another one is "junco.") Chukars are transplanted birds in North America, originally from south Asia. The name is appropriate because it comes from the Hindustani *cakor*, meaning partridge. And the Hindustani name was apparently given because the people of the region thought that's what its call sounded like.

The introductions of Chukars in the U.S. began in the 1930s and was attempted in 42 states for hunting purposes. In only ten of these states, all in the west, were populations successfully established. In Oregon, the first introductions were in the 1950s, east of the Cascades, and in the next 15 years, more than 100,000 of them were released. They like semiarid sagebrush and grasslands country, especially rocky slopes.

Chukars are beautiful birds, and can't be mistaken for anything else. The first one I ever saw was in eastern Washington, and I had no idea such a bird existed. It took many years after that before I saw another one, even though I made many trips to appropriate habitat in the search. When I finally succeeded, it was in a national park (Death Valley), where the birds were unhunted and relatively tame.

In Oregon, I have yet to find one as the result of a deliberate search, but have had them find *me* when I was least expecting it, when one would pop up along the roadside. I am told the best way to find one is to wait in late afternoon by a known watering-hole, but the method has never worked for me. Since there are regular releases of these birds for hunting purposes, you can never be sure whether you are seeing a truly wild bird, or one that has spent part of its life behind a fence.

If you want to see a Chukar, you have to go to the semiarid country where they live. In our region, their population is on the decline. In past years they could be found in the dry rocky country south of Tulelake, but no more. In recent years, they have been seen on the east side of Stukel Mountain, near Klamath Falls. In 1998 there was one at Miller Island, which seems out of expected habitat, but with introduced game birds, anything can happen. In past years, introduction attempts were made in the Rogue Valley which apparently did not succeed, although a couple of them have been seen near Grants Pass, one in the 1970s, and the other in 1999.

## Ring-necked Pheasant (RPHE)
*Phasianus colchicus*

J F M A M J J A S O N D

Ring-necked Pheasants, like Chukars, are introduced birds, and are not native to the U.S. However, they've been in this country so long that I've seen people argue concerning whether they are introduced or not. Attempts to introduce pheasants in North America date all the way back to 1730, but the first success came in Oregon, in 1881. Introductions, for hunting purposes, have been attempted in all of the Lower 48 states, but have been successful in only 12, all in the north and west. Today, the pheasant is the official state bird of South Dakota.

**Ring-necked Pheasant**

The birds in the east came from England, but the birds in Oregon came from China. The Chinese birds have a ring around the neck, but the original eastern birds did not. (Today, they may have rings, because of continued introductions and interbreeding.) The birds in England apparently were brought from Asia centuries ago, and are the same species as ours, neck-ring or not.

Everybody loves the Ring-necked Pheasant, because it is a beautiful bird. The males are gaudy: the neck is a metallic blue-green with a white ring, most of the head is bright red, and the body is a bronze, gold, and iridescent mixture. The tail is two to three feet long, and often is cocked up at an angle. The female is brown and mottled, which undoubtedly helps in camouflaging her as she sits on the nest. Females resemble roadrunners so much, that they sometimes are mistaken for them.

During the spring, if there are pheasants in the neighborhood, you are likely to hear their "love song." This is a loud, penetrating double squawk (sometimes rendered as *kor-kok!*) followed by a flurry of wing beats.

With an introduced species such as the Ring-necked pheasant, the question of competition with native species arises. In the far west, this apparently has not been a problem, but has been troublesome in the middle west, where pheasants are believed to be a culprit in the demise of Greater Prairie-Chickens in some states.

Pheasants are "brood parasites." The female starts laying eggs even before she has prepared a nest. These eggs may be left randomly on the ground, or may be deposited in the nests of other birds, such as prairie-chickens. The pheasant eggs hatch sooner than do the prairie-chicken eggs, and the mother prairie-chicken departs with the chicks, believing them to be her own.

Pheasants have declined in our area on both sides of the Cascades, along with the decrease in grain crops. Pheasants depend upon such crops for both food and cover. The grain that is eaten is mostly waste grain, with weed seeds, leafage, and insects making up the balance. In order to sustain hunting, the state regularly releases pheasants into the field, especially at wildlife areas such as Denman, in the Rogue Valley, and Miller Island, in the Klamath Basin.

## Ruffed Grouse (RUGR)
*Bonasa umbellus*

Hunters often call this bird "partridge," although it is not closely related to the Old World partridges. Ruffed Grouse are found coast to coast in the more northerly states, and up through Canada into Alaska. In Oregon, the species is widespread. There are two color forms: gray, and rufous. The rufous form predominates west of the Cascades, and the gray form to the east.

Ruffed Grouse can be hard to see. In my own case, the first time I saw one was when it exploded from the grass almost at my feet -- a common experience reported by many people. Nevertheless, biologists claim that in spring and summer they are often seen along logging roads, especially in western Oregon. As hunting season progresses (generally from September through December), they become more wary.

They like deciduous/evergreen forests, preferably riparian zones, and forests dominated by alders. They also like disturbed areas, such as areas regenerating from logging, especially if there are small clearings.

In springtime, from late March until May, a male grouse will select a log in the forest, probably the same one that has been used for years, and begin his "drumming." The drumming is produced by wingbeats, beginning slowly, and then building into a crescendo that has been described as the "rumbling of distant thunder." The sound can carry for distances up to a mile, but the source can be difficult to locate. The whole performance may last for ten seconds, and then be repeated after 3 to 5 minutes.

In our region, Ruffed Grouse have been sighted along roads bordering the Rogue River near Prospect, near Lake of the Woods, and at various places around Upper Klamath Lake, such as at Malone Springs, Odessa Campground, and at Wood River Picnic Area.

## Greater Sage-Grouse (GRSG)
*Centrocercus urophasianus*

J F M A M J J A S O N D
East

Until 2000, this bird was just called "Sage Grouse." But in that year, the AOU decided that there was a population of grouse in Colorado sufficiently different from other "Sage Grouse" (for one thing, they were smaller), to be considered a separate species, and gave it the name Gunnison Sage-Grouse. The rest of the "Sage Grouse" in the country, including those in Oregon, were given the name, "Greater Sage-Grouse." In former times it was called the "sage hen," and some people still call it that.

The strutting of males in March and April on their "leks" is a fabled sight. A lek is an open area where the males gather to puff out their beautiful white fronts, spread their tails, and strut for the benefit of the females. Simultaneously, they make weird noises that sound like *plop! plop!*. The females, half the size of the males and very drab, hurry through the collection of males, looking almost furtive as they make their selections of mates.

Sage-Grouse live where the sagebrush is, because they depend upon it for food. During the winter, it forms almost their entire diet. At other seasons, they will eat the blossoms and pods of other plants, plus insects. After the young birds have learned to fly, their mothers bring them down from the dry hillsides to locations where they can find small tender weeds. I was in the ghost town of Bodie in eastern California one summer, and was astonished to find Greater Sage-Grouse right in the streets of the town. All of them were females and youngsters, as far as I could tell, seeking tender young plants.

Greater Sage-Grouse occur in our area, at the Clear Lake NWR in the Klamath Basin, and, to a limited degree in other sagebrush habitat in the region. At one time, it was possible to get a permit to enter and view the birds at Clear Lake, but no longer, because the population is apparently heading toward zero. It is estimated, as of this writing, that there are only about 30 birds left at that location. I am told the reason for their decline is because of the spread of junipers, brought on by fire suppression and grazing, which reduces the sagebrush on which the birds depend. The closest places known to me where Greater Sage-Grouse can be viewed on their leks are: Millican lek near Bend, Oregon (contact BLM at P.O. Box 550, Prineville, OR 97754, phone 541-416-6700); and Shaffer lek, near Susanville, California (see my book, *Birding Northern California*, for directions and a map).

# Blue Grouse (BGSE)
*Dendragapus obscurus*

A Blue Grouse can be easy to hear but hard to find. Yet, at times one of them may walk or run about in plain view, paying little or no attention to nearby humans. Twice, I have watched a male perform his courtship display within a few feet of me, with tail fully fanned, and hurrying to follow a female to show her how gorgeous he was. Once, I tried to keep up with a male as he was following a female, but the forest was littered with fallen trees. The bird negotiated the logs easily, pausing occasionally to spread his tail and puff out his chest, but I was soon left behind.

Outside the mating season, I've had them stick around in full view, paying little or no attention to me, while going about their business. On one occasion, I was sitting on a log, and heard a soft clucking behind me. Here was a female grouse, moving slowly along a log about fifteen feet away, and making no effort to flee. Even after I stood up and took almost a whole roll of pictures, she just continued to amble along the log. (See Plate IV.) I suspect there was a young one down below that she was supervising, out of sight in the grass. This kind of behavior caused old-timers to give this bird the name of "fool hen."

Mostly, you will know there is a Blue Grouse around because of the hollow "hooting" sound the male makes, which sounds to me like short notes from a bull fiddle, given perhaps five or six times in succession. The hooting begins in March and continues into May. It is so ventriloquial that I've never been sure of exactly what direction it is coming from, or how far away it is.

These are big birds, both males and females weighing about 2 ½ pounds. Males are dark gray, and females are gray-brown. Males have a yellow-orange comb over the eye; females do not. The birds can be found in the spring and summer in the Cascades especially in mixed forests of Douglas fir and true fir, often around the edges of stands that have been logged. I've even seen them in summer right up to tree line. In summer they eat berries, insects, buds, and flowers. In winter, their diet consists mostly of tree buds. I haven't seen them in winter, but they apparently spend most of their time roosting in trees, making them difficult to find.

# Wild Turkey (WITU)
*Meleagris gallopavo*

Wild Turkeys are native to much of the Lower 48 states, but historically did not exist on the Pacific Coast. Fish and Wildlife departments in the states that did not already have turkeys set out to remedy the problem.

Doing so was astonishingly difficult. Originally, birds were raised on game farms and then released into the field. That failed. The turkeys simply didn't have enough survival skills to make it in the wild. Then the expedient of trapping wild turkeys in Texas and Arizona (they are native to both states) was tried. After many trials and many failures, the method worked. Oregon today has populations in several areas of the state, generally at low and middle elevations. In 1999, 2,500 of them were taken by hunters, statewide.

**Wild Turkey**

Wild-trapped turkeys from Texas were first released in the Rogue Valley in 1975, and today might be found many places in Southern Oregon at low to mid elevations, where there are trees, and acorns for them to eat. I have seen them congregating next to farmers' fields, and once met one on the trail to Lower Table Rock that didn't seem to want to get out of the way.

The first Wild Turkey I ever saw did not behave that way. I heard him gobble from a distance, and quietly crept up on him. He spotted me instantly and departed, running down the slope like a race horse. Then he took off in a low glide, and disappeared.

The contrast between the behavior of this bird and the one that wouldn't get out of the trail is interesting. Apparently turkeys are smart enough to discover areas where they won't get hunted, such as public parks, and congregate there. My turkey on the trail behaved like most of the other turkeys I've met in public parks -- they just move about, doing their thing, and ignore me unless I get too close.

In early years, turkeys were considered to be easy game, but apparently there was a big change in the latter half of the 19th century, when Dr. William L. Ralph made this observation:

> One can hardly believe that the wild turkeys of today are the same species as those of fifteen or twenty years ago. Then they were rather stupid birds, which it did not require much skill to shoot, but now I do not know of a game bird or mammal more alert or more difficult to approach.

## Family **ODONTOPHORIDAE**: New World Quail

**Mountain Quail** (MOUQ)
*Oreortyx pictus*

**California Quail** (CAQU)
*Callipepla californica*

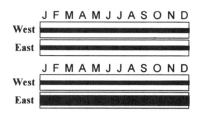

At first glance these two resemble each other, but a closer inspection shows many differences. Probably the most conspicuous things are their plumes. California Quail have teardrop-shaped plumes; Mountain Quail have two long, slender plumes that sometimes coalesce into one. In each case, the plumes on the females are smaller than on the males.

California Quail have narrow white longitudinal bars on their sides, and are scaled on their fronts. Mountain Quail have bold white vertical bars on their sides, and no scales. There are other differences, but the ones mentioned should serve to identify the birds.

Mountain Quail are birds of the far west, and are found in foothill and mountain country throughout Oregon, generally above 1600 feet. In the past, they have been called "plumed quail," and "mountain partridge." They are secretive and seldom seen. When surprised, they tend to melt into the brush and disappear, rather than fly. An interesting trait of Mountain Quail is that the female sometimes lays two simultaneous clutches, with an average of 11 eggs per clutch. The female incubates one clutch and the male incubates the other.

The places I have seen them in our region are in the rolling, forested country on the top of the Cascades, in open areas that have been logged, but with areas of brush. In each case, the sighting was very brief. In spring they are easily heard. Their loud call, *quee-ark,* can be heard a half mile away. In fall, they migrate downhill to get below the snow line.

California Quail, as contrasted to Mountain Quail, are readily seen, provided you are in their brushy habitat. They are residents of the lowlands, and at one time were called "Valley Quail." Many people still call them that. They are native to California and southern Oregon, and have been transplanted to many other parts of the state. Sometimes they are found right in town, and I once saw an enormous flock on the outskirts of Burns. They have even been transplanted to Hawaii and New Zealand.

Often your first intimation that there are California Quail around is when you hear the male's loud call, *shee-CAH-go!* Often, a male can be seen standing on guard on a bush or rock, while the flock forages. When surprised, the birds fly off into brush, their wings giving a loud whir. As a rule, there will be a fairly large flock, and their clucking can be heard as they regroup in their hiding places. In spring, the sight of a pair of quail, followed by a brood of little fluff-balls, is a common sight. The chicks can run almost as soon as they are hatched, and can fly within ten days after hatching.

When I was a kid, we lived in a area where California Quail were abundant. My older brother decided he was going to capture a baby quail, a practice which was probably illegal even then. He succeeded in getting one by throwing his sweater over a flock of chicks as they ran, and then proudly took his prize home to our mother to raise. She had grown up on a farm, and knew just what to do. The quail was raised to adulthood, and ran freely around the house as a pet.

But one day it got caught in a door as it was closing and broke its leg. The leg healed, but the quail walked with a limp after that. Not long after, a flock of wild quail showed up in our yard, and our pet quail abandoned us and joined them. But, from time to time, if a flock of quail passed through our yard again, we might see our "pet" among them, walking along with a limp.

## Family **RALLIDAE**: Rails, Gallinules, and Coots

### Yellow Rail (YERA)
*Coturnicops noveboracensis*

J F M A M J J A S O N D
East

There's little use in describing this bird, because chances are you won't be able to see one. They are notorious for being secretive, and for their unwillingness to be caught in the open. For what it's worth, they are small, they are yellowish, and they are active at night. If you should be lucky enough to glimpse one in flight, look for the white in the secondaries.

The old way of seeing a Yellow Rail is now in disrepute because it is so disruptive to the birds' lives. This was for a fairly large number of birders to gather on a spring night in a marsh where the birds breed. The people waited until they could hear one calling, and then slowly surrounded the bird, moving in closer and closer, until it finally was found cowering at their feet.

The reason this procedure is disruptive is because the marsh in which the birders are tramping around is where the nests are located, and who can tell how many nests get damaged in the process. The accepted procedure now is just to listen for the birds' calling. The call is so distinctive that there is nothing else like it.

Nothing else, that is, except the tapping of two small rocks together, to make a sound like *tick-tick, tick-tick-tick, tick-tick.* It is a perfect imitation, and Yellow Rails will often answer the sound you make with two rocks.

During nesting season they prefer areas with grass that is not too tall, but adequate to provide cover, with standing water perhaps 2 to 3 inches deep. Their usual breeding range is in Canada and a few of the northern states, but there are small breeding groups in Klamath County. It is believed that there are 235 to 285 breeding pairs in the state, most of them in Klamath County, and some in Lake County.

In May and June, they have been heard "ticking" from the wet meadows near Fort Klamath, and along West Side Road near Jack Spring and Mare's Egg Spring. They have also been heard in the Klamath Marsh NWR along Silver Lake Road. Sometimes they start ticking at dusk, but other times it may be as late as 10 p.m. Expect mosquitoes.

Jack Spring is 13.9 miles north of OR 140, on West Side Road. Look for Milepost 3 (on left side of road), and then go 0.3 mile further, where there is barely enough room to park at the edge of the road. Mares Egg Spring is 16.1 miles north of OR 140; there is some paved parking on the road shoulder.

### Virginia Rail (VIRA)
*Rallus limicola*

J F M A M J J A S O N D
West
East

Rails are known for their secretive behavior, but this one at least comes out in the open more than its cousin, the Yellow Rail. Nevertheless, you might have to remain at the edge of a marsh for a long time, holding still, in order to see one. It is a highly vocal bird, especially in spring, so you've got a good chance of hearing one. Its loud, *kid-ick! kid-ick! kid-ick!* can often be heard in daytime. Another sound that it makes is one that resembles the grunting of a hungry pig.

In appearance, it looks like a miniature version of its larger cousin, the Clapper Rail, which we don't have in Oregon. The adult has a general rich chestnut-brown color, with conspicuous vertical stripes on the flanks, altogether making it a very attractive bird. The long down-curved bill immediately distinguishes it from another small rail, the Sora, which has a short bill.

Anywhere there is a marsh, even a small one, there is a chance of finding a Virginia Rail. The Klamath Basin has extensive marshes, and offers much good habitat. Habitat in the Rogue Valley is less extensive, but the Denman WA has good marshes, and in spring and summer I have heard them there.

The Latin name, *limicola*, means "mud-dweller," which seems appropriate, because muddy marshes are where they live. I cannot find any explanation in the literature for the common name, "Virginia." After all, their natural range covers the entire lower 48 states. I suspect when the species was first named, that the type specimen came from Virginia.

Their food consists almost entirely of animal matter such as worms, fish, snails, insects, and even small snakes. A story is related of a Virginia Rail that captured a 12-inch garter snake, and then tried to swallow it. This would seem to take some doing, because the bird itself is only about 10 inches long. The rail attacked the snake with thrusts of its bill, and then, after about 30 minutes of this, attempted to swallow it. The snake wrapped itself around the bird, and the rail quickly disgorged it. For the next two hours, the bird alternately attacked the snake and attempted to swallow it, and in the end, succeeded.

A Virginia Rail in flight looks pitiful. I have witnessed this only one time, in which the rail fluttered on feeble wings from the marsh growth, across a small pond, and into the growth on the other side. Yet, the literature insists that they are capable of long migrations. Those who have seen them in migration (not me) say they fly at night, at a height of only a few feet, and at a speed never witnessed under ordinary circumstances.

I love to read the old literature such as the following, written by John James Audubon in 1840, regarding the courtship of the Virginia Rail:

> Now with open wings raised over its body, it ran around its beloved, opening and flirting its tail with singular speed. Each time it passed before her, it would pause for a moment, raise itself to the full stretch of its body and legs, and bow to her with all the grace of a well-bred suitor of our own species.

## Sora (SORA)
*Porzana carolina*

In contrast to the ticking noise of a Yellow Rail or the *PUMP-er-lunk* of the American Bittern, the Sora has a very pleasing "song" (to me, at least). The song of the Sora starts with a plaintive, high k*er-wee,* with rising inflection, and then shifts to a pleasant whinny that makes me laugh every time I hear it. The whinny has been rendered as *koWEE-ee-ee-ee-ee, ee, ee,* descending in pitch, and slowing down toward the end.

Virginia Rails and Soras live in similar marshy habitat, and are about the same size, with the Sora a little smaller. In our region, any marsh that has Virginia Rails is also likely to have Soras, at least in summer.

The bill of the Virginia Rail is long and down-curved, while that of the Sora is short and stout, and has been likened by some to the bill of a chicken. In an adult Sora, the bill is yellow and the face is black. In a juvenile, both face and bill are brownish. The tiny ones that are still in their downy plumage, fresh out of the egg, are all black. (So are Virginia Rails, by the way.) Since they are about the same size as adult Black Rails, they have been mistaken for that rare species. Black Rails are not known to occur in Oregon.

Soras are sometimes seen sitting at the edge of a marsh, head poking out of the cattails, as if waiting for something -- perhaps prey such as aquatic insects. They do eat insects and mollusks, but almost three-quarters of their diet consists of seeds. They are said to especially fond of wild rice.

Like other rails, they have narrow bodies that permit them to slip off easily among the cattails when they are frightened. The narrow body has prompted some folks to say that their name derives from "thin as a rail," but my dictionary of birds' names says it derives from the Old French, *raale,* "to make a scraping noise." The common name, Sora, is the name used by Native Americans for this species.

Soras, again like other rails, are perceived as slow and clumsy fliers. But these tiny birds undertake long migrations, in some cases to South America, covering perhaps 3,000 miles in the process. They can swim and dive, too. Arthur Cleveland Bent relates one case in which a Sora plunged into a brook about a foot deep, and crossed underwater for about 15 feet by clinging to underwater vegetation.

**American Coot** (AMCO)
*Fulica americana*

**Common Moorhen** (COMO)   Accidental
*Gallinula chloropus*

Both of these species belong to the rail family, although they don't behave much like other rails I have put them together because they superficially resemble each other. Adult coots have white bills and foreheads; adult moorhens have bills and foreheads that are red in summer, but turn blackish in winter. An important mark on a moorhen is the horizontal white line on each flank just above the waterline, that is present on birds of all ages. Juvenile coots and juvenile moorhens resemble each other, except that the juvenile coot does not have this white line. There is one record for Common Moorhen in the Rogue Valley, at Denman WA, and two for the Lower Klamath NWR.

Coots, especially, don't behave like proper rails. Instead of lurking in the cattails, they are generally right out there in the open, swimming about, and diving and dabbling just like they were ducks. Sometimes, it seems, even if there is no other bird life on a pond, there will be coots. They have the largest breeding population in Oregon of any water bird, and in fall may gather in flocks of thousands. In November 2000, a flock of 1600 was seen at Lake Selmac.

Many people disdain coots, I suppose because they are considered common and vulgar. Hunters call them "mudhens," and claim their flesh tastes bad, although some say it is quite palatable. The name "coot" is used by hunters also for the sea-ducks known as "scoters," and it is presumed that both names are derived from the word "scoot," to hurry off.

**American Coot**

I happen to like coots. I find their *kuk-kuk-kuk-kuk* as they poke around in the marsh to be a friendly noise. I love their little ones. The adults may be dark and drab, but the young ones sport gaudy orange heads during their first few weeks. Finally, coots are dutiful parents, and aggressively protect their young from danger.

I was a witness to an event that demonstrates the protectiveness of coots. I had gone to a remote lake in Yellowstone National Park for the purpose of seeing Trumpeter Swans, at a time when Trumpeters were more rare than they are today. A family of six trumpeters -- two adults and four young -- was floating on the lake, providing a perfect image of wild harmony.

Coming energetically from one side were two clusters of coots, each consisting of an adult followed by a little group of eight or nine cootlets. A group of coots was passing close to the swans, when one of the adult swans suddenly lunged at them, beak gaping wide, aiming not for the adult coot but for the cootlets. The swan was joined by the other adult, and they jabbed repeatedly at the young coots, most of whom disappeared under water.

Once the cootlets had been dealt with, the swans turned back to their placid floating. I scanned the lake, trying to see how many of the young coots had survived, but could only see a couple.

Suddenly an adult coot appeared, flying low and fast over the lake, and rammed at full speed into the side of one of the swans. Retreating slightly, the coot banged into the swan again. Another coot appeared, flying at full speed, and slammed into the other swan. There was a wild melee as the coots pressed their attack and the swans counterattacked.

Finally, apparently satisfied with their work, both coots withdrew. The swans settled down to float serenely on their way, acting as if nothing had happened. I noted then, as one of the adult coots swam off, that it was followed by only four baby coots.

Not only do coots tip up like dabbling ducks, they also frequently come out on dry ground and graze like so many chickens. But they also can dive to depths of 10 to 25 feet, remaining under water for up to 15 seconds. The young can stay under even longer -- nearly three minutes, according to one authority.

Coots are easily alarmed, and a whole flock will take off together if they think danger is approaching. Mallards can take off almost vertically when they take flight, but not coots. Coots race over the water, wings flapping against the surface, feet paddling, before they finally become airborne. Sometimes they don't actually get airborne at all, but flap over the surface and settle elsewhere. Nevertheless, once in the air they are strong fliers, and engage in long migrations.

Bald Eagles have been known to prey on coots. Apparently an eagle will not attack if the coots remain together in a tight flock. But if the eagle manages to make them scatter, it will select one and pursue it as it swims under water until it surfaces. The eagle then forces it under again, and is once more waiting overhead as it surfaces. This game is repeated until the coot finally is exhausted, and the eagle wins.

## Family **GRUIDAE:** Cranes

### Sandhill Crane (SACR)
*Grus canadensis*

One of the grand experiences of the natural world is to hear the haunting, mysterious calls of Sandhill Cranes coming from high in the sky. This call has been rendered as *k-r-roo, kr-r-r-roo, ku-kr-r-roo*, but such an English rendering has no chance of eliciting the stirring, primitive feeling that the real thing causes within the soul.

Almost all those who have listened to Sandhill Cranes report their feelings the same way. One observer says it ". . . seems to suggest something prehistoric -- such a call as one might expect was heard in the days when pterodactyls and their kind flew about the marshes." Such thoughts are not entirely fanciful, because Sandhill Cranes are the oldest known currently existing bird; fossil bones nine million years old have been found.

There are two subspecies of Sandhills in the west, the "Lesser" Sandhill Crane, and the "Greater" Sandhill Crane. (There is a third, called "Canadian" Sandhill Crane, that occurs to a small degree.) The "Greater" is only five inches or so taller than the "Lesser," and for most of us, the

**Sandhill Crane**

two can not be told apart in the field. Approximately 30,000 Sandhill Cranes of both subspecies spend the winter in California, about one-fifth of which are "Greaters." But this number is dwarfed by the half million or so that congregate on the Platte River in Nebraska in spring. Most of those on the Platte go on to the high Arctic to breed, but some stop in Alaska.

The "Lessers" that come to Southern Oregon only pause in migration on their way to Alaska. But the "Greaters" remain to breed. They can be found in pairs in wet meadows in places such as the Lower Klamath NWR, along the Lost River in Poe Valley, and in the mountains at various meadows such as the ones at Howard Prairie and near Fish Lake. On their wintering grounds they forage in large groups and are easy to observe, but during breeding season they are dispersed and often are hard to see. Both sexes share in incubation, and often the only thing you will see is a head sticking above the tall grass.

Much has been made of the dancing in which cranes engage, principally on their breeding grounds. One observer has described the dance as a ". . . series of hops and jumps, and of bowing low to the left and right, with the wings limply extended, as if loose jointed, and nearly touching ground." Before and during the dance, they may give their *kr-r-rooo* sound.

Dancing has been commonly supposed to be a part of the mating ritual. And so it is, but it also may occur any time of the year, and sometimes a large group may become involved. Some researchers believe that dancing at this time of year represents a ritualized form of aggression.

## Family **CHARADRIIDAE**: Lapwings and Plovers

**Black-bellied Plover** (BBPL)
*Pluvialis squatarola*

**American Golden-Plover** (AMGP)
*Pluvialis dominica*

**Pacific Golden-Plover** (PAGP)
*Pluvialis fulva*

Some people say *PLUH-ver,* and some say *PLOH-ver.* In my own case, I never know which way I'm going to pronounce it until I hear it coming out of my mouth. My dictionary gives both pronunciations, if that's any help. The name is derived from the Old French *plovier,* meaning "rainy," although there seems to be no particular behavior that justifies the name.

These three are considered together because of the difficulty in distinguishing them, at least in some plumages, and because of their similar size and behavior. Black-bellied Plovers are larger than the others but this may not be evident unless birds of different species are standing near each other.

A characteristic of all plovers is their manner of feeding. They run, stop, hold still with head erect, lean down to peck at something, and then repeat the process. Sandpipers, on the other hand, keep their heads down while foraging.

All three plovers are uncommon to rare in our area. A notable exception was when a flock of more than 500 Black-bellied Plovers were seen in a pasture near Lower Klamath NWA, in April 2000. Most often, they will be found at a water treatment facility (read: sewer ponds), or at a shallow muddy lakeshore.

All of the three breed in the far north, and only one, the Black-bellied Plover, spends the winter at our latitude, where it sticks to the coast. American Golden-Plovers, on the other hand, spend the winter in Argentina, and migrate up through the center of the U.S. in the spring. In the fall, they gather in Nova Scotia and fly directly across the ocean to Brazil, perhaps pausing to rest on the ocean along the way.

Pacific Golden-Plovers are even more remarkable in their migrations. They spend the winter in a huge area ranging from the Hawaiian Islands to Australia, and migrate directly over the Pacific Ocean to their breeding grounds in the far north. In the fall, they again fly directly across the Pacific to their wintering grounds. No wonder both American and Pacific Golden-Plovers are rare and irregular in our area.

In the spring, if we're lucky enough to get any of these birds, they will be making the transition to their breeding plumage. The breeding plumage is not fully developed until the birds arrive on their breeding grounds, but by then all three have black faces and throats and have white stripes down the sides of their necks. The white stripe on the Pacific Golden-Plover extends all the way down to the flank, which is not the case with the other two. A distinctive characteristic of Black-bellieds, seen in flight and present in all plumages, is that they have dark axillaries, or "armpits."

When the birds return in fall, all three species are more or less gray. In fact, in Europe, the Black-bellied Plover is called the "Gray Plover."

Until 1995, the two golden-plovers were combined into one species, called "Lesser Golden-Plover." In 1995, research was published showing that in western Alaska, where both species breed, the two as a rule do not interbreed, build their nests at different elevation levels, and have different breeding displays.

In the fall, in their nonbreeding plumages, the two golden-plovers can have varying amounts of yellow flecks on their backs, so this characteristic is undependable. Assuming you have already settled the question of whether you have a Black-bellied Plover, by the dark axillaries, then you can often separate American from Pacific Golden-Plover by the following: the wing tips of an American will extend well beyond the tip of the tail, and will show four primary feathers; the wing tips of a Pacific will barely extend beyond the tip of the tail, and three primaries will be visible.

These are only a few hints for identification, and there is much more to the story. (See Paulson, 1993, *Shorebirds of the Pacific Northwest,* which has many pages devoted to the topic.)

## Semipalmated Plover (SEPL)
*Charadrius semipalmatus*

|  | J F M A M J J A S O N D |
|---|---|
| West | — — |
| East | ■■■----■■■ |

## Snowy Plover (SNPL)
*Charadrius alexandrinus*

|  | J F M A M J J A S O N D |
|---|---|
| East | --------- |

There is only one word for these tiny birds: cute. Each one weighs about 1.5 ounces, which makes them slightly larger than the small sandpipers that are called "peeps." They sometimes are mixed in with sandpipers on a beach or mudflat, but can be immediately picked out by their customary plover behavior -- run, stop, look, pick; run, stop, look, pick.

The Semipalmated Plover is a bird of the Western Hemisphere, but the Snowy Plover is found around the world. In Britain, they call it the "Kentish Plover." These two are easily distinguished from each other, because the "semi" has a single complete neck ring and a dark back, while the Snowy has only a partial neck ring, and a light back. In fact, on the Snowy, the "ring" is reduced to dark patches on each side of the neck -- black during the breeding season, and gray during the nonbreeding.

It's worth noting that baby Killdeer have sometimes been mistaken for Semipalmated Plovers, because they have only a single neck ring (the adult Killdeer has two), and are about the right size. Where does the name "semipalmated" come from? It is because they have small webs linking the toes, as opposed to full webs such as are found on ducks.

There have been a handful of records of Semipalmated Plovers breeding in Oregon, but they mostly breed in the far north, and winter along the Pacific Coast all the way to South America. Small numbers winter on the Oregon Coast, but in our area they are principally migrants. Snowy Plovers, however, nest on the beaches of the Oregon coastline, and also nest in the interior west at various places, mostly on the edges of alkaline lakes. They have nested, on an irregular basis, at White Lake, in the Klamath Basin.

I once saw a Snowy Plover nest on the edge of a gravel road. The "nest" was only a shallow scrape in the gravel, and contained three eggs. Such a nest is almost invisible unless it is spotted as the tiny bird is in the process of returning to it. The nest was located in a wildlife refuge, so the refuge personnel put 4 x 4 boards around it so autos wouldn't run over it.

The boards worked, because over the time the eggs were being incubated, many motorists drove by and avoided the boards (and the nest), probably not even knowing there was a nest there. After four weeks, two newly hatched birds were seen, and the next day the nest was abandoned. This was considered normal for this species. After the eggs hatch, the nest is abandoned within a few hours.

An interesting part of the biology of this species is that the female typically leaves the male in charge of the chicks, and then goes in search of a new mate. In a mild climate, such as the Oregon coast, a female may produce two or three broods in a year.

## Killdeer (KILL)
*Charadrius vociferus*

Almost everybody recognizes a Killdeer. They seem to be everywhere, in almost any open habitat, on beaches, mudflats, farm fields, and golf courses. Nearly 600 of them were seen in the Rogue Valley during the Christmas count in 2000, and the largest count in North America was recorded not far from us, on the northwest coast of California -- more than 6,000. By contrast, the Klamath Falls Christmas count that same year had only 6, showing that the birds pretty much withdraw from the east side of the Cascades in winter.

The Killdeer is a plover. As such, it has the typical plover behavior: run, stop, look, peck; run, stop, look, peck. The Latin name, *vociferus*, fits them perfectly, because they are indeed noisy. Their loud call *KILL-dee, KILL-dee*, can often be heard from the sky, even at night, as the birds fly about announcing their presence and telling us their name. At times, especially when they are alarmed, this call is shortened to *Keeee! Keeee!*

The two black stripes around the neck identify them instantly; there is no other shorebird in North America that has that mark. Curiously, when they are small chicks they have only one stripe, causing some folks to misidentify them as Semipalmated Sandpipers.

They are beautiful when they fly. Not only is there a vivid white stripe on the wing, but the rump and tail are almost orange. In fact, the predominant impression you may have, as the bird flies away, is of its orange color. They breed as far north as Alaska, but in the west and south they are year-round residents. They are birds of the New World only, although the Old World has some close relatives.

The "distraction display" of the Killdeer is legendary. Other birds also have distraction displays, but I think the Killdeer may surpass them all. In this display, the parent flops along on the ground, dragging a wing as if broken, and uttering distress cries. The orangish rump and tail are never more visible than during this display. The purpose, of course, is to lure you away from the nest site, and it has worked exceedingly well with me. It has worked even though I knew that the nest would not be found near the birds, but somewhere backward along the direction from which they came.

The nests are difficult to find, even though they are right out in the open. Often they are in gravel, such as along a graveled road, in a gravel parking lot, or even on a gravel rooftop. On one occasion, when I saw a parent bird doing its distraction display in a gravel parking lot, I decided not to follow it, but hid behind a car instead. The bird soon stopped its display, and then walked forward and sat down in the gravel.

I had found the nest. But even though I had carefully memorized the location with respect to nearby landmarks, it took a long time before I actually located the nest, with four eggs placed together in the gravel, and blending in so well that they were well-nigh invisible.

I don't know whether the birds succeeded in raising a brood or not, but am hopeful. That particular part of the parking lot was not heavily used, and I returned in a couple of weeks to check the nest. I couldn't find it, even though I remembered the landmarks. I couldn't even find any eggshells, and that is what gave me hope. If the eggs had been squashed by tires, I would expect to find evidence, but Killdeers are known to carry off the eggshells once the chicks have hatched, and discard them some distance away. The reason they do this, it is thought, is that broken eggshells would be highly visible, and might attract predators.

One thing I am sure of is that baby Killdeers are the cutest things in the bird world (see Plate V). The chicks can run almost as soon as they are hatched, and they live a hazardous life. Not only are they exposed to all kinds of predators, but I learned of a new kind of hazard if the Killdeers are nesting on a gravel roof, and if the roof happens to have a parapet. On roofs without parapets, the chicks can jump off the edge and flutter to the ground, even if the roof is 50 feet high. But in this case there was a parapet; the chicks were unable to get over it, and they starved to death.

## **Mountain Plover** (MOUP)  Vagrant
*Charadrius montanus*

This plain-looking plover is misnamed, because it is not associated with the mountains, but with the dry plains. They breed on the plains of Montana, Wyoming, and Colorado, and then most of them migrate *west* to California for the winter. There are a few records in Oregon, mostly on the coast, and there is one from the Lower Klamath NWR in September 1981.

## Family **RECURVIROSTRIDAE:** Stilts and Avocets

**Black-necked Stilt** (BNST)
*Himantopus mexicanus*

Here is a bird that is properly named. The back of its neck is black, and it stands up on such long stilt-like legs that it seems like a mistake has been made. Its bill is long and sharp, and its legs are bubble-gum pink. Altogether, you have a bird that looks like it was designed by Walt Disney.

They are about 14 inches tall, and like to feed out in the open in shallow water. Thus, they are easy to observe, and always fun to see. They breed in the Klamath Basin, and occasionally stage "mini-invasions" into areas west of the Cascades. There is one breeding record for the Rogue Valley, in 1994.

Nests are typically built on the shallow muddy borders of lakes, in open marshes, or on dry ground that is subject to flooding. If the water should rise, the bird will shove almost anything movable, such as sticks and water plants with clinging soil, under the nest to raise it above water. Under such conditions, a nest may be built up until it is 8 to 10 inches in height, painfully obvious in the open, surrounded by water.

Stilts have been reported to place their nests in the middle of cow pastures, and observers have noted with some surprise that the nests seem to come through in surprisingly good shape, with eggs hatching safely almost under the feet of the stock. Bent observed, "[I am] convinced that a stilt simply remains on her nest and by her vociferousness and possibly even with a few vigorous thrusts of her long bill causes a grazing cow to direct her course away from the nest."

In the winter, stilts withdraw to the south, many to California, but some as far as South America. The largest numbers in winter reported on Christmas counts are usually from the San Francisco Bay area.

### American Avocet (AMAV)
*Recurvirostra americana*

The French call this bird *"avocette,"* which seems to be source of our common name. However, the French are not referring to our avocet, which is restricted to North America, but to a related one, called Pied Avocet.

The scientific name *Recurvirostra* means "turned-up bill." This suits the bird perfectly, because the upward bend is sometimes so pronounced it looks like the bill has been subject to an accident. The females are the ones with the most strongly curved bills; the bills on the males are straighter, although they still have pronounced curves.

Avocets are bigger than Black-necked Stilts (about 18" tall), and even flashier, with striking black and white bodies and rusty red heads and necks. The rust color is a feature of the breeding plumage; in winter, the rustiness fades to a light gray. They often forage along with stilts, and prefer the same kind of open shallow water that stilts do. However, they can swim better than stilts, and one wonders sometimes, in observing an avocet, whether it is swimming or is walking on the bottom with its long legs.

American Avocet

Avocets are more inclined to move in flocks than are stilts, and when foraging in the water may do so in a group, advancing in line almost like a drill team. They typically swipe their bills back and forth in the water when foraging.

As with stilts, avocets breed in the Klamath Basin, but are irregular west of the Cascades. They build their nests either at the edges of ponds, or on small mounds in the water. They, too, will shove stuff under their nests to raise them up in case the water rises, just like stilts do. Bent says, of avocets,

"Its favorite resorts seem to be the shallow, muddy borders of alkaline lakes, wide open spaces of extensive marshes, where scanty vegetation gives but little concealment, or broad wet meadows splashed with shallow pools. If the muddy pools are covered with reeking scum, attracting myriads of flies, so much the better for feeding purposes."

The American Avocet is mostly a bird of the American west, but in winter it, like the Black-necked Stilt, withdraws to the south, some of them to the Gulf Coast or to Mexico. As with the stilt, the largest numbers in winter reported on Christmas counts are usually from the San Francisco Bay area.

## Family **SCOLOPACIDAE:** Sandpipers, Phalaropes, and Allies

**Greater Yellowlegs** (GRYE)
*Tringa melanoleuca*

**Lesser Yellowlegs** (LEYE)
*Tringa flavipes*

The combination of long, bright yellow legs, sharp bill, and white rump visible in flight, readily identifies a bird as a *yellowlegs*. But deciding whether it's a Greater or a Lesser may take some additional study.

If the two species are standing side by side, as they sometimes do, there's no problem. The Greater is substantially bigger than the Lesser. Or if there is a bird such as a Killdeer or a dowitcher nearby, you can make a good comparison. A Greater Yellowlegs is much larger than either a Killdeer or a dowitcher; a Lesser Yellowlegs is slightly smaller than either one. We're talking body weights here. A Lesser Yellowlegs may appear to be larger than a Killdeer or dowitcher, but that's because the neck and legs are longer. It's the bodies that need to be compared.

The most reliable marks for separation between the two species are bill length and voice. In a Greater Yellowlegs, the bill is much longer than the head; in a Lesser Yellowlegs, the bill is about the same length as the head, maybe slightly longer. The bill of a Greater may or may not be bent slightly upward; the bill of a Lesser is straight. Also, the basal third or so of the bill in a Greater may be pinkish or light gray, with the rest of the bill black. In a Lesser, the bill is usually all black.

Both birds can be quite vocal. They have a variety of calls, but their loud flight calls are distinctive. The Greater gives a loud, ringing *tew, tew, tew,* slightly descending, usually with three notes, but sometimes four. The Lesser gives a somewhat similar call, but faster, and usually with two notes, *tu tu.*

Neither bird breeds in our area, but go to Canada and Alaska for that purpose. There, they frequently sit in fir trees, a behavior which may look bizarre to someone who has only seen them in our area, when they are almost always seen feeding in shallow water. Both species have the habit of bobbing their heads by alternately shortening and lengthening their necks, when they are nervous and about to take flight.

Mostly, we see them in migration, especially with the Lesser. In winter, both species mostly go to South America, but a few Greaters remain in our area. The average number of Greaters during the Christmas counts in the five-year period from 1996 through 2000, is 43 per year for Klamath Falls, and 17 per year for Medford. On the other hand, there was only one Lesser Yellowlegs counted in winter during the entire five-year period for Klamath Falls, and only two for Medford.

## Solitary Sandpiper (SOSA)
*Tringa solitaria*

|   | J F M A M J J A S O N D |
|---|---|
| West | - - - -     - - - - |
| East |   —           — |

Solitary Sandpipers resemble Lesser Yellowlegs, except their legs are shorter and are greenish-yellow, rather than bright yellow. Other helpful points to remember are that Solitaries have dark backs heavily dotted with white spots, and have dark underwings, visible in flight. Also, the tail is not white, as in the yellowlegs, but is dark in the center with barring on the sides. There is a prominent white eye-ring, bolder than in the yellowlegs species.

This bird, true to its name, usually is seen alone. Also, they seem to prefer small ponds, sloughs, and wooded lakes. They breed in Canada and Alaska, and spend the winter in South America. Thus, we see them only in migration, and then not often.

## Willet (WILL)
*Catoptrophorus semipalmatus*

Willets are familiar to most people because they have seen them on the coast in winter. They are big, and are right out there on the beach in the open, foraging at the edge of the surf. Their plumage is about the dullest thing going -- all drab and gray. That is, until they fly, and then their black and white wing stripes are dazzling. As might be inferred by the scientific name, *semipalmatus,* their feet are partially webbed.

Not many of them spend the winter on Oregon's coast. Mostly, they go south to California and as far as Peru. A part of the western population even migrates to the east coast in fall, although these seem to be the ones that nest east of the Rocky Mountains.

In spring and summer, this is a shorebird that uses the Klamath Basin as a breeding location. It prefers short grass or brushy uplands for nesting, usually near water. Its breeding plumage is mottled in muted shades of brown, with occasional shadings of "pinkish buff." Typically, during breeding season, one will stand on a perch such as a fence post and give a clear, rolling call, *pill-o-will-o-willet,* from which comes the common name. If it flies, the black and white wing stripes are just as dazzling as ever.

The east coast has Willets, too, but they are a different subspecies, are smaller than ours, and pretty much tend to stick to the Atlantic and gulf coasts.

Our Willets nest through the northern part of the interior west, from Oregon and northeastern California to Canada and the Dakotas. One observer (Ernest Thompson Seton, 1890) reported that he found a nest in Manitoba on a dry alkali plain, ". . . which was placed in a slight hollow, shaded on one side by the skull of a buffalo and on the other by a tuft of grass."

## Wandering Tattler (WATA)       Vagrant
*Heteroscelus incanus*

The name "tattler" presumably refers to the occasions when the bird detects the presence of a hunter and gives the alarm call as it flies away, thus "tattling" on the hunter. The name has also been given to other birds, such as the two yellowlegs, which do the same thing.

The name "wandering" refers to its migratory behavior. It breeds in Alaska and Siberia, and winters across a broad area, from the California coast to the islands of Polynesia, and thus wanders long distances. This is the only shorebird that appears entirely dark gray on the upperparts when it flies -- no wing stripes, no white tail, no nothing. Another characteristic is its tendency to bob and teeter as it forages, somewhat like a Spotted Sandpiper.

Tattlers are fairly common in rocky habitat on the coast in migration, but are very rare in our region. There are two records, both on the west shore of Upper Klamath Lake.

## Spotted Sandpiper (SPSA)
*Actitus macularia*

Spotted Sandpipers are widespread breeders across much of North America, but in winter most of them go to the Pacific or Gulf coasts, or all the way to South America. They withdraw entirely from the east side of the Cascades in winter, but a few of them remain on the west. The annual Christmas counts in the Rogue Valley usually produce a few "spotties," especially the Grants Pass count, which sometimes has eight or nine, and once (1996) had 17.

In summer in our area they are seen frequently along streams and lakesides. They typically fly low, with bursts of shallow stuttery wingbeats, followed by glides. Once you learn what that flight looks like, spotties are instantly recognizable on that basis alone. Upon occasion, however, particularly if they fly high, their wingbeats can be steady, and they look like any other sandpiper. When they are foraging, they usually teeter and bob constantly.

In breeding plumage, spotties show many black spots on their breasts, as their name would indicate. In winter they are brown and drab, but they have brown areas extending down the sides of their breasts next to whitish shoulders, and well-defined eyebrows, which help to distinguish them.

As is the case with certain other shorebirds, it is the females who are aggressive in breeding season, and who perform most of the courtship displays. The male may do most of the brooding of the eggs, and supervise the chicks after they hatch. In the meantime, the female may go in search of another mate.

Spotted Sandpipers sometimes behave in unsandpiper-like behavior, such as perching on wires and in trees. One remarkable talent is revealed by the following quote from Bent:

> . . . the bird dove into running water, swam with wings and feet rapidly moving for about 20 feet, and emerged down stream, still flying, and made off in its characteristic way, only a few inches above the water.

## Upland Sandpiper (UPSA)
*Bartramia longicauda*

May be extirpated in Southern Oregon

There are no recent records of this bird in our area, but the first Oregon breeding record is from Fort Klamath, in 1887, and a pair was seen in 1998 at Sycan Marsh in Lake County, which is just over the border from Klamath County. They are hard to find anywhere in Oregon, and the population in our state appears to be on the way to extirpation. Censuses taken over the years show declining numbers, and a census taken in the 1990s produced only 46 individuals, in Grant, Umatilla, and Union counties in eastern Oregon.

Upland Sandpipers are about the size of a Greater Yellowlegs, have long necks, and small-looking heads. They prefer nesting locations that are in ungrazed or lightly grazed grasslands, and they often sit up on fence posts in breeding season.

## Long-billed Curlew (LBCU)
*Numenias americanus*

|  | J | F | M | A | M | J | J | A | S | O | N | D |
|---|---|---|---|---|---|---|---|---|---|---|---|---|
| West |  |  |  |  | ---- |  |  | ---- |  |  |  |  |
| East |  | ■■■■■■■■■■■■■■■ |  |  |  |  |  |  | --- |  |  |  |

## Whimbrel (WHIM)
*Numenias phaeopas*

|  | J | F | M | A | M | J | J | A | S | O | N | D |
|---|---|---|---|---|---|---|---|---|---|---|---|---|
| West |  |  |  |  |  | Vagrant |  |  |  |  |  |  |
| East |  |  |  | --- |  |  |  |  | ---- |  |  |  |

The Long-billed Curlew is appropriately named. Not only is it our largest sandpiper, it has an outrageous bill -- 4 to 8 inches long, gracefully curved downward. The Whimbrel also has a long, downcurved bill, but the length of the bill is only 3 to 4 inches. The Whimbrel is further distinguished from the Long-billed Curlew by its smaller size, and its striped head with a pale median head-stripe.

Whimbrels occur around the world. They nest in the far north, and then most of them migrate to the southern hemisphere, some as far as Tierra del Fuego. A few spend the winter on the Oregon coast. We get them in our area only as migrants, and not very often at that.

Long-billed Curlews, on the other hand, are breeders in the Klamath Basin. They nest in moist meadows or dry prairies, and both sexes incubate the eggs. When one is on the nest, with neck outstretched on the ground, it can be so inconspicuous as to be overlooked.

Curlews breed throughout the American west, and go to the coasts of California and Mexico for the winter, where they often feed right on the beach next to the surf. In the Central Valley of California they often feed in alfalfa fields in large flocks. Their characteristic call is a loud, plaintive *cur-lee! cur-lee!* with rising inflection, from which they get their name.

**Marbled Godwit** (MAGO)
*Limosa fedoa*

|  | J F M A M J J A S O N D |
|---|---|
| West | ---- ----- |
| East | ——— ———--- |

**Hudsonian Godwit** (HUGO)          Vagrant
*Limosa haemastica*

Godwits are large birds with long upturned bills, usually pink at the base. and with a black tip. The two godwits considered here are both North American birds, although they differ in breeding locations and migration patterns.

Marbled Godwits breed in the Canadian prairie provinces, and migrate in winter to the California and Gulf coasts, and to Mexico. In spring, enough of them gather on the northern California coast as to give rise to the annual birding festival known as "Godwit Days," held at Arcata. During migration, in both spring and fall, some of them may stray our way. A flock with 30 birds was seen at White Lake in April 2000, and the truly astonishing number of 145 birds showed up near Ashland in April 1981.

Hudsonian Godwits breed much further north, in Alaska and at Hudson Bay. They migrate mostly through the center of the continent and along the Atlantic Coast, winding up in Argentina. Getting one here is real event. One was at Lower Klamath NWR in May 1993, and another was at Miller Island in May 2000.

**Ruddy Turnstone** (RUTU)
*Arenaria interpres*

|  | J F M A M J J A S O N D |
|---|---|
| West | -- -- |
| East | -- ---- |

**Black Turnstone** (BLTU)          Vagrant
*Arenaria melanocephala*

Both of these birds properly belong on rocky ocean shores, where they do indeed turn stones over while foraging. The are both about the same size, and both show striking black and white patterns when they fly.

Ruddy Turnstones occur around the world, and breed in the far north. Black Turnstones, on the other hand, are strictly Pacific Coast birds, breeding in Alaska, and spending the winter on the coast from British Columbia to Lower California.

Strays of these two species in our area are rare, and are most likely to be found on lakeshores and at sewer ponds. There are three records of Black Turnstone at the Kirtland Sewer Ponds near Medford, all in spring, and a September 2000 record from Tule Lake NWR.

## Red Knot (REKN)
*Calidris canutus*

|  | J F M A M J J A S O N D |
|---|---|
| West | -- |
| East | --- |

## Sanderling (SAND)
*Calidris alba*

|  | J F M A M J J A S O N D |
|---|---|
| West | ---        ----- |
| East | ---    ---- |

These two are so much birds of the sandy ocean beaches, that it seems peculiar that they occasionally show up inland. The Sanderling, especially, is the familiar little clockwork toy that runs along the beach chasing the surf.

They are similar enough to place together, although the Red Knot in breeding plumage is so vivid that it is not likely to be mistaken for anything else. In fall, the Red Knot is much more drab, and looks somewhat like an overgrown Sanderling. Red Knots are similar in size to Dunlins and dowitchers, and in their gray winter plumage might be overlooked in large mixed groups of birds.

A Sanderling in breeding plumage is bright rufous in front, and might be mistaken for a Red-necked Stint. In winter, they are gray on the back and white underneath. Juveniles are somewhat similar to the winter adults, but have bright spangled black-and-white backs.

Red Knots are larger than Sanderlings, but both have a stocky appearance, and have stout black bills of moderate length. Both of them breed around the world in the very far north, and in fall migrate as far the very tips of the southern continents. When they show up in our area, it is likely to be on the muddy shores of lakes or at sewer ponds.

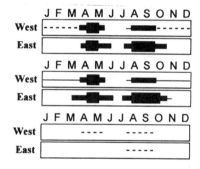

## Western Sandpiper (WESA)
*Calidris mauri*

## Least Sandpiper (LESA)
*Calidris minutilla*

## Semipalmated Sandpiper (SESA)
*Calidris pusilla*

In Europe, these tiny sandpipers are called "stints;" in America, they are called "peeps." Westerns and Leasts, especially, may be looked upon as our "bread-and-butter" sandpipers in the west, because they are so widespread and common. All three are essentially North American birds.

The Western, as its name implies, is a bird primarily of the west, although some of the population winters on the east coast. Except for a slight toehold into Siberia, it breeds only in Alaska. The Semipalmated, on the other hand, is primarily a bird of the east, although it breeds across the entire northern part of the continent. Its migration paths are across the great plains, and then along the east coast; thus, the birds we get here are strays. The Least breeds across the entire northern part of the continent, and seems to be everywhere, in migration.

In winter, if water edges are frozen, or if there is snow cover, these peeps head for the coast or to the south, some as far as South America. Many Westerns and Leasts spend the winter at the Oregon coast, but the most likely place in our area in winter is the Rogue Valley, where the Least Sandpiper is the more likely one to occur.

In migration, these two range from common to abundant on both sides of the Cascades, at sewer ponds, and along muddy lakeshores such as at Agate Lake in the Rogue Valley, and White Lake in Lower Klamath NWR. Picking out the Leasts from the others is fairly straightforward, because the Leasts have yellow legs, and the other two have black legs. A problem with this is, if the Leasts have been mucking about in black mud, their legs may appear black, also.

A difference in feeding behavior can be of help. Western Sandpipers tend to wade into the water to feed, sometimes right up to their bellies, and tend to probe deeper than the other two. Both Least and Semipalmated Sandpipers tend to pick at muddy or even dry surfaces, often away from the water, and are looked upon as "pickers" rather than "probers," although they also may probe upon occasion. Leasts may forage in low grass, looking somewhat like mice running about.

Bill length and shape are useful, but can be unreliable, because of much overlap. Nevertheless, we can make some generalities that will work for the majority of the birds we see. A peep with a long bill, broad at the base but tapered, and slightly drooped at the tip, is almost certain to be a Western. One with a small, slightly drooping bill, finely-tipped, is most likely a Least. One with a bill that is almost straight and tube-shaped, with little taper, and blunt at the tip, is most likely a Semipalmated. But there is so much variation and overlap, that the weasel-words "almost certain," and "most likely," are necessary.

The problem is especially acute with Western and Semipalmated Sandpipers. Arthur Cleveland Bent put it well, when he wrote:

> It is most difficult and often impossible to distinguish between the western and semipalmated sandpipers in life; and I have experienced difficulty in distinguishing between them even in the hand.

There appears to be some differences between the western and eastern populations of Semipalmated Sandpipers that work in our favor. The eastern "Semis" tend to be longer-billed and more pointy-tipped than the western Semis. This causes the eastern Semis to resemble Western Sandpipers, whereas most of the western Semis stick closer to the pattern described earlier, as having tube-shaped bills with blunt tips.

In nonbreeding plumage, all three are studies in brown, gray and white. A helpful clue is that the Least, in nonbreeding plumage, has a brownish "dirty" breast, quite unlike the relatively clean, white breasts of the Western and the Semipalmated. After a person has become accustomed to the nonbreeding plumages of these birds -- the grays and the whites -- it sometimes comes as shock to see a Western or Least Sandpiper in breeding plumage during spring migration, when the upperparts are edged with bright rufous. I've known fairly experienced birders to say, "What on earth is that?"

A similar problem exists with juvenile birds. The Western and Least juveniles both may have rufous tinges to their upperparts as juveniles, much like the fresh adult breeding plumage seen in spring. In fall migration, the adults arrive first, bearing worn breeding plumage. Then the juveniles come in their fresh bright plumages, looking like entirely different species from the adults.

The "semipalmated" in the name of the Semis means that the front toes are slightly webbed, just as it does with the Semipalmated Plover. But wait. The front toes of the Western Sandpiper are also slightly webbed, just like the Semipalmated Sandpiper. Well, that's the way it is with the common names of birds. Anyway, you can't see the webbing between the toes in the field anyway, so for practical matters it makes no difference.

Let's summarize the major characteristics, which will be applicable to the great majority of birds you see, especially in fall and winter. If it's got yellow legs, a small bill, and a dirty-looking chest, it's a Least Sandpiper. (Okay. Long-toed Stints also have yellow legs, and are close lookalikes for Least Sandpipers. But if you really want to start a fight, just claim you've seen a Long-toed Stint. There are only two Oregon records accepted by OBRC.)

If it's got black legs, a fairly long, droopy bill, and a white chest, it's a Western Sandpiper. But if it's got a tube-like bill, blunt on the end, and running around picking at the surface, there's a pretty good chance it's a Semipalmated Sandpiper.

These peeps may occur anywhere in our area where there is suitable open water with muddy shores. It is interesting, that for the rarest one, the Semipalmated Sandpiper, the first verified record in the state came from the Rogue Valley, at Agate Lake, in August 1977.

## Baird's Sandpiper (BASA)
*Calidris bairdii*

## White-rumped Sandpiper (WRSA)
*Calidris fuscicollis*

Accidental

Both of these birds are often referred to as "large peeps," because they are somewhat larger than the "real" peeps such as Western and Least Sandpiper. Both have short black legs and long wings, which gives them a low-slung horizontal stance somewhat like a small tern. The wing tips extend well past the end of the tail. In the fall, Baird's is more likely to be found at higher elevations than other sandpipers.

There are no accepted records in Oregon for White-rumped Sandpiper, but there is a record for Tule Lake NWR (California), in July 1989. A White-rump resembles a Baird's, but has a conspicuous white rump, visible in flight.

## Pectoral Sandpiper (PESA)
*Calidris melanotos*

|       | J F M A M J J A S O N D |
|-------|--------------------------|
| West  |    ---    ———— |
| East  |            ■■■■ |

## Sharp-tailed Sandpiper (SHAS)
*Calidris acuminata*

Vagrant

These two species are about 8.5 inches long, and resemble each other somewhat. They are approximately 50 percent longer than a Least Sandpiper, and about three to four times as heavy. The reason for comparison with a Least, is because the Pectoral Sandpiper has sometimes been described as a larger edition of the Least Sandpiper. Since Pectorals often feed in association with Leasts, the size comparison can be useful.

In many species of birds, females are larger than males, but not with Pectorals. The females average about two-thirds the weight of the males. One way to put it is that males are about the size of a Killdeer, while females are about the size of a Dunlin.

The major thing to look for in a Pectoral Sandpiper, other than size, is the distinctive streaked markings on the breast. The dense vertical streaks stop rather abruptly on the lower edge of the breast, making a sharp contrast with the white belly. The legs are yellowish, which immediately sets a Pectoral off from a Baird's, which has black legs.

The common name of the Pectoral refers to the air sacs on the breast of the male, which are inflated during courtship. Even though we do not see the courtship in our area (Pectorals breed on the shores of the Arctic Ocean), it is worth quoting from the description in Bent:

> [The note of the bird] is deep, hollow, and resonant . . . [It] fills its esophagus with air to such an extent that the breast and throat is inflated to twice or more its natural size, and the great air sac thus formed gives the peculiar resonant quality to the note. . . When not inflated, . . . the skin hangs down in a pendulous flap or fold exactly like a dewlap. . . . The bird may frequently be seen running along the ground close to the female, its enormous sac inflated, and its head drawn back and the bill pointing directly forward . . .

Both Pectoral and Sharp-tailed Sandpipers often forage in low vegetation, and can sometimes be seen when they stop foraging and stick their heads above the grass. Also, they can hold still in the vegetation for fairly long periods of time, thus rendering themselves virtually invisible.

For the Pectoral Sandpiper, both juveniles and adults appear in Oregon during fall migration. But for the Sharp-tailed Sandpiper, all of the records that have been accepted in Oregon by the OBRC are juveniles. A brightly-plumaged juvenile Sharp-tailed can hardly be mistaken for anything else. The cap is rufous, and the breast is a bright orange-buff color, with diffuse streaks, very different from the dense streaking of the Pectoral, with its sharp cut-off.

Both species have a supercilliary mark above the eye, but in the Sharp-tailed this is especially bold, and gets wider behind the eye.

There are only three records for Sharp-tails in our region that are known to me, two in the Rogue Valley, and one near the Lower Klamath NWR, all in fall.

**Dunlin** (DUNL)
*Calidris alpina*

The Dunlins moving north in spring look like an entirely different species from the ones moving south in the fall. In spring, they are quite sporty. Probably the most noticeable thing will be the conspicuous black patch on the belly. Also, they have rufous backs, which caused them once to be known as "Red-backed Sandpiper." They are not likely to be mistaken for anything else.

In fall, they are drab and gray, and the belly patch is gone. At this time, they are about the drabbest of our shorebirds, and this explains the name -- a diminutive form of *dunling,* meaning a dun-colored little bird.

The best recognition marks in fall and winter are their size (about twice the weight of a Western Sandpiper), and their bills, which are moderately long and drooping at the tip. The species with which they are most often confused at this time of year is the Western Sandpiper, unless the two species are side by side. Since the Dunlin has a brownish breast, somewhat like a Least Sandpiper, it apparently is the bill shape that causes the confusion with Westerns.

On the coast, Dunlins may be the most abundant shorebird in winter; flocks as large as 15,000 have been seen. In the Klamath Basin, flocks of perhaps 1,000 have been seen during migration, but in winter, they essentially leave the Basin and move to the coast or to California's Central Valley. They are irregular in winter in the Rogue Valley; small flocks are seen some years during Christmas count

Audubon, writing in 1840, described the restlessness often exhibited by Dunlins:

> There seems to be a kind of impatience in this bird that prevents it from remaining any length of time in the same place, and you may see it scarcely alighted on a sand bar, fly off without any apparent reason to another, where it settles, runs for a few moments, and again starts off on wing.

**Curlew Sandpiper** (CUSA)              Accidental
*Calidris ferruginea*

A male Curlew Sandpiper in breeding plumage is unmistakable. It's about the same size as a Dunlin and has a beak shaped almost like a Dunlin's (a little more slender and evenly curved than a Dunlin's), but is such a bright rufous over most of its body that it couldn't be anything else. The female is less bright, but the long curved bill and rufous front separates her from others.

It's in the nonbreeding plumage, as usual, where the plot thickens. Separation from a Dunlin is the issue, but a Dunlin has shorter legs, a shorter neck, and a slightly thicker bill that droops at the tip, instead of being evenly curved. Also, the Curlew Sandpiper overall is paler, especially in the breast, than a Dunlin. Some people have referred to a Curlew Sandpiper as an "elegant Dunlin."

Curlew Sandpiper is an Asian breeder that winters in Australia. Just how one of them manages to wind up on the Pacific Coast is one of those mysteries, although some people suspect there might be a small breeding population in Alaska. There are only a few records for Oregon, and almost all of these are for the coast, in fall migration. There is one record for the Klamath Basin, at Tule Lake NWR, in August 2000.

## Stilt Sandpiper (STSA)                           Vagrant
*Calidris himantopus*

The species that Stilt Sandpiper most resembles is probably the Lesser Yellowlegs, partly because of the long bill, and partly because of the long, greenish-yellow legs. But it also resembles a dowitcher, because of its "sewing-machine" manner of feeding. However, if a Stilt Sandpiper raises its head, the resemblance to a dowitcher is gone, because a dowitcher's bill is long and straight, and the bill of a Stilt Sandpiper is shorter and droops at the tip. They tend to prefer shallow water, and avoid mudflats.

There are three records of Stilt Sandpiper at small lakes in the Rogue Valley, all of them August sightings. On the east side, there are four records: one in the spring at Klamath Marsh, and three in August and September, at Miller Island, White Lake, and Tule Lake NWR.

## Buff-breasted Sandpiper (BBSA)               Vagrant
*Tryngites subruficollis*

This sandpiper is well-named, because of its buff-colored underparts. The buffy color, plus the short bill, small head with beady black eye, and yellow legs should be enough to identify it. It is about the size of a Pectoral Sandpiper, but the Pectoral has distinct black streaking on the breast.

This bird prefers sparse vegetation, although it is sometimes found on mudflats. It somewhat resembles a plover, and occasionally will run and stop, in the manner of a plover. Mostly, it forages at a walk, with its head up and bobbing like a pigeon, although it may be somewhat erratic, changing direction frequently.

There are four records from the Rogue Valley, three of them from Agate Lake and one from Kirtland Ponds, all in late August or early September. There is one from the Lower Klamath NWR, in September 2001.

# Ruff (RUFF)
*Philomachus pugnax*

Vagrant

Here is another well-named bird, because on its breeding grounds the male has spectacular head tufts and neck plumes. The scientific name, *pugnax*, refers to its pugnacious behavior during the breeding season. This is a fairly large bird, with the males about the size of a Greater Yellowlegs, and the females somewhat smaller. The breeding area is across northern Europe and Asia, and their normal wintering area is Africa and southern Asia, so it is not clear why as many of them come our way as they do.

Many people refer to a female Ruff as a "reeve," but apparently there is nothing wrong with referring to a female Ruff as a female Ruff, since the word "Ruff" not only refers to the male, but also to the species.

Veteran Ruff-watchers say that one of the best ways to pick a Ruff from a crowd of shorebirds is to watch for how it forages. Ruffs frequently (but not always) forage at a run, which is enough to make them stand out. They typically have a lanky look, with somewhat of a pot belly. In adult nonbreeding plumage, both males and females tend to be gray underneath, changing to white on the underbelly, and with a dark back. Juveniles, which constitute the bulk of the birds that show up in Oregon, are buffy-colored. The legs may be greenish to yellow, but sometimes are orange. Some of the males in nonbreeding plumage may show white heads and necks, perhaps as a precursor to acquiring their breeding plumage.

There are several spring sightings at Lower Klamath NWR, and one spring sighting in the Rogue Valley, so it is conceivable we could catch a glimpse of a male in breeding plumage. More likely, we will see a bird in transition, as was the case with one at the Kirtland Ponds in April, 2002, which was showing black spots on the breast. In addition, there are a couple of fall sightings in the Rogue Valley, one in August and one in September.

# Long-billed Dowitcher (LBDO)
*Limnodromus scolopaceous*

# Short-billed Dowitcher (SBDO)
*Limnodromus griseus*

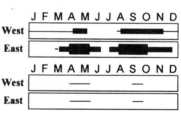

These two species pose one of the most difficult identification problems in birding. Only some of the high points of identification will be included here, but these may help with most of the birds you see. If more detail is desired, check out Kevin Zimmer's book *Birding in the American West*, or Dennis Paulson's book *Shorebirds of the Pacific Northwest*. The former book gives 5 pages to the topic, and the latter gives 15.

Dowitchers of either species generally feed in flocks. Flocks in the thousands have been seen on the coast, but those in our area are more likely to number in the hundreds, in the Klamath Basin, and in the scores, in the Rogue

Valley. The general rule is that Long-billeds favor inland locations and that Short-billeds favor coastal locations, but either species can show up either place.

In shape, dowitchers resemble snipes, and sometimes people call them that. They have the same long bills as snipes, up to three inches long. They also feed like a snipe, bill buried in the mud, and going up and down rapidly like a sewing machine. No wonder people once called them "Red-breasted Snipe."

The first thing to realize is that bill length in general is no help in identification. An extremely long-billed bird might safely be called a Long-billed, and an extremely short-billed bird called a Short-billed, but there is too much overlap to be useful in most cases.

In fall and winter, when the two are in their plain gray-and-white non-breeding plumage, they are almost impossible to separate, except by voice. The Short-billed, in flight, usually gives a call like *tu-tu-tu,* similar to that of the Greater Yellowlegs, but softer and more mellow. The Long-billed gives a sharp *keek!* in flight, but may string several *keeks* together if alarmed. But if the birds don't call, then the advice of most experts is to just identify them as "dowitcher sp.?", meaning it's a dowitcher, but which species is uncertain.

In either juvenal or breeding plumages, the matter is more tractable, but intricate. A part of the problem is that the Short-billed has three subspecies, and one of them, *hendersonii,* strongly resembles the Long-billed Dowitcher.

Broadly-speaking, if it's in the spring, and you see a dowitcher in breeding plumage, look at the belly. If the bird has a white belly, you've got a Short-billed. But if the lower parts are all orange-buffy, with no white belly, you've got a problem. A look at the side of the upper breast may help. If it consists of dark spots on the orange background, it's a Short-billed. If it's barred dark and white on the orange background, it's a Long-Billed. If you can't be sure, then it's a "dowitcher sp.?"

With juveniles, Short-billed and Long-billed can usually be told apart by looking at the tertials. (The tertials are the secondaries closest to the body, and, in most shorebirds, cover the primaries when the wings are folded.) On a juvenile Short-billed, the tertials will have broad buffy edges, and internal buffy markings consisting of irregular lines. On a juvenile Long-billed, the tertials will have narrow buffy edges, and the internal parts of the feathers will be dark. If they're really all dark, you can be confident you've got a Long-Billed, but juvenile Long-billeds once in a while show some markings on the internal parts of the feathers, and then you can't be sure.

Opinions differ concerning the origin of the name, "dowitcher." One tradition says it's a Native American name; another says it's because that's what its call sounds like, but begs the question as to which call. A third is that the name comes from the 18th century, and is a corruption of *Duitsch Snipe* (Dutch Snipe), a name given to distinguish it from the "English Snipe" (today's Common Snipe). Take your pick.

## Common Snipe (COSN)
*Gallinago gallinago*

Some people believe the snipe is a fictitious bird, and is used to play tricks on neophytes at summer camp. But it's a real bird, and a fascinating one at that. In summer, they are conspicuous, either as they sit commandingly on the tops of fenceposts, or as they fly overhead, making their weird "winnowing" sound, *woo-woo-woo-woo-woo*. These displays can be seen and heard at twilight in spring almost anywhere in our region that there are suitable wet meadows, such as at Howard Prairie or the meadows in Wood River Valley.

Common Snipe

Nobody seems to argue any more concerning whether the sound is made with the feathers or with the voice. It's the feathers, although there still may be argument over whether it's done with the wings or the tail. Certainly, as a snipe flies over, doing its winnowing sound, you can see that the tail is spread. As soon as the tail is folded, the winnowing stops. But those who argue for the wings say that the tail may be spread, but it's the vibrating wings doing the job. However, the consensus today seems to be that it's the tail.

In winter, snipes come to lower elevations on both sides of the crest, and then they are much more cryptic than in spring. They often tend to hold very still for long periods of time, and blend so well with their surroundings as to be invisible, even though they may be right out there in the open. As soon as they move, however, they reveal themselves and give away their identity. Nothing but a snipe could have such bold stripes on the head and back, and such a long bill.

Often they will hold still in wet grassy areas, usually next to a pond, and don't move until you get close. Then they are likely to take off with a harsh alarm cry, rendered in English as *scaip* or *scresh*, and fly away on a zig-zag course. The claim is made that the name "snipe" comes from "snip" or "snap," and refers to the alarm cry.

In the past, snipes were hunted so aggressively that fears were expressed concerning their future. In one 20-year period, from 1867 to 1887, one hunter bragged that he had killed 69,087 snipes. His biggest one-day total, for a six-hour period, was 366 snipes. Today, snipes are still hunted in Oregon, but the daily bag limit is eight.

## Wilson's Phalarope (WIPH)
*Phalaropus tricolor*

|  | J F M A M J J A S O N D |
|---|---|
| West | — ------ |
| East | ▬▬▬▬▬▬▬— |

## Red-necked Phalarope (RNPH)
*Phalaropus lobatus*

|  | J F M A M J J A S O N D |
|---|---|
| West | —    — |
| East | ▬▬---- ▬▬ |

## Red Phalarope (REPH)
*Phalaropus fulicaria*

|  | J F M A M J J A S O N D |
|---|---|
| West | ---   -------- |
| East | Vagrant |

Not very often do we have a case where the common name is derived directly from the scientific one, but that is what has happened here. Phalarope (FAL-ar-ope) comes from the name *Phalaropus,* which means "coot-footed." Coots have lobed toes, and so do phalaropes, which is one reason they are such good swimmers. The toes on a Wilson's are less lobed than on the others, which perhaps is consistent with the fact that the Wilson's is more terrestrial than the others.

Swimming is the way we usually see them if, indeed, we see them at all. They are such tiny little birds that they are often overlooked, right when they are out there in plain view. Once your eye gets tuned to them, however, you are likely to spot them right away, because of the way they swim.

They swim lightly and buoyantly on the water, spinning and zig-zagging, and pecking frantically at tiny objects (mostly the larvae of mosquitoes and other insects) on the surface. The Wilson's Phalarope, especially, tends to make complete rotations. On observer counted 247 complete rotations made by a Wilson's as it was feeding. A distinct advantage for those who would observe phalaropes is that they are often very tame and will allow a close approach.

Among phalaropes, the females are larger and more gaudily colored than the males. The females aggressively pursue the males, and females sometimes engage in bruising battles over mates, sparring with their wings and pecking at each other.

Once the eggs are laid, the females take little part in incubation or raising the young, leaving this to the males. In June the females leave the breeding grounds and begin to migrate south, while the males are still tending the young.

The males leave the breeding grounds in late July, and the juveniles leave in August or early September. Just how the juveniles, with no adults to guide them, find their way to their wintering places in the southern hemisphere, is one of the wonders of nature. The Red-necked and Red Phalaropes spend the winter on the open oceans; the Wilson's Phalaropes go to Argentina.

Red-necked and Red Phalaropes mostly migrate at sea, with the Red usually further from the shore than the Red-necked. When you are on a pelagic trip, and the ocean gets rough, it is astonishing to see these tiny birds nonchalantly riding the waves, perfectly at home. The Red Phalarope, especially, is adapted to the sea, and rarely comes ashore except to breed. Both of these species are worldwide, and breed in the far north.

The Wilson's Phalarope, on the other hand, is more a bird of the land. It is strictly a New World bird, and breeds in most of the western states and provinces. West of the crest, we may get them in migration at such places as lakes or sewer ponds, but they are common breeders on the east side. (My notes for a visit to White Lake one April contain the notation, "Wilson's Phalarope -- many.") They have been known to breed as high as 5000 feet, in the southern Cascades.

The other two phalaropes rarely come out to walk on land. In fact, I can't recall ever seeing one do so. But the Wilson's comes out on land frequently. When this happens, and the bird is in nonbreeding plumage, it is easy to be confused, because it can resemble a Lesser Yellowlegs or Solitary Sandpiper. In such a case, look for the Wilson's white breast, and plain, light gray upperparts.

The Red Phalarope is rarely seen in our area, although there are eight records for the Rogue Valley, three in the spring, four in the fall, and one from late December. There are very few records east of the crest anywhere in Oregon, but I once saw a Red Phalarope in full breeding plumage in White Lake, in the month of April. In that same month, there were a number of Red Phalaropes sighted in other inland locations in the west, for reasons that were never understood, because there was no storm at the time that could have driven them inland.

All three phalaropes in breeding plumage are colorful birds. The Red Phalarope is probably the most striking. Most of the body is brick-red, and there is a white patch on the cheek. Wilson's and Red-necked Phalaropes resemble each other in breeding plumage, with varying amounts of red on their necks. In the Wilson's, look for the pale gray crown and black stripe running up alongside the neck. In the Red-necked, look for the much darker head and back, with the back having buffy stripes. In all three, the males are duller versions of the females.

In non-breeding plumage, all three are studies in gray and white. The Red and the Red-necked both have a conspicuous black patch by the eye, which is lacking in the Wilson's. The Red-necked has stripes on the back, whereas the other two have more uniformly gray backs. Finally, the Red-necked and Wilson's both have thin sharp bills, with Wilson's being longer, and the Red has a shorter, more stout bill.

## Family **LARIDAE**: Skuas, Gulls, Terns, and Skimmers

The identification of jaegers ("skuas") and gulls are among the most difficult in the birding world. On the west coast, we frequently see hybrids of Herring, Glaucous-winged, and Glaucous Gulls, and of Western and Glaucous-winged Gulls. Immature birds, especially, are a challenge. David Sibley, in *The Sibley Guide to Birds,* does a good job of showing the many plumages that gulls go through as they mature, and even gives some clues to hybrids. A whole book by P.J. Grant, *Gulls, A Guide to Identification,* will probably tell you more about gulls than you want to know.

**Parasitic Jaeger** (PAJA)                                                   Vagrant
*Stercorarius parasiticus*

**Long-tailed Jaeger** (LTJA)                                              Vagrant
*Stercorarius longicaudus*

The word "jaeger" is the German word for "hunter," and in Britain jaegers are called "skuas." There are three jaegers in North America. Two of them are listed above, and the third one, Pomarine Jaeger, has not been recorded in our region. All three are seabirds, and you generally have to go out on a boat to see them. But once in a while a Parasitic or Long-tailed Jaeger may show up inland in the fall, usually near a large body of water. There are no records from the Rogue Valley, but there are records from the Klamath Basin. In September 1995, a Long-tailed Jaeger showed up at the marina near Moore Park, and stayed several days, and one was seen in September 2001 in the same area.

Identification is fairly straightforward in full-plumaged adults. If you see a bird a little smaller than a small gull, with distinctly two-toned upperwings, an extremely long tail, and a buoyant tern-like flight, you've likely got an adult Long-tailed Jaeger. Unfortunately, the long tail feathers that give the bird its name are often broken or missing in fall, so this most helpful of marks may not be there.

The Parasitic is somewhat larger than the Long-tailed. If it has a strong, falcon-like flight, shows flashes of white at the base of the underwing primaries, and (best of all) has a pair of central, sharply-pointed tail feathers about 2 or 3 inches long, you almost surely have an adult Parasitic Jaeger.

So much for the adults. Juveniles, and color morphs ranging from light to dark, make the situation complicated, requiring that you puzzle through a whole suite of characteristics, too many to deal with here, especially for birds that are so rare in our area. And, even though you may study up diligently on jaegers, some cases are so difficult that you might just have to let them go as "jaeger sp.?"

**Franklin's Gull** (FRGU)
*Larus pipixcan*

|   | J F M A M J J A S O N D |
|---|---|
| West | `----------` |
| East | `———————  -----` |

**Laughing Gull** (LAGU)                                    Accidental
*Larus atricilla*

These two gulls resemble each other in breeding plumage. Both have black hoods, both have red bills, and the gray color of their backs is about the same. Franklin's Gulls are smaller than Laughing Gulls, and some claim they can separate the two on the basis of size alone.

There are several subtle differences between them, but the most useful single characteristic is the wing tips. In an adult Franklin's Gull, there are conspicuous white spots in the black wing tips, and there is a white band separating the black wing tips from the gray in the rest of the wing. In an adult Laughing Gull, the white spots in the wing tips are very small, and the gray of the wing blends smoothly into the black of the wing tips with no separating white band.

Laughing Gulls breed in the Gulf of California, and winter on the coast of the Gulf of Mexico. Any birds we get here are post-breeding wanderers. There are only two accepted records for the entire state of Oregon, one of them an adult in breeding plumage at Lower Klamath NWR, in April 1983.

Franklin's Gulls, on the other hand, breed in the prairie states and provinces, in Idaho, and in eastern Oregon. They were completely unknown in the Great Basin in the 19th century, and made their first appearance at Malheur NWR in 1943. Today, substantial numbers of them breed at Malheur, and a small breeding colony was first detected at Lower Klamath NWR in 1989, where they nested with Forster's Terns. In 1998 there were 4500 nests at Malheur, but they are very sensitive to water conditions -- either too high or too low -- and their numbers have declined since. There are eight records from the Rogue Valley.

Franklin's Gulls migrate in winter to South America, and Laughing Gulls spend the winter on the Gulf Coast. Thus, we are not likely to see either one of these in winter.

**Little Gull** (LIGU)                                    Accidental
*Larus minutus*

This is the smallest of all the gulls, and at 11 inches long is only a little larger than a robin. It is a gull of Europe and Asia, although in recent years it seems to have established a small breeding presence around the Great Lakes, and at Hudson Bay. A scattering of them have shown up in Oregon, mostly on the coast, and mostly in the winter.

Inland, one has shown up at John Day Dam on the Columbia River, at Summer Lake in Lake County, and at Lower Klamath NWR, in June 1998. Identification of a juvenile is easy, because there is a bold dark "M" across the upper side of the wings. This, plus the very small size, clinches the identification. In the adult, the wingtips are pale, and the undersides of the wings are dark.

## Bonaparte's Gull (BOGU)
*Larus philadelphia*

This gull is not named for the Emperor Napoleon, but for his nephew, Charles Lucien Jules Laurent Bonaparte, who lived in the United States from 1822 to 1828. He edited a major reference work on American birds, and is considered the father of systematic ornithology in the U.S.

Bonaparte's Gulls are the smallest gulls we regularly get in Oregon, only 13.5 inches long. (Little Gull is smaller, but is accidental.) They sit high and buoyantly on the water, reminding one of a phalarope, and they even peck at the surface in the manner of a phalarope. When one flies, it is sometimes mistaken for a tern. In summer there is a black hood, which reduces to a black spot behind the eye in winter. Add to this a dainty black bill and red legs, and you've got a lovely little bird.

Bonaparte's is a tree-nesting bird, an unusual trait in gulls, although Mew Gulls occasionally do the same. In their northern nesting grounds, in Alaska or Canada, their nests are typically placed in spruce trees, perhaps 20 feet or more off the ground. We get them in our area in both spring and fall migration, typically near large bodies of water, but sometimes at sewer ponds. Large flocks have occurred in the Klamath Basin. In winter, they prefer southern coastlines, and very few remain in Oregon for the winter.

## Heermann's Gull (HEEG)                                    Vagrant
*Larus heermanni*

These gulls breed in Mexico, and in summer disperse northward. They are almost totally bound to the ocean, and to find one as far inland as our area is a major event. Nevertheless, one occasionally shows up in fall in the Klamath Basin, either at Lake Euwana or at the marina along the lower shore of Upper Klamath Lake. The latest was in fall, 2000.

Heermann's Gulls are unique among gulls, because in the breeding plumage, the body is gray and the head is white. The bill is bright red, with a black tip. Immatures are entirely dark brown or almost black, and have bills that range from pink to red. At first glance, one might be taken for a jaeger.

## Mew Gull (MEGU)
*Larus canus*

Some years ago, the North American version of this gull was considered a separate species called "Short-billed Gull," and the Eurasian version was called Mew Gull, at least by American authors. Today they are merged into one species, which the Americans call Mew Gull, and the Europeans call "Common Gull."

This is a small gull, about the size of a Ring-billed Gull. They nest in Alaska and northwestern Canada, mostly in marshes, but sometimes nest in spruce trees, like Bonaparte's Gulls. They come our way in the fall, most of them to spend the winter on the coast. A few make it to the interior, on both sides of the crest. In spring they head back north, with an occasional straggler lingering until May. One was seen at Tule Lake NWR in the spring of 1992, and another in the fall of the same year at the same location.

As might be supposed, its common name comes from one of its calls, a mewing, querulous, *quee-you, quee-you.* In breeding plumage, the head is very white, and the bill is a clear, unmarked yellow. In winter, the adults get a certain amount of smudginess on the head and neck, and the yellow bill may show a faint dark ring. In an immature bird, this ring may be much more distinct, leading one to think it is a Ring-billed Gull. But the bill is much smaller than on a Ring-billed, and Mew Gulls have a "gentle" look, quite unlike a Ring-billed. Also, Mew Gulls have dark eyes at all ages, whereas adult Ring-billeds have pale irises.

**Ring-billed Gull** (RBGU)
*Larus delawarensis*

**California Gull** (CAGU)
*Larus californicus*

These are our "bread-and-butter" gulls, the ones we have with us most of the time. People are likely to call them "seagulls," but it's probably just as reasonable to call them "landgulls," because they spend just about as much of their time inland as they do at the sea. Some people are even inclined to call them "shopping center gulls," or even "garbage dump gulls," because that's often where you find them. Ring-billed Gulls are distributed from coast to coast, and in many places they are the most common gull. California Gulls, on the other hand, are birds of the west.

Most species of gulls nest on coastlines, but not these two, which nest in many western states and Canadian provinces away from the ocean. In our area, there are (or have been -- the colonies sometimes shift locations) breeding colonies at Upper Klamath Lake, Lower Klamath NWR, Tule Lake NWR, Meiss Lake, and Clear Lake. Often, Ring-billeds and Californias nest together. In most locations, after breeding, the birds drift toward the coast for the winter. In the Klamath Basin, as an exception to the rule, many of them stay around in winter.

When these gulls move west in a post-breeding movement, they generally fly directly over the Cascades, and may be found there in late summer and fall. The Californias, after reaching the coast, tend to move south for the winter, although some of them remain.

Wilson's Phalarope (female in breeding plumage)

American Avocet (in breeding plumage)

Sanderling (in nonbreeding plumage)

Black-necked Stilt

Greater Yellowlegs (in nonbreeding plumage)

Killdeer (chick)

**PLATE V**

**Willet (in breeding plumage)**

**Semipalmated Plover**

**Long-billed Curlew**

**Long-billed Dowitcher**

**Forster's Terns (in breeding plumage)**

**Spotted Sandpiper (in breeding plumage)**

**PLATE VI**

Meiss Lake, in Butte Valley WA, provides an illustration of the manner in which breeding colonies can shift in response to water conditions. Historically, Meiss Lake has had one of the larger breeding colonies of California Gulls. There were almost 3000 nests there in 1999, but there were zero in 2001, because the lake dried up early, in April. As for Ring-billed Gulls, there were 2500 nests in a colony adjacent to the Californias in 1999, and zero in 2001.

The diet of gulls makes a person believe that they will eat anything that remotely appears edible, which accounts for their frequent presence at garbage dumps. California Gulls have even been spotted sitting in cherry trees, eating the cherries, and one was seen to catch a Barn Swallow in flight, and then come down to eat it.

Identifying adult gulls of these two species is fairly straightforward. Even though they resemble each other somewhat, the adult Ring-billed has a broad black ring around the bill, while the adult California has red and black marks on the bill. Also, the very pale gray mantle of the adult Ring-billed Gull can be of help. But if you see one of them flying overhead, and can't get a good look at the mantle or the bill, you may have to just mark it down as "gull sp.?" Even the mantle color may not help, because if the sun is coming from a bad angle, it can make a mantle look either darker or lighter than it really is.

But now the plot thickens even more, because California Gulls from their second summer to the third winter also have black rings around their bills, and are often misidentified as Ring-billed Gulls. Don Roberson, author of *Monterey Birds,* calls this his "Number One Case" of most-misidentified birds.

**Ring-billed Gull**

What can a poor birder do? Well, the California is somewhat larger than the Ring-billed, it has a darker mantle, and -- most useful of all, if you can get close enough to see it -- the California has a dark eye, and the Ring-billed has a pale eye.

But there's always seems to be an exception with birds, especially gulls. It turns out the (usually) pale-eyed Ring-billed has a *dark* eye as a juvenile. However, the subject of juvenile gulls, and immature gulls generally, is too lengthy for discussion here. (See comments under the heading, *Laridae,* on Page 135.)

## Herring Gull (HERG)
*Larus argentatus*

|  | J F M A M J J A S O N D |
|---|---|
| West | -- ------- |
| East | ███████         ███ |

## Thayer's Gull (THGU)
*Larus thayeri*

|  | J F M A M J J A S O N D |
|---|---|
| West | Vagrant |
| East | ----         ---- |

These two gulls resemble each other. The Herring Gull breeds in the north, and winters in our area, mostly on the coast, although it also winters in inland areas to some extent. It is a worldwide species, and can be found in winter at many inland spots across the continent.

The Thayer's Gull breeds in the very far north, even farther north than the Herring Gull. It migrates to the Pacific Coast for the winter, with a few showing up inland. There is a related species, the Iceland Gull, that breeds in a location near the Thayer's, and migrates to the east coast. There is controversy regarding these two, with some authorities considering them to be the same species.

Both the Herring Gull and the Thayer's Gull have very light mantles, pink legs, and large yellow bills with red spots on the lower mandibles. At least the adults do. The Herring Gull is a little larger than the Thayer's, has a slightly larger bill, and has an eye which is not as dark as the Thayer's. These points are helpful, but the best way to tell them apart is in flight.

In an adult Herring Gull, the tips of the wings, seen from above, will be very black, with white spots, whereas in a Thayer's Gull, the black will be mainly on the outer webs of the primaries. The wing of an adult Herring Gull, seen from below, will show a considerable amount of black on the tip. In an adult Thayer's, the underwing will be mostly white, with just a bit of black showing at the tip. A problem with Herring Gulls, as with all the large gulls, is that they interbreed frequently with other species -- especially with Glaucous-winged and Glaucous Gulls, in the case of the Herring.

Many people call attention to the flat-headed look of the Herring Gull, compared to the rounded head of the Thayer's, and this can be helpful. Both species have pure white heads in summer, and have smudgy streaking on their heads and necks in winter

Juvenile and immature birds, as is always the case with gulls, are a problem. For me, the only way to handle this is to find a gull that is willing to stay in one spot for a long time, so I can get out my scope and field guide and ferret out the marks.

In our area, Lake Ewauna in Klamath Falls is a good place to check for gulls. One the west side, they often come into the rocky shallows in the Rogue River next to the fish hatchery that lies just below Lost Creek Dam.

## Western Gull (WEGU)
*Larus occidentalis*

|  | J F M A M J J A S O N D |
|---|---|
| West | -------------------- |
| East | Vagrant |

## Glaucous-winged Gull (GWGU)
*Larus glaucescens*

|  | J F M A M J J A S O N D |
|---|---|
| West | -----               ----- |
| East |  |

These two birds are about the same size and shape, and hybridize frequently. In fact, it has been claimed by Sibley that hybrids may outnumber pure birds, on the Washington coast. Surveys made on the north Oregon coast have shown that about a third of the large gulls are Western/Glacuous-winged hybrids. Furthermore, the proportion of hybrids seems to be increasing. It makes one want to ask the question: If there are so many hybrids, then why are these two considered separate species?

The answer probably is because pure birds of these two species look markedly different from each other. The Western Gull is the darkest-backed gull we have on the west coast, and the Glaucous-winged (except for the occasional Glaucous) is the lightest-backed. The wingtips of the Western are black, with white spots. The wingtips of the Glaucous-winged are light gray, the same color as the mantle, with white spots.

There are all levels of hybrids, including back-crosses, but some of the marks a hybrid might display are: a mantle of an intermediate shade of gray; wingtips that shade from the gray of the mantle into the darker area at the tip; and smudgy streaking in winter on the head and neck. (A pure Western would generally have a white head and neck in winter.)

The reason for dwelling on hybrids is because hybrids apparently appear inland more frequently than do the pure birds. Western Gulls, especially, seem to be reluctant to come inland; Glaucous-wingeds are almost as reluctant. Both of them truly merit the name, *"sea*gulls."

Western Gulls are resident on the Pacific Coast from Washington to California, and breed there in large numbers. Glaucous-wingeds breed more to the north, from Washington to Alaska, but move south in large numbers for the winter. Both are birds of the west, and are rarely seen in other parts of the country.

A good place for gulls on the east side of the Cascades is Lake Ewauna in Klamath Falls, and, on the west side, in the shallows of the Rogue River below Lost Creek Dam, next to the fish hatchery.

## Glaucous Gull (GLGU)                                    Vagrant
*Larus hyberboreus*

There are no records of this gull from the Arctic in the Rogue Valley, but there are two winter records in the Klamath Basin. Look for a large, pale gull that stands out from other gulls. Adults will be clearly distinguishable by the white wingtips, with no black. First-year birds may be a pale brown, and second-year birds are almost white. Immature Glaucous-winged Gulls can also be whitish or a pale brown, but the Glaucous-wingeds have all-black bills, whereas the first and second-year Glaucous Gulls have two-toned bills, pink at the base, and black on the outer third.

## Sabine's Gull (SAGU)
*Xema sabini*

|   | J F M A M J J A S O N D |
|---|---|
| West | -- -- |
| East | -- --- |

Some people say sah-BEEN, but my encyclopedia claims it should be SAB-in. My encyclopedia also says the scientific name *Xema* is a coined word, and doesn't mean anything at all. No matter, this exquisite little gull is always a delight. It is readily recognizable by its three-tone wing pattern -- gray triangle on the inner wing, white triangle in the middle, and black triangle on the outer wing. Both juveniles and adults have the three-tone pattern. In addition, adults in breeding plumage have a black hood.

Sabine's gulls are rare in our area but show up on both sides of the crest with surprising frequency. They nest in the far north, and winter in the southern hemisphere. Normally they migrate at sea, but there seems to be a small contingent that migrates inland. Look for them at lakes and sewer ponds.

## Black-legged Kittiwake (BLKI)     Accidental
*Rissa tridactyla*

Here is another highly pelagic bird from the north that comes south to our coast in the winter, in moderate numbers. It is extremely rare inland, but there is one record from the Lower Klamath NWR. The name "kittiwake" comes from the bird's call.

The wingtips on an adult are solid black, with no white spots, which makes it look as if the bird's wingtip has been dipped in ink. The head is white in breeding plumage, but a dark spot appears behind the eye in winter plumage, reminiscent of a Bonaparte's Gull. The Bonaparte's bill is black, however, and the kittiwake's bill is yellow. It is not likely you would be able to see the black legs on a kittiwake in flight.

Juvenile Black-legged Kittiwakes are extravagantly marked, with a big, black "M" across the top of the wing. The pattern is somewhat like that on a Sabine's Gull, with three triangles -- gray, white, and black, except there is a black line between the inner (gray) triangle, and the middle (white) triangle.

## Caspian Tern (CATE)
*Sterna caspia*

increased dramatically, apparently at the expense of colonies on the east side of the Cascades, including the Klamath Basin.

In the winter, Caspian Terns retreat to the southern coastlines of North America and Mexico. At least our North American populations do. In Europe, they migrate to the Mediterranean, and in Australia and New Zealand they don't migrate at all.

Here is a bird that most people have no problem recognizing. It is almost as big as a large gull, has a black cap all year (dark streaking on top in winter), and has a huge red bill that points downward when it is foraging over water. The wingtips, on the underside, are dark. Probably, the first intimation you will have that there is a Caspian Tern around is its call, which is on a low key, loud, harsh, and grating -- *kaarrr!*

Small fish furnish the major food supply; thus, these terns are generally to be found near large lakes. A Caspian Tern may plunge head first from a height as great as 100 feet, sometimes disappearing under water, to capture its prey. If the fish is intended for the young, it will be carried back intact, rather than being swallowed and regurgitated later in the manner of many other birds. Arthur Cleveland Bent gives a graphic description of the feeding of young Caspians by the adult:

> The adult Caspians carry fish food to the island directly from the sea. . . The moment [the parent] lands on the island there is a commotion among all the young terns. As a rule the rightful heir would seize the fish before it would leave the parent's bill and unhesitatingly get the fish by the head; then with one or two gulps it would disappear head first, and nine times out of ten . . . the youngster would keel over on its back, with its little red feet frantically waving in the air, the fish's tail also waving about . . . while the process of digestion started. . . . This display lasted . . . about three or four minutes.

Toward their own young the Caspian terns are very tender. However tender they are toward their own offspring they are extremely brutal toward the young of others, and I frequently saw the young ones mauled and flung about by the parent birds of other young.

### Forster's Tern (FOTE)
*Sterna forsteri*

### Common Tern (COTE)
*Sterna hirundo*

### Arctic Tern (ARTE)
*Sterna paradisaea*

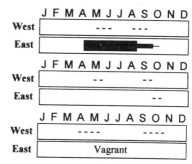

Separating these birds can be difficult, and there are many misidentifications. Zimmer, in *Birding in the American West,* points out that the varying molting patterns between the three species cause numerous complexities. He devotes ten pages to the topic in his book.

We'll try to stick to some of the simpler points, which will help in identifying most birds. First of all, we are not likely to see either Common or Arctic Terns in winter plumage, since these two do not molt into that plumage until they reach their wintering grounds. In the case of the Common, the wintering ground is South America, and in the case of the Arctic, it is the Antarctic pack ice. In fact, the Arctic Tern is the migrating champion of the bird world -- a round trip of 22,000 miles each year.

So, in winter plumage, we have only the Forster's to deal with, and it is readily recognizable because it develops a well-defined black patch around the eye and the auriculars.

Breeding-plumaged birds, which we may see either in spring or fall (summer too, for the Forster's) all have black caps, red bills, and red legs. In a standing bird, you may be able to see that the legs on the Arctic are quite short, and that the line along the bottom of the black cap is more undulating in the Forster's than in the other two, but these are minor points and dependent upon subjective evaluation.

There are two sets of characteristics that will help the most, on breeding-plumaged birds, both of which apply to flying birds. These are overall shape, and wing pattern.

First, on overall shape, an Arctic Tern flying overhead will appear distinctly shorter-headed and longer-tailed than the other two.

Second, on wing pattern. When seen from below, an Arctic Tern will have a very thin black line at the trailing edge of the wing on the outer primaries. On a Common, this black line will be much broader and fuzzier. On a Forster's, the width of the line will be about the same as on a Common, but it will be more gray, rather than black.

One point which is often emphasized in field guides is that the Common Tern will have a well-defined narrow "wedge" extending into the wing from the trailing edge, but this mark can sometimes be duplicated in Forster's Terns.

A useful point is body color. From below, in breeding plumage, both the Arctic and Common Terns are distinctly gray on the underbody. The Forster's Tern is white.

Juveniles can be a problem. All of them can show some brownish or grayish barring on the back, plus incomplete caps, and varying amounts of brownish on the head. The major thing to look for here, in the sitting bird especially, is a very distinct "carpal bar" (at the bend of the wing) on the Common, an indistinct one on the Arctic, and none on the Forster's.

Arctic terns almost exclusively migrate at sea, so we are not likely to get them here. Nevertheless, we have had a few, both in the Rogue Valley and in the Klamath Basin -- near large bodies of water, of course.

We are more likely to get a Common Tern inland than an Arctic. The Commons also migrate at sea, just like the Arctics, but many also migrate over the interior. Arctic Terns mostly nest in the far north, but Common Terns nest closer to us; their breeding grounds extend along the Canadian border through all the southern Canadian provinces, with the exception of British Columbia.

Thus, their migration paths are more likely to include areas like ours, with the Klamath Basin more likely than the Rogue Valley.

Forster's Terns breed widely in eastern Oregon, especially in the Klamath Basin. They winter on the southern coasts of North America, and south to Central America.

There are many accounts by observers who have walked near nesting tern colonies and were subjected to attacks by the parents. In all these accounts, the terns swerved off before making actual contact, but once when I was near a colony of Arctic Terns off the coast of Maine, I was instructed to hold a four-foot long stick in the air over my head as I moved about. The birds indeed drove fiercely at me, screaming all the while, as I walked. Perhaps it is true that the birds would not actually have struck me, but I felt them hit the stick a number of times, and it would be hard to convince me that it wouldn't have been me that got the hits, if it hadn't been for the stick.

**Black Tern** (BLTE)
*Childonais niger*

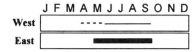

This small, dainty tern is not likely to be mistaken for anything else, especially in its breeding plumage, consisting of an all-black body and gray wings. They rarely plunge-dive after fish like other terns, but zig-zag about the marshes and over the ponds like swallows, chasing insects. In winter, most of the black on the body fades, leaving a partial black cap. But the wings remain dark gray, like no other tern in our area.

Black Terns occur in the Old World also, nesting in northern latitudes and migrating in winter to the coasts of Africa. Ours nest through the northern interior of the continent, including eastern Oregon and the Sacramento Valley of California, and migrate to Mexico and South America. They breed around Upper Klamath Lake, Lower Klamath NWR, in the Klamath Marsh, and at Meiss Lake. They once bred in a couple of places in the Rogue Valley, but do so no longer.

They breed in marshes, and place their nests on almost anything available. They have been known to build their nests on top of other birds' abandoned nests, on piles of mucky grass, and even on old cow pies -- anything to get the nest a couple of inches above water.

## Family **ALCIDAE**: Auks, Murres, and Puffins

**Ancient Murrelet** (ANMU)                             Accidental
*Synthliboramphus antiquus*

Here is another seabird that simply doesn't belong here. However, the Rogue Valley has had two, one in 1966 (specimen at Southern Oregon University), and one in 1992, probably blown in by storms. The "ancient" in the name refers to the whitish or grayish feathers on the head in breeding season.

## Family COLUMBIDAE: Pigeons and Doves

### Rock Dove (RODO)
*Columba livia*

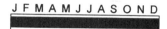

Nobody seems to have a kind word for Rock Doves, or pigeons, as they are familiarly known. They certainly have an affinity for cities, and it is probably their talent for decorating buildings with whitewash that brought them into disfavor with so many people. The highest number on the North American continent in the 2000-2001 Christmas Count was 8,122 in Vancouver, B.C. The highest count in our own area was in 1997 in Klamath Falls, with 932. Yet, in a wild state they nest on rocky cliffs (hence, their name), and I have seen them nesting in such places far from cities.

Rock Doves were introduced on the North American continent very early, in Nova Scotia in about 1606, and then later in Virginia, about 1621. Now they are continent-wide residents. Because the first ones arrived in the early 17th century, they can trace their lineage as North American residents further back than most present-day Americans can. Because the semi-wild populations are believed to have come from escaped domestic birds, the recommendation has been made that they be called "Feral Pigeons."

They come in all kinds of colors, because fanciers in the past have bred them for those qualities. Their original color apparently was gray, and that color is seen frequently in flocks today. Most, but not all, have a conspicuous white spot on the rump. They are very fast fliers. A timing experiment in Great Britain clocked one at 82 miles per hour.

Rock Doves apparently were first domesticated in about 4500 B.C., primarily for their meat, and subsequently for their message-carrying ability. They have been trained to return to their home lofts from distances of hundreds of miles, by progressively releasing them further and further from home.

It is believed that they use for the sun for direction, and have an internal sense that permits them to make proper corrections as the sun advances across the sky. However, tests have shown that other direction-finding means must also exist, because Rock Doves released on cloudy days, when the sun is obscured, also find their way home, apparently using the Earth's magnetic field.

### Band-tailed Pigeon (BTPI)
*Columba fasciata*

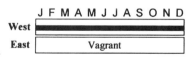

In 1911, in Southern California, it was reported that the "wild pigeon" of the east had unexpectedly turned up in the west. The reference, of course, was to the Passenger Pigeon, which had gone into extinction as a wild bird about ten years earlier. (The last living specimen died in captivity, in 1914.) The western birds, however, were not Passenger Pigeons, but Band-tailed Pigeons. Nevertheless, many people apparently truly believed they were Passenger Pigeons, miraculously restored, not in the east, but in the west. It was reported that there were "millions" of them, although a more conservative observer estimated there were "only" a half million or so.

But that's still a lot of birds. Many years later, it was suggested that the flocks represented most of the Pacific Coast population of Band-tailed Pigeons, drawn by an unusual crop of acorns, coupled with acorn shortages elsewhere.

So what was the response? Instead of celebrating the apparent return of a bird from extinction, hunters flocked to the scene. W. Leon Dawson, writing shortly after the event, said

> By automobiles and railroads they came. The country was aroar with gunfire. The ammunition business jumped in a dozen towns. . . [A reporter wrote that] a Sunday excursion of hunters from San Luis Obispo brought home 1,560 birds. Another man, hunting for the San Francisco market, killed 280 pigeons under one oak in one day. [The destruction of that winter] must have been . . . more than half the entire species.

Arthur Cleveland Bent, writing in 1932, stated that the species was headed for extinction. Fortunately, the federal government acted quickly. Following the shoot-off described above, a five-year moratorium was declared on Band-tailed Pigeons, and hunting the birds was brought under control. Nevertheless, in Oregon, from 1957 to 1987, the hunting take averaged 86,000 birds per year. Today, the daily bag limit is two, and the season lasts only two weeks.

Band-tailed Pigeons in Oregon are found west of the Cascades, and are more numerous near the coast than inland. They are not normally found east of the Cascades, but birds are not bound by human rules, and occasionally turn up there anyway. Superficially, they resemble Mourning Doves, although they have much shorter tails, nothing like the long, pointed tails of Mourning Doves. They prefer forested areas, whereas Mourning Doves prefer more open environments.

They eat many things, from buds to fruit, but are especially fond of acorns. Many birds from the state's population migrate south in winter to California, but some remain in the western valleys for the winter.

Frequently, a single Band-tailed Pigeon may be seen perched in the very top of a tree, apparently alone. But outside of breeding season they tend to gather in small flocks, so there might be others nearby, hidden in the foliage. The single most obvious identification mark, if you're close enough to see it, is a white crescent on the nape of the neck (not present, in juveniles). If one flies, the gray tail band, with a narrower black band above it, helps in the i.d. Their call is a deep, mellow, owl-like *whoo-whoo-hoo*.

# Mourning Dove (MODO)
*Zenaida macroura*

When my wife was a little girl and first heard the name "Mourning Dove," she says she thought it was *Morning* Dove, and that it had that name because it is heard calling so often in the early morning. And they do call early in the morning, often just as it is getting light. It sounds like *ooAAH! woo woo woo,* and many people mistake it for an owl. The first part rises and falls in inflection, but the following *woos* are all on one note and are considered mournful in quality, hence the name. When one flies, its wings give off a distinctive whistling sound.

**Mourning Dove**

This has to be one of our commonest of birds. On nationwide breeding bird surveys, it is exceeded only by the Red-winged Blackbird in number of locations where it has been found, and is second to the Dark-eyed Junco as the bird seen most frequently at feeder stations.

In winter, most of them withdraw from the more northerly locations, but many of them stick around all year in our area. The Christmas Counts for 1999-2000 showed 71 birds in Klamath Falls and 346 in Medford.

The Mourning Dove is classified as a game bird in 31 states, including Oregon, and the estimated annual kill by hunters is on the order of 30 million, nationwide. However, their total population in the United States and Canada is estimated at 400 million, and they are so prolific that the overall population is believed to be fairly stable in spite of the hunting.

Mourning Doves are noted for being lousy nest builders. Occasionally, they may build a good nest, especially if it is built on the top of the nest of some other species left from the previous year. But frequently the nest is just a collection of sticks in a loose platform, which can be dislodged by a moderately strong breeze.

If a nest is destroyed, the pair of birds usually just start over again, and may wind up raising two or three broods per season. Sadly, it has been estimated that 70 percent of the young birds don't make it through their first year, so Mourning Doves compensate by being prolific.

They make attentive parents. One of the parents is in constant attendance, with the male generally doing the incubating and brooding during the day, and the female at night. The nestlings are fed by regurgitation, mingled with a whitish fluid from the bird's crop called "pigeon's milk." The parents continue to attend the young until they are fairly well grown, and one observer stated that a parent will sit crosswise on the young ones at night even when they quite large. They have even been known to start new clutches while continuing to care for the young from a previous brood.

## Family **CUCULIDAE:** Cuckoos, Roadrunners, and Anis

### **Yellow-billed Cuckoo** (YBCU)          Vagrant
*Coccyzus americanus*

The Yellow-billed Cuckoo is in severe decline in the Pacific Coast states. It is estimated that at the turn of the century California had 70,000 pairs. Now, the estimate is 100 pairs. In Oregon, in the earlier part of this century, they were considered to be fairly common, but now the records are few and far between, with most of them coming from Malheur NWR. All of the records are from the summer period, since Yellow-billed Cuckoos spend the winter in South America.

There are three records from our area: one killed by flying into a window in Bonanza, in 1975; one found dead on the west side of Upper Klamath Lake in 1980; and the third photographed at a feeder in the Rogue Valley in 1998.

## Family **TYTONIDAE:** Barn Owls

### **Barn Owl** (BNOW)
*Tyto alba*

> When the sun sinks behind the oak trees and the shadows creep over the valleys, the Barn Owl hurries to the nearest meadow or marsh land on a hunting trip. If it has young at home in the nest, its flight will be swift and noiseless, as it crosses the intervening field at short intervals, carrying mice, gophers and ground squirrels. Nine mice form a meal for the brood, and sixteen mice have been carried to the nest in twenty-five minutes, besides three gophers, a squirrel, and a good-sized rat.

So wrote a naturalist a hundred years ago, at a time when owls were considered by many people to be "vermin," and were shot on sight. The writer of the passage was making a favorable case for the Barn Owl as an eliminator of mice, and that it should be considered a friend of the farmer. The case is a good one, because research has shown that up to 90 percent of the prey taken by Barn Owls consists of mice. They can locate and capture mice even in complete darkness, using their remarkable sense of hearing.

Today, I have known farmers who didn't need any persuasion, and who are delighted to have a Barn Owl or two in their barns. I have had them enthusiastically invite me into their barns, to see "their" owls.

But Barn Owls are not restricted to roosting in barns, although they will do so if there is one handy. I have also seen them roosting in artificial nesting boxes, in patches of thick canes, in holes in cliffs, and in willows almost bare of leaves, where they apparently believed themselves to be invisible.

A Barn Owl would seem to be a fairly good-sized bird, weighing around a pound. But a Great Horned Owl weighs three times as much, and is considered to be the Barn Owl's worst natural enemy. On numerous occasions, Great Horneds have been known to kill and devour Barn Owls.

In our area, Barn Owls are fairly common year-round residents, on both sides of the Cascades. If you think you might know where one hangs out, you might wait until it is dark, and then try making a squeaking noise, like a mouse, in the chance that you might lure it into flying overhead. (I've never been successful at this, but it is claimed that it sometimes works.) One place to find them is in the holes and crevices of the cliffs south of the Klamath Refuges Visitor Center, near where the tour route begins.

People refer to Barn Owls as "monkey-faced owls," because of their peculiar heart-shaped facial disks. They are also referred to as "white owls," or "ghost owls," because from below they are almost white.

They don't hoot, but make a loud, grating *sksch,* causing some people to say that *this* is the owl that should have been named "screech owl." They also make other rattles and clicks, plus a rasping snore that sounds like the bird is being strangled. Nearly a hundred years ago, using the flowery language of the time, a person gave his impressions of the weird noises of the Barn Owl:

> After listening night after night to the harsh screams, and even louder growling, rattling noises he can make, sounds which in the dark hours fairly make the shivers jump up and down one's spine, I can well imagine that the woods could seem haunted and that, in the silent flopping flight of the big whitish bird, any superstitious person could see a ghost or almost any uncanny being of the visionary world . . .

## Family **STRIGIDAE**: Typical Owls

### **Flammulated Owl** (FLOW)
*Otus flammeolus*

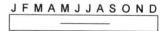

The "Flam" Owl is unique among our local owls because it is a neotropical migrant, meaning it is here only during the summer and migrates to warmer climes for the winter, in this case to Mexico and Central America. Its migratory behavior is directly related to its size and strength, because it is one of the smallest of our owls (about two ounces), and possesses relatively weak feet and talons. As a result, its prey consists almost entirely of insects, such as moths and beetles. In winter, when insects are in short supply in northern areas like ours, the Flam Owl must go south, to where the insects are.

Flammulated Owls are western birds who prefer to nest in forests dominated by ponderosa pine with a relatively closed canopy, but with an open understory for hunting. In the past, it has been thought that they were rare, because they were detected so seldom. However, in recent years biologists have discovered they are much more common than believed, but are simply hard to detect because of their smallness and their retiring nature. Thus, a biologist might consider them to be "fairly common," but a birder is likely to look upon them as "rare."

It's extremely difficult to get a look at one, but their calls can be heard if one goes to the right area at the right time of year. They usually start calling in May, and reach a peak in June. The first hour or so generally is given over to hunting, but then a male may spend most of the nighttime hours in calling, especially if it's a moonlit night.

The call is a low-pitched soft *hoo,* given at intervals of perhaps two seconds, that is far-carrying and ventriloquial in nature. There is a variation consisting of two notes, *hoo-hoo,* with the first *hoo* lower and softer than the second.

They nest in dry forests all over the western states. In our area, they nest on the east side of the Cascades, but also throughout Jackson County in proper habitat, and to the west as far as north-central Josephine County. Their chief enemy is the Spotted Owl, and it is said that when a Spotted Owl speaks, the Flam Owls all go silent.

The name "flammulated" would imply that they have flame-colored plumage, and many of them do have some reddish coloration. But some of them don't, so the same is slightly misleading.

## Western Screech-Owl (WESO)
*Otus kennicottii*

This is a tiny owl, although about twice the weight of a Flammulated Owl. But the two differ considerably in attitude. The Flam Owl is reclusive, while the screech-owl is aggressive. In fact, it has been said that, if the Great Horned owl is a "flying tiger," then the screech-owl is a "flying wildcat."

Screech-owls have been known to kill prey twice their size and more. There is a case on record in which a screech-owl attacked a large hen and attempted to carry it off. And there is another, where one came down a chimney and killed a canary, by pulling it through the bars of its cage.

They also have been known to attack humans when they came too near the nest at night. In one case, people were attacked so frequently, sometimes with blood being drawn, that they took to wearing hoods or baseball masks when going near the nest in the evening.

In contrast to this, if one discovers a screech-owl in the daytime, asleep, it seems almost impervious to external disturbances. And if one has taken up residence in a nesting box, it may come part way out of the hole and bask in the full sun.

There is a nesting box near where I live, and every winter a screech-owl took up residence in it, and could be seen there frequently. Usually, it would have its head out of the box both in the early morning and in the late afternoon, fast asleep. Then, one year, it didn't seem to be there. It was Christmas Count time, and every year this particular screech-owl was counted on to fill out the count. I was asked to monitor the box at dusk, to see if it would show up.

Just as it was getting too dark to see, I thought I saw a bird go into the box. I couldn't be sure, so I went over to the tree the box was in, and scraped the trunk of the tree with a stick. Usually, if you do that, and if there is an owl in the box, it will pop its head out to see what's coming up the tree to attack it. But an owl didn't pop its head out. A flicker did.

Screech-owls often take up residence in old flicker holes, and I have come across references to contests between flickers and owls over who would take possession of a hole. Apparently, a flicker will not enter a hole if an owl is there, but if it is left vacant, even for a short time, the flicker will go in and with its formidable bill sticking out, hold it against all comers.

There seems to be some uncertainty why this bird is called a "screech" owl. According to all the authorities I have consulted, it seldom screeches. Personally, I have never heard one do that. Its usual call consists of a series of hollow hoots, all on one pitch, with long intervals at first and then speeding up, like a bouncing ball. Interestingly, the call of the Eastern Screech-Owl is quite different, which is one of the reasons they are considered to be two separate species. The best description of the Eastern's call is that it sounds like a horse's whinny.

Screech-owls are fairly common permanent residents on the west side of the Cascades, but less so on the east side. They like broken woodlands, and will even move into the suburbs of cities, provided there are proper holes to occupy. They will catch and eat almost anything that moves, and can get a proper grip on. The list includes mice, moles, rats, bats, caterpillars, crickets, spiders, scorpions, frogs, and birds (even as large as quail or grouse), just to name a few.

The principal enemies of the screech-owl are larger owls, especially the Great Horned Owl. A general rule is, if you are trying to attract owls by playing tapes of their calls, be sure to play the screech-owl tape first. If you play the Great Horned Owl tape first, you can forget about seeing a screech-owl.

## Great Horned Owl (GHOW)
*Bubo virginianus*

## Long-eared Owl (LEOW)
*Asio otus*

The only reason these two are put together is because they both have long ear-tufts and are sometimes mistaken for each other. If seen side by side, there would be no mistake, because Great-horneds are much bigger than

Long-eareds. However, it is not likely that a Long-eared would remain near a Great-horned very long, because Great-horneds prey on Long-eareds whenever they have a chance.

A frequently mentioned criterion for separation between the two is the white throat on the Great-horned Owl, which the Long-eared Owl lacks. But if the owl has its head hunched down, this mark may not be very visible. A better criterion is the breast, which is densely marked with horizontal barring on the Great-horned, whereas the marks on the breast of the Long-eared consist more of longitudinal stripes, mixed with bars and checks.

The great naturalist, Ernest Thompson Seton, referred to the "untamable ferocity" of Great Horned Owls, and said he ranked ". . . these winged tigers among the most pronounced and savage of the birds of prey." They can attack and kill surprisingly large mammals and birds, including hares and rabbits, skunks, porcupines, domestic turkeys, and even domestic cats. In one case involving a cat, however, the cat put up a stiff fight, and the owl had to drop it.

Porcupines can be a problem, too. An owl that had attacked a porcupine wound up with more than sixty quills in its body, including some which had penetrated the thick skin of one foot, several that had penetrated the heavy muscles of the breast, and two in an eye-lid. No doubt the bird would have died, had it not been captured and had most of the quills removed. Skunks, however, apparently pose no problem, in spite of the odoriferous spray.

Great Horned Owls are among the easiest of owls to detect, because of the characteristic loud, deep, hooting -- *Hoo! Hoo-hoo! Hoo! Hoo!* The time of most hooting is in the winter, because Great Horned Owls are among the earliest of nesters, usually beginning in January. They don't build their own nests, but generally appropriate the nests of other birds, such as Red-tailed Hawks. The Red-tails may dispute such thefts, but apparently lose the contests about 90 percent of the time.

Great-horneds also are known to give out loud, harsh, blood-curdling screams, but these apparently are the food calls of the young birds, as they follow their parents around demanding to be fed.

A contrasting experience is related by A. Leon Dawson, writing in 1923, who doesn't say whether the owls were young ones or not:

> At three o'clock one morning a horrible nightmare gave way to a still more horrible waking. Murder most foul was being committed on the roof just outside the open window, and the shrieks of the victims (at least seven of them!) were drowned by the imprecations of the attacking party. . . Two weeks later the conflict was renewed -- at a merciful distance this time. Peering out into the moonlight I beheld one of these Owls perched upon the chimney of the church hard by, gibbering and shrieking like one possessed. Cat-calls, groans, and demoniacal laughter were varied by wails and screeches, as of souls in torment . . .

Great-horned Owls are also seen while sleeping in trees during the day, particularly in winter when the trees have lost most of their leaves. In such cases, the owls are highly visible, but other times they roost in dense foliage, if they can find it. Also, they may roost in holes in cliffs, as along the road south of the Klamath Refuges Visitor Center. Often, the best way to locate an owl is to listen for the outraged cries of crows or Steller's Jays, who flock around an owl when they discover one, trying to drive it away.

Things are different with Long-eared Owls, which are among the most secretive of birds, and very hard to locate. They usually roost in the densest foliage they can find, but I have seen them sleeping during the day in willow clumps that were almost leafless, the owls apparently not realizing how visible they were. Sometimes, in winter, several Long-eared Owls will roost in close proximity. A place to look for them, after breeding season, is the willows along the road south of the Klamath Refuges Visitor Center.

When surprised, a Long-eared Owl will fly up from its roost, swirl, and immediately head back down into the brush to seek a new spot. This is quite different from the behavior of a Great-horned when startled from its roost, who will then slowly fly off with great dignity to find a new roosting place.

The hooting of a Long-eared Owl, delivered during mating season, is a series of low, mellow hoots spaced 2 to 4 seconds apart. The number of hoots given in succession may go as high as 100, but more typically is 10 to 30. Another sound is a spooky moan, which rises and falls, and seems properly to belong to a ghost.

Like the Great-horneds, Long-eareds use the old nests of other birds, especially crows, for breeding purposes. They have also used the nests of Black-billed Magpies, which have a roof of sorts over the top, with a hole on the side for access.

Great Horned Owls are widespread permanent residents, and are found in all sorts of forested habitats on both sides of the Cascades, even up to high elevations.

Long-eared Owls are fairly common breeders on the east side of the Cascades, although they are so secretive they are seldom detected. There may be some southward movement in winter. On the west side, they are much more scarce, although they have been found to breed to some extent in the Siskiyous.

## Snowy Owl (SNOW)   Vagrant
*Nyctea scandiaca*

There are two records in our area for this ghostly visitor from the north -- one at White City, in the Rogue Valley, in November 1984, and the other at Rocky Point, on Upper Klamath Lake, in January 1997.

Snowy Owls are irruptive in Oregon, with irruptions having occurred in 1955, 1966, 1973, 1984, and 1996. Both of the occurrences in our area took place during irruption years. The reasons why such irruptions occur are not universally agreed upon. Some say it is because lemmings, which are a major food item for the owls, periodically undergo population crashes, forcing the birds to move south. Others say the irruptions are tied to major weather events. Either way, when they do come south, they favor open environments, such as beach dunes, agricultural areas and airports, although they sometimes have turned up on buildings in populated areas.

## Northern Pygmy-Owl (NOPO)
*Glaucidium gnoma*

This is our smallest owl, and I think it is my favorite. Even though it is about the length of a sparrow, it is nearly three times as heavy (2.5 ounces). To me, it looks like a tiny version of a football linebacker -- burly, big shoulders, and no neck.

Some years ago, when I was just getting into birding, I desperately wanted to see a pygmy-owl. I had read that they were easily attracted by imitating their hooting, which consists of a series of fairly high pitched whistled *toots* about a second apart. I was in a nature preserve with a good system of trails, and there was no one around. I wasn't sure just how good I would be, trying to be a pygmy-owl, but decided to risk it. I walked slowly along the trail, hooting away, hoping to hear a response.

I did. It came from a short distance away in the woods, but out of sight. I hurried in that direction, hooting as I went, and was sure the owl was getting closer, because its hooting was louder. I rounded a bend in the trail, still hooting, and here came another birder hurrying toward me, hooting as he went.

**Northern Pygmy-Owl**

The next time I tried it, things went better. I hooted, and almost instantly a tiny, angry little owl darted into a tree over my head and started hooting at me. Simultaneously, small birds like kinglets and warblers appeared out of nowhere, set up a clamor, and began mobbing the owl. The owl paid no attention to its tormentors, and continued to hoot. It never stopped its hooting as I departed, and I could continue to hear it until I was far away.

The mobbing by little birds is a fascinating thing. There seems to be a general rule: Little owls are mobbed by little birds, such as kinglets and warblers; big owls are mobbed by bigger birds, such as crows and magpies. It's never been clear to me what is being accomplished by the mobbing. If the purpose is to drive the owl away, it doesn't seem to work very well, because the subjects of the mobbing usually are unfazed by it. Perhaps it is just instinctive, when the small birds get an opportunity to vent their rage on an ancient enemy and get away with it.

The Northern Pygmy-Owl is a westerner, ranging from Alaska to Mexico. It is a year-long resident of forests and canyons, but not of dense forest. I have only been successful a few times in getting them to come to me by imitating their call; more often I have discovered them by chance, as they sat on a open tree branch, carefully examining the territory for prey items. Under such circumstances, they may allow fairly close approach.

They often hunt in the daytime, and their principal prey is small birds, although they will also take insects and small mammals. They are ferocious hunters, and frequently take prey twice as big as they are. One will hunt from a perch, holding perfectly still except for its head, which turns constantly this way and that, seeking prey. It can turn its head completely around, of course, and when it does, the false "eyes" on the back of the owl's head become visible.

The false eyes look remarkably like real ones, and I suppose the function is that, if something wants to jump on the pygmy-owl when it's looking the other way, it won't do so, because even if the owl is looking the other way, there are the eyes in the back of its head, glaring directly at the would-be attacker.

A. Leon Dawson, in his flowery way, gave this summary of the pygmy-owl:

> Fiend he is from the top of his gory beak to the tips of his needle-like claws; but chances are you will forget his gory character at sight and call him "perfectly cunning," just because he is tiny and saucy and *dégagé* [meaning pert, perky, and free; I had to look it up].

## Burrowing Owl (BUOW)
*Athene cunicularia*

|  | J | F | M | A | M | J | J | A | S | O | N | D |
|---|---|---|---|---|---|---|---|---|---|---|---|---|
| West | - | - | - | - |  |  |  |  |  |  | - | - |
| East |  |  | - | - | - | - | - | - | - | - |  |  |

People almost universally find Burrowing Owls to be captivating little creatures. They are easy to see (if you can find one). They stand right out there in the open, all owly-eyed, serious-looking and apparently unafraid, looking almost like little toys. And they even come out in the daytime where people can see them, instead of only at night like most other owls.

They are only a little over nine inches long -- about the same size as robins. But they are stockier than robins, and in fact weigh about twice as much. And, like most owls, they can be terrors. Major Bendire kept a pair of owls in captivity, and fed them with four Townsend's ground squirrels a day. He described what happened:

> As soon as a squirrel was turned loose in the room with the Owls, one of them would pounce on it, and, fastening its sharp talons firmly in the back of the squirrel, spread its wings somewhat, and with a few vigorous and well-directed blows of its beak break the vertebrae of the neck, and before it was fairly dead it commenced eating the head.

Many owl researchers agree that Burrowing Owls are probably capable of digging their own burrows in soft earth, but prefer to adapt burrows created by mammals such as badgers. This has its dangers, because it has been found that depredation by badgers on the eggs and young of the owls is a frequent cause of nest desertion.

Some people believe that Burrowing Owls and rattlesnakes live together in the same burrows. Certainly, owls and snakes have been observed going in and out of the same burrows, but the snakes are probably after a meal. A factor which has undoubtedly contributed to the rattlesnake story is that young owls, concealed inside their holes, often make noises that sound like rattlesnakes.

The nesting burrows appear to be attractive to many kinds of insects. Earwigs and crickets occur abundantly in occupied burrows, but this seems to work to the owls' advantage, because the bugs provide a convenient food source. Also, the burrows almost invariably abound in fleas.

Burrowing Owls are pretty scarce in our area, although they still seem to be holding their own in eastern Oregon, except in places like Bend, where the owls get displaced by human developments. They used to nest in the Rogue Valley, but not any more. An attempt was made in the 1980s to reestablish the owls at Denman WA, but it did not succeed. Once in a while, one or two will show up in winter in the Rogue Valley, to take up temporary residence near man-made culverts. (See Plate VII.)

**Burrowing Owl**

References to "colonies" in the old literature would make it appear that Burrowing Owls live in dense communal groups, but this appears generally not to be the case. During a study in eastern Oregon, it was observed that nest desertion was most frequent when two pairs nested within 110 meters of each other, because of insufficient prey to support both nests. In the latter portion of the breeding period, the adults and several of their offspring may be observed clustered about a single burrow, giving the impression that a large group of owls is nesting communally.

## Spotted Owl (SPOW)
*Strix occidentalis*

## Barred Owl (BDOW)
*Strix varia*

Here are two more species that are sometimes confused. The Barred Owl is larger, of course, but that may not be useful when looking at a lone bird. Both have dark eyes, both have round facial disks, both are earless. The clue is in the name: The Barred Owl is, well, barred, and the Spotted Owl is spotted.

The spotting or barring is on the chest and belly. In the Barred Owl, there is a set of pronounced horizontal bars across the throat and upper breast, changing to dark vertical streaks on the lower abdomen. In the Spotted Owl, there is creamy white mottling, or spots, on both breast and abdomen.

There is little confusion telling them apart when they are calling. The Barred Owl has the most famous owl call in existence -- a loud *Who cooks for you? Who cooks for you-allllll?* The Spotted Owl, on the other hand, has a call consisting of four emphatic hoots in a characteristic pattern: *Hoo . . . HoHoo . . . Hoo-o-o.* Both are likely to answer calls played by a tape player, sometimes in the daytime.

My first experience with a Barred Owl was memorable. I was camping near a swamp in Georgia and heard a Barred Owl in the distance. (In the South, they are called "swamp owls.") It was pitch dark, but I took my tape player and hurried in the direction of the call. I played the tape once, and sensed a shadow passing near me. I played it again, and the shadow came so close I felt it was going to take my head off. It was a Barred Owl, all right, and it appeared to be so annoyed with being duped that it sat in a tree nearby and let loose with an avalanche of loud screams and haunted-house noises.

The range expansion of the Barred Owl is one of the great ornithological events of recent years. At one time, it had been thought of as a bird of the east and south, with a penetration across Canada. But that penetration grew. By 1943 Barred Owls had been found in British Columbia, and by 1974 the first one was detected in Oregon, in the Blue Mountains. They showed up in the southern Cascades in 1981, and now they have moved down into Northern California, almost to the latitude of Lake Tahoe.

Today, their range just about overlaps that of the Northern Spotted Owl, and much concern has been expressed concerning the future of Spotted Owls. Barred Owls aggressively chase Spotted Owls, and sometimes kill them. And, in a role-switch, they sometimes mate together. Many hybrids have been seen, raising the concern that the Barreds may hybridize the Spotteds out of existence.

Both species need lots of room. Pairs of Spotted Owls, for example, are generally one to two miles apart. Thus, it takes a lot of effort to find one. Once found, a Spotted Owl shows little fear of humans. In every case where I've come across a Spotted Owl, it has never flown. In fact, in each case I gained the impression the owl was bored, and only wanted to be left alone so it could sleep. Barred Owls are more wary of humans.

Both species are permanent residents in coniferous forests. Undisturbed old forest is preferred, although both will make some use of logged lands coming back into new growth. Both species are in the southern Cascades, but Barred Owls have apparently penetrated to the west of the Cascades to a relatively minor degree. They are rare in the Siskiyous, at least so far, and one was heard near Wolf Creek, in Josephine County.

The subspecies of Spotted Owl called "Northern Spotted Owl" is a celebrity in the news media, and has been declared "threatened" by the federal government. A survey spanning the 1985-93 period suggested that both the population and the adult survival rate were in decline. A later survey, extending through 1998, still showed evidence of population decline, but there was no evidence of declines in survival or reproductive rates. Estimates of population trends are certain to be hotly contested, of course, regardless of whether they are up or down. In the meantime, the Northwest Forest Plan of 1994 has set up a network of reserves to provide appropriate habitat for Spotted Owls.

## Great Gray Owl (GGOW)
*Strix nebulosa*

Not long ago it was thought that this owl was largely a Canadian resident, with only modest range extensions into the United States. Any that were seen in Oregon were thought to be winter wanderers. But now it has been determined they are year-round residents many places in Oregon, including the Blue Mountains, the Cascades, and the Siskiyous. In the Cascades, they are usually found east of the crest above 3000 feet, mostly in old lodgepole forests, or in mixed lodgepole/ponderosa. Somewhere nearby there are sure to be meadows for hunting, ranging from 15 to 250 acres in size.

In the Siskiyous, however, they are found at elevations between 1400 and 3000 feet, in proximity to north-facing slopes with Douglas fir, with more open, drier, south-facing slopes nearby. In winter, they prefer to be in areas with less than 16 inches of accumulated snow, presumably because deep snow makes hunting more difficult.

Even though these are our biggest owls in terms of length, they average only about two-thirds the weight of Great Horned Owls. Even so, they look huge, with unusually large facial discs, and have a muted gray pattern on the body. They are rare and reclusive, roosting during the day in heavy forest. They are notorious for being hard to find, which means that they are correspondingly high on most birders' "wish lists."

I've come upon them twice in Southern Oregon, after about ten failed tries. The first time was not far from Howard Prairie. I had been playing a tape, with no success. The call on my tape is a series of deep booming hoots, about ten of them, tailing off at the end, which I understand is the courtship call of the male.

I had put my tape player away, and was in the process of giving up and departing when I heard a muffled deep *hoot* from the nearby forest, somewhat like the sound on my tape. The *hoot* was repeated, and then again. I walked carefully into the forest, and the *hoots* kept being repeated, at intervals of three or four seconds. I was led thus directly to the owl, which was only about 100 yards away, and perched perhaps 50 feet off the ground on a short branch. As soon as I appeared the hooting stopped, but the owl just sat there looking at me, and even tolerated being photographed. (See Plate VII.)

The other time was different. This was on the west side of Upper Klamath Lake in a fairly dense forest, when I became aware of four highly agitated Steller's Jays, sounding off at something in a the dense foliage of a tree. As I got closer, a Great Gray Owl bounded out of the tree and flew up the slope, either because I was getting too close, or because it couldn't stand the jays any more.

## Short-eared Owl (SEOW)
*Asio flammeus*

|  | J F M A M J J A S O N D |
|---|---|
| West | ------                              ---- |
| East | ======================= |

I've never been able to see the ears on a Short-eared Owl, so they must be short indeed. Occasionally I've spotted one hiding in the grass, but most often they've been flying overhead. They have a characteristic, moth-like flight, which helps to distinguish them from male Northern Harriers, who often hunt the same territories at dusk. Their most useful marks, seen in flight, are the dark carpal marks at the "wrists."

In our area, the best place to see them is in the marshes of Klamath County, where they are more or less resident. Their preferred hunting time is dusk, but they also are often seen in the daytime. In the Rogue Valley they sometimes are found near the Medford Airport in winter, and have been seen west of Grants Pass. Airports are favorite locations, because airports often have extensive grassy fields around them that are relatively unused by humans.

**Short-eared Owl**

Short-eared Owls live on every continent except Australia. Some of the population migrates to the Arctic to breed, and some stay put. In the winter, resident populations are augmented by those coming down from the north.

The unpredictable nature of the owls' movements is demonstrated by the results of banding studies. In some cases the results were consistent with what one would expect -- north in the spring, south in the fall. Some of the birds didn't move at all, as was expected, but others moved transversely. For example, a bird banded in North Dakota in June was found six months later in Oregon, a thousand miles west.

And then there was the case of two birds banded in British Columbia a day apart in September. A little less than two months later, one of the birds was found in Southern California, whereas the other was still in British Columbia.

Short-eared Owls are rarely found roosting in trees, although they may sit on fence posts or tree stumps and use them for hunting perches. Arthur Cleveland Bent reported on an instance where he had been scanning tree stumps for owls and had given up, when one "stump" suddenly opened its wings and flew away. Mostly, however, Short-eared Owls roost on the ground during the day, usually in the shade of tall grass.

## Boreal Owl (BOOW)                         Accidental
*Aegolius funereus*

Believe it or not, the first verified Oregon record of this elusive bird came from Fort Klamath, in March 1902. It was not found again in the state until one was seen in northeastern Oregon 85 years later. Not much is known about this rare little owl, but there seems to be a resident population not far north of our area, in the subalpine forests near Bend.

The scientific name *funereus,* meaning in this case, "mournful," refers to the sound of its call, which has been considered as melancholy by some. But others have likened it to ". . . the tolling of a soft but high-pitched bell and sometimes to the dropping of water . . "

## Northern Saw-whet Owl (NSWO)
*Aegolius acadicus*

|  | J F M A M J J A S O N D |
|---|---|
| West |  |
| East | ▰▰▰▰▰▰▰▰▰▰▰▰ |

Whenever the word "northern" appears in a bird's name, the implication is that there must be a "southern" version somewhere. And so there is in this case: an owl that lives in Mexico and Central America, called the Unspotted Saw-whet Owl. Some authorities think they are actually the same species.

This tiny little owl is closely related to the Boreal Owl, and is often confused with it. But the expression on the Northern Saw-whet Owl is described by some as "surprised," while the expression on the Boreal Owl is described as "angry." Furthermore, the black outline of the facial disc is much more pronounced in the Boreal Owl, and the bill in the Boreal is yellowish, whereas in the saw-whet it is black. The breast and belly of the saw-whet has reddish-brown streaks.

Saw-whets are considered by biologists to be fairly common in the forests of the Cascades, although they are so nocturnal and retiring that birders are likely to look upon them as rare. In winter, they withdraw from the heavy snow areas, because their principal prey, mice, live in tunnels in the snow and are not accessible to the little owls.

The harsh "saw-filing" noise for which the bird is named is heard most frequently in spring, generally just before dawn. It has been rendered as *skree-aw, skree-aw, skree-aw,* almost always in threes. (Some say the bird is not named for the "saw-filing" call at all, but that the name comes from the French word *chouette,* meaning a small owl.) There is another call, somewhat similar to the repetitious *toots* of a pygmy-owl, but much more rapid.

Much has been said and written about the tameness of this owl, and my own experiences certainly support that view. In the first case, I saw it light on a branch near my deck, visible as a silhouette against the small amount of light remaining from the setting sun. It apparently saw me, because it cocked its head a few times as if to get a better look, but it was still in the same location after it became too dark to see.

On another occasion, one was spotted sleeping in a small tree. Although a half-dozen birders busied themselves about the tree, trying to get good looks, the owl never opened its eyes.

An even more remarkable occasion was when a neighbor called several of her birder friends to come over and "see the cute little owl in her breezeway." The owl remained in position for more than an hour, waiting for mice that were known to reside in the breezeway, while a half-dozen birders peered at it through an open door, only ten feet away. (See Plate VII.)

## Family **CAPRIMULGIDAE**: Goatsuckers

The family name of "goatsuckers" comes from an old legend that claimed these birds sucked milk from goats at night, whereas the truth is that they feed almost exclusively on insects caught in flight. The family consists of two subfamilies, the "nighthawks" and the "nightjars," the latter of which includes our Common Poorwill. The nightjars got their name from the harsh, jarring notes of the English Nightjar, which makes a *churring* noise that apparently can go on most of the night.

### Common Nighthawk (CONI)
*Chordeilis minor*

| | J F M A M J J A S O N D |
|---|---|
| West | ▬▬▬▬ |
| East | ▬▬▬ |

A nasal *peent! peent!* coming from somewhere above announces the presence of a nighthawk. Then one will be spotted, sometimes high in the sky, bounding erratically about on long slender wings, going about its business of sweeping insects into its huge, gaping mouth. The transverse white bar midway on each wing will instantly confirm its identity.

One of the principal items of prey is flying ants. In a study of the contents of the stomachs of 24 nighthawks, the number of ants ranged from 200 to 1,800. Other prey items are grasshoppers, beetles, locusts, and mosquitoes. The stomach of one bird was found to contain 500 mosquitoes.

Besides the *peent! peent!* call, there is a noise generally referred to as a "boom," made by the male during courtship. The male, starting from a point high above where the female is located, goes into a plunge dive, and pulls out sharply at the bottom with his wings spread forward, and produces a loud "booming" sound by the vibration of his primaries. However, some people question whether the word "boom" is appropriate, and claim it sounds more like blowing across an empty bottle. This noise is partly responsible for its popular name, "bull-bat," the "bat" part referring to its bat-like flight.

Nighthawks are most abundant in eastern Oregon, in sagebrush and rocky scablands. However, they occur throughout the state in breeding season. In winter, they leave the state entirely, and migrate to South America. For nesting, they prefer open areas, including dry creek beds, burned areas, and human-created landscapes such as unused gravel roads and abandoned parking lots. As recently as the 1970s they nested on gravel roofs in urban areas in Oregon, but apparently have ceased doing so. Speculation about the reasons include predation by crows, and less mosquito prey in urban areas because of pest insect reduction programs.

For foraging, they need places with plenty of bugs, and will frequently be seen over riparian areas or open water, because that's where the bugs tend to be. Most of their foraging is at dawn or dusk, but they are also frequently seen during the day. A special characteristic is that, if one of them roosts on the branch of a tree, it almost always will take a position parallel to the branch, rather than crosswise.

## Common Poorwill (COPW)
*Phalaenoptilus nuttallii*

|  | J F M A M J J A S O N D |
|---|---|
| West | ———▬▬▬▬——— |
| East | ——————▬▬▬▬▬— |

The first time I ever saw poorwills I had no idea what they were. I was driving on a little-used gravel road in the darkness before dawn, on my way to a Sage Grouse lek on a sagebrush plain. In the darkness, these little birds kept flying up from the road in my headlights and disappearing into the sagebrush. It wasn't until many years later, when I'd had more experience with the species, that I realized what I had seen.

On another occasion, I had stayed well after dark at a location near Mono Lake, hoping to hear or see Long-eared Owls. As I was exiting from the parking lot onto the main road, I observed a strange-looking object lying on the pavement, in the glare of my headlights. At first I thought it was a piece of crumpled paper, and then I thought it might be a reptile like a horned lizard. Whatever it was, it didn't move.

Thinking it might be something that would warrant a photograph, I picked up my camera, got out of the car cautiously, and walked toward it. It still didn't move, and, as I got closer it looked even stranger, something like a peculiarly shaped rock. At the moment when I was beginning to bring my camera to bear, a car came along the road at high speed. The "rock," startled into action, flew up into the air and away, easily recognizable now as a Common Poorwill.

This willingness of a poorwill to allow close approach is commented upon frequently in the literature. In one instance, eight observers came close to a poorwill, some as close as two feet, during which it continued to sit tight. A poorwill will often sit in the middle of a road, provided there isn't any traffic, waiting for insects. Then, when your car comes along, its eyes, reflected in the beams of your headlights, show up as two glowing pink spots.

Their name comes from their call, which is a loud *poor-WILL! poor-WILL!* sometimes repeated many times. At dusk, in poorwill country in the spring, their calls can often be heard coming from different directions, and can be heard for long distances. On one occasion In Arizona, I heard a poorwill some distance away, and walked toward it. It was completely dark, but with my flashlight I soon discovered the bird on the edge of a sandy wash, perched on a rock, calling repeatedly. I came to within 20 feet of it, and then withdrew. During the whole time, it never ceased its repetitive calling, and I could still hear it until I was far way.

Common Poorwills can be found in sagebrush and juniper-covered hills in the Klamath Basin, and have been seen on both sides of Upper Klamath Lake. They can also be found in the Rogue Valley, on dry hillsides with ceanothus and manzanita. In winter they leave our area entirely and go south. The species is highly unusual, in that a couple of individuals in the southwest deserts have been found in states of hibernation during winter.

## Family APODIDAE: Swifts

**Vaux's Swift** (VASW)
*Chaetura vauxi*

| | J F M A M J J A S O N D |
|---|---|
| West | ━━━▬▬▬▬━━━━ |
| East | ▬▬▬▬▬▬ |

**White-throated Swift** (WTSW)
*Aeronautes saxatalis*

| | J F M A M J J A S O N D |
|---|---|
| West | - - - - - - - - - - |
| East | ────── |

**Black Swift** (BLSW)
*Cypseloides niger*

| | J F M A M J J A S O N D |
|---|---|
| West | - - - - - - - - - |

First, about pronunciation. William Samson Vaux, for whom Vaux's Swift is named, was a native of Philadelphia. According to my encyclopedia, he pronounced his name as "vawks," so we presumably should do the same, and say "vawks's swift.". (Some people pronounce it "voze swift," giving it the original French pronunciation.) Vaux's Swifts are the most common of the swifts in Oregon. They are principally forest dwellers, where they build their nests inside hollow trees. They are the smallest of the three, and have been described as little brownish "flying cigars."

Swifts cannot perch on twigs or wires, which is one of the big differences between swifts and swallows. Another difference in is their appearance while flying. Swifts have long narrow wings that are swept back like a scimitar. The typical flight of a swift is a series of rapid wingbeats, followed by a glide. They may appear jerky, compared to swallows.

They have strong claws, and can cling to vertical surfaces. They build their nests, made of small sticks cemented in place with saliva, on the inside walls of hollow trees, chimneys, or deep in cracks in cliffs. They spend only a brief time here in the summer, and migrate to Central or South America for the winter.

Though primarily hollow-tree nesters, Vaux's Swifts may nest to some extent inside chimneys, just as do Chimney Swifts, their eastern counterparts. The Vaux's Swift is a western bird, so confusion between the two normally does not arise. Since chimneys are usually not in use during the summer breeding season, problems would not be expected to arise for the birds. With Chimney Swifts, it has been observed that if an off-season fire is constructed, the young ones either fall into the fire or into the living room. The same would presumably befall Vaux's Swifts under similar circumstances.

During migration, Vaux's Swifts may roost in flocks in large chimneys overnight. Arthur Cleveland Bent describes one such instance in which the swifts began to gather an hour or two before sunset. At a certain stage of twilight, the birds rapidly began to enter the chimney, and, in Bent's words, resembled a long black rope dangling in the chimney's mouth.

Though Vaux's Swifts are primarily forest birds, they may be hard to see when foraging over a forest. They are more likely to be visible when foraging over a stream or a pond, sometimes in company with swallows.

White-throated Swifts are less widespread in Oregon than are Vaux's, and mostly are to be found on the east side of the Cascades in open country, wherever there are nesting cliffs nearby. They have a black-and-white pattern on the underparts, that sets them apart from the other two. Some people have said the black-and-white pattern makes them resemble little killer whales.

In the past, a few pairs of White-throated Swifts have nested on Sheepy Ridge, south of the Klamath Refuges Visitor Center. In the Rogue Valley, there have been reports of birds near Lower Table Rock. They may also occur at Crater Lake. When they are foraging they can be very high, and it may be necessary, even in a good location, to watch the sky for a long time before spotting one.

The White-throated Swift is reputed to be the fastest of all the birds. One was observed escaping from the dive of a Peregrine Falcon at a speed estimated at 200 miles per hour. When diving into their nesting crevices in a cliff, they come at the cliff at great speed and disappear without seeming to slow down. I witnessed an event like this once. The swifts were foraging in a loose flock not far overhead when it began to rain. Instantly, the swifts dove at full speed toward the nearby cliff face where the crevices were located, and disappeared as if by magic.

Black Swifts are all dark, as their name implies, and are twice the size of Vaux's Swifts. The status of Black Swifts in Oregon has been described as "enigmatic." They are believed to nest at Salt Creek Falls in the Cascades and at other nearby locations, but no nests or young have been found. When they are foraging, they may travel many miles away from their nest sites, and fly so high they are difficult to detect. In our area, they have occasionally been spotted during migration, usually from some high-elevation hawk-watch site.

## Family **TROCHILIDAE**: Hummingbirds

The adult male hummingbirds we get in our area are reasonably straightforward to identify. The females and juveniles are a different matter. In general, they can only be identified by applying a group of subtle characteristics, and even then some can not be separated in the field. For certain species it gets down to the manner in which the tail feathers are shaped. The subject is too detailed for this book, so we'll stick to the readily identified adult males.

Hummingbirds are birds of the New World. There are more than 300 species, most of them in the tropics. Twenty-one of these enter the U.S., but only eight penetrate very far beyond the Mexican border. We get seven of these in our area, three of which breed here. The one we don't get is the Ruby-throated, which in the east is the only commonly-occurring hummingbird.

It is often believed that hummingbirds eat only nectar, but they actually consume many insects, mostly gleaned from the flowers they visit. They will even frequently fly out from a perch and capture an insect on the wing, like a flycatcher. They are also known to eat the sap of trees.

Almost all of them are neotropical migrants, and one of them, the Ruby-throated, migrates 600 miles each way across the Gulf of Mexico, spring and fall. One observer in a boat in the Gulf of Mexico saw six of them heading north, after they had already flown hundreds of miles from Yucatan. Their flight was direct and rapid, about 25 feet above the water, and they showed no signs of exhaustion, or made any attempt to light on the boat. That's not bad stuff for a little mite that only weighs one-tenth of an ounce.

Hummingbirds don't have many natural enemies. Perhaps their worst enemy is ants. Cases have been documented where ants got into the nests and killed and ate the nestlings. There also have been somewhat extraordinary cases where hummingbirds have been swallowed by fish or frogs, and one case of a hummingbird that got caught in a spider's web and was thoroughly trussed up by the resident spider as if it were a giant fly. The last case had a happy ending for the bird, if not for the spider, because a human came along, killed the spider, and carefully unwrapped the bird.

## Black-chinned Hummingbird (BCHU)
*Archilochus alexandri*

J F M A M J J A S O N D

The Black-chinned is primarily a resident of the southwest, although its breeding range extends northward to the Canadian border and includes eastern Oregon. They occur in the Rogue Valley and the Klamath Basin on an irregular basis, but have not been confirmed as breeders, although the Breeding Bird Atlas program found one "possible" breeding site in the southwest part of Klamath County. They are rare to uncommon along the Klamath River below Iron Gate Reservoir, and are believed to nest there. In winter, Black-chinneds move south, mostly into Mexico.

The male Black-chinned has a black chin, exactly as its name would suggest. Below that, it has a purple gorget that shows up when the sun hits it exactly right but otherwise looks black, like the chin. Below that is a white band, that separates the gorget from the grayish underparts.

Male hummingbirds have various courtship displays, each of which is more or less specific to a given species. The one for Black-chinned, for example, consists of a series of U-shaped arcs. The female sits on a branch, and the male displays in front of her. He starts from a point perhaps 20 feet above her, swoops down in an arc with a whizzing noise, and then comes to a halt about 20 feet above her at the other end of the arc. He then repeats in the opposite direction, and carries through on several repetitions.

# Anna's Hummingbird (ANHU)
*Calypte anna*

Who was Anna? She was the Duchess of Rivoli, and wife of Prince Victor Massena. A French naturalist, Rene Lesson, in 1829 discovered a new hummingbird in a collection from Mexico belonging to the Prince. Lesson named the bird to honor Anna, the Prince's wife. Whether he sought thus to ingratiate himself with the Prince, or with the Prince's wife, history does not say.

Anna's Hummingbirds are the "standard" hummingbirds in the Rogue Valley, summer and winter. They are the only ones that winter mainly in the United States. Amazingly, until a few decades ago they were not present in Oregon, although they were common in California. The first record for Oregon was in 1944. In the 1960s they began expanding rapidly north, and now they are found all the way up into Washington, mostly west of the crest.

**Anna's Hummingbird**

One of the factors that has led to the range expansion of Anna's Hummingbirds is the widespread use of feeders, especially in winter. In addition to this, they are hardy creatures, who seem to be able to get along even when the temperatures get below freezing.

No doubt the ability of hummingbirds to go into a state of torpor on cold nights helps them to last through cold periods. During such a state, the temperature drops from a normal 105° F, to 55° F, and the heartbeat drops from 250 beats per minute (this is the resting rate; it rises to 1,250 when flying) to only 50. Nevertheless, during prolonged periods of unusually cold weather, there is generally a large die-off of Anna's Hummingbirds. Upon occasion, during cold weather, they have been known to roost overnight near chimneys or near lights, for heat.

The male is spectacular, and is unmistakable. Not only does he have a gorgeous rose-red gorget, the red also goes up over the top of the crown. There is some possibility of confusion with a male Costa's, where the color of the gorget also goes up over the top of the crown. But the color in the Costa's is purple, not red, and the gorget extends down the sides of the throat in long "whiskers". The gorget on an Anna's also extends somewhat down the sides of the throat, but not as long as in Costa's.

A slight complication is that the rose-red gorget of the Anna's may show flashes of purple in certain lights, but the dominant color will be red. All of these gorgeous red and purple colors will just appear black most of the time. It is only when the sun is just right, that the colors appear.

The nuptial flight of the male is spectacular. The female sits quietly in a bush, while the male flies upward until he is almost out of sight. Then he dives downward at tremendous speed, and curves into an arc close to the ground, uttering an explosive *CHIP!* at the lowest point. He terminates his arc close to the location of the female, hovers for a few seconds, and gives his "song." Then he rises once more to a great height, and repeats the performance.

It has been said by some that the Anna's Hummingbird is the only one, out of the seven species of hummers that enter our area, that can be said to possess a song. However, the high-pitched whistled notes of the Costa's Hummingbird are somewhat similar to the song of the Anna's, but are not delivered as often, nor are they as sustained. It should be added that the "song" of the Anna's might not be recognized as such by many, because it is a high, squeaky performance that sounds more like the filing of a saw than anything else.

Cases have been reported in which hummingbirds will fly right up in front of a person's face and hover there, as if selecting which eye to attack. I've not come across a case where an attack actually took place, although I had a remarkable experience with a hummingbird in the large walk-in aviary at the Arizona-Sonora Desert Museum, near Tucson. A female hummingbird flew up in front of my face and hovered there, with her bill pointing first at one eye and then the other. But instead of attacking, she approached my chest, where my binoculars were hanging, and carefully settled down into one of the eyecups, as if it were a nest. She stayed there for a long time, apparently testing the fit. While I was wondering what to do next, she decided it would not do the job, and departed.

## Costa's Hummingbird (COHU)
*Calypte costae*

|  | J F M A M J J A S O N D |
|---|---|
| West | - - - - - - - - - - - - - - - - - |
| East | Vagrant |

By all rights, this bird shouldn't be in our area at all, because it is looked upon as a resident of the desert southwest. But it has been recorded on both sides of the Cascades in our area. There have been a number of records in winter and spring, and at least one in summer, most of them at feeders. There was even a nesting attempt near Brookings, on the coast, although the attempt failed.

Here is another case in which the adult male should not be confused with anything else, assuming you get a good look in good light. (Note slight possibility of confusion with a male Anna's, mentioned in the account for that species.) The gorget is purple (Anna's is rose-red), and the color goes up over the top of the head, as it does in Anna's. The gorget extends down the sides of the throat in long streamers, much further than the gorget on an Anna's.

## Calliope Hummingbird (CAHU)
*Stellula calliope*

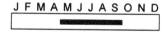

J F M A M J J A S O N D

This is the smallest bird in the U.S., but is not the smallest in the entire world. That honor goes to the Bee Hummingbird of Cuba, which is one-quarter of an inch shorter.

But where did the name come from? The *Stellula* of the scientific name works fine; it means "little star," and applies to the colorful streamers of the gorget. But the "calliope" part is mysterious. None of my sources seems to be sure of what the person who bestowed the name had in mind. Did he mean Calliope, the Greek muse of epic poetry? It doesn't seem likely. One source suggested that he simply meant pleasant, or beautiful of voice. Hummingbirds aren't exactly noted for the beauty of their singing, so that doesn't seem to work either. Or did he mean the kind of calliope that is a sort of steam-driven organ? That seems even less likely. We are left with a mystery. Maybe we shouldn't even care. It's a lovely name for a lovely little bird.

Superficially, the male Calliope resembles the male Costa's in that it has a purple gorget. However, unlike the Costa's, the purple does not extend to the top of the head. Also, the purple is distributed down the throat in long streamers, which some have referred to as a "peppermint candy effect." There is a white line below the eye, that extends all the way from the gape to the neck.

The nuptial display consists of a set of "U" curves somewhat like those of the Black-chinned. The male dives from a point as high as 60 feet above the female, who sits on a bush. He shoots down on a "U"-shaped path, barely missing the female, and then ascends to an equal height at the other end of the "U." As he passes the female he utters a short little sound -- *bzzt* -- described as like a bee being held down.

The birds arrive from their Mexico wintering grounds in the latter half of April, and the males, at least, are gone by the first part of July. The females and immatures are gone by September. While they are here, they principally inhabit the middle elevations of the Cascades and the Siskiyous, where they seek out areas with flowers. As the season progresses, they follow the flowers to the higher elevations.

It is very difficult to confirm nesting, but they are classified as "probable" breeders many places in southern Oregon, and as "confirmed" in a couple of locations. Major Bendire, writing in 1895, said that Calliope Hummingbirds at Fort Klamath at that time outnumbered the Rufous Hummingbirds three to one. In fact, the first documented record of breeding in Oregon was made by Bendire, near Fort Klamath.

**Broad-tailed Hummingbird** (BTLH)
*Selasphorus platycercus*

| | J F M A M J J A S O N D |
|---|---|
| West | ----------- |
| East | Vagrant |

This is the hummingbird of the Rocky Mountains, and it occasionally strays to our area. There are records on both sides of the crest, usually of birds seen at feeders. The Breeding Bird Atlas program confirmed a couple of nesting locations in eastern Oregon, close to the Idaho boundary. A scattering of locations in the state were designated as "possible," including one in the Rogue Valley.

At first glance, a male Broad-tailed might be taken for an Anna's, except that the male Anna's has red on top of the head, which the Broad-tailed lacks. Be aware, though, that an immature male Anna's may have some red on the throat but not yet have red on the head, until it develops its full mature adult plumage.

Another helpful mark is that the male Broad-tailed has white underparts and green sides. The most helpful sign, though, will be the loud trilling noise made by the wings of the male Broad-tailed as it flies. The sound has been described as "like a cicada," and it is much louder than the buzzing sound made by other hummingbirds.

**Rufous Hummingbird** (RUHU)
*Selasphorus rufus*

|  | J F M A M J J A S O N D |
|---|---|
| West | ▬▬▬▬▬ |
| East | ▬▬▬ |

**Allen's Hummingbird** (ALHU)      Vagrant
*Selasphorus sasin*

These two hummers are among our most attractive. The males of both species are green and rufous, and have brilliant gorgets that shine like burnished gold when the light is right. Sadly, there is a lot of uncertainty in the separation of these two, even with the males. With the females, it is generally agreed that it is impossible to distinguish between them in the field.

Allen's Hummingbird is a species that usually is not found very far from the coast, although there are occasional strays. Rufous Hummingbird breeds mostly inland, but also breeds on the coast. In our area, an Allen's is considered a real rarity, and great care needs to be taken in identification.

The problem lies in the amount of rufous on the back. If the *back and rump* are entirely rufous, it is clearly a male Rufous Hummingbird. If the *back* is all green, it is probably a male Allen's Hummingbird. But the tail on an Allen's is rufous, and the rufous color sometimes extends upward onto the rump, so the back may be partially green and partially rufous. In Rufous Hummingbirds, some individuals may have the same pattern.

To be sure of the identification, with a part-rufous and part-green hummingbird, you have to look at the tail feathers, which you probably can't do in the field. In the Rufous, the second tail feather out from the center will be more or less notched; in the Allen's, there is no notch. Also, in the Rufous, the outermost tail feathers will be broader than in the Allen's. This is not likely to be helpful to the average birder, so it will probably be necessary to pass on individuals with mixed rufous/green backs, with the notation *Selasphorus* sp?

Rufous Hummingbirds arrive in our area in March or April, the males before the females. They are common in both the Cascades and the Siskiyous in open forests and meadows, depending upon the availability of flowers, although breeding may not commence there until June. The males, after breeding, may follow the flowers up to timberline, and then begin to migrate southward along the mountains. By August, they are mostly gone south. The females and immatures remain longer, but are essentially gone by September.

Allen's have only been seen a few times in our area where the identity was unquestioned, and then only in the extreme western part of the region. There have been a few netted and banded right on the border of Josephine County and

Curry County, at Bear Camp. One was banded at Horse Creek Meadow, and there have been a couple of sight identifications of birds that were entirely green-backed, one near Cave Junction, and the other near Grants Pass.

Rufous Hummingbirds mostly prefer red flowers, such as paintbrush, columbine, and penstemon, but will also go after the white flowers of the madrone. It has been observed that they will investigate almost anything red, such as an empty salmon can, or a red handkerchief. I had one come up and investigate every wrinkle on the red shirt I was wearing, as I sat on a high ridge in British Columbia.

Arthur Cleveland Bent says:

> All observers seem to agree that jealous courage and pugnacity are among the chief attributes of the rufous hummingbird; it seems to be the dominant species in the vicinity of its nest and about its feeding places, driving away, not only other hummingbirds, but other species of larger birds and animals; it seems to love to fight and often appears to provoke a quarrel unnecessarily.

## Family **ALCEDINIDAE**: Kingfishers

### Belted Kingfisher (BEKI)
*Ceryle alcyon*

Almost everybody recognizes a kingfisher, and most people also recognize the call, a loud rattling noise made as the bird flies from one place to another. One thing that helps in kingfisher-watching, is that they make a regular practice of sitting on exposed branches or rocks, where they can be readily seen.

The huge head, large bill, and shaggy crest are parts of what marks a kingfisher so recognizable. What is not so easily recognizable, however, is how to tell a male from a female. Here is one of those cases where the female is more ornately decorated than the male. She is the one with the extra band across the chest -- the rufous one. She also has some rufous on the flanks. The male has no rufous, and the single band across the chest is blue.

They are year-round residents in our area, and can be found wherever there is any fishable water. They dive, either from a perch or from the air for their prey, which principally consists of fish. Sometimes they

**Belted Kingfisher**

disappear under water in the process. Once obtained, the bird takes its prize to a perch and beats it into insensibility, tosses it into the air, and swallows it head

171

first. Arthur Cleveland Bent reports a case where a fish was too large to swallow all at once. The tail was left protruding from the mouth until the process of digestion permitted the bird to work it down. When fish are not available, as during a drought, the birds may turn to lizards, frogs, small snakes, grasshoppers, young birds, mice, and even to berries if things get really tough.

The nest is placed in a burrow anywhere from 3 to 15 feet long. The burrow is constructed in a soft earthen bank by both parents, working alternately, using their powerful beaks to loosen the earth, and their feet to kick it out the opening. The burrow may be 3 by 4 inches in cross section, and terminate in a small room 6 or 7 inches in height, and 12 inches in diameter. The young are almost helpless at first, but have enough agility to wrap themselves around each other in a tight ball, as a stratagem to keep warm.

Once the young birds leave the nest, the parent has to teach them how to fish. This she does by catching a fish, beating it into insensibility, and then dropping it into the water where the young can see it. Eventually, one of them, presumably the hungriest, makes a dive for it, at first missing the mark as often as hitting it. The parent bird keeps this up, perhaps relenting enough to feed them a bit, but finally refusing to feed them the fish directly, and forcing them to dive for it on their own. In a week or so, they are proficient enough to catch their own live fish.

## Family **PICIDAE**: Woodpeckers and Allies

Most of the woodpecker species share certain common traits. For example, all of them have stiff tail feathers that they use to support themselves against tree trunks. All have stout bills that they use to make their nesting holes, or to pry off pieces of bark. Almost all (the Lewis's Woodpecker is a notable exception) have a flight behavior that consists of several wingbeats followed by a swooping glide with wings folded, then again several wingbeats, and a glide.

Woodpeckers move up a tree in a more or less vertical posture -- head up, tail down. They don't run in all directions like nuthatches do, who will often have their heads pointed downward, although a woodpecker may move onto the lower side of a branch with its back to the ground. They have what are called *zygodactylous* feet, with two toes forward and two backward. (The "perching birds," or *Passerines,* have three toes forward and one backward.) Exceptions to the "four toes" rule are the Black-backed Woodpecker and Three-toed Woodpecker, both of which are missing one of the rear toes.

Sapsuckers are part of the woodpecker family, and they literally eat sap. They bore small holes in the barks of trees to stimulate sap flow, and then lap it up. Subsequently, other woodpeckers may come and take advantage of this food source, and so do hummingbirds.

Sometimes a "sapsucker tree" may look like it is completely girdled with holes, raising concerns about the welfare of the tree. Individual branches on trees have been killed by sapsuckers, and even perhaps an occasional tree. However, because sapsuckers will pick out a particular tree for their attentions, filling that one tree full of holes and ignoring others, the damage is limited. Many trees full of holes seem to survive, although they may look disfigured.

Woodpeckers excavate holes in trees for their nests, some of them choosing dead trees and stubs, and others preferring live trees. They also use such holes for roosting at night. Other hole-nesting species, who are incapable of making their own holes, will often use abandoned woodpecker holes for nesting purposes.

A special characteristic of woodpeckers is their drumming, using a dead tree, a utility pole, or even a metal surface for the purpose. Both males and females drum, and the purpose of the drumming seems to be one of communication, perhaps to establish a pair bond, or as a defense of territory.

## Lewis's Woodpecker (LEWO)
*Melanerpes lewis*

Lewis's Woodpeckers sometimes act as if they don't want to be woodpeckers, but would rather be flycatchers. Much of their food consists of insects, which they capture by flying out from a perch and returning to it, just like a flycatcher. Observers have noted that a Lewis's can spot a flying insect 100 feet away, fly straight to it and capture it without fail, and fly directly back to the original perch. Often one will take up its post in the very top of a tree, to facilitate its fly catching.

In the fall, after insect season declines, they eat other things such as fruit, and have been accused of doing major damage in fruit orchards. In winter, they rely mostly on acorns, and share the trait with their cousins, the Acorn Woodpeckers, of storing acorn meats. However, instead of storing complete acorns in round holes, the way Acorns do, they strip off the outer shells, break the acorns into pieces, and store the pieces in bark crevices for future use.

They don't fly with the usual flap-flap-flap and wing-closed swoop of most woodpeckers. Instead, they fly in a crow-like manner, and are often mistaken for crows. From a distance they look all black, which further causes them to be taken for crows.

Up close, however, a Lewis's Woodpecker is seen as a beautiful bird. The back is a metallic greenish-black, there is a silvery gray collar around the neck, some suffused red on the face, and a lovely rose-red belly.

Finding a Lewis's Woodpecker can sometimes be an exercise in frustration. First, they are on a declining population trend in Oregon; second, they are notorious wanderers in winter, in pursuit of a suitable food supply. One winter they will seem to be everywhere, and the next year there may be none. The Medford area is one of the more reliable spots. I examined the Christmas Count records from 1994 to 2000, and the Medford count had them every year, ranging in numbers from 10 to 121.

In two of those years, Medford had the highest winter count of Lewis's Woodpeckers in the nation. In the years when Medford wasn't the highest, then either the Etna count (southeast of Yreka about 25 miles) or the Lyle count (in Washington, on the Columbia River between Hood River and The Dalles) had the highest.

For nesting, Lewis's Woodpeckers prefer either open ponderosa pine forests, or cottonwood groves along streams. Probably the most likely place to find nesting Lewis's in our area is in the Klamath River canyon, in the stretch from Iron Gate Reservoir down to Horse Creek. In the mating season, they utter a harsh *churrr,* but during the rest of year are rather silent.

## Acorn Woodpecker (ACWO)
*Melanerpes formicivorus*

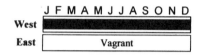

| | J F M A M J J A S O N D |
|---|---|
| West | ■■■■■■■■■■■■ |
| East | Vagrant |

Like its close relative, the Lewis's Woodpecker, this bird often acts like a flycatcher. Much of its food in summer is obtained by flycatcher behavior -- flying out from a perch to catch an insect and then returning. It also shares the Lewis's attraction to acorns, although the Acorn Woodpecker stores its acorns by drilling holes in trees (or telephone poles) into which the acorns fit tightly.

**Acorn Woodpecker**

Each acorn is inserted into its own hole, and is fitted so tightly it cannot be removed without destroying it. As the acorns age, they shrink, and acorns may be moved several times to better-fitting holes. A tree was once found in which it is was estimated that 50,000 acorns were embedded.

Such a tree is referred to as a "granary tree," because the birds depend upon them in winter for most of their food. (A notable example of such a tree is a large ponderosa pine located at the eastern end of the picnic area at Touvelle State Park, on the Rogue River.) At one time it was thought that the woodpeckers were mostly interested in whatever grubs the acorns might contain, but research has shown it is truly the acorn meat they are after.

Acorn Woodpeckers obviously are hard workers, and their energy may sometimes work against them. In one case, some Acorns were attempting to store their acorns in a tree that happened to be hollow. As they pounded their acorns into their holes, the nuts pushed through and fell into the hollow interior. Later, the hollow tree was found to be filled with acorns to a depth of almost 20 feet.

Acorn Woodpeckers live in tightly knit social groups, organized around granary trees. A group is made up mostly of family members, and may have up to 15 birds. All group members help to drill holes and store acorns, and they join together in incubating, brooding, and feeding the young. Apparently, it is not clear whether communal mating also takes place.

"Immigration" into the groups does occur, but things are not easy for the immigrant. Each group has a clearly defined territory, and if a prospective immigrant crosses the boundary it is chased away, or even physically attacked. However, if the immigrant is persistent, the chasing may gradually diminish, and the immigrant be allowed to join the group.

Acorn Woodpeckers are common west of the Cascades, wherever there are oaks. It is easy to know when they are around, because they are so noisy. Their loud *ya-cob! ya-cob! ya-cob!* is one of the most familiar of bird calls. Their plumage is also unmistakable, consisting of a gaudy red, white, and black pattern on the head that makes them look like clowns. When they fly, they show conspicuous white spots on the wings and rump.

Did you know you can tell male from female by the pattern on the head? Here's another case in which the female patterning is more elaborate than the male's, because she has *three* colors on the top of her head, instead of the two colors of the male. Both have red and white on the head, but in the female there is a black strip across the crown that separates the white from the red.

Joseph Grinnell and Tracy Storer, two of the grand old western naturalists, had this to say of the instinct of Acorn Woodpeckers to remain vertical:

> When alighting on a tree trunk, these birds assume a vertical posture, head out, tail appressed to the bark. They move up by a hitching process -- head in, tail out; up; tail in, head out. If a bird perches on a small horizontal branch, his position is more likely to be diagonal than directly crosswise. If a bird alights on the square top of a fence post, he seems ill at ease and soon backs over the edge into a more woodpecker-like posture.

## Williamson's Sapsucker (WISA)
*Sphyrapicus thyroideus*

One of the interesting things about this species is that the male and female look so different from each other. The male is mostly black, with white stripes on the head, a red chin, a bright yellow belly, and a conspicuous white longitudinal stripe on the wing. The female, on the other hand, looks sort of like a watered-down flicker, except that she, too, may have some yellow on the belly. The female was discovered by science first, and given a scientific name. Later, the male was discovered (on the shore of Upper Klamath Lake, by the way) and was given a different scientific name. All this had to be sorted out later, of course, but it took 15 years to discover the mistake.

These birds are summer residents in the higher elevations on the east side of the Cascades, and possibly in the Siskiyous, in a variety of coniferous forests with fairly open canopy. They make their nesting holes in trees that are soft and rotten internally, but which generally have live exteriors. In such a tree they may make multiple holes; one tree was found with 38 woodpecker holes in it. In winter, apparently some of them move to more southern locations, while others remain, perhaps moving down slope.

They are shy and retiring, and often hard to spot. However, when alarmed they give a loud cry, very much like that of a Red-shouldered Hawk -- *kree-e-e!*

*kree-e-e! kree-e-e!* The very first time I heard this call I was convinced I was hearing a hawk, perhaps a goshawk, and wondered what a goshawk and a sapsucker were doing in the same tree. It wasn't until later, when I saw a sapsucker in the act of giving the call that I realized how badly I had been misled.

In true sapsucker style, they eat the sap of trees, and also eat the inner layers of bark. For this they apparently prefer lodgepole pines, but also eat the sap of red and white firs, Jeffrey pines, and aspens. In addition, they eat insects, especially ants. In an examination of the stomachs of 17 birds, 86 percent was found to be ants, and the rest was from the cambium layers of trees.

## Red-naped Sapsucker (RNSA)
*Sphyrapicus nuchalis*

| | J F M A M J J A S O N D |
|---|---|
| West | ‐‐‐‐‐‐‐‐‐‐‐‐‐‐‐‐‐‐‐‐‐‐‐ |
| East | ‐ ‐ ‐ ‐ ‐ ——————————— ‐ ‐ ‐ ‐ |

Red-naped Sapsuckers are principally birds of the Rocky Mountains, but are found in Oregon, primarily east of the crest. They closely resemble the birds with which they once were lumped -- Yellow-bellied Sapsuckers. Yellow-bellieds, even though they are eastern birds, do occasionally occur in Oregon. In fact, one was photographed at Gilchrist, in Klamath County, in 1983. Since Gilchrist lies along the Little Deschutes River, and is technically not within the scope of the Klamath Basin, Yellow-bellied Sapsucker has not been included as a separate species for this book. Nevertheless, one could show up, so identifications should be approached with care.

There is enough plumage variation in these two species, plus the possibility of hybrids, that some individuals might not be classifiable. The thing to do is to look for several i.d. marks. The red spot on the nape is obviously a mark to look for, but should not be used as the sole basis for identification because there are exceptions, as often seems to be the case in the bird world. Some Yellow-bellieds, which are not supposed to have the red spot, might have it anyway, and some Red-napeds might not, even though they are supposed to. Both males and females of both species have red on the top of the head, so that doesn't help. Also, either species could have some yellow on the belly, so that doesn't help, either.

The best thing to look for is the pattern on the cheek, chin and throat. The female Yellow-bellied is white on the chin and throat, whereas the female Red-naped has a white chin and a red throat. The males of both species have red chins and throats, but in the Yellow-bellied, the red is completely enclosed by a black border which separates the red from the white stripe on the cheek. In the Red-naped, the black border is incomplete, so that the red bleeds through into the white stripe.

Got all that committed to memory? I do at the moment, because I am writing about it. But the next time I go into the field, I probably will have forgotten which is which, and have to look it up.

# Red-breasted Sapsucker (RBSA)
*Sphyrapicus ruber*

This bird has so much red on the head that many people want to call it "Red-headed Woodpecker." Of course the Red-headed is the best-known woodpecker in the country, but it is an eastern bird, and looks strikingly different from this one. Sometimes eastern birds of various species turn up in Oregon, but there are no records of Red-headed Woodpecker on the "Accepted" list of the OBRC for the state.

The Red-breasted Sapsucker is our "workaday" sapsucker -- the one we are likely to see most frequently. Since we usually see them from the back, we are likely to notice the red on the head more than on the breast, although the red extends far enough down the breast to justify its name. They are summer breeders in the Coast Range and Cascades, but only breed in scattered locations in eastern Oregon. West of the crest, they inhabit mixed forests of deciduous and coniferous trees. East of the crest, they often are found in aspen-ponderosa forests. In the winter, most appear to migrate downslope to lower elevations, although some move south out of the state.

During the Breeding Bird Atlas project, many hybrid sapsuckers were found, especially in the southern and eastern part of the Cascades, along the border of Klamath and Lake counties. Most of these appeared to be Red-breasted/Red-naped hybrids.

Over the decades, those who classify birds apparently had trouble making up their minds about the Red-breasted Sapsucker and two of its close relatives -- the Red-naped Sapsucker and the Yellow-bellied Sapsucker. Prior to 1931 they were considered three species. Then, from 1931 to 1983, they were lumped into one, with the name Yellow-bellied Sapsucker. Now they are three species again.

Their nests are placed in whatever trees are locally abundant, including aspens, cottonwoods, firs, and others. For food, 67 species of trees have been known to be tapped, including orchard fruit trees, although some observers have noted a preference for willows. They not only collect sap from the holes they make, but also capture insects that come for the sap. In some cases, the diet of the birds has been found to be more than half of insects, mainly ants.

Red-breasteds tend to be very quiet birds -- not nearly as vocal as some other woodpeckers. Often, one will advertise its presence by a very quiet tapping noise, and then you may discover it's a lot closer than you thought.

In 1895, Major Bendire wrote eloquently as follows, presumably discussing Red-breasted Sapsuckers, but in the process sounding very much like a chamber of commerce brochure for Fort Klamath:

> Fort Klamath, . . . although but 4,200 feet above sea level, has a very cool summer climate, frosts occurring in almost every month in the year. The surrounding country is very beautiful at that time. Heavy, open forests of stately pines and firs, among these the graceful and beautiful sugar pine, are found on the mountain sides and reaching well down into the green, park-like

valleys. Interspersed here and there are aspen groves of various extent, their silvery trunks and light-green foliage blending artistically with the somber green of the pines. These aspen groves are the summer home of the Red-breasted Sapsucker.

## Nuttall's Woodpecker (NUWO)             Accidental
*Picoides nuttallii*

Nuttall's Woodpeckers are common less than a hundred miles below the border with California, but there are only four records for Oregon. The first one was collected in the Umpqua River Valley in 1855. The next two, a male and a female, were collected near Ashland in 1881. The fourth one was found dead near Trail, in 1991. The first specimen is in the U.S. National Museum, the next two are in the British Museum, and the last one is in the museum at Southern Oregon University. One could argue that, if you are a Nuttall's Woodpecker, and yearn to be in a museum collection, the thing to do is cross the border into Oregon.

Nuttall's is one of the "ladder-backed" woodpeckers, meaning that it has conspicuous black and white barring on the back. It is difficult to separate from the species that actually has the name, Ladder-backed Woodpecker. However, the Ladder-backed is a sedentary species of the southwestern desert, and as far as I know has never come within 500 miles of Oregon. And the Nuttall's has given us exactly one bird in the last 120 years, so we won't attempt to go into the tricky i.d. marks that separate them.

## Downy Woodpecker (DOWO)
*Picoides pubescens*

## Hairy Woodpecker (HAWO)
*Picoides villosus*

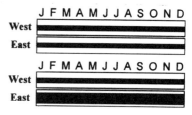

Here are two more look-alikes. True, the Hairy is much bigger than the Downy, but that may not be of much help when you see a woodpecker by itself, which usually is the case. The names "Downy" and "Hairy" presumably refer to the downy plumage of one and the rough plumage of the other, but these differences have not been apparent to me in the field.

In both species, the male has a red spot on the nape, but the female doesn't. Both species have conspicuous white stripes down their backs. The only other woodpecker that comes even close to having a white stripe down the back is the Three-toed Woodpecker, and its stripe has barring across it, unlike the Downy or the Hairy. The stripe on the back of the Hairy, which is white in birds of the interior, becomes washed with brown as one gets closer to the coast.

Juvenile Hairies of both sexes have an unusual characteristic, because they may have red, orange, or even yellow crowns, up to the time of their first fall after hatching. If the crown is yellow, this sometimes causes them to be mistakenly identified as Three-toed Woodpeckers.

Field guides sometimes emphasize that Downies have dark bars on their outer tail feathers and Hairies don't. Unfortunately, sometimes Downies don't have the bars, and in the Northwest, some Hairies might. It is better to use overall size, bill size and shape, and the call.

Hairies are almost 40 percent longer than Downies, and more than twice as heavy. The bill on a Downy looks tiny and delicate, and on a Hairy looks huge and formidable. The call of a Downy is a low, flat *pik;* the Hairy gives a much sharper, louder *peek!* Downies also give a whinnying sound like a small horse. Hairies have a "rattle call" that sounds like a lot of the *peek!* calls in rapid succession, sometimes written as *peekikikikikik!.*

Foraging behavior also might be helpful, but should be used as a hint, not as a definitive mark. Downies are often found softly tapping on small twigs, and sometimes even on weed stalks. Hairies generally won't stoop to such behavior, perhaps because their weight is too great. They usually are found on the main trunks of trees or on their larger branches. Hairies are much shier than Downies, and are quicker to fly off when a birder appears.

Both species are full-time residents throughout Oregon. Hairies tend to prefer higher elevations, but are found to some extent in valleys. Downies prefer lower elevations, especially riparian habitats. Both species may build roosting holes in addition to nesting cavities, for sleeping at night. One nesting hole for a Downy was in a dead tree limb 5 inches in diameter. The Downy made a hole that was just large enough to get into, leaving only a shell in the tree limb. The hole faced downward so water couldn't enter.

Woodpeckers, like all wild creatures, have many enemies, but some of the enemies might be different than anticipated. Often, these enemies are other birds that want to appropriate the woodpeckers' nesting holes, but are incapable of making their own. Starlings are well known for this kind of behavior, and often drive the woodpeckers from their holes and destroy their eggs. A somewhat less obvious enemy is the House Sparrow. One was once observed systematically carrying newly hatched woodpeckers from their hole and dropping them in a nearby stream to drown. And a most unlikely enemy was a tree squirrel, which was observed sitting near a woodpecker hole, eating a naked baby bird. Such are the day to day realities of the bird world.

## White-headed Woodpecker (WHWO)
*Picoides albolarvatus*

The White-headed Woodpecker is truly a westerner, and many eastern birders have it high on their wish lists when they come to the Pacific Coast. Both males and females have white heads, but their bodies otherwise are black, except for white spots in the wings. The male has a red spot on the back of the head, but the female's head is almost entirely white.

They are uncommon permanent residents on the east side of the Cascades, usually in ponderosa pine forests or in forests dominated by ponderosas. They prefer relatively open forests with large diameter trees. Even logged areas are okay, provided some large ponderosas are present. In the Siskiyous, southwest of Ashland, there is a small population in true fir forest. They can sometimes be located by their "rattle call" that sounds very much like a Hairy Woodpecker, consisting of *pik!* calls in rapid succession, sometimes written *pikikikikikik!*

For half or more of their food, they rely on seeds of the ponderosa pine, although they also consume a lot of insect grubs. They often get at their prey by prying off layers of bark, thus exposing the grubs, rather than by hammering. They also search the crevices in the bark of a tree for insects and their eggs, starting at the bottom of a tree and working up toward the top, before repeating the process on another tree.

For nesting, they prefer the dead standing stumps of pine trees. The tree must have been dead long enough for the pitch to have hardened so that the outer shell is firm, whereas the interior must have been softened by decay. Apparently, to find the proper conditions, they must make many tests, leaving behind them numerous unfinished holes. One stub that was found had 5 finished holes in it, but also had 11 unfinished ones.

I once sat near a dead tree to have my lunch, and intermittently could hear a woodpecker tapping away somewhere. But I couldn't see it, no matter how much I tried. I then noticed that the nearby dead tree had a woodpecker-sized hole in it, and that the tapping seemed to be coming from that direction. At last it dawned on me that the tapping was coming from *inside* the dead tree, and after a bit, sure enough, a White-headed Woodpecker flew out of the hole.

## Black-backed Woodpecker (BBWO)
*Picoides arcticus*

## Three-toed Woodpecker (TTWO)
*Picoides tridactylus*

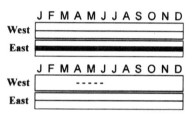

Both of these woodpeckers have three toes, and, once upon a time, the Black-backed was called the "Black-backed Three-toed Woodpecker." Bent called it "Arctic Three-toed Woodpecker," and its scientific name certainly implies it is a resident of the Arctic. However, its range, though a northerly one, barely reaches the Arctic. The range of its close relative, the Three-toed Woodpecker, actually extends further north than does the range of the Black-backed.

The Three-toed Woodpecker was once called the "Northern Three-toed Woodpecker, which certainly recognizes its northerly range. It does not have a completely black back like its close relative. There is a long whitish stripe down the middle of the back, somewhat reminiscent of a Hairy Woodpecker, except that in the Three-toed, the white stripe has black barring across it. (In the Rocky Mountains, most of the black barring in the white back stripe is missing, increasing the resemblance to a Hairy Woodpecker.)

The males of both species have yellow crowns, which sets them off from other woodpeckers. Both sexes in both species have barred flanks. Both species seem to prefer lodgepole pine forests, and especially forests that have been recently burned, or those with heavy bark beetle infestations.

Both species engage in loud drumming in the breeding season. Both have a *peek!* call, somewhat similar to that of a Hairy Woodpecker, and both give a descending rattle call -- *peekikikikik!*.

Black-backed is uncommon on both sides of the crest, and on the west side is primarily found near the summit. Its center of abundance in Oregon is believed to be in the lodgepole pine forests on the east side of the Cascades between Bend and Klamath Falls, and in the mountains around Fort Klamath. Three-toed is harder to find than Black-backed. Reports of Three-toed in our region are scarce, principally centered in the high-elevation lodgepole forests around Crater Lake and Mount McLoughlin.

Both live principally on the larvae of wood-boring beetles, and find their food most abundant in areas with trees that have recently (3 to 5 years) been killed by fire and have the bark peeling off. They usually work by using glancing blows that cause pieces of bark to peel off, exposing the grubs. It has been noted that, when foraging, a bird may lay its head against the tree as if listening for the presence of grubs.

Nests are usually placed in dead trees. However, one observer reported on a case of a nest in a live tree, where a bear had attempted to get at the nestlings. The noise made by the nestlings had apparently attracted the bear, and it had bitten off pieces of the tree around the hole to an inch deep, but had finally given up. If the nest had been in a dead tree, things might have been different.

## Northern Flicker
*Colaptes auratus*

### "Red-shafted Flicker" (RSFL)

### "Yellow-shafted Flicker" (YSFL)

The Northern Flicker is one of our commonest birds, and one of the most broadly known. It is an intriguing bird, partly because of its behavior, and partly because of its tangled nomenclature history.

The first thing to know about flickers is that they are prodigious hole-makers. Sometimes the holes are for nests, but sometimes they are just for roosting. Many other hole-nesting creatures use old flicker holes and in fact depend upon the existence of such holes, but people become irate when the holes are drilled into their houses. Arthur Cleveland Bent quotes from one of his contributors, concerning this trait:

> When once a house has been selected it seems that nothing short of death will cause them to cease their drilling operations until one, and in some cases three or four, holes been cut through the outer wall of the building. Whether these holes, which are generally made in the winter, are excavated for roosting

places or simply through a sort of nervous energy seems a matter of doubt; but certain it is that the birds spend much time in them as soon as they succeed in completing their work.

As an example of how persistent a flicker can be, Bent cites a case in which an observer saw a flicker attack a wooden casing that surrounded a large iron pipe. The space between the wooden casing and the pipe was filled with sawdust to protect the pipe from freezing. The flicker drilled through the wood, and then began digging out the sawdust, which caved in from above as soon as any was removed. A month after seeing the flicker at work, the observer returned to see what had happened in his absence. He discovered about a bushel of sawdust on the ground, and the flicker was busily going in and out of the hole it had made, taking food to its young.

Most people recognize flickers when they see them. The brown-barred back and black crescent across the breast make them unmistakable. Our western subspecies has pink-orange underwings, and once was considered a separate species, the "Red-shafted Flicker." When a flicker flies away from you, it flashes a lovely identification mark -- a conspicuous white rump.

Often, you will know a flicker is around because of its loud, explosive, *KEER!* You may also hear its long *wik wik wik wik wik* call, or "song," delivered principally in breeding season, but also at other times of the year. This call can be difficult to separate from a similar call of the Pileated Woodpecker. Both sound much alike, but the Pileated's is louder and has a "reedy" quality to it. Also, the flicker's call tends to remain at one pitch through most of the call, whereas the Pileated's often tends to rise and fall.

Flickers do much of their foraging on the ground, more like a robin than a proper woodpecker. The bulk of their food consists of insects, mostly ants. However, perhaps 25 percent consists of fruits and seeds.

Now, about the nomenclature history. There are two principal groups, each group containing several subspecies. These "groups" were once considered to be separate species. These are our western bird, the "Red-shafted Flicker," and the eastern one, the "Yellow-shafted Flicker." In the region where the two meet, there is extensive interbreeding, producing all sorts of hybrids. As a result, the AOU some time ago combined the two into one species.

But why the choice of the name "Northern" Flicker? Is there a southern one? Well, it turns out there are lots of southern ones, depending upon where you look. Arthur Cleveland Bent described no less than nine flickers. In the fashion of the day, each one of these had a separate name, even though there were three species involved, and a bunch of subspecies. One of the names he used was "Red-shafted Flicker," but nowhere to be found, in Bent's list, was a "Yellow-shafted Flicker."

Instead, Bent divided the "Yellow-shafted Flicker" into "Northern Flicker," and "Southern Flicker." Obviously, he considered the "Northern Flicker," which was found in the more northerly states in the east, to be the important one, because he gave far more pages to it than to any other. My guess is, that when it came time for the AOU to pick a name for the lumped species, combining "Red-shafted" and "Yellow-shafted," they chose the name with the widest usage, which was "Northern Flicker." For whatever it's worth, there are some "southern" flickers in Mexico and Cuba that might (or might not) be separate species from the Northern Flicker.

Flicker hybrids cause lots of problems, and we occasionally get them on the Pacific Coast. Three of the key features to look for are underwing color, malar stripe, and the crescent on the nape. In the western "Red-shafted," the underwing color is reddish, the malar stripe on the male (females have no malar stripe) is red, and *there is no crescent on the nape.* In the eastern "Yellow-shafted," the underwing color is yellow, the malar stripe on the male (none, on the female), is black, and there is a red crescent on the nape in both male and female. Hybrids characteristically show mixtures of these features.

Bird banders keep track of Red-shafted and Yellow-shafted separately, and use codes as follows: RSFL for "Red-shafted Flicker," and YSFL for "Yellow-shafted Flicker." Also, during Christmas Counts, the participants keep track of the two groups separately.

## Pileated Woodpecker (PIWO)
*Dryocopus pileatus*

J F M A M J J A S O N D

First, as to pronunciation: My encyclopedia says it's pronounced either PIE-lee-ayted, or PILL-ee-ayted, so I guess you can pronounce it any way you want. I do note, however, that the scientific name is supposed to be pronounced pie-lee-AY-tus, so I've been trying to train my tongue to say PIE. However, PILL-ee-ayted sometimes slips out anyway.

Most people recognize this bird immediately, partly because of its size, about like a crow, and partly because of its spectacular red crest, which both sexes have. It is an uncommon permanent resident of mixed conifer forests in the Cascades and Siskiyous. It prefers older forests, because that is where large diameter trees, needed for nesting holes, are to be found. That's also where dead and decaying trees are located, with insects in them.

The Pileated Woodpecker is an elusive bird, difficult to locate even after you have more or less pinned one down by its call or its hammering. The call consists of a rapid series of *wik wik wik wik wik* notes, very much like a flicker. (See Northern Flicker account.) It is heard often in the forest, especially in spring, while the bird itself remains unseen. Many observers have noted how alert and furtive Pileateds are, and how quick one is to move to the opposite side of a tree when you show up.

Pileateds chisel off huge chips as they bore into trees, mostly looking for insects such as carpenter ants. Typically, they make huge rectangular holes in the process, measuring perhaps 6 by 10 inches, and as much as 6 inches deep. Their nesting holes are correspondingly large, with entrance holes 3 or 4 inches in diameter, and the nest hole itself perhaps 20 inches deep. A pair usually will build a new nesting cavity every year, although the cavities are sometimes

183

used again in a following year. At night, they will often utilize unused nesting holes for shelter.

## Family **TYRANNIDAE:** Tyrant Flycatchers

With the flycatchers, we enter the world of the passerines, of the order *Passeriformes.* All of the species from the flycatchers to the end of the AOU list are considered to be passerines. These are the so-called "perching birds," and the term "songbirds" is sometimes applied loosely to all of them, although some people restrict the term "songbird" to the true singers. Note that, by the definition that includes all the passerines, a crow is a "songbird."

The name "tyrant" given to the family refers to the audacious behavior of some of its members. Outstanding among these are the kingbirds, which are known for their willingness to attack larger birds such as crows and hawks, and drive the intruders away from their territories.

Almost all of the flycatchers are neotropical migrants, meaning that they leave the U.S. in winter and migrate to Mexico, South America, or islands in the Caribbean. A few, such as the Vermilion Flycatcher (which occurs in Oregon only as a vagrant), winter along the U.S./Mexico border. Only the three phoebes have all-year ranges that extend to any extent into the U.S.

Flycatchers of the genus *Empidonax* ("empids," for short) are notoriously difficult to identify. It is generally agreed that the most reliable indicator is voice, but this means that the birds must be singing. There are a number of visual characteristics that can be applied to silent birds, but these require experience, and even then it may not be possible to identify every species. Kevin Zimmer, in *Birding in the American West* gives 15 pages to the identification of empids.

### Olive-sided Flycatcher (OSFL)
*Contopus cooperi*

It has been said that Western Wood-Pewees call out *BEER-r-r,* that Alder Flycatchers call out *FREE beer-r-r,* and that Olive-sided Flycatchers call out *Quick! THREE beers!* There are no accepted records of Alder Flycatchers in Oregon, but we get the other two, and *Quick! THREE beers* is certainly a good way to remember the Olive-sided's song.

In Oregon, Olive-sideds have been found to be most abundant in the Cascades, although they are widespread, and have even been found right down to sea level. They prefer evergreen forests, preferably more or less open, with tall trees or snags from which to fly out and snatch insects. Their habit of flying out from a perch to capture something, and then to fly back to the same perch, has been referred to as "yo-yo flight." The "something" that they catch turns out to be bees and wasps more than anything else. Western Wood-Pewees forage in the same manner, and at first glance the two can be confused.

An Olive-sided is chunkier looking than other flycatchers, with a large head and short neck. If you can see them, there are white spots on the flanks, visible in flight. Viewed from the front, there is a whitish line down the middle of the breast, separating the darker sides, looking somewhat like an open vest.

The wonderful thing about Olive-sided Flycatchers is that in spring you can hear their songs everywhere in the high country. They can often be spotted while singing, in the very top of a conifer or on a snag. Apparently, not everyone appreciates them. Arthur Cleveland Bent says, "Its notes are so constantly uttered at times that they become fairly tiresome," and reports on the owner of a mountain resort who asked for someone to shoot an Olive-sided, because it made so much noise it annoyed the guests.

## Western Wood-Pewee (WEWP)
*Contopus sordidulus*

The Western Wood-Pewee is our most common flycatcher. You know that spring has arrived when you start hearing its slightly buzzy, nasal, down-slurred call, *peer-r-r* coming from the forest. Be aware, however, that starlings have learned to produce an almost exact imitation of this call. Also, it has been noted that the call sounds something like a Common Nighthawk, so it's a good idea to look for the bird before making a positive i.d. Usually, the pewee will be found sitting on an exposed branch, periodically doing its "yo-yo" flight to sally out and capture an insect.

The full song of the pewee consists of several syllables, with the downslurred buzzy *peer-r-r* as the last one. Arthur Cleveland Bent put this in his book as *tswee-tee-teet, tswee-tee-teet, bzew,* of which the *bzew* is the one described as a downslurred *peer-r-r*. Bent expressed the view that it seemed to be a melancholy song.

We are not likely to see the eastern counterpart, the Eastern Wood-Pewee, in our area, but there is one record of it at Malheur NWR, so anything is possible. Visually, the two species are identical, but if the bird you are looking at goes *pee-ah-weee?* in a thin whiny voice, falling and then rising at the end, take another look, because that's the song of the Eastern Wood-Pewee.

Pewees have an indistinct eye-ring, which usually looks like no eye-ring at all. This helps to separate them from some of the empids, many of which have conspicuous eye-rings. One empid, though, that can be confused with the Western Wood-Pewee is the Willow Flycatcher. However, Willows usually perch low in brushy habitats, while pewees usually perch high, on exposed perches. Note the word "usually," because there is no law that prevents a bird from temporarily entering another's traditional surroundings.

Western Wood-Pewees occur statewide in open groves of trees, or on forest edges, at all elevations, although they are rare in dense forest. They live almost entirely on insects and spiders, mostly captured by typical flycatching behavior. They often place their nests in rather open locations. I once came across one placed on a horizontal branch squarely over the middle of a gravel road that carried much traffic, only a few feet above the passing cars and trucks.

# Willow Flycatcher (WIFL)
*Empidonax traillii*

Here's another bird with a tangled nomenclature history. Arthur Cleveland Bent called it "Little Flycatcher," although why he chose that name is not clear, since it is one of our larger empids. Later, its name became "Traill's Flycatcher." Even later, "Traill's" was split into two species, Alder Flycatcher and Willow Flycatcher. These two are impossible to separate on the basis of visual marks, and their songs are generally used to identify them.

In the case of the Alder Flycatcher, the main song is harsh and burry and is usually written as *fee-BEE-o*, or as *rreeBEEa*, with the accent on the second syllable. The call note is a flat *pit*. In the Willow Flycatcher, the main song is an explosive, sneezy *FITZ-bew!* with the accent on the first syllable. Unfortunately, the Willow occasionally may give a song that sounds a lot like the Alder, without the sneezy quality of the first syllable. This has given rise to reports of Alder Flycatcher in Oregon, none of which have been accepted by the OBRC.

Willow Flycatchers are associated with shrubby habitats for nesting, especially willows. However, other plants have also been used, such as Himalayan blackberry and bracken fern. In our area, the Oregon Breeding Bird Atlas lists them as "confirmed" breeders in a couple of locations, and as "probable" in many. Breeding is difficult to confirm, because the observations of males apparently feeding young may actually be of males feeding females.

Joseph Grinnell and Tracy Storer say, "[It] adheres closely to the cover of thickets; it must be looked for beneath the level of the willow tops." According to Major Bendire, "They never remain long in one place, but move from perch to perch, snapping up insects as they fly; they are pugnacious, quarrelsome little creatures, making up in courage and determination what they lack in size."

Willow Flycatchers do not have conspicuous eye-rings, which immediately separates them from the other empids in our area, which do have eye-rings. (Note that Western Wood-Pewee, which also does not have an eye-ring, is not an empid, but is a member of the genus *Contopus*.) The call note of the Willow is a liquid *whit,* and is very similar to that given by Dusky and Gray Flycatchers. The habitats of the latter two species, however, are quite different from the preferred habitat of the Willow. Leon Dawson, quoted in Bent, says, "Traill's [Willow] gives an impression of brownness, where the Western [now split into Pacific-slope and Cordilleran] is yellowish green, Hammond's blackish, and Wright's [now Dusky] grayish dusky." Dawson's statements could be helpful, but shouldn't be used as the last word.

Virginia Rail

Northern Saw-whet Owl

Northern Pygmy-Owl (head turned, to show false "eyes")

Great Gray Owl

Western Screech Owl (in box)

Burrowing Owl (by drainage culvert)

**PLATE VII**

**Black-chinned Hummingbird**

**American Dipper**

**Western Kingbird**

**Red-naped Sapsucker**

**Bank Swallow**

**Western Scrub-Jay**

**PLATE VIII**

# Hammond's Flycatcher (HAFL)
*Empidonax hammondii*

# Dusky Flycatcher (DUFL)
*Empidonax oberholseri*

# Least Flycatcher (LEFL)
*Empidonax minimus*

Vagrant

Hammond's and Dusky are strictly westerners, and form one of the more difficult pairs to identify. Both of them are found in the Cascades and the Siskiyous, with the Hammond's usually at higher elevations, and the Dusky at lower elevations, although it, too, can be found at higher elevations. The Hammond's prefers mature moist forests, and tends to avoid clearcuts, while the Dusky prefers drier, more open habitats, including logged areas, provided the bushes and trees are growing back. Hammond's generally prefers the upper portions of trees, while Dusky's are likely to be found lower, although there is no law that says they can't sometimes do the opposite.

They have similar plumages and are about the same size, they both have eye-rings, both have wingbars, both might or might not have a slight yellowish wash on the underparts, and both get their insect prey by flycatching. It is generally accepted that the only way to separate them is by structure and voice.

Hammond's generally looks big-headed and short-tailed. Sometimes the head looks sort of squarish. The bill is smaller and narrower than on the Dusky, and usually looks quite dark. The "primary projection" (the projection of the primary tips beyond the tertial tips) is greater than on the Dusky; and this is what makes the tail look short. The male Hammond's gives a sharp *pit*, similar to the note of a Pygmy Nuthatch. Hammond's are active birds, constantly flicking their wings and tail somewhat like a kinglet. A Dusky may also flick its wings, especially when changing perches, but doesn't do it as habitually as a Hammond's.

A Dusky Flycatcher generally looks round-headed and long-tailed. The bill is longer than on Hammond's, and the lower mandible is usually pale orangish at the base, with a dark tip. The "primary projection" is shorter than on a Hammond's. The call note is a liquid *whit*, similar to that of the Willow Flycatcher.

The "song" of the Hammond's usually has three parts, written in various fashions by different authors, but more or less in the sequence, *se-put* (uttered rapidly), *tsur-r-r-p* (roughly burred), and *grr-vik*, sometimes given with "monotonous regularity," in Bent's words. The song of the Dusky may have three or four parts, and is somewhat similar to that of Hammond's, but with the last note a clear *psuweet*, similar to the call of the Pacific Slope Flycatcher.

Got all that? Don't be surprised, when you're out there identifying flycatchers, if all of these identifying characteristics fail you, and you might have to record a sighting as *Empidonax* sp?

Least Flycatcher is basically an eastern bird. The first Oregon record was at Hart Mountain in Lake County, in 1972. Now it has tenuously established itself as a breeding bird at Clyde Holliday State Park, on the John Day River, and is suspected of being a "possible" breeder elsewhere in eastern Oregon. We have one record for Southern Oregon, of a singing bird at Petric Park, near the Wood River Wetlands, in July 2000.

The Least Flycatcher closely resembles Hammond's. Both are small (the Least qualifies as being "least" by being ¼ inch shorter), are big-headed and have small bills. However, the bill on the Hammond's is usually all dark, while on the Least, the lower mandible is mostly flesh-colored. The best way of identifying a Least is by its "song," which is a thin, dry *cheBEK cheBEK cheBEK,* repeated rapidly over and over.

## Gray Flycatcher (GRFL)
*Empidonax wrightii*

The Gray Flycatcher, even though it is a member of the confusing empid group, has three saving graces. First, in breeding season, it lives in an entirely different habitat than its lookalikes. Second, it has the habit of repeatedly bobbing its tail downward, a characteristic shared with no other empid; other empids may occasionally bob their tails downward, but not habitually. Third, it has a loud, characteristic two-syllable song.

You have to go out into the sagebrush and juniper country, south and east of the Klamath Basin, to find this bird in breeding season. In the Devils Garden area east of Clear Lake I found it to be fairly common in April among the junipers. It is easily located by its song, an emphatic *chir-RUP! chir-RUP! chir-RUP!,* that sometimes has a high-pitched *seep* interspersed. It is an overall gray color, and it has an eye-ring and wing-bars just like the other empids it gets confused with. Dusky Flycatchers can be rather gray in late summer and fall, so in migration these two birds can look somewhat alike. Look for the downward tail-bobbing, on the Gray.

As with some other empids, the early nomenclature of this bird is a tangle. Because of mistaken identification of specimens, the bird we now know as Dusky Flycatcher got the name of *E. wrightii,* and was called "Wright's Flycatcher." Later, it was discovered that the specimen which had been used for naming "Wright's Flycatcher" was in fact a Gray Flycatcher. So Gray Flycatcher got the name *E. wrightii,* and Dusky Flycatcher was re-named and given the scientific name *E. oberholseri.* The problem of confusion with the empids apparently goes back a long way.

## Pacific-slope Flycatcher (PSFL)
*Empidonax difficilis*

## Cordilleran Flycatcher (COFL)
*Empidonax occidentalis*

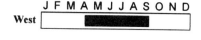

Not too long ago, these two were one species, under the common name "Western Flycatcher," and with the scientific name *difficilis*. The name, of course, means "difficult," which prompted one ornithologist to say, "very appropriate." The name became even more appropriate following the split, because these two are impossible to tell apart visually. They are separated on the basis of their call notes and their songs, and, to some extent on the basis of their ranges, at least in breeding season.

Before the split which produced Pacific-slope and Cordilleran, there was another split, which created the Western Flycatcher from its eastern counterpart, Yellow-bellied Flycatcher. So here is yet another complicated lineage involving flycatchers.

The characteristics that are used to separate Pacific-slope and Cordilleran are their principal call notes, referred to as "position notes." In the Pacific-slope, the male gives an upslurred *pseeyeet!* In the Cordilleran, it is a two-syllable *pit sweet!* There is another call note, often given by females, which is similar in both species -- a sharp *seet*.

The so-called "advertising song" of the Pacific-Slope consists of three syllables -- *pssSEET ptsick seet!* The *ptsick* note has two syllables, the first one low and the second one high. The Cordilleran gives the same song, but the syllables of the *ptsick* note are reversed, with the first one high and the second one low. Got all that? Stay tuned, because there are problems.

In eastern Oregon, some individuals have been observed to give the call notes of both species, or notes that are intermediate. Also, other vocalizations have been observed upon occasion to be intermediate. This causes the status of Cordilleran Flycatcher in Oregon to be unclear, and some people recommend that members of both species be referred to as "Western type." In fact, in the Oregon Breeding Bird Atlas project, the editors stated: "For purposes of this atlas project, no attempt was made to separate Cordilleran from Pacific-slope Flycatcher because of the unreliability of field identification by sight or song," and the results were simply presented for "Western Flycatcher."

There are certain visual qualities that can be used to separate "Western type" flycatchers from others in the empid group. One is that "Western types" often have more yellow on the undersides than do Hammond's, Dusky, or Gray, although much of the yellow may be gone by fall. Another is that they tend to have a peak on the rear of the head. Also, the lower mandible is entirely orange.

The eye-ring on a "Western type" tends to be flattened on the top and flared out at the rear, giving a "tear-drop" shape. Many of these characteristics are shared with Yellow-bellied Flycatcher, but to date no sightings of

Yellow-bellied Flycatcher have been recorded for Oregon. One final factor that might help in singling out a "Western type" is its tendency to sit on the limb of a tree in deep shade, giving its call monotonously, and occasionally darting out for an insect.

Pacific-slope Flycatchers are widespread in Oregon, most often in mature, shaded forests. Cordilleran Flycatchers are considered to be birds of the Great Basin and Rocky Mountains, and are typically found in higher and drier habitats. The usual assumption is that birds on the west slope are Pacific Slope, and on the east slope are Cordilleran. That assumption has been reflected in the bar charts above. However, the uncertainty and controversy described above should be borne in mind, in dealing with *difficilis*.

## Black Phoebe (BLPH)
*Sayornis nigricans*

|  | J F M A M J J A S O N D |
|---|---|
| West |  |
| East | vagrant |

The Black Phoebe is unmistakable, with its black upperparts and breast, contrasting with a white belly. It is a fairly rare bird in Oregon, and occurs regularly only in the southwestern corner of the state. It first became established in Oregon in 1932, and has been slowly expanding its range since that time. In the Rogue Valley, it is a rare year-round resident.

**Black Phoebe**

Black Phoebes are almost always found near water, where they advertise their presence by frequent crisp *tsip!* notes. I've seen them next to irrigation ditches and even near puddles, just to be near water. They are almost always alone, except for mated pairs in breeding season. One will frequently forage by sitting on a rock near the water, waiting for its insect prey, whereupon it swoops out, collects its prey, and swoops back. Occasionally it will lower its tail and raise it, something like a Gray Flycatcher. Black Phoebes eat a higher percentage of insects in their diet (99.4 percent) than any other flycatcher.

The song is a plaintive, drawn out *fee-wee, fee-wee,* sometimes sliding upward, sometimes down, which could be interpreted as the bird saying its name. For nesting purposes, phoebes need a rock face or wooden wall against which to place their nests, using mud to hold them together.

They generally require some sheltering projection over the nest site, and it is believed that the building of bridges over creeks has been advantageous to them, resulting in an increase in the population. Arthur Cleveland Bent tells of a case where a phoebe built a nest on the inside wall of an unused well, and continued to sit on the nest even after a pump was put down the well and water pumped every day.

### Eastern Phoebe (EAPH)                                                            Vagrant
*Sayornis phoebe*

There are only a few records of Eastern Phoebe for the entire state of Oregon. There are records from Valley of the Rogue State Park, and from Malone Springs, both in June. It has about the same shape as a Black Phoebe, and has a dark head, but is much grayer overall and does not have the conspicuous black hood coming down over the upper breast like the Black Phoebe does.

### Say's Phoebe (SAPH)
*Sayornis saya*

The Black Phoebe loves water, but the Say's Phoebe loves the opposite. Don't look for it in heavy forest. It prefers the open spaces -- sagebrush plains, rocky foothills, and dry fields. Its call, a soft, plaintive *phee-ur,* is heard often in such country. In its flycatching, it tends to perch low, on rocks, weedstalks, and fenceposts. It is a restless bird, constantly shifting from perch to perch, but fairly tolerant of the presence of humans.

Say's Phoebe is attractive, with its gray upperparts, black tail, and peach-colored belly. It generally doesn't use mud in building its nests, as does the Black Phoebe. The nests may be placed in crevices in cliffs, tree cavities, on rafters under bridges, in old mine shafts, or in deserted ranch buildings. Nests have even been placed in the burrows of Bank Swallows, and Arthur Cleveland Bent cites a case where a pair drove away a pair of Barn Swallows from their nest and appropriated it for themselves.

Say's Phoebes are breeders east of the Cascades. Most of them withdraw to the south in the winter, perhaps going no further than Southern California. But a few stick around, and some of them show up in the Rogue Valley in winter.

### Ash-throated Flycatcher (ATFL)
*Myiarchus cinerascens*

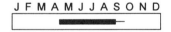

*Myiarchus* flycatchers represent another sticky problem in identification. A peek in your field guide will show that there are four lookalikes in the genus. But we don't have a problem in Oregon, because Ash-throated Flycatcher is the only member of the genus that we normally get. There is a record on the coast of a Dusky-capped Flycatcher, which is one of the *Myiarchus* group, but that's it.

The first sign that there is an Ash-throated Flycatcher around is likely to be its loud, burry *ka-WHEER!* repeated periodically, sometimes varied with a *ker-brick!* Soon the source is spotted, sitting on an exposed branch, waiting to dart out for an insect. It has been said that, with their erect posture, they lend a "touch of elegance" to the surroundings.

Their preferred habitat is brushy slopes with trees, or hillside oak groves, where there is open ground for foraging and trees for perching. They are easily recognized, with their large, brown bushy heads, whitish throats ("ash-throated"), pale yellow underparts, and reddish tail.

They are cavity nesters, and will accept almost anything that resembles a cavity. They will, of course, nest in natural cavities in trees and old woodpecker holes, if they can find them. But they have also been known to build nests in roof drainpipes, old tin cans, empty mail boxes, and almost any other box-like opening.

Some odd nesting locations have been selected. In one, an old pair of overalls was hung on the line to dry. There was a hole in one leg, and a pair of Ash-throated Flycatchers began carrying nesting material into the hole, but the material immediately fell out the bottom of the leg. The owner saw what was going on, and tied up the bottom of the leg, whereupon the birds finished their nest and ultimately raised a brood in it.

In another case, a pair built a nest in an opening on the underside of the boom of a power shovel which was in use almost every day. The nest site may have been chosen at a time when the shovel wasn't being used, but the birds stuck with their nest, even when the shovel was in operation, and successfully raised their brood.

## Western Kingbird (WEKI)
*Tyrranus verticalis*

## Eastern Kingbird (EAKI)
*Tyrranus tyrranus*

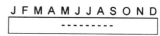

These two birds don't resemble each other much, but are placed together because of similar habits and shape. The Western Kingbird has a pale gray head, dark wing coverts, yellow underbelly, and a black tail with white outer tail feathers. My references claim that there is a tiny red crown patch, but I've never been able to see it. The Eastern Kingbird has a black head, is white on the underparts, including a white throat, and has a conspicuous white tip to the tail. There is not much chance of confusing these two, unless you see the bird only in silhouette, in which case they look much alike.

There is another kingbird that occasionally enters Oregon, although all the records to date except one (Malheur NWR) have been along the coast. This is the Tropical Kingbird, which breeds in Arizona. For some reason, a fair number of these birds, following breeding season, wander up the coast in fall as far as British Columbia. A Tropical Kingbird can be told from a Western by its much larger bill and by the pronounced fork in the tail. Tropical Kingbirds don't have white outer tail feathers, and Westerns do. However, in late fall much of the white might be worn off the feathers, so you can never be sure that a kingbird is a Tropical, just because it doesn't have white outer tail feathers.

Western Kingbirds are nesting opportunists. They like open country, but would prefer to have trees nearby for nesting. If they can't get them, they will use many kinds of sites, including human structures such as windmills, outbuildings, and even farmhouses. A pair once built a nest on a ledge over the kitchen door of a farmhouse, even though the door was used 50 times a day. In a different case, an observer noted that, as soon as telephone poles appeared in his area, the kingbirds took to them immediately.

Kingbirds don't have the name *Tyrranus* for nothing. They are the original tyrants for which the family was named. Arthur Cleveland Bent quotes an observer as follows:

> The ... kingbird is a masterful, positive character, and when you come into his neighborhood you are very likely to know it, for he seems to be always screaming and scrimmaging. ... A passing enemy is allowed no time to loiter but driven from the field with impetuous onslaught and clang of trumpets.

The Western Kingbird was once called "bee-martin," and was accused of lingering about beehives in order to snap up the bees. A research project, however, found that only 5 percent of the food eaten by the kingbirds consisted of honey bees, and of these, almost all were drones. An observer at the time claimed that the parent birds somehow must be able to teach the babies that worker bees have stings, and drones don't.

### Scissor-tailed Flycatcher (STFL)     Accidental
*Tyrranus forficatus*

It seems strange that this bird, which mostly lives in Texas, should turn up in Oregon, but there are seven Oregon records, mostly on the coast, and including one at Davis Lake, in northern Klamath County. There is one record from the Klamath Basin, on the California side of the border, at Butte Valley Wildlife Area, in June 1984. The incredibly long tail of this bird, two-thirds of its total length, makes it instantly recognizable.

## Family **LANIIDAE:** Shrikes

### Loggerhead Shrike (LOSH)
*Lanius ludovicianus*

### Northern Shrike (NSHR)
*Lanius excubitor*

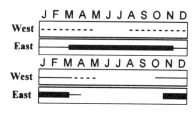

Here is another pair that sometimes gives trouble in identification. In the Northern Shrike, the bill is longer than in the Loggerhead, and it has a stronger hook on the end. The mask over the eye is narrower, and does not extend above the eye. Finally, in the Northern, there is usually is some very fine barring across the breast, especially in the juvenile. Beware, though, because the juvenile Loggerhead also has some barring on the breast.

In the Loggerhead Shrike, the bill is much smaller, almost stubby-looking, and there is less of a hook. The mask is broad, and extends above the eye. The fine barring on the breast is absent, except in the juvenile.

**Loggerhead Shrike**

Both species like open country of fields or marshes, with small trees for hunting perches. They often will perch on the top of a bush or on a wire, in order to get a good look at the surroundings. Often, when disturbed, one will simply move down a ways and assume a similar posture on the next bush.

Shrikes have been referred to as the only truly predatory songbirds. They are the terrors of the fields in which they live, at least as far as insects, other small birds, and mice are concerned. As for the "songbird" part, we normally might not think of shrikes in that fashion, but they are members of the Passerines, or "perching birds," and the Passerines are loosely called songbirds.

A shrike cannot capture a bird in flight like a falcon does, but may strike it a blow, force it to the ground and then kill it with a series of sharp bites on the neck. A popular name for them is "butcher-birds," because they impale their prey on thorns for future use, calling to mind the custom of butchers putting their meat on hooks.

One observer watched a shrike as it perched by the opening of a House Sparrow nest and extracted the fledglings one by one. Shrikes are apparently irresistibly drawn to canaries in cages. One will fly at the cage, and the canary, rather than withdraw to the center of the cage where it is safe, instead flees to the opposite side of the cage and sticks its head out between the bars, trying to escape. The shrike then darts to that side of the cage and clips off the canary's head with a series of sharp bites. One person claimed she lost three canaries that way.

They have been reported to enter bird-banding traps, kill all the birds inside, and not even bother to eat any of them. Their ability to dispatch sparrows once caused the authorities in Boston many years ago to post men in the parks to shoot the shrikes, in order to protect what were then called "English Sparrows," now called House Sparrows. It was popular at that time to try to get European species established in the U.S., and the shrikes were about to wreck the program to get House Sparrows established. Today, when many people look upon House Sparrows as pests, some may wish the shrikes had won.

In the past, shrikes were occasionally referred to as "French Mockingbirds," because their overall gray color and white wing patches cause them to resemble mockingbirds when in flight. ("French," perhaps, because they have fancier plumage than ordinary mockingbirds.) They have also been called "mouse hawks", and have been called "cotton pickers" because they sometimes use cotton in their nests.

## Family **VIREONIDAE**: Vireos

### Bell's Vireo (BEVI)                                                  Accidental
*Vireo bellii*

This is a brush-loving bird of the southwest and midwest. Any that we get have overshot their spring migration path by a long ways. There are two records from Fields, in Harney County (May 1980 and June 1998), and one from Tule Lake NWR (June 1980). If you should be lucky enough to see one, you can identify it by the following: It is a tiny bird, about the size of a goldfinch, with varying amounts of yellowish underneath or none at all, depending upon which subspecies it is. It has a broken eye-ring and faint spectacles, with a faint dark eye-line running through the eye.

If you really want to get picky, look at the underside of the lower mandible, which is pale in most individuals, instead of being black. This may take some doing, because Bell's Vireos are noted for being hyperactive, and staying out of sight in the bushes. Most important is its song, which is a rapid, jumbled *jeedle-jeedle-JEE,* frequently repeated. Sometimes there is a rising inflection on the last syllable, as if asking a question, and sometimes there is a downward inflection, as if answering it.

### Cassin's Vireo (CAVI)                                    J F M A M J J A S O N D
*Vireo cassinii*

### Plumbeous Vireo (PLVI)                                              Vagrant
*Vireo plumbeus*

In 1997, what was then known as "Solitary Vireo" was split into three species: Cassin's Vireo, Plumbeous Vireo, and Blue-headed Vireo. The breeding range for Cassin's is the Pacific Coast states, with an overlap into Idaho and Montana; for Plumbeous it is the Rocky Mountains and Great Basin; and for Blue-headed it is the east and all the way across Canada through Alberta.

Cassin's is our regular breeding vireo. But all three are long-distance migrants; thus, if the two who don't breed here somehow mess up their directions, we can get them in our area as vagrants. Blue-headed has occurred at least 7 times, ranging from the coast to Malheur NWR, but with none in our area. Most of these occurrences have been in the fall, which suggests that these birds might have come from Alberta or a neighboring province, are migrating south, and have gotten their compasses out of whack.

Plumbeous has occurred 10 times, with almost all of the cases east of the Cascades. Two of these have been in the Klamath Basin, one near Klamath Marsh NWR, and one near Stukel Mountain. There also is an observation west of the crest, in the Applegate Valley. The great majority of the records have been in late spring, suggesting that the birds overshot their normal breeding range in the process of migrating north. The Oregon Breeding Bird Atlas shows a "possible" breeding record for Plumbeous in the Klamath Basin, and a "probable" on the border of Klamath and Lake counties.

These three can be difficult to tell apart. All three have prominent "spectacles," all three have wing bars, and all three have a similar-sounding song, which consists of a slow series of *chur-YEE, CHEER-iyeer,* with variations, often sounding like a question and answer.

Our local Cassin's and the Blue-headed resemble each other, with bluish-gray heads, backs that are usually greenish, and white underparts with some yellow on the flanks. Generally, a Cassin's will be duller in appearance than a Blue-headed, but a Cassin's in fresh, bright, new plumage can look a lot like a Blue-headed. The thing to check is the degree of contrast on the cheek, between the blue of the head and the white of the throat. In Blue-headed, the contrast is strong, while in Cassin's it is weak

A Plumbeous Vireo is gray on the upperparts and white on the underparts, usually with a grayish wash, but sometimes with a bit of yellow, on the flanks. It is not likely to be mistaken for a Blue-headed, but a Cassin's in worn plumage can be very gray, and look a lot like a Plumbeous. The distinction to look for is that the edges of the secondaries on a Plumbeous will be grayish, whereas on a Cassin's they will be greenish-yellow.

What all this means is, if you think you've got an out-of-range Blue-headed or Plumbeous, you need to get a close enough look to see the contrast on the cheek, or the color of the edges of the secondaries.

Cassin's Vireos prefer mixed coniferous/deciduous woodlands, and breed throughout the southern Cascades on both sides of the crest, and also in the mountains to the north and south of the Rogue Valley. They tend to forage both high and low in the trees, moving in a deliberate way, while gleaning insects from the twigs and leaves. They can be quite inconspicuous, and could be overlooked entirely except for their singing.

## Hutton's Vireo (HUVI)
*Vireo huttoni*

| | J | F | M | A | M | J | J | A | S | O | N | D |
|---|---|---|---|---|---|---|---|---|---|---|---|---|
| West | ■ | ■ | ■ | ■ | ■ | ■ | ■ | ■ | ■ | ■ | ■ | ■ |
| East | | | | | Vagrant | | | | | | | |

The main lookalike for this bird is Ruby-crowned Kinglet. The two are about the same size, have about the same coloration, have two wing-bars, and have conspicuous eye-rings. First, as to behavior, the kinglet will usually be the more hyperactive of the two, flicking its wings constantly while it darts from branch to branch. Hutton's Vireo, though it may be more active than some of the other vireos, is more deliberate than the kinglet. If it is agitated, it, too, can flick its wings and jump about, but does not do so as habitually as the kinglet.

196

The bill on the Hutton's is thicker than on the kinglet, and it has a slight hook at the tip. The bill on the Ruby-crowned looks thin and sharp. A major mark to look for is the pattern on the wing-bars. On the Hutton's, the two bars will be about equally bright, and the area between the bars is the blackest portion of the wing. On the Ruby-crowned, the lower bar is typically more conspicuous than the upper one, and there is a small black area below the lower bar.

Of course, if it's a male Ruby-crowned Kinglet, and becomes agitated enough to raise its little red crest so it is visible, the game is settled right there. Also, an agitated Ruby-crowned (and they are often agitated), will give an irritated little chatter, that may begin with a single *jit,* and then continue in a rapid series of *jit-jit-jit-jit-jit.*

In breeding season, a Hutton's Vireo will identify itself by its song, which is a loud *tsuweet tsuweet tsuweet* (upward inflection), repeated many times before switching to a variation, *tsuwheer twuwheer tsuwheer* (downward inflection). The Oregon Breeding Bird Atlas shows the principal breeding locations of this bird, at least as far as our area goes, to be in forests dominated by Douglas-firs, in Josephine County and on the western side of Jackson County. There are some "probable" breeding locations on the border of Jackson and Klamath counties, north of Mount McLoughlin.

## Warbling Vireo (WAVI)
*Vireo gilvus*

|  | J F M A M J J A S O N D |
|---|---|
| West | ▬▬▬▬ |
| East | ▬▬▬▬▬ |

When I was first getting started into birding, I was sitting near a tree with a large crack in the trunk, and observed a pair of birds approach. The birds were brownish and (to me) unidentifiable. One of them went inside the crack and suddenly sang from inside the tree, in a bubbling torrent of song. Somewhere, I had read that a Warbling Vireo's song was long, melodius, and warbling, and that the male would sometimes sing while sitting on the nest. Therefore, I concluded there must be a nest inside the tree, and that what I heard was a Warbling Vireo singing from the nest.

I'm not even embarrassed by this story any more. I just think it's funny. What I had seen and heard, of course, was a pair of House Wrens, but there is a point to this story, which is not to go on the basis of single trait in identifying a bird. For one thing, in addition to plumage, behavior is important. Warbling Vireos indeed may sing from the nest, but I've never seen one do it, probably because the nests are hard to find. In any event, a Warbling Vireo nest would not be located in a tree cavity. And in other ways, Warbling Vireos don't even begin to behave like House Wrens. They tend to remain in thick foliage, moving slowly from branch to branch, frequently high in the trees, usually out of sight, singing their song. House Wrens bounce around in the open restlessly, more or less "in your face," pausing on a branch to let loose a bubbling torrent of song, and then zip off to another place.

I love Warbling Vireos partly because of where they live -- in the mountain forests, often in alders or aspens. Their song is a repeated set of warbles, each set usually ending with the last note going up, as if it's a question. One birder said it sounds as if the bird is saying, *"What's on the menu? Whattaya wanna order? Whattaya wanna eat?"* [1] The song can be confused with that of the Purple Finch, but the Purple Finch's song is much faster and more energetic than the somewhat leisurely song of the Warbling Vireo.

Warbling Vireos are not very flashy birds. No wing-bars, no eye rings, no special colors -- just kind of drab grayish-olive, with perhaps a little yellow on the sides. There is a whitish eyebrow, and a slight eye-line that terminates in pale lores. Altogether, the facial expression has been described as a "blank" look, but which another observer has described as "innocent."

## Red-eyed Vireo (REVI)    Vagrant
*Vireo olivaceus*

This widespread vireo breeds throughout most of the United States, including the northeast corner of Oregon. There are three reports from the Rogue Valley, and one from the Klamath Basin, in the Klamath River Canyon. All of the reports were in late spring or summer. It prefers riparian zones with large cottonwood trees, where it reveals itself by its repetitive song, which has been rendered as *Here-I-am, where-are-you? Here-I-am, where-are-you?* delivered at a faster rate than in the Cassin's Vireo. Sometimes the singing is kept up all day long. It keeps singing its song even as it is feeding, and was described by Bent as "a happy laborer, whistling at his work."

The head has a striking pattern, unmistakable if seen well. The crown is gray with a black border above the eye. Nest to the crown is a white eyebrow, and there is a black line through the eye. This gives the effect of a white eyebrow with black borders top and bottom. The bill is large and the head has a long flat crown. The iris of the eye is indeed red, but the color is hard to see. Getting a good look may be a chore, because this vireo likes to work high in the trees, its green body looking pretty much like one of the leaves.

## Family **CORVIDAE**: Crows and Jays

People generally recognize crows when they see them, although there might be some uncertainty between crows and ravens. Likewise, they usually recognize a jay, although they are likely, if the jay is colored blue, to call it a "Blue Jay." But there are seven species of jays in the U. S. that are colored blue, and four of them occur in our area: Steller's Jay, Blue Jay, Western Scrub-Jay, and Pinyon Jay. The one that truly bears the name Blue Jay is a midwestern and eastern bird, and is only a vagrant in our area.

---

[1] Thanks to R.J. Adams.

# Gray Jay (GRAJ)
*Perisoreus canadensis*

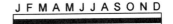

Here's another bird that has gone by many names. "Canada Jay" and "Oregon Jay" are two of them, although some authorities believe these two, currently considered to be subspecies, might actually be separate species. The "Oregon Jay" is distributed along the Pacific coast and through the Cascades, and the "Canada Jay" is in northeastern Oregon, through the Rocky Mountains, and into Canada and Alaska. The two differ from each other principally in the amount of white on their heads. The "Oregon Jay" has an extensive amount of black on the head and a white forehead. The "Canada Jay's" head is mostly white, with a moderate amount of pale gray.

But there are even older, time-honored names. "Camp Robber" is one, which needs no explanation. Another one is "Whiskey Jack," which apparently has nothing to do with whiskey, but is considered to be a corruption of an Indian name for the bird: "wiss-ka-chon." This, the story goes, was turned into "Whiskey John," and then into "Whiskey Jack."

Old-timers claim the "camp robber" will eat anything from soap to plug tobacco. Whether it actually will eat those things is unclear, but they have been known to steal them and carry them off. It certainly is omnivorous. Besides camp scraps, it will eat bugs, seeds, berries, mushrooms, birds' eggs, and carrion. They have been known to eat from skinned carcasses hung by deer hunters, making holes through the dried surfaces large enough to admit their heads, eating one to two pounds of meat from each hole.

Much of the food is carried off and hidden in caches, for use during the winter. One such cache was found in which three holes, presumably made originally by flickers, had been filled with about a quart of bread scraps. As soon as the birds found their cache had been discovered, they removed everything, and presumably cached it somewhere else.

Their preferred habitat is the evergreen forests of the Cascades and Siskiyous, including true fir-hemlock forests. My impression of these birds is that they arrive silently, almost as if appearing from nowhere, and don't advertise their presence like other jays. Once in view, they aren't particularly nervous, but seem to hang around to see what is going on. Some observers have said they will follow a human, out of curiosity. It has also been said that they will come to the sound of an ax, because it suggests making camp, and that means food.

Even though it is usually a silent bird, it is capable of making noises, one of them a loud *wheeet!* It also occasionally makes a scream very much like that of a Blue Jay, but whether this is an imitation or an innate call, my sources don't say. Just to make things confusing, my sources do say that they sometimes may give a soft sweet song, but I've never been privileged to hear it.

## Steller's Jay (STJA)
*Cyanocitta stelleri*

Western birders sometimes become rather apathetic about Steller's Jays because they are so common. This seems to me to be unappreciative, because the Steller's Jay is a gorgeous bird, with a black crest and head, and deep blue wings and back. Our local subspecies usually has blue streaks on the forehead; the subspecies to the north of us, in southwest B.C. and Alaska, has few or no blue streaks, and the one in the Rocky Mountains has white streaks.

It is said that, when a western birder goes east, the "most-wanted" bird is a Northern Cardinal, and, when an eastern birder comes west, the "most-wanted" bird is a Steller's Jay. I met a pair of birders in Washington once, who had been birding on the west coast for two weeks. They were due to return to Michigan the next day, and had not seen a Steller's Jay on their trip -- a major disappointment.

I asked my friends from Michigan if they had looked for Steller's Jays around campgrounds or picnic grounds, and they said no. This gave me the clue, because if they were looking in the deep woods, that's where Steller's Jays tend to be shy and elusive. In camp and picnic grounds they are highly visible, as if they have learned from experience that they are safe in such surroundings.

They are lovers of evergreen forests, and are not often found away from that habitat. They may, however, wander into lower elevation areas where oaks and evergreens meet, and may move downslope in winter when snow covers the ground. In their normal evergreen surroundings, their call is often heard -- a rapid *shek-shek-shek-shek* that is usually given in flight, and one which always lifts my spirits when I hear it.

Other calls consist of a typical loud *jaay! jaay!* and a scream that sounds like a Red-tailed Hawk. Most people believe this is a deliberate mimicry, but some have expressed the view that it is actually a true jay call. There is also a soft "whisper song," a sort of warbling mixed with some trills, that sounds very un-jaylike.

Steller's Jay is named for Georg Wilhem Steller, a German zoologist who was a member of Vitus Berings's Arctic expedition of 1741. Steller was the first European to see a Steller's Jay, and it was originally named "Steller's Crow" in his honor. Other animals named for Steller are Steller's Sea-Eagle, Steller's Eider, and Steller's Sea Lion.

## Blue Jay (BLJA)    Vagrant
*Cyanocitta cristata*

Here we have the "original" Blue Jay, with its crest, dramatic blue and white colors, and a scream that sounds like a rusty screen door hinge. Traditionally, we have thought of this as an eastern bird, with its range extending as far west as Colorado and Wyoming.

However, since the 1950s, more and more of these birds have been showing up in other western states, and it is now believed that a range expansion may be under way. The first Oregon reports were in 1973, and in the fall of 1976 there was a major influx. Since Blue Jays are not long-distance migrants, these appearances cannot be explained by migratory overshoot or faulty orientation, but appear to consist of birds who are simply moving beyond their assumed "boundaries."

The Blue Jay is now looked upon in Oregon as a rare but regular visitor from September to April, primarily in northeastern Oregon. It is believed it may even have become a permanent resident in the Grande Ronde Valley, although breeding has not been confirmed anywhere in Oregon.

In our area, there are two records in the Rogue Valley, one in January 1978 and the other in November 1998. There also was one in Klamath Falls, in late November 2000. It has been noticed that Blue Jays are often harassed by Western Scrub-Jays, and that the scrub-jays may be a limiting factor in the range expansion of the Blue Jays.

## Western Scrub-Jay (WESJ)
*Aphelocoma californica*

J F M A M J J A S O N D

This was the first bird species I ever learned, as a kid. It was then called "California Jay," and somewhere, I understood, there was a "Florida Jay" that resembled it. A few years later, I discovered these two had been lumped into one species, "Scrub Jay." I didn't like the new name. It seemed like a put-down, and I wondered why the "powers-that-be" had done it.

Many years later, I discovered why. Under the prevailing classification criteria, if two sets of birds could interbreed successfully, they were deemed to be one species. The two sets in question, even though separated by thousands of miles,

**Western Scrub-Jay**

presumably could interbreed, so they were lumped. The choice of the common name "scrub" was fairly straightforward: The "Florida" bird had been described and named before the "California" bird, so its name had priority. The term "Scrub Jay" was the name used widely in Florida for the bird, because it inhabited Florida scrub, consisting of thickets of sand pines, shrub oaks, and palmettos, so that was the name chosen.

Subsequently, the AOU reversed itself, partly because of the geographic isolation of the Florida group, but also because of other evidence. In the process, it created three new species -- Western Scrub-Jay, Florida Scrub-Jay, and Island Scrub-Jay, the last one an isolated group on Santa Cruz Island, off

Santa Barbara. The range of the Western Scrub-Jay is huge, extending from the Pacific Coast to Texas. But there still remains an issue, with respect to the Western Scrub-Jay. Is it one, or two species?

The birds of the Pacific Coast subspecies, including ours, have strongly defined, though incomplete, blue breastbands, or "necklaces." The birds of the interior subspecies, some of which have shown up in southeastern Oregon, have only faint blue necklaces. There are other differences, but the necklace is the main one. The AOU, in its checklist, holds out the possibility that the interior subspecies may be a separate species, and the name "Woodhouse's Jay" has been used for it in the past. Arthur Cleveland Bent used that name for it, and said, "this is the shiest, most secretive, and most elusive of all the jays that I have seen in my life."

Because of the existence of "Woodhouse's" in southeastern Oregon, the possibility of them occurring in the eastern part of the Klamath Basin has occasionally been suggested, but their presence there has not yet been demonstrated.

Arthur Cleveland Bent relates a case concerning the intelligence of scrub-jays, involving a photographer, who said:

> I have never worked with birds that appeared to show as much intelligence. We set up our blind near their nest, which was in a young oak. . . . Although the birds had become used to the blind and were nowhere to be seen when we entered, still they appeared to know that we were there. They came back very quietly, slipping through the trees and alighting near the blind. Then one of them leaned over and peered through the small opening through which the camera was focused. After looking very carefully, he saw us and set up a great outcry.

There is no doubt that scrub-jays can make great outcries. Their loud *SHRACK! SHRACK! SHRACK!* is well known. What is not so well known is the crooning noise a jay may make near its own nest, which has been described as pleasing and ventriloquial, and can only be heard for a short distance.

There is also no doubt concerning scrub-jays' aggressiveness. If a bunch of small birds are at my feeder and a scrub-jay shows up, the small birds scatter. Perhaps they know well that scrub-jays can turn into serious predators.

Instances have been reported in which scrub-jays knocked smaller birds right out of the air and killed them. Many people seem to react with horror when a scrub-jay does that, but don't seem to react so negatively when a Cooper's Hawk does the same thing.

And they do steal birds' eggs. Many people condemn them for that. But some species of squirrel do the same thing, and wrens are well known for their tendency to go about destroying other birds' eggs, apparently to reduce competition. And perhaps humans shouldn't be so judgmental, because we steal birds' eggs, too, except we generally get a farmer to do it for us.

## Pinyon Jay (PIJA)
*Gymnorhinus cyanocephalus*

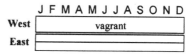

As its name suggests, this bird likes to be around pinyon pines. But there aren't any pinyon pines in Oregon, so they have to make do with junipers and ponderosas. Their principal range in Oregon is the central part of the state, ranging down to Lake County. But we get them in our area, too, although they are less numerous. One place to look for them is in the junipers and pines on the eastern side of the Klamath Basin.

There have been a few occurrences in our area in places where they wouldn't normally be expected. One was at Howard Prairie Lake in 1987, and another at Emigrant Lake in 1991. The most remarkable record is one at the 8,000-foot level on Garfield Peak, in Crater Lake NP, in 1990.

Pinyon Jays usually move in tightly knit flocks, and, outside of breeding season can often be detected by their loud crow-like calls. In fact, they were originally called "Blue Crow," because of their flocking habits and otherwise un-jaylike behavior. Arthur Cleveland Bent says, "A dull-blue, crowlike bird, with a short tail and a long, slender bill, could hardly be anything else but a pinyon jay, especially if seen flying about, or feeding on the ground, in flocks."

When they don't have pinyon pine nuts to eat, they resort to the seeds or tender young cones of other pines, particularly ponderosa pines. They will eat grain if they can find it, wild fruits, insects, and the eggs and young of other birds. They generally nest in loose colonies, and engage in a certain amount of communal feeding, with the parents assisted by kin.

Since they move in large flocks, you can look for them for a long time without success, and then suddenly be inundated by them. It is claimed that they are able to distinguish between the calls of their own flock-members and those made by others. In the breeding season they can be difficult to find because they are less vocal, and don't engage in territorial song.

## Clark's Nutcracker (CLNU)
*Nucifraga columbiana*

If you want to see a nutcracker, go to Crater Lake. It's as simple as that. Near the parking lot in the village on the rim, they fly back and forth among the hemlocks, sounding out their harsh *kr-r-r-ack* calls, looking for handouts from the tourists. Their harsh voices aside, they are lovely birds -- pearly gray, with black and white wings and tail.

I once camped at high elevation in Utah, and was prepared to enjoy a delightful afternoon in camp. There were two nutcrackers flying about, a new fledgling pursuing a parent, and demanding to be fed. The fledgling was as large as the parent, and kept up a constant barrage of *kr-r-ack, kr-r-ack, kr-r-ack*, which at first I thought was delightful. After two hours of this, without even a sign of a letup, it was no longer delightful. Arthur Cleveland Bent says, "They follow the adults with a persistence truly wonderful, awakening the echoes . . ." And indeed they do.

Nutcrackers can be found in other locations in the Cascades and Siskiyous, generally at the higher elevations, but Crater Lake is the most reliable. In winter, some of them may descend to lower elevations, but apparently some do not. Ronald Lanner, in his book about nutcrackers (*Made for Each Other: A Symbiosis of Birds and Pines*) reported on cases in which nutcrackers had burrowed through snow, sometimes as much as a meter deep, and succeeded in finding previously cached pine nuts about 75 percent of the time, evidently using visual clues.

Nutcrackers eat the nuts of several kinds of pines and firs, and also eat acorns and juniper berries. Other items of food are large black ants, beetles, snails, and, of course, the eggs and nestlings of other birds. However, they apparently have a special relationship with the whitebark pine -- the pine that is customarily found at timberline. The birds store pine nuts by the thousands, far more than they can eat, though they have a remarkable memory for where they stored them -- most of them, anyway. One researcher says they remember locations by utilizing nearby landmarks, and essentially use a process of triangulation to pinpoint the exact spot. This implies a remarkable amount of intelligence.

The birds cram the whitebark pine nuts into the earth or into crevices. Some of them are never recovered, and eventually sprout. It is claimed that the whitebark pine is almost entirely dependent upon the nutcracker for seed dispersal, since the seeds of the whitebark lack wings. The seeds of many other pines have wings attached, and can be dispersed by wind, but not the whitebark. Since whitebark pines are an important part of some of the loveliest scenery in the west, it has been said that the Clark's Nutcracker "is the caretaker of some of our most scenic vistas."

## Black-billed Magpie (BBMA)
*Pica hudsonia*

Black-billed Magpies are birds of the open country -- grasslands, pastures, sage steppe, and junipers. We tend to think of them as birds of the Great Basin, although their range extends as far east as Nebraska and as far north as Alaska. Until recently, our bird was lumped with those all around the world, with the scientific name *Pica pica*. But now, our American version has been split from the rest. (David Sibley, in his monumental book, *The Sibley Guide to Birds,* published in 2000, gives its name as "American Magpie." On his Internet web page, Sibley explained that, as his book approached publication, he knew the AOU was considering the possibility that the name "American Magpie" would be chosen as a result of the split, and wanted his book to be as up to date as possible. But the committee decided to stick with Black-billed Magpie, after it was too late for Sibley to make the change. Later printings of his book contain the correction.)

In Southern Oregon, magpies are common on the east side of the crest, but rare on the west side. Generally, if they are to be found on the west side at all, it will be in the dry foothill country to the west of Ashland. A major surprise was the discovery of breeding in that location, in 1999.

Magpies are usually recognized by most people, with their flashy black and white coloration and long tails. They are fairly noisy, and their *cah-cah-cah-cah* call, slightly higher than a crow's, is instantly recognizable. They build their nests in loosely associated colonies, and generally move about in groups.

Magpies eat the usual foods of their relatives in the Corvid family -- insects, carrion, seeds, fruit, and small mammals. They will ride the backs of deer and domestic animals, searching for ticks. And they have been known to open the sores on domestic animals and eat the flesh of the animals, sometimes even resulting in the deaths of their unwitting hosts. They find the kills of coyotes so quickly, that some people believe they deliberately follow coyotes for that purpose.

**Black-billed Magpie**

Their nests can be awesome. Sometimes they are three or four feet in diameter, formed of tightly woven sticks, generally completely roofed over, usually with more than one entrance. William Leon Dawson, one of the grand old ornithologists of the early 20th century, said:

> Magpies are the most abusive and profane of birds. When a nest of young birds is threatened . . . they denounce, upbraid, anathematize, and vilify the intruder, and decry his lineage from Adam down . . . When these run dry, they fall to tearing at the leaves, the twigs, the branches, or even light on the ground and rip up the soil with their beaks, in the mad extremity of their rage.

Magpies are sometimes kept as caged pet birds, and are capable of mimicking human speech. Dawson relates the story of a captive magpie that had learned to imitate its owner's voice. The bird's cage was near the stable (this was the early 1900s). On one occasion, when the magpie's owner was attempting to hitch up his horse, the magpie clucked to the horse, *"ck, ck, ck,"* and then said, *"Get up, Peter, get up."* This was followed immediately with, *"whoa, boy, whoa,"* getting the horse so confused it didn't know what to do.

The Black-billed Magpie has a close cousin, the Yellow-billed Magpie. The Black-billed ranges across most of the continent, but the Yellow-billed is confined completely to the interior valleys of California. The ranges of the two don't come any closer to each other than about 50 miles. Except for a few vagrants that may be escaped cage birds, the two species are not found in each others' territories.

There is lots of speculation concerning how these two became differentiated, and how they got here. It is believed by some that both originated in Asia, and made a transit across the Bering land bridge. There is even some speculation that, when the Black-billed reached California, the Yellow-billed was already there, perhaps even transported by prehistoric humans.

In all the speculation, there don't seem to be any good ideas concerning why the Black-billed stopped their expansion before they got to the interior of California, or why the Yellow-billeds never engaged in a range expansion of their own, outside California. Maybe the birds know.

## American Crow (AMCR)
*Corvus brachyrhynchos*

## Common Raven (CORA)
*Corvus corax*

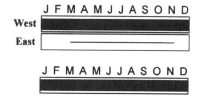

Arthur Cleveland Bent claimed that if a person knows only three birds, one of them will be the crow. He's undoubtedly correct, but in spite of this, people sometimes confuse crows and ravens. If the two are side by side, there is no problem, because ravens are about 35 percent longer than crows on the average, and outweigh them by more than two to one.

If one of the birds is soaring high in the air like a hawk, you can be pretty sure it's a raven, because crows don't do that as a normal thing. Again, if the bird is passing overhead, and you can see the wedge-shaped tail, you know it's a raven. But if the bird is sitting in a tree or standing on the ground, you might not be so sure, especially if the only look you get is as you speed by on the highway.

The problem is with two of the classic marks we use for ravens -- bill size, and shagginess on the throat. Ravens that live in the far north have larger bills and are shaggier than those in our area. The range in bill lengths for the subspecies that lives in our area almost meets the range in bill lengths for our subspecies of crow. The upper end of the range for our crow is 1.58 inches, and the lower end for our raven is 1.66 inches. Since ravens are so much larger than crows, if one of them happens to have a short bill, on the larger body it could make it look an awful lot like a crow. If it's not particularly shaggy, you might not be sure what it is.

If the bird vocalizes, of course, that usually should remove any doubt. Most people are familiar with the *caw caw caw* of a crow. The typical call of a raven is a low, baritone *croake-croake.* On the other hand (it seems there is always an "on the other hand," with birds), both crows and ravens are so versatile in their calls, that they can produce uncertainty in the observer. One of the calls of the crow is a kind of rattle, which has been likened to the gritting of teeth, apparently given as a part of courtship. Another is a pleasing sound that suggests the cooing of a pigeon. And they are good imitators, and have been known to imitate the whine of a dog, the cry of a child, and the crowing of a rooster.

In our area, crows are more likely to be found on the west side of the Cascades, especially in agricultural areas, than on the east side. They tend to stay away from montane forests, unlike ravens, which may appear anywhere. For crows, breeding has been confirmed in the Rogue Valley, but not in the main part of the Klamath Basin. Breeding has been confirmed, however, in Lake County, and on the boundary between Klamath and Lake counties. Breeding for ravens has been confirmed in many places throughout Southern Oregon, especially in the Cascades and Siskiyous.

Much has been said about the intelligence of both species. Concerning the crow, Henry Ward Beecher allegedly said that if men could be feathered and provided with wings, very few would be clever enough to be crows.

Arthur Cleveland Bent had this to say on the subject:

> No bird has been the subject of more heated controversy than the crow, and none of our birds have been more violently persecuted by man. In spite of incessant persecution the crow has been able to outwit his human adversaries by its unusual intelligence and instinct of self-preservation, to the extent that it has been able to maintain its existence in all parts of its wide and diversified range. For this the crow commands our admiration.

Much research has been done, and many anecdotes have been told, concerning the birds' intelligence. Both crows and ravens are well known, for example, for dropping clams on rocks at the beach, to break them open. The anecdote I like the best was witnessed by a licensed wildlife rehabilitator. She had hung a suet cage by a chain from a branch, rendering it unreachable by all but the most agile birds. But one of the crows learned to pull the chain up with its beak and hold it with one foot while reaching down with its beak to grab the chain and pull it up again, repeating the performance until it got at the suet.

Ravens have been observed in combat with hawks, and sometimes have come out at least even. In one case, related by Bent, a Peregrine Falcon dove on a raven in the air. But, just before the blow was given, the raven flipped over on its back with its feet in the air, and the falcon veered off. The raven righted itself, and continued on its way. The falcon tried again, and again the raven flipped over and warded off the blow. The falcon attempted eight times to hit the raven, with the same result each time, and finally gave up.

If we need proof that ravens are survivors, even under extremely adverse conditions, we should consider the case of the annual Christmas Count at Prudhoe Bay, Alaska. Prudhoe Bay is on the edge of the Arctic Ocean, and every year, one species is recorded: Common Raven. In the Christmas count of 2000, 73 of them were counted at Prudhoe Bay.

# Family ALAUDIDAE: Larks

## Horned Lark (HOLA)
*Eremophila alpestris*

This is a bird of the open spaces, of sparse vegetation, bare ground, and plowed fields. In the Cascades, they use alpine and pumice habitats. Some people assert that they have never seen one perch in a tree, and I have to admit neither have I. The best I have seen them do is perch on a fence post.

They are hardy, to say the least, and most of them, at least in our area, stay on their breeding grounds through the winter. Weed seeds and wheat kernels are their main food when they can get them, and when the snow is on the ground they pick the seeds off any weed stalks that protrude. After those are gone, they turn to the strawstacks and barns of the ranches. One writer said:

> [I have] met them on an open prairie when the temperature was nearly 30 degrees below zero, and though a fierce gale was blowing from the northwest they did not exhibit the least sign of discomfort, but rose and flew against the wind, then circled around and alighted on the highest and most windswept place they could find.

They form flocks in the winter and it might be supposed that, since they favor bare ground, they ought to be easy to see. But this is not the case, as demonstrated by Bent's comments:

**Horned Lark**

> As we walk across . . . some bare stubblefield . . . we may be surprised to see a flock of these birds arise from the ground, where their quiet movements and concealing coloration had rendered them almost invisible. They rise all together, and we hear their faint sibilant twittering as they circle about, now high in the air in scattered formation, now close to the ground in more compact order, showing a bright glimmer of white breasts as they wheel away from us, then suddenly disappearing from our view against the dark background as they turn their backs toward us, and finally vanishing entirely as they all alight on the ground not far from where they started.

Seen up close, the Horned Lark is a gorgeous little bird. There are many subspecies, differing somewhat in appearance, but all sharing a dark breastband, dark mask, and tiny black "horns." Sometimes several subspecies will be represented in a single flock.

Breeding has been confirmed several places in the Klamath Basin, and one especially noteworthy confirmation was in Crater Lake National Park. They formerly bred in the Rogue Valley, but no breeding has been confirmed there in recent years.

## Family **HIRUNDINIDAE**: Swallows

**Purple Martin** (PUMA)
*Progne subis*

| | J F M A M J J A S O N D |
|---|---|
| West | - - - - - - - - - - |
| East | ▬▬▬▬▬▬ |

Purple Martins in the past were distributed more widely in Oregon than is the case today. The reasons may include a decrease in the cavities they need for nesting, and competition from House Sparrows and European Starlings. In Southern Oregon, they formerly nested fairly commonly in the Rogue Valley and the Klamath Basin. The 2001 Breeding Bird Atlas only shows one confirmed nesting site for southern Josephine County, and there has been nesting in the recent past at Lava Beds National Monument, in the rocks of collapsed lava tubes.

They nest in cavities in snags, in natural crevices or those in man-made structures, and in nest boxes expressly put up for them. I once saw Purple Martins nesting in drain openings on the underside of a freeway overpass. In the east, people regularly put up boxes on poles, and in one case reported that if the box wasn't erected in time, that the martins could be observed hovering in the air in the spot where the box was supposed to be, looking for it.

The male Purple Martin is a bigger-than-normal swallow, bluish-black all over. The female is bluish on the back, but grayish underneath. In flight, either one of them could be mistaken for a starling, especially if only visible in silhouette.

Indians in the southeastern part of the U.S. regularly hung hollowed-out gourds for the martins, because the birds provided protection for their poultry. If a hawk showed up, the martins would attack it en masse, and drive it away. In more recent times, people have erected colonial nesting boxes, sometimes containing as many as 20 or 30 "rooms."

Starlings are perhaps one of the worst enemies for martins, because they are so aggressive in taking over nesting holes. But there are other enemies, such as screech-owls. In one account, a screech-owl would light at the entrance of one of the nesting boxes, peer inside, and then reach in and drag out a martin, repeating the performance at other boxes and thus acquire as many as a half-dozen victims in one night.

**Tree Swallow** (TRES)
*Tachycineta bicolor*

**Violet-green Swallow** (VGSW)
*Tachycineta thalassina*

Both of these swallows breed widely in Southern Oregon, utilizing somewhat similar nesting sites. Both of them use tree cavities and nest boxes. The Violet-green is more likely to use niches in cliff faces, and also is more likely to use nest boxes in urban locations. Both may nest in riverine woodlands, but the Violet-green is more likely to nest at higher elevations. One of them even nested near the summit of Mount Thielsen, at an elevation of about 9000 feet.

It is quite easy to make a mistake in identification between these two. If it is a perched male, there shouldn't be a problem, because the white around the eye of the Violet-green surrounds the eye entirely, whereas in the Tree, the eye is entirely surrounded by black. Female Violet-greens and female Trees look a lot alike, because both of them have dark backs. In some female Violet-greens, the white around the eye may not be as distinct as with the males. The juveniles resemble the females.

If the swallow is flying, and happens to be a male, and you can see the color of the back, there again is no problem, because the back of the male Violet-green is emerald-green and the back of the male Tree is blue-green. But we often see swallows from below or from the side, as they flash by. Then is when we look for the white flank spots of the Violet-green. The trouble is that Tree Swallows also have white flank spots, although they are not as large.

My own feeling is that if you are not sure that the flank spots are big enough for Violet-green, then you are probably looking at a Tree Swallow. In addition, it has struck me that when the white spots are so extensive that they appear to nearly join on the back, *that's* when you've got a Violet-green.

Both species form large flocks for migrating in the fall. I once saw a flock of migrating Tree Swallows that I estimated had 3,000 birds in it. And there was a migrating flock seen in late July, 1989, near Rocky Point on Upper Klamath Lake, that was estimated at more than 20,000 birds, mostly consisting of Violet-green Swallows. Even this number seems almost trivial when compared with the size of flocks that have been reported from the east coast. In one case, it was estimated that the number of Tree Swallows migrating past during the day was in the hundreds of thousands, perhaps millions.

Both species have responded positively to nest boxes, and their populations have increased as a result. But both of them have to battle not only members of their own species for the boxes, but also other species, principally House Sparrows and European Starlings.

I once came into possession of a nesting box that I was assured had a hole in it of just the right size for Tree Swallows, but which was too small for starlings to enter. We put the box up, and a pair of House Sparrows immediately claimed it. All of the expert advice is, if you want Tree Swallows to come, then you have to rid the box of House Sparrow eggs on a regular basis. Neither my wife nor I could bring ourselves to do that, so we waited. One morning, as my wife watched, she saw a starling come to the hole, struggle to enter, and succeed. It remained inside for a while, and then came out, once more struggling in the process. So much for "starling-proof" nest boxes. We might be willing to put up with House Sparrows, but not with starlings. The box came down.

Sometimes, in battles between starlings and swallows, it is the swallows who win. Arthur Cleveland Bent tells a tale of a pair of Tree Swallows, who, once they had occupied a box, left at least one of the pair constantly on guard, usually perched on the roof of the house. If a starling appeared, the swallow would immediately enter the box and sit with its head sticking out of the hole, blocking the entrance. The starlings finally gave up.

Tree Swallows migrate south to Mexico for the winter, but in some years, one will get recorded on the Medford Christmas Count. Thus, at least a few of them apparently stick around during the winter. They are the only ones in the swallow tribe that eat berries and seeds as well as insects, so perhaps this trait is what makes it possible for them to stay during the winter.

## Northern Rough-winged Swallow (NRWS)
*Stelgidopteryx serripennis*

This is the plainest of our swallows -- plain brown above, pale underparts, and drab, buffy throat. One thing to be alert to is that the broad white undertail coverts sometimes are visible from above, which, with a fleeting look, might resemble the white flank patches of a Violet-green Swallow. Another thing to look for is that Rough-wings tend to have a more deliberate, flowing flight than some of the other swallows.

The 2001 Breeding Bird Atlas shows them as sparsely distributed breeders through most of Southern Oregon. They prefer stream, lake, and pond shorelines, primarily because that's where the banks are that they dig their nesting tunnels in. In this respect they resemble Bank Swallows, but they do not nest in large colonies like Bank Swallows do. The birds dig their own tunnels, but have been known to re-use tunnels made by kingfishers. Sometimes the tunnels are shallow, only a foot or so, but usually are deeper, up to 4 feet.

When they can't find a soft bank to dig a tunnel in, Northern Rough-winged Swallows have been known to adapt to other kinds of cavities -- holes in masonry, quarries and caves, crannies and ledges under bridges, and even gutters and drainpipes. In one astonishing case, a pair built a nest on a buttress beneath the deck of a river steamboat (this was in the east), and then followed the boat on its daily trips in order to feed their young.

About the name: The "rough-winged" comes because there is a little hook on one of the primary feathers, and the "northern" comes because there is another "rough-wing" to the south, in Central America.

## Bank Swallow (BANS)
*Riparia riparia*

There's little doubt about the meaning of the scientific name. *Riparia* refers to the fact that these birds like to live in the banks along streams, i.e., in riparian settings. However, I can think of at least three Bank Swallow colonies I have seen that were not in riparian settings. One was in a sandy cliff facing the ocean, one was in a road cut, and another was in a big pile of dirt sitting in a garbage disposal dumpsite.

It is the almost perpendicular bank, of course, that is important, and along streams is where many of these banks are. Bank Swallows live in dense colonies, and a bank where a colony is located is typically peppered with holes, not all of them necessarily in active use. These holes, dug by the swallows themselves, may be 2 or 3 feet deep or even deeper, depending upon how soft the soil is. Usually, the burrows run at right angles to the cliff face, but sometimes they do not, and two burrows may come together and end in a common chamber. When this happens, it seems to be that the usual outcome is for both pairs of swallows to build their nests in the common chamber.

Colony sites may be reused year after year, but the swallows may have to abandon a site and move elsewhere, usually for one of two reasons: (1) the bank becomes unstable, perhaps because of river erosion; (2) the burrows may become so infested with mites that the swallows move out. In situations of the latter type, the swallows sometimes move back again later, presumably because the mites have died.

The identification of a Bank Swallow is straightforward: the back is dark brown and the underparts are white, and there is a conspicuous dark band running across the breast, that comes together in the center with a distinct dark "V" pointing downward. Juvenile Tree Swallows also have dark bands across their breasts, but the band is diffuse and not as well defined as in the Bank Swallow, and the downward-pointing "V" is absent.

Bank Swallows occur in Britain, too, where they are called "Sand Martins." Some have advocated that we should change the name of our bird so it is the same as the British one, in the spirit that the English common name of a bird should be the same everywhere in the world.

## Cliff Swallow (CLSW)
*Petrochelidon pyrrhonota*

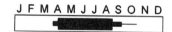

Punctuality on the part of Cliff Swallows concerning their return in the spring is one of our cherished bits of folklore. And punctual they are, at least within a swallow's terms of reference. Their fabled return to San Juan Capistrano on the exact same date, March 19, each year -- even at the exact same hour, according to some enthusiastic reporters -- has been well chronicled. And they do generally arrive within a day or two of the expected time.

There is such a thing as arriving too early. A case has been reported (in the east, not at Capistrano) in which the swallows arrived early, after a warm spell. The warm spell was followed by a prolonged cold spell, and it was estimated that 90 percent of the swallows died, both from the cold, and from the absence of flying insects for food.

Cliff swallows are the ones who build those gourd-shaped nests, the ones that look like an Eskimo igloo with a hole on top, gathered together in closely packed colonies. Two elements are needed, in order to build their nests: (1) a convenient vertical surface, reasonably protected from the elements; (2) a nearby source of mud.

They fly down to the mud, barely touching the surface, with their wings fluttering, and scoop up a ball of mud. This they take back and fit it into place. It has been estimated that it takes on the order of a thousand trips, to build one of the nests. In one case, an observer noted that a particular female swallow did not make any trips to the mud source. Instead, she remained at her own partially completed nest, and as soon as a nearby swallow had deposited a gob of mud and departed, she would go get the mud and use it in her own nest. As if this particular kind of larceny is not enough, the birds also engage in brood parasitism, laying their eggs in the nests of neighbors. They have even been observed transferring their eggs by mouth, into neighbors' nests.

The nests do not contain much reinforcing material such as straw, and thus are vulnerable to rainstorms. To protect against this, the swallows try to place their nests with some overhead protection. They especially like the undersides of bridges and culverts, and, as humans have built more and more of these, the Cliff Swallow populations have responded by expanding their ranges.

They also place their nests on dams and buildings, sometimes irritating the owners of the buildings. They might even put them on cliffs -- the traditional locations -- if they can't find something better.

They breed widely in our region and in the state as a whole, although not usually at the higher elevations. They advertise their presence by their numbers as they fly in and out of a nesting location such as a bridge It is easy to recognize one, by its squared-off tail and orange rump patch. Our local subspecies has a whitish forehead, but one in the southwest, called "Mexican Cliff Swallow," has a chestnut colored forehead.

The most serious enemy of the Cliff Swallow appears to be the House Sparrow. The sparrows have been observed to take possession of the nests and drive the swallows away, tossing out the eggs and nestlings of the swallows. Ants are another enemy. Nests deserted by the swallows have been examined in which dead nestlings were found, covered by ants.

# Barn Swallow (BARS)
*Hirundo rustica*

A Barn Swallow is instantly recognizable by its long forked tail and cinnamon-colored underparts. It is probably the best-known of the swallows. For nests, they build open cups of mud (unlike Cliff Swallows, who build closed dome-like mud nests), reinforced with straw, with some sort of overhead cover. Before Europeans arrived, they probably used rocky caves, crevices in cliffs, or rocky shelves with some protection from above. Today they use human-built structures almost entirely for their nests, and only occasionally use natural sites. Wherever they may locate, there must be a nearby mud supply.

**Barn Swallow**

Their nests may be placed on either a vertical or a horizontal surface, in the angle of a framing brace, or in a corner where two sides are supported. They will place their nests inside buildings if they are accessible, under eaves, but especially under bridges. They don't nest colonially in the fashion of Cliff Swallows, but several Barn Swallows may place their nests close together in a favored location.

They may use material other than straw for their reinforcement. One analysis of a nest produced the following list: 1635 rootlets, 139 pine needles, 450 pieces of dried grass, 10 chicken feathers, and 2 human hairs. Both parents share in incubation duties, changing places frequently during the day. At night, the female apparently does the incubation, with the male perched close by.

They are common throughout our region, and throughout the state. They are present in low-lying areas, but also may be found at higher elevations, provided there are suitable nesting sites. I once saw a nest with nestlings in it located next to the front door of a mountain lodge, at an elevation of 5000 feet.

As is always the case with wildlife, they are subject to lots of risks. A long spell of cold weather is a major risk. I was told of a case where early-arriving Barn Swallows were caught by a long spell of cold rain, and for shelter and warmth crowded into boxes that had been set out for Wood Ducks. House Wrens have been known to puncture the swallows' eggs and appropriate their nests. There is even a bizarre case of a swallow being captured by an enormous bull frog. A human saw the frog with the tips of a bird's wings protruding from its mouth, captured it, and discovered that the bird was an adult Barn Swallow.

Barn Swallows spend most of their time in the air capturing insects on the wing, as do other swallows. In 1831, an ornithologist attempted to calculate how many miles a swallow might fly in a lifetime, using the following assumptions: speed -- 60 mph; daily effort -- ten hours; life span -- ten years. The answer? Two million miles. Many have scoffed, saying the estimate is too high. Okay. Cut it in half. Then it's one million miles.

## Family **PARIDAE:** Chickadees and Titmice

**Black-capped Chickadee** (BCCH)
*Poecile atricapilla*

West: J F M A M J J A S O N D (all months)
East: (none)

**Mountain Chickadee** (MOCH)
*Poecile gambeli*

J F M A M J J A S O N D (all months)

Everybody knows the chickadee, but problems might arise sometimes in separating these two. The Mountain Chickadee has a white eyebrow, which the Black-capped lacks, although the eyebrow can be worn and indistinct by late summer, and may even disappear altogether. Also, Black-cappeds on the Pacific Coast have a strong pinkish-brown wash on their flanks when in fresh plumage, whereas Mountains are grayish. (Black-cappeds in the Rocky Mountains have less pinkish wash on the flanks than those on the Pacific or Atlantic Coasts.)

The familiar *chick-a-dee-dee* calls of the two are similar, and so are the high, whistled *fee-bee* songs, with the first note higher than the second. The Black-capped often just does the two syllables *fee-bee,* but sometimes may make it three: *fee-bee-bee.* The typical song of the Mountain is the three syllable *fee-bee-bee* song, with sometimes four or five syllables.

The ranges of the two species in general do not overlap. The Black-capped is mostly a lower elevation bird, found primarily west of the Cascades in the river valleys and in urban areas, especially those dominated by hardwoods. Mountain Chickadees are exactly what the name implies, and are year-round residents of coniferous forests, especially at the higher elevations. The 2001 Breeding Bird Atlas shows them as confirmed breeders in the Cascades and Siskiyous, and throughout Klamath County.

Both species eat mostly insects in summer, but seeds in the winter. Both of them cache seeds (and are good at finding them again), and it is the caches which help the Mountain Chickadees get through the winter. Even so, in some winters, they may show up in the lower valleys. After the nesting season is over, chickadees may join up with other birds in loose flocks, often including warblers and nuthatches.

Both species usually excavate their own nests, typically choosing the dead stub of a tree, and removing the decayed wood to make a hole. They also may use old woodpecker holes, and will use nesting boxes. In one case, a Mountain Chickadee entered through a space at the lower edge of a cabin and built a nest on one of the floor joists.

## Chestnut-backed Chickadee (CBCH)
*Poecile rufescens*

J F M A M J J A S O N D

Chestnut-backed Chickadees are commonly thought of as birds of the coast, and so they are. But they also breed throughout western Oregon, especially in forests dominated by Douglas-fir. In Southern Oregon they are found in the Siskiyous and in the Cascades, and breed as far east as the vicinity of Crater Lake.

From below, they look pretty much like a Black-capped Chickadee, but a glimpse of the back reveals the rich chestnut color that gives the bird its name. The ones in our region also have chestnut on the flanks, but toward the south, in Central California, the flanks become grayish.

Chestnut-backs have a *"chick-a-dee"* call, but it is thinner, higher, and buzzier than in the Black-capped. They also have a high-pitched *tseet tseet* call that has been likened to that of a Golden-crowned Kinglet. They apparently do not have a "fee-bee" song of the type given by the Black-capped and Mountain Chickadees.

Like other chickadees, they mostly make their own nests by excavating decayed wood from dead trees, but in situations where the outer shell of the tree is still hard. They occasionally use woodpecker holes, and will use nesting boxes if placed near evergreen trees.

Chestnut-backs are often seen in small flocks, and will form loose associations with other species, especially Golden-crowned Kinglets, but also including nuthatches and warblers. They sometimes will respond to squeaking sounds with the lips on the back of the hand.

## Oak Titmouse (OATI)
*Baeolophus inornatus*

J F M A M J J A S O N D
West
East

## Juniper Titmouse (JUTI)
*Baeolophus ridgwayi*

J F M A M J J A S O N D
East

These two recently-split species (formerly known under the combined name of "Plain Titmouse") pose an interesting situation for Oregon birders. First of all, even though both are widely distributed throughout the west, in Oregon they occur only in the southern part of the state. As far as Oak Titmouse is concerned, the Rogue Valley is their stronghold in Oregon, and it is an isolated population. Titmice don't normally occur much further north, and there is a big gap between this population and those further to the south, caused by the extensive coniferous forests around Mt. Shasta

Juniper Titmice are known to occur in southern Lake County, east of Lakeville. There, along Highway 140, is the classic place in Oregon to look for them. But what about the birds in the Klamath Basin? Exactly where, in this region, do the two species come in contact? Carla Cicero, who did the basic research that resulted in the split into two species, placed their zone of contact near Mt. Dome, which lies in California, south of Lower Klamath NWR and west of Lava Beds NM.

More recent evidence suggests that the zone of contact may be Lava Beds NM itself. In this zone, birds that are brownish and birds that are grayish appear, the former suggesting Oak Titmouse and the latter Juniper Titmouse. Furthermore, there are birds in this zone exhibiting characteristics of both species.

The best opinion, until further research is done, seems to be that the birds found to the west of Lava Beds are Oak Titmice, including those found around Klamath Falls, and those down the Klamath River Canyon. The ones found to the east, in Langell Valley and around Clear Lake NWR, are Juniper Titmice.[1] A special problem with Juniper Titmice is that they tend to be very sparsely distributed and are not easy to find.

Oak Titmice, on the other hand, are reasonably easy to find, with their chickadee-like calls, and loud whistled *pe-to pe-to peto* spring songs. They are browner than Juniper Titmice, which are quite gray. As far back as 1923, Joseph Grinnell thought that the bird we now call Juniper Titmouse was a distinct form, and said he was almost tempted to propose full species status for it. He called it "Gray Titmouse."

The spring songs of the two are similar, but the song of the Juniper is lower pitched and more rapid. Also, the Juniper Titmouse has a "rattle" call, and I was able to get my very first look at one by following that call. A few years later, however, I was startled to hear an Oak Titmouse give a similar call, although that was the only time I've ever heard one of them do it, so maybe it's not habitual. In the meantime, we should enjoy our Oak Titmice, since we are the only ones in Oregon who have them. And we certainly should enjoy our Juniper Titmice, providing we can find them.

## Family **AEGITHALIDAE**: Long-tailed Tits and Bushtits

**Bushtit** (BUSH)
*Psaltriparus minimus*

J F M A M J J A S O N D

"Tit" is an old Middle English word meaning "small," and the name is certainly suitable for the Bushtit, because it is one of the smallest birds in North America. In Britain, they call all chickadee-type birds "tits."

During most of the year, Bushtits travel in medium-sized flocks, with 20 to 50 birds in a flock. The first indication you have that any of them are around is when you hear their continuous twittering sound, used to keep the flock together. Joseph Grinnell made a careful study of their call notes, and concluded they have five different calls: (1) their usual twittering "location" calls; (2) a louder twittering, when they are traveling rapidly and not feeding; (3) an even louder call, used by an individual that has become separated from

---

[1] I am indebted to Kevin Spencer and Don Roberson for this information.

the flock; (4) a loud alarm note, used when an enemy is discovered; (5) a shrill quavering trill uttered continuously by the entire flock, apparently used to confuse an enemy such as a Cooper's Hawk, because individual sources cannot be picked out.

When a flock comes into view, several birds will be spotted in a nearby tree, actively foraging for insects, hanging upside down as often as in any other position, with stragglers moving from tree to tree, so that the whole flock has a forward advance. They arrive, they are all around you, and then they are gone.

In breeding season, they separate into pairs and become much more quiet, and are harder to find. They industriously build their incredible nests, sometimes taking weeks to do so. The nest is a hanging gourd-shaped structure 7 to 10 inches long, with an opening on the side toward the top.

The birds make their nests by starting at the top with a shallow bag woven into the branchlets of a tree, and then make it deeper by getting inside and forcing the bag to stretch downward, subsequently filling in the thin parts with more material. Toward the bottom, the walls of the nest may be an inch thick, providing a secure, warm place for the young. After the eggs are laid, both parents spend the nights inside the nest.

Such a nest, even though suspended in the open in plain view, may be hard to spot, because the mosses and lichens used in its construction may make it look like just so much litter hanging from the branches. So-called "helper" Bushtits may stick around the nest area, assisting to build the nest, feeding the young, and occasionally even participating in incubation.

Bushtits are common breeders throughout Southern Oregon at the lower elevations. They are rare at the higher elevations. The eyes of the female are pale yellow, but in the males are dark. Juveniles of both sexes have dark eyes, generally through the month of August. The overall color is brownish-gray, but the birds in our area are brownish on the tops of their heads. To the east, from eastern Oregon on through the interior, the heads are grayish.

## Family **SITTIDAE**: Nuthatches

**Red-breasted Nuthatch** (RBNU)
*Sitta canadensis*

**White-breasted Nuthatch** (WBNU)
*Sitta carolinensis*

Nuthatches are fun. They dash about on tree branches, rush headlong down trunks, search crannies in the bark, and hang upside down like chickadees, in never-ending searches for nuts, insect eggs and larvae, all the while calling out energetically to their colleagues.

It seems almost to be a rule that, before you see a nuthatch, you will hear it. If you are in the high country, the *ank! ank! ank!* of the Red-breasted Nuthatch seems to come from everywhere, sounding for all the world like a little tin horn. The sound is deceptive, and often makes it seem as if the bird is a long distance off, when in fact it may be close by.

On the other hand, if you are lower down, in the oak country, it is the White-breasted Nuthatch you will hear. The call of the White-breasted is similar to that of the Red-breasted, but is subtly different. Unfortunately, field guides are likely to render both calls as *yank! yank! yank!* but the Red-breasted seems somewhat more resonant to me like, well, a little tin horn. The White-breasted is more raspy, to my ear at least.

The main reason for putting these two birds together is that there is sometimes some confusion in identifying them. The trouble arises from the term "red-breasted." The Red-breasteds are indeed reddish on their breasts, but White-breasteds generally have some reddish underneath also, on the flanks. A look at the face will settle the matter. The face of the White-breasted around the eye is white. The face of the Red-breasted has stripes: a white stripe over the eye, and a prominent black stripe right through the eye.

**White-breasted Nuthatch**

Both species are widely distributed in Southern Oregon. The general rule is: Red-breasteds are at the higher elevations in the conifers, especially in the firs; White-breasteds are at lower elevations in the oaks and ponderosas. In the winter, Red-breasteds often descend to lower elevations.

For nesting, both use natural cavities and old woodpecker holes, and sometimes use nest boxes. Red-breasteds do more of their own excavating than do White-breasteds. Another peculiarity of Red-breasteds is that they have the habit of smearing pitch from conifers around the entrances to their nesting cavities.

Both species eat insects and insect eggs, usually found by means of their foraging activities in scurrying about on tree trunks and branches, investigating all the crannies. White-breasteds are considered to be "tool-users," because they sometimes use flakes of bark to pry off other pieces of bark.

Red-breasteds have been observed catching insects in the air, flycatcher-style. In winter, both species eat nuts, with the White-breasted favoring larger nuts like acorns, and Red-breasted favoring the nuts of conifers. Thus, the "nut" part of their name is obvious, and the "hatch" part is believed to be a corruption of "hack," referring to the habit of some Old World nuthatches to hack seeds and nuts open with their bills. New World nuthatches do not do this as often as the birds from the Old World, although Red-breasteds have been observed to wedge pieces of nut meat into bark crevices and then hack them into smaller pieces.

Because nuthatches so often proceed head first, down the trunk of a tree, they undoubtedly find many items of food overlooked by woodpeckers and creepers, who do their foraging with their heads pointed *up* the trunk. You may sometimes find a woodpecker hanging upside from a horizontal branch, but I don't think you are likely to see one going down a trunk head first, nuthatch-style.

## Pygmy Nuthatch (PYNU)
*Sitta pygmaea*

|  | J F M A M J J A S O N D |
|---|---|
| West | - - - - - - - - - - - - - - - - - - - - - - - |
| East | ███████████████████████ |

Pygmy Nuthatches sort of look like chickadees, but behave more like Bushtits. They busily flit about in loose flocks like Bushtits do, keeping up a constant twittering, again much like Bushtits, all the while drifting from tree to tree. A major difference from Bushtits is that they are likely to be found high in pine trees, whereas Bushtits are more likely to be found low, in bushes and small trees. A behavior trait that marks Pygmy Nuthatches off from the other nuthatches is that will go right out onto the outer twigs and pine needles in their foraging, something the other nuthatches generally don't do.

Two things make them resemble chickadees: they have black caps, and they often hang upside down on the branches. A close look will show that they don't really look like chickadees at all. For one thing, they don't have black bibs, and for another, their tails are very short, not at all like the long tails of chickadees.

These birds are found primarily east of the crest, and are strongly associated with ponderosa pines, moving about in flocks whenever they are not directly engaged in nesting activities. Other birds, such as chickadees and warblers, often move with the flocks.

They are confirmed breeders in many areas of Klamath County, but breeding has not been confirmed in either Josephine or Jackson counties. They are hole nesters like the other nuthatches, and usually excavate their own nests in the rotting centers of dead trees or dead branches, but will also use old woodpecker holes. Often, there are "helpers" about the nest, generally young birds from the previous season, who help with feeding. It has been observed that nests with "helpers" have a better success rate than those without.

They are not migratory, although they may range outside their breeding territories after breeding is over. On very cold winter nights, bunches of them may jam into cavities together to maintain warmth, and may even go into a state of torpor until morning comes.

Pygmy Nuthatches sometimes show amazing tolerance for the presence of humans. Arthur Cleveland Bent relates a case of a nest that was placed in a partially decayed post next to a boardwalk. People were passing constantly and workmen were repairing a drain nearby, but the birds seemed unfazed by all this, and went about the job of raising their brood. He relates another case in which an ornithologist was attempting to reach into a nest to examine the eggs, but the bird, whenever it saw a chance, would light next to the hole and dodge inside past the ornithologist's hand.

## Family **CERTHIIDAE**: Creepers

### Brown Creeper (BRCR)
*Certhia americana*

This bird is perfectly named, for it is indeed brown, looking almost like a loose flake of bark, and creeping is what it does for a living. They are so well camouflaged that they can go unnoticed except for one thing. As they creep along the trunk of a tree, looking for insects and spiders, they regularly emit thin little *tsss* notes. This is usually the first indication there is a creeper nearby. The high-pitched note is similar to that of a Golden-crowned Kinglet, except that the kinglets usually repeat their notes -- *tss tss tss*.

Unfortunately, if you don't hear high frequencies well, then you won't be able to detect its thin little call note. I understand that men are more likely than women to lose their ability to hear high frequencies as they get older, so whenever I am in the forest I listen intently, to see if I can still hear a creeper.

They also have a high, thin song, that sounds like *zee zee zoodle-dee zee,* and has been rendered as "trees, trees, beau-ti-ful trees." To me, this sounds very much like the song of the Black-throated Green Warbler, which is an eastern bird. On one occasion, I pursued this song down the edge of the Rogue River without being able to pinpoint its source, just about convinced I had discovered the presence of an eastern rarity. I finally caught sight of the bird, and it was a Brown Creeper.

Creepers have a characteristic foraging behavior. One will fly to the base of a tree and then move upward on the trunk, generally foraging in a spiral path as it proceeds upward, using its tail as a prop like a woodpecker. I have never seen one turn its head downward like a nuthatch does, or even hitch its way back down like a woodpecker. Once in a while, a creeper may give a little backward hop, but mostly it will proceed diligently up the trunk until it gets near the top. Then it flies down to the base of a neighboring tree and begins the process all over again.

Brown Creepers are widespread breeders and year-round residents in Southern Oregon. They usually build their nests under loose bark of large-diameter dead trees, although they have also been observed to use old woodpecker holes if loose bark is not available.

The ability of these birds to camouflage themselves when danger threatens is remarkable. In one case an observer was watching a creeper when a hawk screamed. The creeper flattened itself against the trunk, and, even though the observer had been watching through a scope, he was unable to make out the contours of the bird, and to be certain it was not just a lichen.

# Family **TROGLODYTIDAE**: Wrens

**Rock Wren** (ROWR)
*Salpinctes obsoletus*

Rock Wrens are well named. They do like rocky outcrops, cliffs, lava fields, and the rocky faces of earth-fill dams. These are primarily birds of eastern Oregon, although a small contingent comes west of the crest. Their nests are usually placed in the crevices between the rocks and can be difficult to locate, although their habit of "paving" the entrances to their nests with small flat stones can be a clue.

A few places where they have been found is the rocky cliffs south of the visitor center near Tule Lake NWR, Table Rocks in the Rogue Valley, and at Emigrant Lake, near Ashland. When I looked for them at Emigrant Lake, I searched the area of the rocky dam diligently without success, and then came across a pair in the campground.

The scientific name *obsoletus* makes it sound like the bird is obsolete, but it actually means "indistinct," for the bird's dull coloration. The color blends in well with its rocky surroundings, but the Rock Wren's habit of moving restlessly about, often perching on the tops of rocks, and giving its buzzy *brzzt!* call at intervals, makes it easy to spot. When it flies, the light buffy tips on the tail, except for the central feathers, are visible.

When one sings, it sounds much like the repetitious song of a mockingbird. The song has been interpreted as *chur-wee chur-wee chur-wee, chee-ur chee-ur chee-ur chee-ur, deedle deedle deedle,* and so on. There is also a call note that sounds like *tick-ear!* It is said that the total repertoire of the species exceeds a hundred song types.

**Canyon Wren** (CANW)
*Catherpes mexicanus*

I'll stick my head out, and say here that I think the Canyon Wren's song is the most beautiful bird song of all. Dr. William Beebe in 1905 described it thus: "It is a silvery dropping song of eight or ten clear sweet notes, becoming more plaintive as they descend . . ," and Arthur Cleveland Bent added that it fills "the whole canyon with delightful melody."

Canyon and Rock Wrens inhabit somewhat similar surroundings -- rock piles and rocky canyons. The Rock Wren tends to run around more in the open than does the Canyon Wren, who has a habit of disappearing among the rocks and then suddenly appearing elsewhere, apparently having traveled through some hidden set of crevices. Frequently, as it travels, it gives out a penetrating *bzzzt!* that resembles somewhat the call of a Common Nighthawk. Hearing the harsh *bzzzt,* one wonders if this same bird is truly the source of that ethereal cascading song.

Canyon Wrens are more brightly colored than Rock Wrens, with rufous both above and below, a gray head, and a gleaming white throat that stands out like a little searchlight, even though the rest of the body might be obscured by shadow. If there is one recognition point that stands out above all others with the Canyon Wren, it is the gleaming white throat. (Except for the wonderful song, of course.)

Canyon Wrens are sparingly distributed in Southern Oregon, mostly east of the crest, although they are also present in scattered areas of the Siskiyous, and have been heard singing at Upper Table Rock. They have been found in the rocks and cliffs near the visitor center at Tule Lake NWR, and in the Klamath River canyon.

**Bewick's Wren** (BEWR)
*Thryomanes bewickii*

I've heard the name of this bird pronounced a number of ways, but my encyclopedia says it should be BEW-icks, as in the automobile. It is an accomplished songster, and has such a variety of songs that it is sometimes difficult to be certain that it is a Bewick's doing the singing, and not something else.

Bewick's Wrens and Song Sparrows can sound a lot alike. Both may start off their songs with two or three notes, all on the same pitch, and then move into a more complex set of notes and trills. In fact, there may be cases where you can't tell them apart. They also are capable of mimicry, and an observer found one that occasionally gave the spring song of a chickadee.

Generally, though, the Bewick's Wren's song will end with a rapid series of notes all on the same pitch, sometimes given as a trill. There often will be a *bzzz* at the beginning, or sometimes in the middle of the song, similar to the bird's scratchy call note. There is much variation, with birds on the east coast the most likely ones to sound like Song Sparrows. A typical song might be rendered as *pit pit bzzz deedledee* (ending in a trill).

Bewick's Wrens like brushy areas, especially in riparian habitats, and breed widely in such locations on the west side of the Cascades. They are much less common in eastern Oregon, except in the Klamath Basin, where they are common in appropriate habitat. They are readily recognizable by the bold white eye-stripe, brown back, long tail, and light gray underparts.

For nesting, a cavity of some sort is needed. Sometimes a cavity is used in the roots of an upturned tree where an embedded boulder has fallen out. But they also have been found nesting in old woodpecker holes, bird boxes, under slabs of peeling bark, and even in tin cans. In the east, Bewick's Wrens are considered to be in a state of decline, but in Oregon the population appears to be increasing.

# House Wren (HOWR)
*Troglodytes aedon*

|       | J F M A M J J A S O N D |
|-------|--------------------------|
| West  | ────▬▬▬──────            |
| East  | ───▬▬▬▬▬▬▬───            |

House Wren

*Troglodytes,* of course, means "cave dweller," and it's not a bad name for this cavity-nester. Its definition of what constitutes a cavity is indeed broad. Not only are natural cavities such as crevices in stumps or in caves utilized, but so are bird boxes, and old woodpecker holes. Also, convenient nooks in buildings, tin cans, boxes, pails, crates, empty stove pipes, and coats left hanging in sheds will do. Probably the most remarkable example I have come across was of a pair of wrens that built their nest on the rear axle of an automobile. When the automobile was moved, the wrens went along, and ultimately hatched a brood.

After a nest is completed and occupied, a male House Wren may start another nest, and sometimes acquires a second mate to go along with it. Or it may be that the original female moves over to the new nest and starts a second brood, while the male attends to the original brood. Or she may select an entirely different nest constructed by a different male, and desert the original brood, leaving it to the care of the original male. There even are cases in which unmated birds will satisfy the urge to care for offspring by helping to care for the young of other species. Life in the House Wren's world can be complex.

Their song is a delight. It is loud and long, and consists of rattles and trills in a bubbling cascade. During breeding season it is heard frequently, usually from a highly visible perch. It is claimed that House Wrens sometime mimic the song of a Bewick's Wren, but I've personally never caught one doing that. Maybe they do such a good job of it that I have been completely fooled.

There is a dark side to the House Wren. When nesting sites are scarce, and the numbers of the birds are high, some males take to puncturing the eggs and killing the young of other birds, presumably to reduce competition for scarce resources. In the 1920s, a battle apparently raged in ornithological circles over whether House Wrens should be condemned for such tactics. One ornithologist, defending the wrens, said, "Tried in a court of men and he no doubt would be convicted of the charges made against him; but a court of Wrens would dismiss the case and commend the culprit."

House Wrens breed widely in Southern Oregon, in the valleys, the foothills, and even in the higher elevations. Contrary to what might be expected, they even are found in regenerating clearcuts, where they apparently find the brushy spots and open spaces to their liking. East of the Cascades, they are often found in aspen groves and open forests of Douglas fir and ponderosa pines. Following breeding, there may be some temporary dispersal to higher elevations, and as winter approaches, they migrate south.

## Winter Wren (WIWR)
*Troglodytes troglodytes*

Whoever named this little bird must have liked it so well he named it twice, *Troglodytes troglodytes*. Actually, it was named by Linnaeus in the 18th century, and was probably given the double name because it is the only wren in the Old World. In the New World there are 59 species of wrens, and it is believed they originated here. The Winter Wren is presumed to have made its way to the Old World via Alaska and the Bering land bridge. Along the way, it managed to establish an isolated outpost of Winter Wrens on the Pribilof Islands, in the middle of the Bering Sea. In Britain, because it's the only wren they have, they simply call it the Wren.

There are three outstanding things about this bird, besides its tiny size: first is its preferred surroundings, which consists of deep shady forest with tangled undergrowth; second is its short tail, carried sticking straight up in the air, and sometimes even cocked so far forward it almost sticks over the bird's head; third is its song, which has been described by many writers in loving detail, as one of the loveliest of bird songs.

The song does have an almost out-ot-this-world quality, sounding much like a rapid high-pitched tinkling of tiny bells. It typically goes on so long that you wonder how such a tiny body can hold so much breath. The length of the song has been timed at lasting from 8 to 17 seconds, and once at 23 seconds. The song is usually given from the top of a stump or from a low-hanging dead branch. When not singing, the birds bustle about in the underbrush, generally out of sight, and give a frequently repeated call note -- *chik! chik-chik! chik-chik!*

Like most wrens, they like to use some sort of cavity for nesting, a cranny in upturned roots, under the bark of a decaying log, or under the roots of a standing tree. For reasons best known to the wrens, the males often build extra nests, sometimes called "decoy nests," because they are generally not built as well as the real nests. It has been suggested that these nests represent an excess of nest-building zeal, although others believe the male may be trying to appropriate all the available nesting sites in the vicinity.

Winter Wrens are widespread in Southern Oregon, and have been confirmed as breeders in the Cascades and Siskiyous in moist conifer forests, often near streams. In winter some may migrate south, but others move down slope from the higher elevations and find such shelter as they can. In a case in western Washington, the shelter was a small birdbox, 6 inches square, into which 31 Winter Wrens were seen to crowd at dusk.

The name "winter" wren may have come from the birds' behavior in the east where most migrate south, but a few stay around in the more northern latitudes and stick out the winter.

# Marsh Wren (MAWR)
*Cistothorus palustris*

When you are near a marsh of cattails and bulrushes in spring, one of the most persistent noises will be that of Marsh Wrens. You may hear three or four of them at once -- all of them invisible. Furthermore, the sounds may move rapidly from place to place, but with their sources remaining unseen.

If you stand still for a moment, the noisemaker may briefly show itself, clambering to the top of a cattail, all the time singing lustily. But make any motion, and the singer disappears instantly.

The "song" has been described in different ways, depending upon the outlook of the observer. Bent quotes one observer who said, "The song begins with a scrape like the tuning of a violin followed by a trill with bubbles, gurgles, or rattles . . . at times liquid and musical, at other times rattling and harsh, but always vigorous."

**Marsh Wren**

Another was less kindly disposed and said, ". . . you hear a low, crackling sound, something similar to that produced by air bubbles forcing their way through mud or boggy ground when trod upon."

If you have an older bird book, it may show this bird as "Long-billed Marsh Wren." There also used to be a "Short-billed Marsh Wren," an eastern bird that is now called Sedge Wren. The two current names are quite appropriate for the two species, because Marsh Wrens are almost completely bound to wet marshes, whereas Sedge Wrens tend more to prefer wet meadows.

Marsh Wrens build globe-shaped nests over water by binding a bunch of cattails or bulrushes together and constructing the exterior of the nest with cattail leaves and stems. The nest is domed, and has an entrance on one side. A pair may work on several nests at once, but only build an interior lining in one of them, a task which is carried out by the female. The rest are called "dummy nests," and their exact purpose is unclear.

Sometimes as many as a dozen dummy nests might be constructed, mostly by the males, and many of them are never finished. Since Marsh Wrens are known to be polygynous (where a male has more than one mate), one could guess that is the reason behind all the extra nests.

Marsh Wrens are present in our area wherever there is an adequate marsh, especially in the Klamath Basin. Any small wren found in a marsh and singing lustily can safely be taken to be a Marsh Wren. However, there is a visual mark that is worth mentioning. This is the highly visible black and white striping on the upper back. The eastern Sedge Wren has similar striping, but the rest of our wrens do not.

# Family CINCLIDAE: Dippers

## American Dipper (AMDI)
*Cinclus mexicanus*

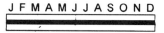

In 1911, John Muir wrote the following, in his famous essay called "The Water Ouzel":

> Among all the countless waterfalls I have met in the course of ten years' exploration in the Sierra, whether among the icy peaks, or warm foot-hills, or in the profound yosemitic canyons of the middle region, not one was found without its ouzel. No canyon is too cold for this little bird, none too lonely, provided it be rich in falling water. Find a fall, or cascade, or rushing rapid, anywhere upon a clear stream, and there you will surely find its complementary ouzel, flitting about in the spray, diving in foaming eddies, whirling like a leaf among beaten foam-bells; ever vigorous and enthusiastic, yet self-contained, and neither seeking nor shunning your company.
>
> If disturbed while dipping about in the margin shallows, he either sets off with a rapid wfiir to some other feeding-ground up or down the stream, or alights on some half-submerged rock or snag out in the current, and immediately begins to nod and curtsey like a wren, turning his head from side to side with many other odd dainty movements that never fail to fix the attention of the observer.

Today, of course, we know the "Water Ouzel" as the American Dipper. I always have had a sentimental attachment to the name "Water Ouzel," and was sorry to see it go, even after I learned that "ouzel" comes from an old Anglo-Saxon word for "blackbird."

Southern Oregon abounds with "Water Ouzel" streams in the Cascades and Siskiyous, just as much as in the "yosemitic" canyons of which Muir wrote. For example, the Audubon Society's annual winter trip to the little stream that flows through Lithia Park, in Ashland, typically produces 6 or 7 of these birds in a three-mile stretch of creek.

Dippers are so attached to rushing water that when they fly they almost invariably will follow the course of the stream, and prefer not to fly over land even for a short distance. One will dive into fast rushing water as if it were a placid pond, forage while walking on the bottom, and then pop out again to stand on a rock, bobbing its body up and down in the fashion that gives it its name "dipper." In doing this, the bird vertically moves its whole body as a unit, instead of teetering or bobbing its tail as some other birds do.

The typical nest of a dipper is about a foot in diameter, consisting mostly of moss, domed over, and with a hole in the side. Invariably, the nest is near water, usually placed on a vertical rock surface, and often so close to a tumbling waterfall that it is kept constantly wet. However, I have also seen them built on the trusswork under wooden bridges, and saw one once that had been built onto the vertical concrete wall belonging to the control valve of an irrigation ditch. The nests are reputed to be kept very clean. The young birds eject their fecal matter enclosed by a membrane, called a "fecal sac." The parents remove these sacs and discard them some distance from the nest.

One summer, my wife and I were in Yosemite Valley and decided to take a nature walk with a park naturalist. The naturalist had a distinct New York accent, which made me think he might be a city boy, and I wondered where he had obtained his knowledge of western bird life. As we walked, he casually pointed to three Brewer's Blackbirds, foraging at the edge of a mud puddle. He said, "Those are Water Ouzels. It's unusual to see that many at once." His statement about seeing so many at once was certainly true, but one of the three birds was a glossy black male Brewer's, with brilliant yellow eyes. Of course we bailed out at the first opportunity. Ever since, my wife and I have referred to male Brewer's Blackbirds as "yellow-eyed Water Ouzels."

## Family **REGULIDAE**: Kinglets

**Golden-crowned Kinglet** (GCKI)
*Regulus satrapa*

Here is a bird that is far more often heard than seen. Even though they almost always come in small flocks, they can be hard to see. They are tiny, and they tend to flit about high in the trees, so that what you can generally see from below is just a silhouette.

The first sign that there are Golden-crowned Kinglets around is likely to be the high-pitched call: *tsee-tsee, tsee-tsee-tsee.* The call is at about the same high frequency as that of the Brown Creeper, but the difference is that the creeper usually gives a single call, and the kinglet tends to give calls in doubles or triples. The kinglet also has a spring song, that starts with several notes like the high-pitched call and ends in a chickadee-like chatter. People with high-frequency hearing loss may not be able to hear the songs or the calls.

Once in a while, a Golden-crowned may come down into the lower branches, occasionally quite close, since they don't seem to fear humans much. Then you can get a glimpse of the head pattern, and realize what a gorgeous little bird this is. The crown is bright yellow in the female and yellow with a bit of orange in the male. Below this is a black stripe, then a white stripe, and then a black stripe through the eye. In all, it is a highly distinctive head pattern, and instantly identifies the bird.

Golden-crowneds are common year-round in Southern Oregon in coniferous forests. Many stay at the higher elevations throughout the winter, and seem to find enough insects and insect eggs there to survive. Some descend to lower elevations, where they might be found in deciduous trees. At night, in order to survive, they may spend the cold hours in old squirrel's nests, or huddled together in a sheltered spot. Even so, in a prolonged cold spell considerable mortality can occur.

# Ruby-crowned Kinglet (RCKI)
*Regulus calendula*

Unlike Golden-crowned Kinglets, which tend to forage high in the trees, Ruby-crowneds are often found low, almost "in-your-face" in some instances. If the bird is agitated, it is highly likely to give out its scolding chatter, often written as *jit-jit-jit-jit-jit*. And it the bird is *really* agitated, and is a male, the little red feathers on the crown may be lifted in a conspicuous tuft, resembling a miniature Indian headdress.

Telling a Ruby-crowned from a Hutton's Vireo can sometimes be a challenge. Both have eye-rings, both have wing-bars, and both have a similar olive-green color. The kinglet will usually be more active than the vireo (some would say *hyper*active), and does a lot of wing flicking as it darts around among the branches. The bill on the kinglet is thin and sharp, and lacks the small hook on the tip of the bill that the vireo has.

A major mark is the pattern on the wing-bars. On the Hutton's, the two bars will be about equally bright, and the area between the bars is the blackest portion of the wing. On the Ruby-crowned, the lower bar is typically more conspicuous than the upper one, and there is a black area below the lower bar.

**Ruby-crowned Kinglet**

Ruby-crowneds are likely to be found alone, instead of in a flock like the Golden-crowneds. As a part of their foraging technique, they may hover at the edges of the outer branches gleaning for insects, much as some warblers do.

In the winter we may hear only the scolding chatter of the Ruby-crowned, but a transformation occurs on the breeding grounds, where this tiny creature delivers a song that sounds like it is coming from a bird five times the size. The song, usually delivered from a high perch, starts out with a few thin, high notes that are at the border of audibility, and then suddenly bursts into a series of loud, rich, rolling phrases. Sometimes, portions of this song can be heard on the wintering grounds, as the birds are preparing for migration.

Ruby-crowneds were listed in the 2001 Breeding Bird Atlas as "probable" breeders in high elevation forests in the Cascades and Siskiyous, and as "confirmed" in eastern Klamath County. In the past, they have been found breeding in Crater Lake NP, primarily in lodgepole pines or in other dry forests. In winter, they are common in the valleys west of the crest. Most of these wintering birds probably breed far to the north of us, in Alaska or B.C.

# Family SYLVIIDAE: Old World Warblers and Gnatcatchers

**Blue-gray Gnatcatcher** (BGGN)
*Polioptila caerulea*

The Blue-gray Gnatcatcher has sometimes been called the "Little Mockingbird" because of its superficial resemblance to the larger bird. Most of the features are duplicated -- the blue-gray upperparts, the white underparts, even the white outer tail feathers. A few features don't fit: mockingbirds don't have conspicuous eye-rings the way that Blue-gray Gnatcatchers do, and the white wing spots of mockingbirds are lacking in gnatcatchers.

Southern Oregon has long been thought of as the most northerly outpost on the Pacific coast of the Blue-gray Gnatcatcher. However, some scattered breeding sites have shown up in other parts of Oregon, which suggest that the bird might be expanding its range. In the Rogue Valley, gnatcatchers are generally found in ceanothus thickets, although they typically build their nests in white oaks, and in the Klamath Basin they seek out thickets of mountain mahogany.

Gnatcatchers do catch gnats (as well as other insects), sometimes catching them in the air like a flycatcher. However, gnatcatchers are more likely to make a vertical sally of a few feet after an insect, rather than fly out a long distance like a flycatcher might. Besides gnats, they eat ants, wood-boring beetles, spiders, and other such things.

Gnatcatcher pairs are known for their tendency to tear down partially completed nests and start over in different locations, perhaps as many as three times, using the materials from the old nests to build the new ones. Whether this is because something has upset them about the site they are working on, or whether they simply find a spot they like better, is not clear.

A gnatcatcher typically betrays its presence by its hyperactive behavior, flitting about in the brush, flipping its tail from side to side. Also, there is a frequent high-pitched, thin, nasal call note, that is sometimes written as *zee* and sometimes as *tsee*. The "song" of the Blue-gray, such as it is, consists of a squeaky, nasal series of these call notes, interspersed with chips and slurs. One writer characterized the song as "more curious than beautiful."

# Family TURDIDAE: Thrushes

**Western Bluebird** (WEBL)
*Sialia mexicana*

**Mountain Bluebird** (MOBL)
*Sialia currucoides*

There is not much chance that males of these two species will be confused. The Western Bluebird is a deep blue on the wings and back, and has a chestnut-colored breast. The Mountain Bluebird is sky blue all over, except for white undertail coverts. Telling the females apart is another matter, because the distinguishing marks are subtle.

One clue is behavioral. Western Bluebirds feed extensively in trees, mostly on insects, although they also do some foraging on the ground. Mountain Bluebirds don't forage in trees as much, and do most of their foraging on the ground. Also, Mountain Bluebirds frequently hunt for insects while hovering in place, perhaps 10 feet off the ground, after the manner of a kestrel.

Female Westerns may have brownish tones to the back, which Mountains lack. The chin on a female Mountain is paler than the surrounding areas, and she has clean white undertail coverts that contrast with the gray flanks. The flanks, belly, and undertail coverts on a female Western are grayish.

In our area, a broad generalization can be made about breeding ranges, but there are so many exceptions that it is not very useful. Western Bluebirds breed mostly to the west of the crest, and Mountain Bluebirds breed mostly to the east. However, both species breed to some extent on both sides of the crest, and Westerns breed in the Siskiyous, although Mountains also breed there to some extent.

As another broad generalization, Westerns tend to favor white oaks, and the edges of cutover or burned over forests. Mountains like junipers, open pine forests, and the edges of meadows in the true fir zone. They, too, seem to favor cutover or burned over lands. After the breeding season, there may be some upslope movement by Westerns, to higher elevations. Most members of both species withdraw to the south in winter, although some remain.

Both species have a soft *chew* call note, often repeated. The "songs" mostly consist of repetitions of the call notes, with other notes interspersed: *Chew. Chew. Chew. Chew-chew-chewee? Chew. Chew. Chewee?* Or so I am told, but I have to admit I've never heard the "song" of either species. I might feel bad about this, but many of the veteran field observers in Arthur Cleveland Bent's books say the same thing: they've never heard either a Western or a Mountain Bluebird sing. Clearly, they don't sing much.

Both are cavity nesters, and will use nest boxes, as well as cavities in decayed wood and old woodpecker holes. A shortage of nesting cavities has been a major cause of the decrease in Western Bluebirds in Oregon, primarily because of competition with starlings for places to nest. Starlings are not the only competitors. Competition has been observed from Tree and Violet-green Swallows, House Sparrows, Ash-throated Flycatchers, and flickers.

Both species are primarily insect-eaters, although Bent, in his writings made a special point of saying, regarding the investigations of stomach contents in Western Bluebirds, that "no honey bees were found." This was at a time when beekeepers were concerned that insect-capturing birds around their hives might eat too many bees and hurt their livelihoods.

Both species eat berries to some extent, the Western more so than the Mountain. Of particular interest is the fact that Westerns eat lots of mistletoe berries. The soft outer pulp of the mistletoe berry is digested, but the seed is passed through the bird's system. The seeds have sticky coatings on them that also survive digestion, and if the seed adheres to the branch of a tree, a new mistletoe plant can take hold.

## Townsend's Solitaire (TOSO)
*Myadestes townsendi*

The solitaire has been said to be many birds wrapped up into one. It has been likened to: a flycatcher, because of its flycatching behavior; a mockingbird, because of its gray color, slender shape, light-colored wing spots, and white outer tail feathers; a shrike, because of the way it may sit on a fence post, waiting to pounce upon an insect on the ground; and a thrush, because of its beautiful song. Some people have wrapped this up by calling it the "Flycatching Thrush."

Its song is certainly one of its most outstanding attributes. The song, delivered from some high outpost such as the very top of a conifer, is long and enthusiastic, consisting of a rapid progression of warbled notes. In length and speed, it resembles the lovely song of a Winter Wren, although it is louder and a little lower in pitch, very much like a Purple Finch. There have been some differences in opinion concerning just when the solitaire sings. Some claim never to have heard it sing in spring and summer, but only in fall and winter. Others claim just the opposite. In my own case, it's been spring when I've heard the song, although it appears clear that it does sometimes sing in fall and winter.

Its call note, which is fairly loud, has been written as *tink! tink! tink!*, sometimes repeated at such length as to become monotonous. Some say it sounds to them something like a pygmy-owl, and others say it sounds like the distant bark of a ground squirrel. Major Bendire said it sounded to him like "the occasional sound produced by an axle of a wagon just about commencing to need greasing."

Solitaires, at least during breeding season, do tend to be somewhat solitary, although some say the name is given because of their elusive habits. They also are seen in family groups, and in late fall may gather in small flocks. Unlike some of their relatives, their food consists more of wild fruit and berries than of insects, and in the winter they have been known to exist almost entirely on juniper berries.

For breeding, solitaires prefer open coniferous forests, burned areas, and clearcuts, all the way to timberline. They are found breeding on both sides of the Cascades, in the Siskiyous, and in most of Klamath County, although they apparently don't choose juniper woodlands for breeding. They are year-round residents in our area, but descend to lower elevations in winter.

**Swainson's Thrush** (SWTH)
*Catharus ustulatis*

**Hermit Thrush** (HETH)
*Catharus guttatus*

**Veery** (VEER)
*Catharus fuscescens*

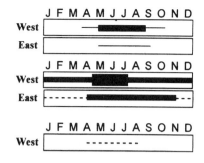

These three can be hard to tell apart, unless they sing. It is said that the Swainson's song spirals up the scale, the Veery's spirals down the scale, and the Hermit's is in the middle. The songs all have an ethereal quality, and they all are beautiful.

For many years, our family's favorite place to go camping was on the Oregon Coast, and there, in early summer, the song of the Swainson's Thrush was our constant companion. The trouble was that I could never see the bird, even though its song was everywhere, and we had no idea what kind of bird was doing the singing. In later years I've learned that my difficulty in locating a Swainson's was not just a peculiar personal failing, but that most people report a similar problem. Only once in my life have I ever actually watched a Swainson's as it sang, when for some reason it came right out on a bare branch. Usually, they sit very still in the dense growth, or fade away unseen. The song is an absolute i.d. for the bird, and its call note is helpful -- a liquid *whip,* sounding something like a drop of water falling into a pool.

Swainson's Thrushes are often considered to be birds of the coast, but they also breed in the Cascades and Siskiyous, at lower elevations than their close relative, the Hermit Thrush. Hermit Thrushes are birds of the higher mountains, and they breed widely in the Cascades and Siskiyous. I have watched them sing many times, since they are more likely to sit on an exposed perch while singing than is a Swainson's. Their song is even more ethereal than the Swainson's, starting with a fairly long note, and then moving into a tremolo which is slightly higher. As soon as one song is done, the bird sings it again, this time at a different pitch. And then again, at a different pitch yet. Some people have described the song as "serene," and "hymn-like." As with the Swainson's, the song is an absolute i.d. The Hermit's call note is highly distinctive -- a sharp, dry *chup!*

The Veery is a different matter. It breeds in northeastern Oregon, but is a vagrant in our area. There are a half dozen spring records from the 1960s and 70s in the Rogue Valley, but none since. Its song, once heard, will never be forgotten. It is a reverse rendition of the Swainson's song, spiraling downward instead of upward, sounding almost eerie and ventriloquial.

The Swainson's and Veery are both neotropical migrants, and leave Oregon entirely in winter. Many Hermit Thrushes, however, stick around in the winter, and any thrush of the *Catharus* genus seen in winter is almost certainly a Hermit. There often are reports of Swainson's Thrushes on

Christmas Counts, but none has ever been verified in Oregon that satisfied the OBRC.

These birds can be tricky in identification, with so much overlap and individual variation that experts say there may be some individuals that cannot be identified with certainty, even with good views. I won't go into all the details, but some hints are given below that will help with most of the birds you may see. (For exhaustive detail, see the articles in *Birding* magazine by Daniel Lane and Alvaro Jaramillo, April 2000, pp. 120-135, and June 2000, pp. 242-254.)

Swainson's Thrushes come into two forms -- the "Russet-backed" of the west, and the "Olive-backed" of the east and almost everyplace else, including central Oregon. The "Russet-backs" usually can be told from Hermits by the rather uniform rufous color from head to tail, whereas Hermits usually show a contrast between the reddish tail and the brown back. Both species have eye-rings, but the Swainson's has a stronger "spectacled" effect, and usually has more of a buffy wash across the front than a Hermit. Also, a Hermit generally will prefer a drier habitat than a Swainson's, and has a habit of cocking its tail up and dropping it slowly, and of simultaneously flicking its wings. The other *Catharus* thrushes may do the same thing, but not as regularly.

Veeries are often confused with "Russet-backed" Swainson's Thrushes, partly because they like similar dense habitats and are hard to see, and partly because with their uniform russet backs they can resemble each other. As compared to Swainson's, Veeries typically have a less marked "spectacled" look, have less of an eye-ring, which is often reduced to a crescent behind the eye, and have grayish flanks instead of buffy-tinged flanks. The call note of the Veery is a down-slurred *veer*.

**American Robin** (AMRO)
*Turdus migratorius*

**Varied Thrush** (VATH)
*Ixoreus naevius*

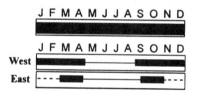

When the English first arrived on the east coast of America, they apparently tended to call any bird with a red breast a "robin," after their own beloved bird back home. Thus, the bluebird was called a robin, so was the thrush that we know today as American Robin, and so was the Eastern Towhee, which was called "ground robin." They even went so far as to call the Red-breasted Merganser the "sea robin." The name in the New World finally became associated only with the American Robin, with the "American" added on because there are several other closely-related robins in the New World. The Old World Robin, by the way, is only about half the size of our American Robin.

This is probably the best-known bird in the U.S. It is distributed over almost the entire North American continent, and its wintering range includes all of the lower 48 states, plus Mexico. Its spring breeding song is one of the most familiar. Many people, even non-birders, have seen their nests, because

**Clark's Nutcracker**

**Mountain Chickadees (parent feeding fledgling)**

**Ruby-crowned Kinglet**

**Pygmy Nuthatch**

**Bewick's Wren**

**Cedar Waxwings**

**PLATE IX**

Yellow-rumped Warbler (male in breeding plumage)

Nashville Warbler

Black-headed Grosbeak (male)

Mountain Bluebird (male)

White-crowned Sparrow

American Robin

PLATE X

robins often build them in highly visible locations. And people, even those who otherwise are mostly unaware of birds, have seen and remarked upon their huge winter flocks.

About those winter flocks: I was impressed by the huge number that showed up on the Grants Pass Christmas Count in 2001, when more than 22,000 robins were seen. I went back through other Christmas Count records, to see how this stood up against the largest number ever seen anywhere in the country. I discovered that in 1997 there were 1,200,000 of the them recorded on the Christmas Count in Taney County, Missouri. Question: How do you count 1,200,000 birds? Answer: You make a guess, hopefully an educated one.

The most familiar part of the robin's plumage is the brick-red breast, more intensely colored in the male than the female. A less familiar part is the amount of white in the undertail coverts that shows up in flight. Robins in the east generally have a deeper shade of rufous in the breast than the ones in the west. Also, it sometimes comes as a surprise to westerners to learn that robins in the east have spots of white in the corners of the outer tail feathers, visible in flight, which are rarely seen in western birds.

The robin's song is familiar to many people, although it can be confused with some other songs that resemble it, especially the song of the Black-headed Grosbeak. The song is a simple one, consisting of repeated phrases that have an up-down, up-down pattern, sometimes represented as *tweedledee?* (up), *tweedledum* (down). The song often ends with a squeaky high note. Robins have several characteristic call notes: a "whinny," a squeal, a *chuck! chuck!,* and a rapid *tut-tut-tut.*

Like all wild creatures, robins face many hazards. Cats are a major hazard, because robins spend so much of their time foraging on the ground. A writer in one of Bent's books estimated that a cat will kill on the order of 50 birds a year, many of them robins. Other birds are also a hazard, especially because robins' nests are often in rather exposed places.

A pair of robins built a nest on one of the downspouts under the eaves of our house one spring, and the female could be seen sitting on the nest from our front window. One day, as we watched, a pair of starlings appeared and went straight for the nest, pecking at the female with their sharp, dagger-like bills, until she was driven off. They pursued her to the ground and continued to peck at her until they decided she was properly subdued. Then they flew up to the nest and consumed the eggs. Yes, I know the starlings were just following Rule Number One in the natural world, which is survival, and probably face many hazards of their own. Nevertheless, it was a vivid lesson in what daily life is like for wild creatures.

A different kind of story is related by Bent. A female robin on the nest was being pestered by a Steller's Jay, which was after the eggs. The robin fought back, and by a lucky thrust of her bill to the jay's head, succeeded in killing it. Screaming her alarm cries, she leaped upon the dead jay, and began to pummel it. Her cries drew other birds, including her mate, who dashed into the fray and joined in punishing the jay's dead body until it became a shapeless mass.

Robins, of course, are well known for hunting for earthworms on lawns. What is not well known is that in earlier times such "lawn-type" foraging grounds, in the west at least, existed primarily in the mountains during breeding season, in the form of meadows. Thus, robins were seldom found breeding in the lowlands, although they would appear there in large flocks in the winter. All of this is coupled with the fact that robins need animal-food such as worms and insects (found by foraging on lawns) for their young in the breeding season, but eat mostly berries and fruit in winter. With the expansion of human dwellings, many "proper" foraging areas, that is, lawns, came into being. The robins responded by expanding their breeding areas into the lowlands. In Southern Oregon, they are probably the most widespread breeding bird.

Varied Thrushes are relatives of the American Robin, and are so strikingly marked that it would seem that they never could be mistaken for anything else. Nevertheless, they are sometimes mistaken for robins, because of a similar shape, ground-feeding behavior, and overall coloration, especially if seen from the back. Seen from the front, the Varied Thrush has a pale orange breast, and the male has a vividly marked black band across the breast. The female also has a band, but it is so pale it might escape notice. Both sexes have a bold orange supercilium and orange wing-bars.

Varied Thrushes are primarily birds of dense forests, and are often seen just as they are drifting away into the undergrowth. They have been confirmed breeding in Southern Oregon in only a few widely separated locations, but are classified as "possible" breeders throughout the Cascades and Siskiyous. They are beautiful birds, but the most remarkable thing about them is their song. This consists of a haunting, vibrating, flute-like note, held for a long time at a constant pitch, that comes from some hidden spot in the forest. A few seconds later, it comes again, this time at a different pitch. And then, after a pause, it comes again, at a different pitch yet. It seems to be the perfect Voice of the Forest.

## Family **TIMALIIDAE**: Babblers

**Wrentit** (WREN)  J F M A M J J A S O N D
*Chamaea fasciata* West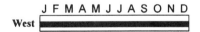

When I first made the acquaintance of this bird, it was in the dry chaparral country of southern California, and I gained the impression that this was exclusively a bird of that region. Wrong. In the many years since, I have found it to be distributed all up the Oregon coast, often in rather wet habitats, and even in the inland valleys of Southern Oregon, in heavy underbrush along streams. It is found in the Klamath River canyon and in many places west of the crest, especially along the Rogue River. It is sometimes found at higher elevations, even as high as 4000 feet, where it favors natural brush fields and regenerating clearcuts. The range expansion into interior Oregon has occurred in the last 70 years, but whether the interior birds originated from the coast or from the south, is not known.

When I say I made the acquaintance of the bird, I should be more precise: I made an acquaintance with the bird's *song,* and it was many years before I got a glimpse of the bird itself. This is easy to understand, because their song is a series of loud, ringing staccato whistles that starts with three or four notes on the same pitch, and then accelerates and drops in pitch, finally becoming a trill. This song is usually given by the male, and it can be heard year-round.

The song has sometimes been described as having the cadence of a ping-pong ball that is dropped onto a table. The female gives a somewhat similar song, consisting of a series of whistles all on the same pitch, and *not* accelerating toward the end, or ending in a trill. Often, when a Wrentit is alarmed, it will give a grating call from an invisible source in the brush, which I have sometimes referred to as a "growl."

In contrast to the loud nature of the song, the birds themselves are very shy, and seldom make more than a brief, furtive appearance. They are small birds, almost more like mice than birds except for their long wren-like tails, generally held cocked at an angle. The overall color is dark brown, sometimes washed with a bit of cinnamon, and the eye is very pale. As one proceeds north along the Pacific Coast from southern California, the birds get darker. In Oregon they are very dark brown, and have appeared to me to be almost black, whenever I've been lucky enough to actually see one.

According to those who have done extensive research on Wrentits, a typical territory is only two or three acres in extent, and is inhabited year-round by a pair. If a Wrentit ventures into the territory of an adjacent pair, it is immediately met by the "owners" and a dispute occurs, usually ended by the withdrawal of the invader. Also, there are usually some unmated "wanderers" passing through territories, looking for cases where one member of a pair has met with an untimely end, in which case the wanderer is prepared to fill the vacancy.

## Family **MIMIDAE**: Mockingbirds and Thrashers

### Gray Catbird (GRCA) — Vagrant
*Dumetella carolinensis*

This bird is gray almost all over, as its name implies, but has a black cap and rufous undertail coverts. It has a song that to some degree resembles the song of a mockingbird, except that it less melodic, with many squeaky-sounding notes, is slower, and is less repetitive. It has a call, frequently given, that sounds very much like a cat. Gray Catbirds breed in northeastern Oregon, and are "probable" breeders in Deschutes County. They favor dense riparian growth, and often are very hard to see. One showed up in our area in summer,

1985, near Ashland, and one spent the winter of 1998-99 near Keno, southwest of Klamath Falls.

## Northern Mockingbird (NOMO)
*Mimus polyglottos*

|  | J F M A M J J A S O N D |
|---|---|
| West | — ---------- — |
| East | --------- |

The Northern Mockingbird is actually a rather southern bird, occurring primarily through the southern half of the U.S. It is "northern" in the sense that there are other mockingbirds in the Western Hemisphere that are more southerly, such as the Blue Mockingbird of Mexico. When Europeans first came to the American west, these were birds primarily of desert and chaparral areas, but they quickly adapted to human surroundings as those became available.

The first mockingbird reported in Oregon was from the Steens Mountain area, in 1935. There has been a range expansion since then, and mockingbirds are reported with fair frequency in many parts of the state, because humans alter the environment in ways that appeal to the birds. In Oregon, they are the most regular in the Rogue Valley, where they have recently been confirmed as breeders. Other confirmed breeding locations in the state are in the eastern part, where the habitat is similar to the dry habitats the birds originally occupied. In the Klamath Basin they are occasionally reported from suburban neighborhoods, and have been seen near the Klamath Basin Refuges Headquarters.

The song is familiar to most people, consisting as it does of loud phrases, some of them melodious, some of them not, with the elements of each phrase repeated three or four times. The song is almost always delivered from some high point -- the top of a tree, a telephone pole, or a TV antenna. On moonlit nights, the singing may go on all night. Many people are also familiar with their characteristic white wing spots and white outer tail feathers, visible in flight, although they sometimes confuse them with shrikes, which have a similar pattern. They are known for their ability to mimic other birds, but they also have been known to imitate the cackling of hens, the squeaking of unlubricated wheels, and the barking of dogs.

Mockingbirds are aggressive, and seem to be willing to attack anything that is perceived as an enemy. They frequently will attack their own reflections, and have been known to pester dogs so much, landing on their backs and pecking at them, as to drive them to shelter.

## Sage Thrasher (SATH)
*Oreoscoptes montanus*

|  | J F M A M J J A S O N D |
|---|---|
| West | Vagrant |
| East | ---- ▓▓▓▓▓▓▓▓ ---- |

This bird was known to old-timers as the "Mountain Mockingbird," partly because it has a long, beautiful song, and partly because in general outline it resembles a mockingbird. However, it is not a bird of the mountains, and it is not a mocker, but has its own original song. And its resemblance to a mockingbird is superficial, since it is brownish instead of gray, is heavily striped in front, and lacks the striking white patches in the wings. It does, however, have white on the outer tail feathers, although the white is restricted to the corners.

The Sage Thrasher is almost as firmly tied to sagebrush as is the Sage Grouse, although it may extend its sphere of interest to include other kinds of dry brushy habitat. In Oregon, it is found in the dry sagebrush plains of the eastern half of the state, mostly on the flats, but also up into the foothills. Wherever this kind of habitat exists in our own region, such as in the sagebrush country to the east and south of the Klamath Basin, it is worthwhile to look for this bird. West of the crest it is rare. There are three records on the west side, in open habitats containing bushes, all of them in late summer.

The best time to look for them on their regular range is in the spring, when the birds are singing. At other times of the year they are notorious for disappearing by running away from the source of the disturbance (which is probably you) concealed by the brush, or by flying low between the bushes. But when one is singing, it will usually occupy a perch on the top of a bush and pour its heart out. Arthur Cleveland Bent offers a lyrical description:

> Scarcely visible in the distance, a gray-brown bird mounts to the top of a tall sage and pours out a flood of glorious music, a morning hymn of joy and thanksgiving for the coming warmth of day. . . . In the solitude of such drab surroundings it is soul-filling, satisfying, and inspiring.

In more prosaic terms, the song is a series of warbles, low trills, and changing combinations, typically carried on for a long time. In one case, it was timed to last for 2 1/2 minutes without letup. The song is sometimes given in flight.

## Brown Thrasher (BRTH) — Vagrant
*Toxostoma rufum*

This handsome vagrant from east of the Rocky Mountains has appeared in Oregon a number of times, usually in winter. The back is rusty-brown and the breast is heavily striped. Its song resembles that of the mockingbird, except that the Brown Thrasher tends to repeat a phrase once or twice, whereas a mockingbird typically repeat a phrase three or more times.

There is one record on the west side of the crest, from Medford, and three on the east side. One of those on the east side remained for several days at Rocky Point, in November 2001.

## California Thrasher (CATH)
*Toxostoma redivivum*

J F M A M J J A S O N D
------------------------

This is primarily a California bird, as its name implies. It almost qualifies as a vagrant, but a few of them live in the Klamath River canyon, downstream from Henley, and in Shasta Valley, disjunct from the rest of the population in California.

Most of the birds in the "mimid" family are considered to be sedentary, and are not long distance migrants. In North America, only the Gray Catbird, Brown Thrasher, and Sage Thrasher qualify as true migrants, which enhances their chances of becoming vagrants. The California Thrasher is about as sedentary as any in the family, but a handful of them have made it over the Siskiyous into the Rogue Valley, for an average of about one bird every seven years. The latest was a roadkill near Upper Table Rock, in May 1996. It is easy to identify because of the huge recurved bill, unlike anything else that occurs in our region.

## Family **STURNIDAE**: Starlings

### European Starling (EUST)
*Sturnus vulgaris*

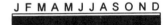

Almost everybody knows that the European Starling is not a native North American bird, but was introduced to this continent in the 19th century. What is not commonly known, however, is that about ten unsuccessful attempts were made, starting in about 1850, before an attempt in 1890 in New York City was finally successful. That's the one that started the population explosion which has now spread over almost all of the continent. One of the unsuccessful introductions was in Portland, Oregon in 1889 by the Portland Song Bird Club. The birds lasted until 1902, and then disappeared.

In light of the Portland introduction, it is interesting to note that the first subsequent detection of starlings anywhere on the Pacific slope was in Siskiyou County, in 1942, when a flock of 40 were found. This has caused people to speculate that the birds were survivors from the Portland introduction, and not invaders from the east, but no one will ever know for sure.

Hardly anyone has a good word for starlings. They are aggressive, they are noisy, they keep filthy nests, they destroy crops, they are superabundant, and above all, they are not native. It has been estimated that there are 200 million of them in the country. An eradication program in California in the 1960s destroyed 9 million starlings, but hardly made a visible dent in the population.

In winter, starlings often form large flocks. Sometimes these flocks are so large and cohesive they look like clouds of smoke. In the 2000 Christmas Count, 2966 starlings were counted in Medford, 3574 in Grants Pass, and 5852 in Klamath Falls. This is nothing, compared to the counts in Portland during the 1960s, which were sometimes on the order of 1 million. The dubious distinction of having the highest all-time Christmas Count anywhere in North America is from Pine Prairie, Louisiana, which reported 20 million starlings in 1990.

Starlings don't even have lovely songs, that might cause people to favor them. The "songs" are a variety of high-pitched squeaks and rattles, plus a harsh chatter, and a rising-and-falling whistle that has been dubbed a "wolf whistle." They are noted for their mimicking abilities, and have been known to make sounds like Killdeers and chickadees, among others. Birders have sometimes been misled by their imitations of Western Wood-Pewees. In spring, the juvenile birds pursue their parents with their "feed me" cry, which has been described as "disagreeable, harsh, rasping, and insistent." Juveniles are sort of drab and gray, but the adult plumage is striking. In the breeding season they are a glossy iridescent greenish-black, and the bill is a vivid yellow; in winter they are intricately spotted, and the bill is dark brown.

Starlings are aggressive and competitive. They are cavity-nesters, and usually succeed in taking over any cavity they may desire from the current occupants. Arthur Cleveland Bent reports on cases where starlings watched a flicker while it excavated its hole, and then, when the hole was complete, moved in and took it over. The flicker thereupon constructed a new hole, and as soon as it was complete, a different pair of starlings did it all over again. There have been cases in which the starling took over the nest even when there were eggs or young flickers in it. In such a case they remove the eggs, or, if there are nestlings, they carry them out and throw them on the ground. Starlings have even been observed to kill adult flickers, by striking them on the head with their sharp bills.

Starlings have been known to out-compete bluebirds, tree swallows, titmice, wrens, and Acorn Woodpeckers in the battles for nesting cavities. However, I did hear of one case where a starling attempted to enter the nesting cavity of an Acorn Woodpecker, whereupon the woodpeckers ganged up on the starling and killed it.

By the way, the word *vulgaris* in the scientific name doesn't mean that the bird is vulgar, whatever we may think. It means "common."

## Family **MOTACILLIDAE**: Wagtails and Pipits

**American Pipit** (AMPI)
*Anthus rubescens*

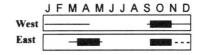

In older books, this bird is called "Water Pipit." The name got changed when it was decided that "Water Pipit," which occurred in both the Old and New Worlds, should be split into two species. The one in Eurasia kept the old name, and the one in North America had to have a new name: American.

Pipits don't breed in Southern Oregon. They are breeders of the tundra, whether in the Arctic or the high mountains of the west. The closest confirmed breeding locations in Oregon are in the high Cascades, at Mount Hood, Three Sisters, and Diamond Peak. Other known breeding locations in Oregon are in the Wallowas, and on Steens Mountain.

Pipits are sparrow-sized birds, brownish on the back, with a white chin and pale buff, heavily-streaked underparts, and with dark legs. There is a very rare subspecies with pinkish legs, a vagrant from Asia, but we are not likely to see that one. The subspecies that breeds in eastern Oregon and the Rocky Mountains is more pinkish on the underparts, with less streaking, but we are not likely to see that one, either. However, with birds, anything is possible.

The pipits we get in Southern Oregon arrive mostly during fall migration, on their way to the Central and Imperial Valleys of California. However, we do get some that stay around in the winter, primarily on the west side of the crest. During the 2000 Christmas Count, Medford reported 102, Grants Pass reported 97, and Klamath Falls reported zero. By contrast, in the prior year, Medford and Grants Pass had zero, and Klamath Falls had one.

The first intimation that there are pipits around may be their characteristic calls coming from the sky -- *pip-IT! pip-IT! pip-IT!* When the flock is on the ground, they may be almost invisible until you walk right into them, whereupon they jump into the sky and form a loose, undulating flock, flying in a wide circle and then disappearing on the ground at some distant point. Or, just as likely, they may fly in a large circle and come right back to where they started from.

They prefer open areas. Short grass fields and muddy edges seem to appeal to them. When they forage, they run about actively on the ground, their bodies swaying, and their tails also usually swaying in synchronism with the bodies. Observers disagree about the tail motion. Some say the birds' tails are constantly in motion, and other say they seldom see any particular tail bobbing or wagging. In my own observations, it seems to me that tail motion of one sort or another has generally been apparent.

When I was a kid, and struggling to identify birds, I saw some brownish birds in open fields that had white outer tail feathers. I looked in my book, trying to find a bird with white outer tail feathers, and came across "Water Pipit." I decided I had seen some "Water Pipits," based upon that sole field mark, and duly recorded them as such in my journal. Today, I realize I had been looking at meadowlarks, which display obvious white outer tail feathers as they coast in for landings.

I also realize, today, that I don't often get to see the white outer tail feathers of pipits, because I don't generally see them coasting to a landing like I do meadowlarks. This may be because they are simply too far away when they decide to come down, which seems to be a pipit habit. Or, if they light in my vicinity, they land from all directions, and don't necessarily orient themselves in the proper direction to see the tail feathers.

Once, when I was at Badlands National Park, I saw lots of meadowlarks about, and took due note of their white outer tail feathers. Later, when I was in the visitor center, I overhead a visitor asking the ranger at the desk, about all those birds he had been seeing with white outer tail feathers. The ranger did precisely what I did when I was first learning about birds. He picked up a field guide and thumbed through it until he found a bird with white outer tail feathers. It was a Yellow Wagtail, a bird that breeds in Alaska, and is extremely rare in the Lower 48. The visitor departed happily, convinced he had been seeing dozens of wagtails.

Having related that story, which tends to make the ranger look like an ignoramus, maybe I should relate another one, even though the subject isn't birds, but is about elk. This happened at Sequoia National Park, at the visitor center. A visitor asked if there were any elk in California, and the young ranger on duty answered "no." Another ranger nearby heard this exchange, and leaped in to correct the first ranger, that there were indeed lots of elk in California. This made the first ranger look like an ignoramus -- which he certainly was -- but the point of the story is that the ignoramus young ranger was me. Maybe that also explains why, when the ranger at the Badlands communicated his own piece of misinformation about the wagtails, I didn't say a word.

## Family **BOMBYCILLIDAE**: Waxwings

**Cedar Waxwing** (CEDW)
*Bombycilla cedrorum*

**Bohemian Waxwing** (BOWA)
*Bombycilla garrulus*

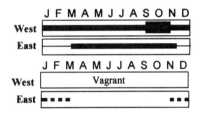

Again, here are two species than can be confused. The major identification hint is: check the color of the undertail coverts. These are whitish in the Cedar Waxwing, and rufous in the Bohemian. When you are looking up at a bunch of waxwings in a tree, the undertail coverts may be the parts that are easiest to see. There are other differences. Bohemians are bigger than Cedars, they are grayer, they have white in the wings which Cedars lack, and they have yellow-tipped primaries.

When you are birding, keep your ears open for the slightly buzzy, extremely high-pitched call notes of the Cedar Waxwing, *ssee ssee ssee ssee ssee,* repeated constantly. These are not audible to some people, because the frequency may be too high. If you hear it, look around, to see if there are some Cedar Waxwings perched in the top of a nearby tree. Often, they sit so quietly you could overlook them if it weren't for the high-pitched call. The Bohemian's call note is lower and buzzier.

Cedar Waxwings breed widely in Southern Oregon, but avoid heavy forests and extensive open areas. However, Bohemians breed in Canada and Alaska. There is only one known breeding record in Oregon, in Clatsop County, near the coast. In winter, Bohemians appear regularly in northeastern Oregon, but if they appear in Southern Oregon at all, it will be in a so-called "invasion" year, when flocks wander in search of food. Sometimes, Bohemians are mixed in with Cedars, so it may be worthwhile to search through a flock for those rufous undertail coverts. Since both species eat lots of berries in winter, including madrone and juniper berries, it could pay off to check such areas.

Even though two-thirds of the diet consists of fruit, waxwings are expert flycatchers, flying out to snatch an insect, and then returning to the same perch. A large flock was once even seen pursuing and capturing whirling snowflakes, as if they were insects. Whether they were after the snowflakes because of the water they offered, or were simply amusing themselves, was not clear. They also sometimes eat flower petals, and have been observed passing a petal back and forth between a pair, in what seemed to be a courtship ritual.

Cedar Waxwings are here all year long, but in some years their numbers are augmented by migrants, and the flocks in fall can get large, especially if the birds find a good food source. One fall I saw a flock near Medford that I estimated had 500 birds in it, and larger flocks have been reported.

Incidentally, the "cedar" part of the name presumably comes from the way the birds flock to "cedar" trees in the winter, for the berries. ("Cedar" is a name that has been frequently applied in the west to juniper trees.) "Bohemian" comes from wandering behavior of the flocks in winter, "like gypsies," and "waxwing" comes from the small red oblong appendages, resembling sealing wax, that the adult birds have on the tips of the secondaries.

## Family PTILOGONATIDAE: Silky-flycatchers

### Phainopepla (PHAI) — Vagrant
*Phainopepla nitens*

**Phainopepla**

Phainopeplas are thought of as birds of the desert southwest. And so they are, but they have a migration pattern that is believed to be unique among North American birds: They have a "normal" nesting in the desert in March and April, and then move north into California and Nevada and nest again in June and July. Some authorities question the double-nesting part. They agree the movement takes place, but believe only one nesting cycle occurs, either in the south or in the north.

In California, their northward movement regularly carries them as far as the foothills surrounding the Sacramento Valley. Thus, the vagrants we get in Southern Oregon might represent "overshoots" of this northward movement, meaning we should expect them in June or July. But all of the records in our area have been in the period from December to April, so something else must be going on. Five of these have been in the Rogue Valley, and one in Klamath Falls. Since some Phainopeplas don't migrate at all, but remain through the winter in their more northerly locations, the ones we get may be simple wanderers, pushing the boundaries, so to speak.

"Phainopepla" is a Greek word meaning "shining robe," and is a reference to the male's glossy black plumage. Here is one of those rare cases where the scientific name and common names are the same. ("Vireo" and "Junco" are two others.) When the male flies, it shows prominent white patches in the wings. The female is a soft, pearly gray. Both the male and the female have red eyes, and prominent crests.

Since these birds are generally found closely associated with mistletoe, with which the Rogue Valley abounds, it might be worthwhile to keep an eye on mistletoe clumps, just in case one of these rarities shows up again. Sometimes they hide in mistletoe clumps and are invisible. But other times they have the habit of sitting still, right in the top of a tree, making a highly visible black dot against the sky.

## Family **PARULIDAE**: Wood-warblers

Some of our wood-warblers have attractive songs, but it's hard to claim that any of them actually "warble." More often, the songs consist of thin squeaks and buzzy notes. Nevertheless, they are among our most beautiful birds, and most appreciated by humans. They tend to have thin bills, as opposed to the heavier bills of the sparrows and finches.

From the birdwatcher's point of view, warblers can be frustrating, because they are mostly nervous, tiny, quick-moving birds that flit around in the brush or high in the trees, making it difficult to bring one's binoculars to bear. Some humorist has declared that warblers operate in accordance with a four-step sequence: (1) they light on a branch; (2) they look around; (3) they snatch an insect; (4) they're gone. This parallels the birder's four-step reaction, which is: (1) *"*Oh!" (2) "Look!" (3) "What?" (4) *"Damn!"*

### Tennessee Warbler (TEWA)   Vagrant
*Vermivora peregrina*

Since this warbler breeds all the way across Canada into British Columbia, it is not surprising that it frequently shows up on the Pacific Coast as a vagrant. Oregon has had so many records that it is no longer on the "review list," meaning that it is not considered to be all that unusual. California gets a lot of reports -- 80 to 90 per year, with the majority of them in fall. Most are on the coast, but there are many inland records. Thus, it is surprising that there is only one record from our area that I have found, a singing male near Juanita Lake, above Butte Valley.

Tennessee Warblers are rather indistinctly marked, and are often mistaken for Orange-crowned Warblers or Warbling Vireos. This may be a part of the explanation for the lack of reports. Tennessees are usually quite white on the underparts, while Orange-crowneds are more yellowish. A possibility for confusion comes in the fall, when some Tennessees are yellowish below, and some Orange-crowneds are whitish. However, a look at the undertail coverts can be helpful, provided you can get the warbler to hold still. On the Tennessee these are whitish, and always are more white than the breast, whereas the undertail coverts on the Orange-crowned are yellow. Also, Tennessees are shorter-tailed than Orange-crowneds.

As for Warbling Vireos, they are not as green on the back as Tennessee Warblers, have heavier bills, usually move more sluggishly than a warbler, and there is a pale arc under the eye, which a Tennessee doesn't have.

## Orange-crowned Warbler (OCWA)
*Vermivora celata*

This is one of the drabbest of our warblers. It breeds from coast to coast, but is more abundant in the west than in the east. In Oregon it is widespread, including Southern Oregon, where it prefers dense brush for breeding, preferably near water. When foraging, it often frequents oak trees, and moves about fairly high in the foliage, seeking insects.

Our local breeding subspecies is yellower than some of the other subspecies, which tend toward olive-gray. There is usually some indistinct streaking on the underparts, a weakly developed supercilium, and an indistinct eye-ring that is split by a thin dark eye-line. The orange crown is practically never visible in the field. Only once can I remember seeing it, and that was only because the bird obligingly leaned forward so that I had a direct view of the top of its head. Even then, the "crown" was only a thin orange line.

The song is a rapid trill, somewhat like that of a Chipping Sparrow or Dark-eyed Junco. The difference is that the trills of the other two species are usually held at a steady pitch, whereas that of the Orange-crowned tends to fall off at the end, either in pitch or frequency, frequently both, as if running out of energy. This criterion is not infallible, however. I once tracked down a song that fell off at the end, convinced that it was an Orange-crowned Warbler, and it turned out to be a junco.

In the east, the bird most frequently confused with the Orange-crowned is the Tennessee Warbler. In the west, the most likely ones to be confused with it are Yellow Warbler and MacGillivray's Warbler. Yellow Warblers are sometimes not as yellow as might be expected, and the males have dusky streaking on the breast that might resemble that on an Orange-crowned. However, Yellow Warblers, both male and female, have plain face patterns, unlike the Orange-crowned, and the dark eye stands out prominently on the face.

The reason that Orange-crowneds are sometimes confused with MacGillivray's doesn't involve our local breeding subspecies, but involves those that appear in fall migration. These may sometimes have grayish heads, which accounts for the confusion with MacGillivray's, which also have gray heads. MacGillivray's Warblers, however, are much yellower underneath, and have much more conspicuous eye arcs.

Most Orange-crowneds migrate to the south for the winter, but occasionally one will turn up on a Christmas Count, on either side of the crest. After breeding is complete, they generally drift upslope as far as timberline before moving to the south.

## Nashville Warbler (NAWA)
*Vermivora ruficapilla*

J F M A M J J A S O N D

## Virginia's Warbler (VIWA)
*Vermivora virginiae*

Vagrant

The Nashville Warbler is a neat, clean little warbler that has reasonably clear-cut recognition marks. Its head is gray, its throat and most of the underparts are yellow, and there is a conspicuous full eye-ring. The undertail coverts are yellow, as is the belly, but there is a whitish patch on the lower abdomen, separating the yellow undertail coverts and yellow belly. The male has a chestnut crown patch, but it is seldom visible in the field.

Nashville Warblers occur coast-to-coast, but there are two subspecies, one eastern and one western, whose breeding areas are separated by almost the entire province of Alberta and the state of Montana. The name "Nashville" has no particular significance. The original type specimen, from which the species was named, was collected near Nashville, Tennessee.

In Oregon, the stronghold of the species is our area -- Southern Oregon, including the mountains east of the Cascades in Klamath and Lake counties. It nests widely in our region in mixed conifer/hardwood forests and in recovering clearcuts, mostly below 4000 feet. However, it may occur sparsely up to subalpine areas. It tends to favor somewhat dry areas with madrones and black oaks, but shuns stands of white oaks and chaparral.

In constrast to some warblers, Nashvilles place their nests on the ground, or close to the ground. They tend to forage in the understory of the forest, or low in the forest canopy. Almost all the birds leave our area in the fall and migrate to Mexico and Central America. Before migration, there is an up-slope movement to higher elevations after breeding is over.

The song of the Nashville Warbler is usually characterized as "sweet," but fairly loud, starting with a series of two-syllable notes, and ending with a series that may vary with each rendition: *seetah, seetah, seetah, sweet sweet, tsyuu*.

The description of the Nashville Warbler is also a pretty good description of its close relative, the Virginia's Warbler. The major differences are that the Virginia's has much less yellow below, and is gray on the back. Nashville Warblers have greenish backs. Virginia's Warblers are primarily southwestern birds, but their breeding range covers most of Nevada. There have been about nine records in Oregon, mostly in the eastern part of the state, with one record in 1980 near Stukel Moutain, in Klamath County.

Who was Virginia? She was the wife of the man who discovered the bird in New Mexico. in 1860.

## Lucy's Warbler (LUWA)  Accidental
*Vermivora luciae*

To have a Lucy's Warbler in our region is an astonishing event, since its normal breeding range is so far away, in the desert southwest. Nevertheless, we had one in May 2002, in the company of a flock of Yellow-rumped Warblers, near Emigrant Lake in Jackson County. Oregon's only other record is from winter, 1986-87, in Lane County.

Lucy's Warbler is our smallest wood-warbler, and is a very plain gray little bird, bearing a general resemblance to Virginia's Warbler, and sometimes even to very plain female Yellow Warblers. Some marks that will help are the chestnut crown and rump patches, if you can see them, more distinct on the male than on the female. Also, a Virginia's Warbler will show yellow undertail coverts, lacking in the Lucy's.

## Northern Parula (NOPA)  Vagrant
*Parula americana*

This beautiful little bird has everything: blue head, yellow throat, eye-arcs, wing-bars, and a black and rufous band across the yellow breast. Everything, that is, except a beautiful song, which is an unmusical buzzy trill, rising in pitch, and then abruptly dropping at the end, with a closing *tsup!*

The Northern Parula is a bird of the eastern part of the country that has shown up in Oregon a number of times, usually in the April to June period. Most of the records are from the eastern part of the state, although there are a few on the coast. In our area, there is one record from Klamath Falls, in May 1981.

As to pronunciation, some people say *par-OO-lah,* and some say *PAR-you-lah.* My enclyopedia gives *PAR-you-lah* as the pronunciation.

## Yellow Warbler (YWAR)
*Dendroica petechia*

Arthur Cleveland Bent called this bird "a rich yellow flame" in the forest. It's hard to disagree with this statement. The male has a bright yellow breast with reddish streaks, a yellow-green back, and a plain yellow face in which the dark eye stands out prominently. This gives the bird a rather "beady-eyed" look. The female is a somewhat subdued version of the same pattern, but lacks the reddish streaks. Immature females can be rather dull, even grayish. A unique characteristic of both sexes is that they show yellow spots in the tail as they fly. The yellow is not the same as the yellow panels in the tail of a female American Redstart, but is more distributed, on the inner edges of the tail feathers.

Yellow Warblers are widespread breeders in Oregon, favoring lowland riparian woods, especially those with willows and cottonwoods. They are fairly common in proper habitat on both sides of the Cascades, at least in Southern Oregon. They have declined substantially in numbers from former times, partly because of loss of riparian habitat, and partly because of parasitism by Brown-headed Cowbirds.

Experience in some areas has shown that unregulated cattle-grazing can seriously reduce the presence of willows, which are preferred Yellow Warbler nesting habitat. In some areas of impacted habitat, when grazing was subsequently controlled so that riparian habitats were not damaged, the willows returned and so did the warblers.

Parasitism by Brown-headed Cowbirds is a serious problem, but Yellow Warblers have developed a defensive response which is unusual among parasitized birds. Because of long experience with cowbirds, many Yellow Warblers can recognize cowbird eggs. When they detect one, the response is either to abandon the nest, or to build a new nest over all the eggs, their own included, and lay a new clutch. Nests with as many as six "tiers" have been found, with a cowbird egg in every tier.

Some species of warblers can be classified by whether they tend to forage low, close to the ground, or high in the trees. The Yellow Warbler does both -- low in the willows and high in the cottonwoods.

Yellow Warblers are highly vocal in breeding season, and have a variety of songs. These are mostly variations on the following pattern, in which the first few notes are all on the same pitch: *see see see see tititi see.* This has been rendered into English words, for better recall, as *sweet sweet sweet sweet, I am so sweet.* The "I am so" is on a lower pitch, and the last "sweet" may rise in pitch to the same level as the first few notes, or may drop in pitch. Western birds, as opposed to those in the east, are more likely to drop in pitch on the last note. The notes are delivered rapidly, and the song has been characterized as "cheerful and perky."

## Chestnut-sided Warbler (CSWA)           Vagrant
*Dendroica pensylvanica*

This warbler, as its name implies, has strong chestnut markings on the sides, and the male has a yellow crown in breeding season. Non-breeding and immature birds are lime-green above. The normal breeding range extends across Canada, as far west as central Alberta.

There are 34 records in Oregon, most of them on the east side of the Cascades. In Southern Oregon, there is one record on the west side, in Ashland, on September 30 1982, and three on the east side -- Mare's Egg Spring, in July 1995, Wood River Wetlands, in July 2000, and 7 Mile Creek in July 2001.

## Black-throated Blue Warbler (BTBW)                    Vagrant
*Dendroica caerulescens*

The male of this species is a dark blue on the upperparts and has a black throat, as its name implies. The female is quite subdued, mostly in shades of gray. In almost all plumages, however, both males and females have a giveaway mark -- a white spot at the base of the primaries, visible when the wing is folded.

The breeding range of this warbler is in the east, and does not extend into western Canada in the way many warblers do. Nevertheless, there are numerous records in Oregon, mostly to the east of the Cascades, and mostly in the fall. There is a record for Southern Oregon, in Medford, in October 1986.

## Yellow-rumped Warbler
*Dendroica coronata*

### "Audubon's Warbler" (AUWA)

### "Myrtle Warbler" (MYWA)

The Yellow-rumped Warbler is probably the best-known, most widespread, and most abundant warbler in the U.S., causing some people to dub it the "ubiquitous warbler." A few years back, this species was considered to be two separate species -- "Audubon's Warbler," and "Myrtle Warbler." Some people believe they should again be treated as separate species, even though there is extensive interbreeding where their summer ranges meet, in British Columbia and Alberta. Many birders, even though they are well aware that these are two forms of a single species, use the names "Audubon's" and "Myrtle" for the birds they see. Also, bird-banders keep separate records for these two, and have separate codes for them. In addition, Christmas Counts report them separately.

Yellow-rumped Warbler

Both forms have the universal badge of the Yellow-rumped Warbler -- a conspicuous yellow spot on the rump that is present in all plumages and seasons. The rump is sometimes not visible when the wings are folded, but if the bird lets the wings drop a little bit, the yellow rump becomes exposed, and it is highly visible as the bird flies away.

In breeding plumage, the two forms are recognizable by the color of the throat -- yellow in the "Audubon's" and white in the "Myrtle." Interbreeding can play tricks with these marks, of course. Also, in the winter some female "Audubon's" may have whitish throats, and thus resemble "Myrtles." However, there is a fairly reliable mark for such cases, that is good for all seasons. This is that the white throat of the "Myrtle," in both sexes, tends to extend back from the throat and curl up around the auriculars in what some people call a "smile mark." Even this mark can get messed up by interbreeding, so there might be some birds that can't be absolutely identified in the field, as to which form they belong to.

It is the "Audubon's" which is the breeder in our area. It breeds widely in Southern Oregon, preferring conifer forests at the higher elevations of the Cascades and Siskiyous, especially true fir forests. The southern Cascades has one of the highest breeding densities of these birds anywhere in Oregon.

Most Yellow-rumps migrate south in the fall, but a few stick around, and move down into the valleys. In fact, the Yellow-rump is the only warbler that is present in winter in our area on a regular basis. (Townsend's Warblers are uncommon in winter on the coast, but are rare and irregular inland in winter.) Most of the wintering Yellow-rumps in our area are "Audubon's," but some "Myrtle Warblers" show up in winter in the interior valleys west of the crest, on an irregular basis.

During breeding season at the higher elevations, especially in conifer forests with broken canopies, this is one of the most frequently encountered birds. Their song is hard to put into words, and is somewhat variable. Frequently, it opens with a loosely spaced trill, followed by a jumble of up-and-down notes: *chee chee chee chee cheedle cheedle.* In one of the variations, the opening notes are two-syllabled: *seedl seedl seedl seedl,* followed by the up-and-down notes. Sometimes the birds are so high in the trees, and concealed by the branches, that it is difficult to spot the singer. Just as you think you've got the location pinned down, you see a little dark spot fly off, and then the song comes from a different place. Their call is a fairly loud frequently repeated *tchip!,* and is often the first indication that there are Yellow-rumps around.

Besides engaging in the usual warbler practice of flitting about in the branches, gleaning for insects, the Yellow-rump also often "hover-gleans," by which it is meant that the bird hovers at the outer edge of the leaves and moves from spot to spot to pick off its prey. I once spotted a small bird that was visible against the sky only as a dark silhouette, engaged in hover-gleaning, and confidently identified it as a Yellow-rump because of its size and behavior. A friend put a spotting scope on the bird, and then said, "But it's got an eye-ring." It turned out to be a Ruby-crowned Kinglet.

## Black-throated Gray Warbler (BTYW)
*Dendroica nigrescens*

West — J F M A M J J A S O N D
East

## Black-and-white Warbler (BAWW)
*Mniotilta varia*

Vagrant

These two warblers superficially resemble each other, but are easy to tell apart if you know what to look for. Both of them have patterns of black and white striping, and have striping on the sides of their breasts. A Black-and-white has a white stripe down the center of its crown that the Black-throated Gray lacks, and has black-and-white streaks on its back. The Black-throated Gray lacks the white streaks on the back, although it may have black streaks on a gray background. Finally, the Black-throated Gray has a yellow spot in front of the eye, which is lacking in the Black-and-white. There is a superficial resemblance to chickadees, but chickadees don't have striping on the sides of their breasts.

There is an important behavioral aspect of the Black-and-white Warbler that can be a clue to its identity. A Black-and-white tends to scramble around on the trunks and larger branches of trees much like a nuthatch -- not at all like proper warbler-like behavior. This has caused some people to call it the "Nuthatch Warbler." Black-throated Grays forage by gleaning through the foliage like most warblers do.

The Black-and-white Warbler breeds east of the Rocky Mountains, but its breeding range extends into Alberta, so we have gotten quite a few strays in Oregon, both in spring and fall. There have been a couple of records on the west side of the Cascades in Southern Oregon, and a few on the east side. One of the latter was at Kimball State Park, in 1974, and was the first verified record in the state of Oregon.

Black-throated Gray Warblers are westerners, although they may show up in the east as vagrants. Males have black throats, but females and immatures have white throats, or at least have a reduced amount of black. They breed in the drier mixed and deciduous woods west of the crest, and sometimes are found on the east side, where they may show up in ponderosa pine stands. They often are found in canyon live oaks and in mature chaparral, and even in brushy habitats in regenerating clearcuts. They may forage at any level in the canopy, and often come down where they can be seen.

Black-throated Grays have a buzzy song that has a number of repeated notes at the beginning, rises toward the end, and then abruptly falls on the last note, generally in a downslur. Sometimes the initial notes have one syllable and sometimes two: *zee zee zee zee ZEEA zoo*, or *zeea zeea zeea ZEET chew*. The song can vary in both pace and pattern, and may differ from region to region. Sometimes it cannot be distinguished with certainty from the song of the Hermit Warbler. Townsend's Warblers have a similar pattern in their songs, but are usually higher and wheezier.

## Black-throated Green Warbler (BTNW)          Vagrant
*Dendroica virens*

Here's yet another eastern warbler whose breeding range extends across Canada as far as Alberta. There are a number of records in Oregon, mostly in the eastern part of the state. There is a record from the Rogue Valley in May 1996.

This warbler is patterned very much like the Townsend's Warbler, and in fact is closely related to it. Both birds have bright yellow faces, but the auricular patch on the Townsend's is black, and on the Black-throated Green is olive. Also, the Black-throated Green has yellow in the area of the vent that the Townsend's lacks.

## Townsend's Warbler (TOWA)
*Dendroica townsendi*

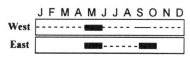

This is one of our more attractive warblers, with lots of yellow, and conspicuous black striping. It is a western species, and only appears in the east as a vagrant. It is a close relative of another westerner, the Hermit Warbler, with which it frequently hybridizes. (See section on Hermit Warbler, for some comments on hybrids.) It is a very close lookalike with an eastern relative, the Black-throated Green Warbler. A Townsend's Warbler can be told from the Black-throated Green, however, by the black auricular patch (as opposed to olive, in the Black-throated Green) and the extensive yellow on the front. Male Townsend's have black throats; females have white.

The breeding range of the Townsend's Warbler primarily is to the north of us, in British Columbia and Washington. However, they do breed in Oregon in the northern Cascades and the mountains of the northeastern part of the state. In our area, breeding has been confirmed in the mountains directly to the east of the Klamath Basin, and is considered "possible" in the southern Cascades.

During migration, Townsend's Warblers may be observed in all kinds of habitats, and at all levels in the foliage, but in the breeding season they favor coniferous forests at the higher elevations. At this time, they can be difficult to observe, because they often forage high in the canopy.

Townsend's Warblers are unusual within their family, because there are two major wintering ranges: Mexico, and the coasts of Washington, Oregon, and California. In the inland valleys in winter, however, they are rare.

The song of the Townsend's is higher and wheezier than those of its relatives, typically with a pattern such as *weazy weazy weazy dzhee*. The song typically rises in pitch, and then drops off at the end. There is much variation, however, and it often is difficult to distinguish the song from that of the Hermit Warbler, and sometimes it is impossible.

## Hermit Warbler (HEWA)
*Dendroica occidentalis*

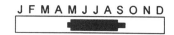

The Hermit Warbler is another westerner, although it, too, has shown up as a vagrant in the east. Its breeding range is less wide than that of the Townsend's Warbler, and is pretty much restricted to the three Pacific Coast states. There is much hybridization between the two species in the areas where the breeding ranges meet, in Washington and as far south as the central Cascades in Oregon. The hybridization zone in central Oregon may be moving toward the south.

They nest widely in Southern Oregon in the Cascades and Siskiyous, and are common in Douglas-fir and true fir forests. They will also occupy ponderosa pine forests, provided there is a Douglas-fir understory. Much of their time is spent in foraging high in the forest canopy, and they can be hard to see unless they come down for water. In late summer, mud puddles or springs in the forest can offer opportunities to see them at ground level.

A adult male is unmistakable, with a yellow face, black throat, and white, unstreaked underparts. The female is a somewhat muted version of the same pattern, and the black in the throat is reduced or absent. Hybrids may show a variety of combinations of the key markings of the two species. One kind of hybrid, for example, may show the face pattern of the Hermit, and the yellow, streaked underparts of the Townsend's. Another kind may show the face pattern of the Townsend's but have no yellow on the breast, and little streaking on the sides.

Hermit Warblers sing songs of two types, with variations. In one, the song starts with some repeated notes in a sort of trill, has some intermediate notes, and then ends decisively: *zeee-zeee-zeee see-see zee!* Sometimes the ending is sharply downward, sometimes upward. In the second type, the opening and intermediate notes are similar, but the end consists of two or three repeated notes. A given male may have variations on a song, and the songs may differ among populations. The songs are almost indistinguishable from those of Townsend's Warbler, and some of the Hermit songs are difficult to distinguish from those of the Black-throated Gray Warbler.

## Bay-breasted Warbler (BBWA)                    Vagrant
*Dendroica castanea*

Here's another "eastern" warbler that breeds as far west as Alberta. There are seven records in Oregon, mostly in eastern Oregon, all of them except one in spring or summer. There is one record for September. The first verified record for Oregon was on the west side of Upper Klamath Lake, in June 1963, of a male in breeding plumage. There is a second record for Southern Oregon, of a singing male, from Grizzly Campground at Howard Prairie Lake, in June 1976.

Males in breeding plumage are highly distinctive, with deep chestnut on the throat, sides, and on the top of the head. Females are duller. Immature birds in their first fall plumage are very plain, and can be confused with Blackpoll Warblers. (There are more than 30 records of Blackpoll Warblers in Oregon, mostly in the eastern part, but none in Southern Oregon.)

## American Redstart (AMRE)  Vagrant
*Setophaga ruticilla*

The American Redstart breeds across most of the North American continent, including in many areas close to Oregon, such as Washington and Idaho. It even breeds sparsely in northeastern Oregon, where it is looked upon as unpredictable, and probably declining. In addition, it has been found as a breeder in a few other locations, including Deschutes County, Curry County, and even near Medford, in July 1970. There are a few other records in various locations in Southern Oregon, on both sides of the crest. In August 1997, a male and a female were found at Odessa Campground, near Upper Klamath Lake.

American Redstarts are easy to identify. The male is black and orange and the female is gray and yellow. Both sexes habitually spread their tails and hold them spread for a second or so, so that the colorful panels in their tails can be seen -- orange in the case of the male, and yellow in the case of the female.

I once was on a boat which was returning to port from a pelagic trip, when a pair of redstarts flew out of nowhere and landed on the boat We were still about 10 miles from port, so I assumed they would gratefully accept the opportunity to be transported back to the safety of the land. But no. After resting for a few minutes, they both took off and headed southwest across the Pacific Ocean, and to certain death.

The fall migration of American Redstarts occurs across a broad front. Many migrate via a land route to Mexico and Central America. But those in the east, and perhaps even some from the west, migrate across the Gulf of Mexico, both in spring and fall. My guess is that the ones I saw heading across the Pacific Ocean were internally programmed in such a way that if they came to an ocean, their instincts told them they should head across it and in a few hours would reach land, such as Cuba or the Yucatan Peninsula. Not that they thought it out in those terms, but generations of their ancestors had followed that procedure, had lived through it, and had passed the internal programming on to later generations.

It probably would have worked out just fine, if they had been heading on the correct compass course, and had indeed arrived at the Gulf coast. Birds have remarkable navigational skills, and apparently use some kind of internal compass which is based upon the sun, the stars, the Earth's magnetic field, or a combination of all three. But, as occasionally happens with long-distance migrants, these two apparently had gotten their internal compasses mixed up, and were heading southwest instead of southeast, a "mirror-image" mistake.

## Prothonotary Warbler (PROW)            Accidental
*Protonotaria citrea*

The Prothonotary (pro-THON-o-tary) Warbler has been called "one of the most stunning of warblers," because of its golden-yellow head and underparts. It has also been called the "Golden Swamp Warbler," because of its preference for dark, swampy woods. Just how this bird of the southeastern part of the country gets all the way to Oregon is not clear, but it has happened a handful of times, mostly in the eastern part of the state. It is included here on the basis of one record, a bird that was netted and banded on July 2, 2001, at Odessa Creek, next to Upper Klamath Lake.

## Ovenbird (OVEN)            Vagrant
*Seiurus aurocapillus*

Here is a bird that is heard far more often than it is seen, and when you do see one, it is more likely to be running on the ground than up in the trees. In fact, even though it is grouped with the warblers, it is often described as "thrushlike." Its conspicuous eye-ring, olive upperparts, and white, spotted underparts certainly makes it resemble a thrush, but the narrow orange crest and blackish lateral crown stripes immediately tell you, "this is not a thrush." Its loud *TEAcher! TEAcher! TEAcher!* song is one of the most characteristic sounds of the forests where it breeds. Sometimes, instead of the emphasis being on the first syllable, it will go the other way: *cher-TEE! cher-TEE! cher-TEE!*

There have been many records of Ovenbirds in Oregon, so many that the OBRC no longer keeps individual records. Most of the records are in eastern Oregon, which is not too surprising, because their regular breeding range comes as close as western Montana. However, there are no confirmed breeding records in the state. There have been 7 records in the Cascades of singing territorial males, but with no females detected.

Some Southern Oregon records are: Wolf Creek, in June 1983; near Eagle Point, in June 1988; Ashland, in March 1996; Odessa Creek Campground, in July 1997, near Provolt, in June 2001; and in Tulelake, in June 2001.

## Northern Waterthrush (NOWA)            Vagrant
*Seiurus noveboracensis*

The Northern Waterthrush is believed to be a breeding bird in Oregon, but just barely. There are a couple of probable breeding locations in northeast Oregon, but the principal location is in the vicinity of Highway 58, near Willamette Pass. Here, a few pairs are presumed to breed each season, along the Little Deschutes River and Crescent Creek in northern Klamath County, and along Salt Creek on the west side of the pass, in dense willows. However, a nest has never actually been found, because of the impenetrable habitat.

Because of the habitat, and because of the tendency of waterthrushes to do most of their foraging on the ground, it is difficult to get a view of one.

There are no known breeding locations for Northern Waterthrush in Southern Oregon, but there are a number of sight records on both sides of the crest, in the May to August period. On the west side, these have come from places like Whiskey Springs and Ashland Pond, and on the east from places like Wood River Day Use Area. Because of their affinity for water, and because of their constant tail-bobbing behavior, they are sometimes confused with Spotted Sandpipers. However, a waterthrush has a much more prominent supercilium than a Spotted Sandpiper, and has dense streaking on its underparts, instead of spots.

## MacGillivray's Warbler (MGWA)
*Oporornis tolmiei*

William MacGillivray was a Scottish naturalist who never saw America. Audubon named this warbler *macgillivrayi,* after his Scottish friend, either ignoring or overlooking the fact that Townsend, who discovered the bird, had already named it for W.T. Tolmie, a surgeon with the Hudson's Bay Company. Townsend's naming had priority, so we are left with the rather curious situation that "Tolmie" stayed with the scientific name, and "MacGillivray" survived as the common name. For years, naturalists in the west referred to it as the "Tolmie Warbler."

Whatever its name, this is a lovely little bird, quite unlike any other western warbler. The male has a dark gray hood that covers the head and extends down over the upper breast, becoming almost black at the lower edge. The hood on the female is a lighter shade of gray, and becomes whitish on the throat. Both sexes have conspicuous white arcs above and below the eyes, and a dark line that extends from the eye to the bill.

The eastern Mourning Warbler has shown up a few times in Oregon as a vagrant, and closely resembles the MacGillivray's. However, it lacks the conspicuous eye-arcs of the MacGillivray's. Even so, individual variations can cause difficulty in separating some MacGillivray's from some Mournings. Also, some subspecies of the Orange-crowned Warbler have grayish hoods and can be mistaken for MacGillivray's Warblers. These can have an indistinct split eye-ring resembling eye-arcs, but the eye-arcs are not as conspicuous as in the MacGillivray's.

This bird is a skulker, and often provides only brief glimpses, as it flits about in the brush. It is a widespread breeder in Oregon in the mountains, and builds its nest in thick underbrush close to the ground. It forages in similar habitat and favors locations close to water. It appears to thrive in areas that are recovering from logging, provided there is brushy habitat.

The typical song is two-parted, and consists of three or four quickly given notes on about the same pitch, and then by some at a lower pitch. One form is *che-che-che-che-cheweet-cheweet-cheweet.* The tempo is rapid, but not as rapid as that of a Wilson's Warbler. There are variations, and sometimes the last notes are on a higher pitch rather than on a lower.

MacGillivray's Warblers do much of their singing from invisible sources in the brush, but one may gradually work its way up to a higher perch to sing, until it suddenly takes alarm and drops into the brush. Their song helps to locate them in April and May, when courtship is in progress, but once the breeding is seriously in progress, in the words of one observer, they slip "through the thickets like shadows."

## Common Yellowthroat (COYE)
*Geothlypis trichas*

The male yellowthroat is unmistakable. It has a yellow throat, of course, but also has a conspicuous black mask, outlined above by a line of white. Its song, too, is distinctive, and is typically represented as a rolling, whistled *witchety witchety witchety*. However, there is much variation between regions, and even with individuals.

The immatures and females, on the other hand, are rather plain, and can be confused with other plain warblers. However, some of the others with which they might be confused generally show all yellow underparts. The immature and female yellowthroats usually have some white on the belly.

This is probably the most widespread warbler in North America. It breeds in all 49 mainland states, and all the Canadian provinces and territories. In Oregon, it nests in many locations throughout the state. In Southern Oregon, it nests on both sides of the Cascades, and is fairly common in the Klamath Basin. It especially likes cattails and other dense emergent vegetation, but may also nest in other wet and shrubby habitats. A Common Yellowthroat is not often seen up in the trees, but prefers the low, open growth, preferably with water.

The male is given to frequent singing, often from a conspicuous perch. During breeding season the male may express its alarm upon the appearance of an intruder by uttering a staccato rattle, all on one pitch. Sometimes this rattle is the first indication you have that there is a yellowthroat nearby.

Arthur Cleveland Bent puts things nicely when he says:

> When invading its haunts one is impressed with the vigorous personality of the male. He nervously raises his alarm with a variety of scolding, interrogative chirps and chattering notes and his dark inquisitive eyes sparkle with excitement through the black mask. He darts with nervous animation from place to place, then disappears in the dense cover only to appear again to denounce the intrusion.

Migration is a major hazard for these birds, and, in fact for all migrants, many of whom migrate at night. I found a number of examples involving yellowthroats in the east, but the dangers for western birds are probably similar. Bad weather, tall buildings, and lighthouses are major dangers. In one case I came across, many birds were killed in a bad storm, but many others were killed by running into tall buildings. In another case, involving a storm at sea, observers on a boat off the Texas coast saw large numbers of land birds perish, many of which were yellowthroats. Even those that attempted to save themselves by landing on the boat were immediately washed into the sea again.

## Hooded Warbler (HOWA)                          Accidental
*Wilsonia citrina*

This eastern warbler has shown up 8 times in Oregon, mostly at inland locations. There is just one coastal record, in Curry County. A male was netted and banded near Upper Klamath Lake at Odessa Campground, in September 1998, and one week later was netted again. The male is easy to recognize, with a black hood enveloping most of his head and neck, and a bright yellow face. The female echoes the same pattern, but is more subdued.

## Wilson's Warbler (WIWA)
*Wilsonia pusilla*

This active little warbler is such an intense yellow color on the face, breast, and underparts, that ornithologists of the last century called it the "Golden Pileolated Warbler." My dictionary doesn't include the word "pileolated," but it lists "pileated," which means a crest covering the pileum. "Pileum" is a word for the top of the head of a bird from the bill to the nape. Thus, the word "pileolated" referred to the black cap on the head of the male. Not to be content with that, ornithologists at one time called it the "Wilson's Black-capped Flycatching Warbler," thereby putting almost everything into the name, including one of its methods of capturing insects.

The female is not as intense a yellow as the male, and the cap is not as dark, and sometimes is missing. There is a characteristic feature, however, that can help in identifying both males and females, and that is the beady black eye which stands out on the yellow face. Yellow Warblers have beady eyes, too, and a female Wilson's that happens to lack a grayish cap can look a great deal like a female Yellow Warbler.

The Wilson's is one of the most abundant warblers on the coast of Oregon, and is common in Southern Oregon. It breeds on both sides of the Cascades in montane areas, from low elevations to timberline, and breeds sporadically in the Siskiyous. It prefers tall, dense shrub growth, forests with rich understories, and riparian thickets. The nests are on or near the ground.

Wilson's Warblers forage from low to middle levels of the vegetation, and are seldom found far from damp situations, either over boggy ground or near a stream. Arthur Cleveland Bent offers this description of its behavior:

> It gives us the impression of extreme alertness as it flits about in the trees and shrubbery, fluttering among the foliage, dashing into the air to capture

flying insects, restless, full of energy, symbolizing, in spring, its characteristics by its brisk, vivid song.

The song is indeed brisk, and is characterized by a rapid series of 10 to 15 high-pitched staccato notes, frequently speeding up toward the end, sometimes with a slight dropping of pitch: *chchchchchchchchchchcheh*. The song is as rapid as a trill, yet is not a trill, but consists of a rapid series of chips. The song is fairly loud, and often is given from the depths of brushy vegetation. You may hear it many times before you are finally rewarded with a glimpse of the flashing yellow source.

## Canada Warbler (CAWA)   Vagrant
*Wilsonia canadensis*

There is only a handful of Oregon records accepted by the OBRC, for this handsome little warbler. The breeding range extends all the way from the east coast across Canada to the edge of British Columbia, so one could conceivably expect more vagrants than this in our area. There is only one record from Southern Oregon, of a bird that hit a window in Gold Hill, in the Rogue Valley, in September 1990. The specimen is at Southern Oregon University.

The male Canada Warbler is blue-gray above, is mostly yellow below, has a conspicuous eye-ring, and has a characteristic black "necklace." The female looks very much like the male, although the necklace is fainter.

## Yellow-breasted Chat (YBCH)
*Icteria virens*

|  | J | F | M | A | M | J | J | A | S | O | N | D |
|---|---|---|---|---|---|---|---|---|---|---|---|---|
| West |  |  |  |  | ▬ | ▬ | ▬ |  |  |  |  |  |
| East |  |  |  |  |  | — |  |  |  |  |  |  |

This bird is classified with the warblers, but doesn't seem to fit. It is bigger than the other warblers, and weighs more than twice as much as most of them. It somewhat resembles a tanager, and sounds more like a mockingbird than a warbler. Some say the song sounds like a mockingbird with a sore throat. Its inclusion with the warblers has frequently been questioned, but recent genetic evidence seems to confirm its placement there.

Sometimes, in looking for the bird, the male's song is all you get, because this bird lives in thick tangles, and is good at keeping out of sight. The song consists of a series of whistles, rattles, clacks, and squeals, given slowly and with pauses in between. It has been rendered as *C-r-r-r-r-r;* (pause) *quack;* (pause) *chuck;* (pause) *jedek;* (pause) *yit yit yit; tr-r-r-r;* (pause) *caw, caw; mew;* (pause) *chrr chrr chrr,* and so on, with infinite variations.

Usually, the song seems to come from the center of a blackberry tangle, and the bird is invisible. But sometimes the male abandons his skulking ways and sings from an open perch. Occasionally, the male will even sing his song in flight, in what appears to be a courtship ritual. A description in Bent, written a hundred years ago, gives the picture:

... he flings himself into the air -- straight up he goes on fluttering wings -- legs dangling, head raised, his whole being tense and spasmodic with ecstasy. As he rises he pours forth a flood of musical gurgles and whistles that drop from him in silvery cascades to the ground, like sounds of fairy chimes. . . . He holds his hovering position for an instant, then the music gradually dies away; and, as he sinks toward the ground he regains his natural poise, and seeks another perch like that from which he started. What mistress could turn a deaf ear to such love-making as that?

When seen well, the bird is spectacular, with an intensely yellow front, and vivid face markings. Males and females resemble each other. The top of the head is gray, there is a conspicuous "spectacled" effect around the eyes with a white line leading to the bill, dark lores below the stripe, then a white malar stripe, and finally, the yellow throat and breast.

Chats breed in many locations in Oregon, but the Rogue Basin, where it is a fairly common breeding bird, is apparently one of their strongholds. In the Klamath Basin it is primarily a transient, although it is a breeder in the Klamath River canyon. Chats prefer lowland tangles and thickets along rivers, often with a open overstory. Thickets of Himalayan blackberries are perfect for their purposes, and their nests are often placed in the middle of such impenetrable places. Their diet consists almost entirely of insects in the spring, when the fledglings need protein, but shifts to about 50 percent fruits and berries in the fall, including madrone berries, thimbleberries, and Himalayan blackberries.

The greatest threat to chats is the removal of their habitat, including loss of blackberries. Another threat is Brown-headed Cowbirds, which frequently parasitize chats. However, some chats apparently have learned to distinguish cowbird eggs from their own, and will either remove them, or abandon the nest.

## Family **THRAUPIDAE**: Tanagers

### **Western Tanager** (WETA)
*Piranga ludoviciana*

The male of this species in breeding plumage is easily identified. It is looked upon by many as the most beautiful western bird, with its red head, bright yellow body, and black and white wings. On the breeding grounds, which is mainly within coniferous forests, the male is highly conspicuous when in the open, but can be surprisingly obscure in the shade, given its coloration.

The females and immatures lack the red color, and their yellow is more subdued. Males in the nonbreeding season lose almost all of their red color, and resemble females. People sometimes mistake the females and nonbreeding males for female orioles, except the bill on a tanager is stout and of medium length, whereas on an oriole the bill is long and sharp.

In spring migration, the birds tend to be highly visible, especially the colorful males. But in fall migration, the males, females, and immatures can all look a good deal alike, and are studies in yellow, black, and white.

Western Tanagers breed widely in coniferous forests in Oregon, including Southern Oregon. In the western Cascades, they tend to be more numerous in the south than in the north. They like Douglas-firs and ponderosa pines, but seem to avoid dense forests for breeding, and also avoid forests where the trees are far apart. After the breeding season is over, they may appear in a greater diversity of habitats.

The loud *pit-ick!* call of the Western Tanager is heard frequently among the conifers during the breeding season, and it sometimes may be difficult to discover the source high in a tree. Its song resembles that of a robin, with short up-and-down phrases, but it is slightly burrier and not quite as sweet as the song of the robin. Both species deliver their songs in short phrases followed by pauses.

For many years this bird was known as the "Louisiana Tanager," and its scientific name *ludoviciana* means "of Louisiana." All this seems very strange, because the bird is rare in Louisiana. However, the first specimen, found by Lewis and Clark in Idaho, was within what was then known as the Louisiana Territory, hence the name.

## Family **EMBERIZIDAE**: Emberizids

The emberizids include the sparrows, which are the classic "little brown birds." Sometimes this term is abbreviated "LBBs," and sometimes "LBJs," meaning "little brown jobs." In identification, some of the features that get emphasized are: presence or absence of breast streaking; presence or absence of central crown stripe; the pattern of stripes on the head; whether the lores are dark or light; presence or absence of an eye-ring; presence or absence of white outer tail feathers; the appearance of the auricular patch and whether it is heavily outlined or not; the streaking on the back; the appearance of the nape and rump; and, of course, the song.

Breast spots such as those on a Song Sparrow or Fox Sparrow, which are caused by the coalescing of streaks on the breast, are useful but can be variable. The "Song Sparrow" type of breast spot is to be distinguished from the so-called "stickpin" type of breast spot exhibited by American Tree Sparrow, Lark Sparrow, and others, which is a dark spot in the middle of an otherwise clear breast.

### Green-tailed Towhee (GTTO)
*Pipilo chlorurus*

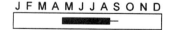

J F M A M J J A S O N D

This western towhee likes the mountains, and prefers dense brushy areas, typically composed of sagebrush, manzanita, or buckbrush, on open slopes with ponderosa pines or junipers. In Southern Oregon they are found in the

Siskiyous, and in the Cascades from the crest eastward. They may range as high as 6000 feet. Flat, low-lying expanses of sagebrush generally are not utilized, nor are the lower chaparral slopes of the Rogue Valley, although Green-taileds may occur occasionally in those places as transients.

The adult bird is quite striking, with a bright rufous cap, white throat with black malar stripe, and greenish-yellow wings and tail. The two sexes look pretty much alike. Typically, the male sings from the top of a bush with its cheerful whistled song, starting with a *wheet-chur*, and which then goes into a complex set of notes that usually includes a trill. One problem is that the song sometimes sounds like that of a Fox Sparrow, which lives in a similar habitat. It is believed that the two species may actually learn some of their songs from each other. The call note of the Green-tailed is a cat-like, plaintive *me-u?* which is not as buzzy as the Spotted Towhee.

Green-tailed Towhees do most of their foraging on the ground, and scratch for their food using a "double scratch," in which both feet are used to scratch backward simultaneously. Other birds in this family do the same thing, but towhees do it habitually. When disturbed in the act of singing, a Green-tailed typically dives into a bush, or may drop to the ground without opening its wings.

## Spotted Towhee (SPTO)
*Pipilo maculatus*

Older field guides show this bird as "Rufous-sided Towhee," from a time when the Spotted Towhee of the west and the Eastern Towhee were considered to be one species. "Rufous-sided" certainly fits both species, because they both do indeed have vivid rufous sides. On the other hand, "Spotted" is a very good name for our western bird, because it has conspicuous white spots on the wings that are missing on the eastern bird. All of them, whether western or eastern, have dark blackish hoods, with the hoods on the females in our area slightly browner than on the males. All of them have red eyes except for a subspecies in the southeastern part of the country that has white eyes. All show conspicuous white corners to their tails when they fly.

It is claimed, when the Eastern Towhee sings, that it is saying, *"drink your teeeeea,"* in which the third note is higher than the other two. The Spotted Towhees of the west show a lot of regional variability on this basic song. Some of them may have anywhere up to 8 introductory notes before getting to the *teeeeee*, but our local birds generally skip the introductory notes altogether, and just go *teeeeeee*, in a buzzy trill that has a resemblance to the song of a Chipping Sparrow. When singing, the male will generally occupy a fairly high position in a tree, and become highly visible. The call note is a buzzy *meeeuw*, somewhat like a cat.

Spotted Towhees are among the commoner of birds west of the Cascades, in open woods, suburban areas, and shrublands in valleys and foothills, and are year-round residents there. They inhabit similar areas east of the Cascades, but avoid extensive areas of sagebrush. Many of those east of the Cascades move to the south in winter, but some remain.

Spotted Towhees scratch with both feet simultaneously like other towhees, and can be very noisy when foraging. They like the brush, but are not as secretive as some of their relatives, often coming out to forage on the ground where they can be seen. Their buzzy call note is often a giveaway to their presence.

## California Towhee (CALT)
*Pipilo crissalis*

This was one of the first birds I learned to recognize as a kid, and I especially learned to take note of the rich cinnamon-colored area on the undertail coverts, which relieved the overall brownness of the bird. I also learned the bird's name was California Towhee.

A few years later, I learned it wasn't the California Towhee any more, but was the "Brown Towhee." I was ignorant of the reasons for this change, of course, but I later learned that it had been lumped with another species that resembled it, from Arizona, New Mexico, and Texas. As a lumped species occurring in many states, it could hardly bear the name of just one state, so "Brown Towhee" was adopted.

In 1988, more careful studies found that these two species weren't as closely related as had been thought, and the two species were split back apart, into California Towhee and Canyon Towhee. Today, the California Towhee is recognized as exclusively a resident of Upper and Lower California, with one exception: there is an isolated year-round range in Southern Oregon. This range is in the Rogue, Applegate, and Illinois Valleys, and in the Klamath Basin in brushy locations such as along the Link River, around the Tule Lake NWR, and in the Klamath River canyon. A few birds occasionally appear as far north as Roseburg,

California Towhees don't like to be very far away from dense brush, but will come out and forage at the edges, usually in shaded areas. Their sharp, metallic *chink!* call is characteristic, and is often heard, especially when the male is patrolling the breeding territory. The song is a loud, fairly long set of piercing staccato chip notes, usually on one pitch and accelerating toward the end, sometimes rendered as *chip chip chip tic-tic-ti-ti-ti-ti-ti,* but there are variations. The purpose of the call apparently is to attract a mate, so as soon as this objective is accomplished the males tend to stop singing.

## American Tree Sparrow (ATSP)
*Spizella arborea*

American Tree Sparrows breed in the far north, but are widely distributed throughout the lower 48 states during winter. In the east they are one of the commonest of sparrows, and are regular in winter in the northeastern part of Oregon. In Southern Oregon they are rare on the east side of the Cascades, and are vagrants on the west side. On the 2000 Christmas Count, one was reported at Klamath Falls, and another one at Medford.

This is a member of the *Spizella* genus; five members of the genus have occurred in Oregon. (A sixth member, the Field Sparrow, has not been recorded in Oregon.) Three of these are difficult to tell apart in winter (Chipping, Clay-colored, and Brewer's Sparrows), and will be discussed in the next section.

The American Tree Sparrow, if seen well, is fairly straightforward in identification. It has a rufous cap (so does the Chipping Sparrow in breeding plumage), which it retains in the winter. Some individuals may have a grayish median stripe on the crown in winter. There is a small rufous stripe behind the eye (a "postocular" stripe), and a small dark spot in the middle of a plain gray breast. There are rufous areas on the sides of the breast next to the bend of the wing, fading to a warm beige on the lower flanks.

Tree sparrows are skulkers. They are strongly associated with willows near water, in country which is more or less open, where they typically creep along grassy edges. They may perch on bushes and fences, but are rarely seen very high in the trees.

**Chipping Sparrow** (CHSP)
*Spizella passerina*

**Brewer's Sparrow** (BRSP)
*Spizella breweri*

**Clay-colored Sparrow** (CCSP)
*Spizella pallida*

Vagrant

These three birds are fairly easy to distinguish in breeding plumage, but their nonbreeding plumages can present problems, which is why they are grouped here together. Two of them, Chipping and Brewer's Sparrows, are widespread in Oregon in breeding season, but their habitats and songs will help to tell them apart. The Clay-colored Sparrow, on the other hand is a rarity in Oregon. It has been recorded in the state a number of times, mostly in fall and winter, and mostly on the coast. There are a couple of records from Southern Oregon: one in early spring of 1992, near Medford, and one in June 1998, near Cave Junction.

The Chipping Sparrow is one of our most familiar summertime sparrows. It is a widespread breeder in most of Oregon, and in Southern Oregon breeds from the foothills to timberline, wherever there are trees and open clearings. During the breeding season, they sing persistently, usually from fairly exposed perches. The song, from which the bird gets its common name, is a long mechanical trill of chips all on one pitch. It resembles that of the Dark-eyed Junco, except that the chipping notes of the junco are more musical. The scientific name, *passerina,* by the way, means "sparrow-like," so that means the Chipping Sparrow is the "sparrow-like sparrow."

The Chipping Sparrow's breeding plumage is instantly recognizable, because it has a bright rufous cap, a white supercilium, and a black eye-line that extends through the eye to the bill. Almost all the Chipping Sparrows leave Oregon for the winter, but a few may remain west of the crest. In the fall, the bright crown changes to a rufous-tinged brown and develops some dark streaking, and the white supercilium loses some of its brightness. It is at this time that the confusion with Brewer's and Clay-colored Sparrows can occur.

Brewer's Sparrows are birds of the sagebrush and buckbrush. They are fairly common in sagebrush country east of the crest, and it is surprising to find a few of them apparently breeding west of the crest, some of them high in the Siskiyous, and others right down on the floor of the Rogue Valley.

This has been called one of the most nondescript birds in Oregon, but compensates for it by having one of the most remarkable songs. The song is typically delivered from the top of a bush, and consists of a series of buzzes and trills on different pitches, sometimes resembling a canary, that run together in a continuous stream. It typically goes on for so long it seems the bird must run our of breath. Brewer's Sparrows leave the state entirely for the winter, but in the fall can be confused with the other two in this group.

Here are some hints on telling these birds apart in their nonbreeding plumages, although there may be some individuals that don't fit the patterns, and thus be unidentifiable.

In the Chipping Sparrow, in all plumages, the dark eye-line extends through the eye and to the base of the bill, which means that the lores are dark. In the other two, the lores are pale.

The auricular patches of the three are different: In the Chipping Sparrow, the auricular patch is sharply defined on the upper side, but the dark line defining the lower edge is indistinct or nonexistent. In the Clay-colored, the dark lines above and below the auricular patch are very distinct, and the line below the patch widens toward the rear. In the Brewer's the auricular patch is outlined both above and below, but the lower line does not widen as it does in the Clay-colored.

It's worthwhile to check the collars and napes, too. In the Clay-colored the head is set off from the body by a well-defined, unstreaked gray collar. In the Chipping Sparrow, the collar is not as well-defined and is less conspicuous. In the Brewer's Sparrow, the nape is heavily streaked, breaking up the gray collar.

Just to render the picture more complicated, there is a subspecies of Brewer's Sparrow that may become a full species in the future, called the "Timberline Sparrow." The breeding range of this bird is in the mountains of Alaska and Canada, at or near timberline. It is hypothesized that some of these birds may migrate through our area, but they resemble Brewer's Sparrows so closely that they might not be detected.

## Black-chinned Sparrow (BCSP)
*Spizella atrogularis*

|  | J F M A M J J A S O N D |
|---|---|
| West | ------ |
| East | Vagrant |

This is an intriguing little bird, looking somewhat like a slim "Gray-headed Junco," except that the junco has a rufous mantle, and the sparrow has a brownish back streaked with black. In Oregon, its occurrences are well beyond the normal range of the species, which extends into the foothills surrounding the Sacramento Valley of California. It is has been recorded twelve times in Oregon, and seven of those appearances have been in the Rogue Valley. Five of them have been in the same location -- Roxy Ann Peak, near Medford.

There are two records in the Klamath Basin, both near Stukel Mountain. There is one in Lake County, and one near Steens Mountain. All these records are in southerly locations in Oregon, but there is one which really pushes the envelope to the north, in Clackamas County. Breeding is believed to have taken place at the Roxy Ann Peak site, and at Stukel Mountain.

The male has black around the bill, and especially on the chin. The female is similar, but lacks the black around the bill. The song is distinctive, and is usually the first clue concerning the presence of the bird. It is generally given from an exposed perch, and starts with a slow *sweet sweet sweet,* and then continues in a rapid trill, sometimes rising, sometimes falling. The preferred habitat is brushy, dry, rocky slopes.

## Vesper Sparrow (VESP)
*Pooecetes gramineus*

Sparrows like to hide in grassy fields and brushy places, and this one is no exception. However, when a Vesper Sparrow is singing, it mounts to the top of a shrub, or perches in a tree next to a field, and sings a lovely song that reminds one of a Song Sparrow. The song opens typically with two long clear notes, followed by a variety of flutelike trills. Some people think it is more plaintive than a Song Sparrow. The name "Vesper" was given because this bird presumably does most of its singing at dusk, but it actually may sing any time of day, including dusk.

For habitat, Vespers seek open situations, with weedy or brushy conditions. They like sagebrush/grass habitats at relatively high elevations, open ponderosa groves, and subalpine meadows. They have been found, apparently breeding, in montane habitats surrounding the Rogue Valley, and in the mountains and fields of southern Klamath County. In migration, they might be found in small, loose flocks.

If you get a good look, Vesper Sparrows are readily identified. Their closest lookalike is the Savannah Sparrow, but the Vesper has white outer tail feathers, that the Savannah lacks. Also, the Vesper has a thin, but distinct, eye-ring, and a small chestnut shoulder patch that is sometimes not visible. The auricular patch is heavily outlined in black, surrounded below by white, which makes the patch stand out. Some individuals may have a breast spot, so breast spots cannot be relied upon for certain identification.

## Lark Sparrow (LASP)
*Chondestes grammacus*

There are several candidates for the title "most beautiful sparrow," and this is certainly one of them. The pattern on the head is vivid and striking, consisting of white, black, and chestnut stripes in what has been referred to as a "harlequin clown" face pattern. Add to this white outer tail feathers and a nice little dark "stickpin" in the middle of the white breast, and you've got about as neat a little sparrow as could be asked for.

Lark Sparrows breed widely in Southern Oregon at the lower elevations, in grassland, sagebrush, and open woodlands, especially east of the crest. West of the crest, they are fairly common breeders in the Rogue Valley and surrounding foothills. In the fall and winter, they typically form medium-sized flocks, often near agricultural fields. Frequently, a passing car will startle such a flock, whereupon many of them will fly to the adjacent fence lines and perch on the wires.

The song is highly variable, and consists of a loose mixture of whistles, trills, and buzzes. Mostly, it has a musical quality, but occasionally some of the notes sound as if they have been borrowed from a Yellow-breasted Chat.

## Black-throated Sparrow (BTSP)
*Amphispiza bilineata*

Here is another candidate for "most beautiful sparrow." The head has a vivid pattern of black and white stripes, and the throat has a conspicuous black patch that extends over the breast. The outer tail feathers have narrow white edgings and white tips. This bird cannot be mistaken for anything else.

The Black-throated Sparrow is mostly a bird of the southwest deserts, and is at the northern limits of its breeding range in Oregon. It is an uncommon and variable breeder in southeastern Oregon, where it seeks dry, sunny, rocky slopes with scattered vegetation. It is a sparse and irregular breeder in appropriate habitat in the Klamath Basin, such as on Stukel Mountain. It has the ability to get the water it needs from the insects and plants in its diet, compatible with its desert habitat. There have been rare influxes into western Oregon, and the Rogue Valley has produced a handful of records, all in May or June.

The song, which is usually delivered from the top of a bush, has a pleasant tinkling quality. The quick opening notes are clear and distinct, followed by a buzzy trill: *pip pip chup chrrrrrrrr.* There are many variations on this theme, even from a given individual.

## Sage Sparrow (SAGS)
*Amphispiza belli*

| | J F M A M J J A S O N D |
|---|---|
| West | Vagrant |
| East | --------- |

There is a good chance that this species will be split into two in the near future: the "Bell's Sparrow" of California, and the "Sage Sparrow" of the rest of the bird's range in the interior west. James Rising, in his book *The Sparrows of the United States and Canada,* has already split them. He gave the scientific name of *Amphispiza belli* to the "Bell's Sparrow," and the scientific name of *Amphispiza nevadensis* to the "interior" Sage Sparrow. In Rising's classification, the "Bell's Sparrow" had priority for the name used for the lumped species, because it been found and described first, in 1850. The "interior" Sage Sparrow wasn't described until 1873. As of the writing of this book, the AOU had not yet decided whether to follow Rising's classification.

Sage Sparrows of the "interior" type breed widely in southeastern Oregon, mostly in sagebrush, but also in other similar brushy habitats. As breeders, they are found in our area only in the eastern part of the Klamath Basin, near Clear Lake NWR. They are notoriously secretive, preferring to run on the ground, out of sight, rather than fly. In breeding season, however, the male will mount to a perch on a bush and sing, and this is the best time to find one. The songs vary, but one version consists of a series of thin, whistled, somewhat plaintive notes -- *sit sit syeoo tsyeoo tsit,* with the first three notes more or less on the same pitch, the *tsyeoo* falling and rising, and the final note on a higher pitch.

About 14 strays have occurred in Oregon west of the Cascades, including one near Emigrant Lake in the Rogue Valley, in March 1989. It is not known whether this latter bird was of the "Bell's" type or the "interior" type. The "interior" is a long-distance migrant, and therefore is the more likely one to stray. The "Bell's" is resident in its California range, and therefore is presumed to be more sedentary, although members of this group have been known to wander after breeding. Since the range of "Bell's" extends quite far north in the Coast Range of California, a stray in southwest Oregon from that source seems possible. If the AOU officially makes the split, the identity of strays, especially west of the crest, will become of great interest.

The two strongly resemble each other, except that the "interior" Sage Sparrow is paler than the "Bell's." Both birds have vividly marked black and white face patterns, a small amount of streaking on the sides of the white breast, and an isolated dark spot in the center of the breast. There is black streaking on the back in both birds, but the "Bell's" is so much darker on the back than the "interior," that the streaks don't stand out as much. Thus, on the "interior," they are much more visible. Finally, the black malar stripe on the "Bell's" is wider and darker than on the "interior." In the latter, the malar stripe is thin and less contrasting.

## Lark Bunting (LARB)         Vagrant
*Calamospiza melanocorys*

Lark Buntings are birds of the Great Plains, but there have been 14 records in Oregon. Two of these were in the Rogue Valley, in November 1961 and in May 1999. One was at Miller Island in the Klamath Basin, in August 1983. About half of the records have been in the spring, and the May 1999 sighting in the Rogue Valley was of a male in summer plumage.

The summer plumage of the male is striking. There is no other North American bird like it -- a large black sparrow with white wing panels. In winter, the male develops a brown and gray streaked appearance, but still has prominent white wing panels. Females are brown and streaked, and have white edges to the greater wing coverts. They can be confused with female longspurs, but the Lark Buntings have heavier bills.

## Savannah Sparrow (SAVS)
*Passerculus sandwichensis*

Why should a bird be named *sandwichensis?* It's because the first specimen known to science was taken at Sandwich Bay, in the Aleutian Islands. Since James Cook, the English explorer, named the "Sandwich Islands" (Hawaii) in 1778 in honor of the Earl of Sandwich, we can assume Sandwich Bay derived its name from the same source. The "Savannah" part comes from the fact that an early specimen in the Lower 48 came from Savannah, Georgia.

This is one of our most abundant sparrows, and is found across the entire continent. I have heard them singing in the Rogue Valley (where I regularly mistake their song for that of the Grasshopper Sparrow), and have had them almost underfoot on the edge of the Arctic Ocean in Alaska, where they ran about making complaining noises because I was too close to a nest.

They are widespread breeders in Oregon. They are confirmed breeders in many places in the Klamath Basin, and are confirmed or possible breeders in a number of places in Josephine and Jackson counties.

They are birds of the open country, and can be found in meadows, agricultural fields, roadside edges, and meadows, where they form flocks in the nonbreeding season. Like all sparrows, they have a remarkable ability to disappear in the grass, but by close inspection they can usually be discovered foraging about like mice. When you are driving along a road, they often will fly up from the road edge and perch in plain view on a fence.

Its song is similar to that of the Grasshopper Sparrow, but is slightly louder, and a little lower in pitch. Like the Grasshopper, it generally opens with two or three *tsip* notes, then goes into a long buzz, and usually has a final note that the Grasshopper lacks: *tsip tsip tsip trzzzzzzzzz tsip.* Sometimes the final note is missing, which makes it seem all the more like a Grasshopper Sparrow.

Besides being abundant and widespread, Savannah Sparrows are also highly variable, with 14 subspecies. Three of these have distinctly different appearances, and may eventually be split into separate species: the very dark "Belding's Savannah Sparrow" of the Southern California coast; the very pale "Ipswich Sparrow" of the Atlantic Coast; and the "Large-billed Savannah Sparrow," of the Salton Sea area in Southern California. It's not likely that any of these three will appear in our area.

Our Savannah Sparrows generally have brown streaked backs, white underparts with fine streaking across the top of the breast and down the flanks, small to moderately small bills, and a supercilium that is usually yellowish, and sometimes is quite yellow, depending upon the subspecies. Occasionally, the streaking on the breast coalesces into a dark spot, after the manner of a Song Sparrow.

## Grasshopper Sparrow (GRSP)
*Ammodramus savannarum*

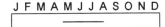

It comes as no surprise to learn that the Grasshopper Sparrow gets its name from the insect-like buzz of its song. The song is so soft that it can be hard to hear, especially in the presence of other birds' songs. This, coupled with its general reclusive nature, makes it a difficult bird to find. The song sounds something like that of a Savannah Sparrow, but is thinner and higher. It typically starts with a couple of soft opening notes, followed by a buzz: *tsck tsck tsrrrrrrrrrr.* The song is generally delivered from an elevated perch on a flower stalk, or on a fence post.

This is a short-tailed, flat-headed, large-billed sparrow. A prominent black eye stands out in a mostly unmarked buffy face. The underparts, at least in the adult, are unstreaked and have a buffy color, blending into a whitish belly. The back can have an intricate pattern of chestnut-colored spots, caused by the chestnut tips on many of the feathers.

The breeding range extends from coast to coast, but the birds apparently have their greatest abundance in the Great Plains. In Oregon, they have been recorded as breeding in a few locations, principally in the Columbia Basin. The preferred habitat is grassy fallow fields, or lightly-grazed pastures. In the presence of heavy grazing, they go elsewhere.

In Southern Oregon, Grasshopper Sparrow has been confirmed as a breeder in the grassy meadows north of Upper Klamath Lake, and in a couple of grassy locations in the Rogue Valley. It is unpredictable and irregular. It may nest for a few years in a particular location, and then for no discernible reason disappear from that location, perhaps to reappear after a few years. Some believe that it may be more numerous than is realized, because it is so difficult to detect that it may often be overlooked.

# Fox Sparrow (FOSP)
*Passerella iliaca*

**"Thick-billed Fox Sparrow"**
*(Passerella megarhyncha)*

**"Slate-colored Fox Sparrow"**
*(Passerella schistacea)*

**"Sooty Fox Sparrow"**
*(Passerella unalaschcensis)*

**"Red Fox Sparrow"**          Vagrant
*(Passerella iliaca)*

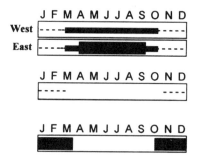

The "Fox Sparrow Complex," as it is sometimes called, is indeed a complex subject. There are either 17 or 18 subspecies of Fox Sparrow in North America, depending upon who you listen to, falling into four fairly well defined groups, shown above in quotation marks. In the Seventh Edition of the *Checklist of North American Birds,* the AOU listed the four groups shown above, and identified them by the scientific names shown in parentheses. The AOU said, ". . . the groups may represent biological species, but there is at least limited hybridization among them, especially between the *schistacea* and *megarhyncha* groups. Additional study is needed in areas of contact of members of the groups. Three of the four groups were treated as separate species by Rising, who considered the *schistacea* and *megarhyncha* groups to be conspecific." Thus, we can expect either three or four new species to emerge in the future from the Fox Sparrow Complex, depending upon what the AOU decides to do.

The currently recognized subspecies *Passerella iliaca fulva* breeds in central Klamath County in the eastern Cascades. The currently recognized subspecies *Paserella iliaca megarhyncha* breeds in the Cascades in the southwestern part of Klamath County and in the Siskiyous. It is believed that the lowlands of the Klamath Basin may be a natural break between the breeding ranges of these two subspecies.

In the winter, the breeding subspecies essentially leave the state, and are replaced in our area by the very dark "Sooty Fox Sparrow," that breeds from northern Washington up to Alaska. The "Red Fox Sparrow" breeds across the northern part of the continent from Alaska to the Atlantic Coast, and occurs in our area only as a vagrant in winter.

**"Thick-billed Fox Sparrow"** and **"Slate-colored Fox Sparrow"** resemble each other, differing in the size of the bill, of course. The head is grayish in both, the wings are a rusty brown, and the spotting on the breast extends down the flanks, but the white belly is usually unspotted. The spotting on the breast may coalesce into a larger spot, as in the Song Sparrow. Narrow wing-bars may be present.

The **"Sooty Fox Sparrow"** is very dark, almost black in some cases. The head is dark brown or almost black, the wings are very dark brown with no wing-bars, and the underparts are heavily streaked or spotted with dark triangular spots. The belly is whitish, and often is spotted. The streaking on the breast sometimes coalesces into a central breast spot.

The **"Red Fox Sparrow"** is the common Fox Sparrow of the east. It has a pattern of rufous and gray, with rufous streaks on the breast and flanks. In fact, the name "Fox" Sparrow was originally given because of the reddish fox color of this bird. It looks so different from those in the other groups that there is not likely to be any confusion.

Summer or winter, Fox Sparrows like dense, low shrub growth. The "Thick-billed" breeds in montane brushland, including brushy spots in clearcuts. The song, given from the top of a bush or small tree, typically starts with two or three whistled notes, *wheet-chur,* or *too-wheet-tyoo,* followed by some warbling or buzzy notes. The song is variable, and sometimes resembles the song of a Green-tailed Towhee. Since these two species live in similar habitat, some song mimicry may be involved. In winter, the "Sooty" types still love brushy places, but at lowland locations, where they "double-scratch" with both feet at once, like towhees.

## Song Sparrow (SOSP)
*Melospiza melodia*

J F M A M J J A S O N D

Song Sparrows are widely distributed across the continent, and are among the best-known of birds. There are 29 described subspecies, displaying an enormous amount of variability, from the very dark birds of the Pacific Northwest, to the very light ones of the desert southwest. Birds breeding to the east of the Cascades are generally brighter than the darker ones to the west, but all the subspecies show intergradation where the populations meet. Some of the breeding birds in Southern Oregon move southward in winter, but other birds coming down from the north augment the normal wintering population.

The dark-plumaged Song Sparrows can be mistaken for the dark-plumaged Fox Sparrows, but Song Sparrows have gray superciliums and conspicuous dark malar stripes, lacking in Fox Sparrows. A Song Sparrow also might be confused with a Lincoln's Sparrow, but the Lincoln's is smaller, has much finer stripes on the breast and flanks, has a buffy wash to the breast, and is less likely to have a central breast spot.

Song Sparrows are most likely to be found in brushy habitats near water, although in winter they might also be found in marshes, moist ravines, and in brush piles. They are opportunistic feeders, and eat insects, seeds, berries, and even small minnows. They have a fairly loud *tchip!* call note, and readily respond to pishing. When singing, they come up to an exposed perch, where they can readily be seen.

There is much variation in the song, but it usually opens with two (sometimes three) rather loud whistled notes, all on the same pitch and sounding somewhat deliberate, followed by a complex series of warbled notes, often including a buzzy trill. The bird traditionally has been described as singing, "Maids, maids, maids, put on your tea kettle, kettle, kettle."

## Lincoln's Sparrow (LISP)
*Melospiza lincolnii*

No, it's not named for Abraham Lincoln, but was named by Audubon for a colleague of his, Thomas Lincoln. Audubon wrote that, while in Labrador, he came upon a bird unfamiliar to him, and heard ". . . the sweet notes of this bird as they came thrilling on the sense, surpassing in vigour those of any American Finch with which I am acquainted, and forming a song which seemed a compound of those of the Canary and Wood-lark of Europe." Having thus written lyrically of the beauty of the song, he wrote, "Chance placed my young companion, Thomas Lincoln, in a situation where he saw it alight within shot, and with his usual unerring aim, he cut short its career."

Lincoln's Sparrows are breeding birds of montane meadows in the Cascades and the Siskiyous, generally above 3000 feet, and as high as 6000 feet. A typical nesting habitat is a wet meadow with a lush cover of sedges and forbs, with dense willow thickets, and scattered firs and lodgepole pines. In the winter the birds descend to lower elevations, mostly in the valleys west of the Cascades. In the breeding season they can be located because of their singing, but in winter they are skulkers in dense brush or tall grass, although they may respond to pishing.

The song is loud, sweet, and bubbly, reminding one of a House Wren's song, and is generally delivered from a bush or small tree where the singer may be partly concealed. Superficially, the Lincoln's Sparrow resembles a Song Sparrow, but it has much more delicate streaking on the upper breast, a broad gray supercilium and grayish face, a thin malar stripe instead of a broad one, and a buffy wash across the upper breast.

## Swamp Sparrow (SWSP)                                             Vagrant
*Melospiza georgiana*

Swamp Sparrow's closest lookalike is the Lincoln's Sparrow. If we were in their breeding territory we could tell them immediately by their reddish caps and Chipping Sparrow-like song, but they don't breed anywhere in Oregon. We get them in winter, mostly along the coast or in the Willamette Valley. Over the decades, the numbers of them found each year have been increasing, but whether this is because there are more of them, or because birder activity has become more intense, is not clear. There is a handful of winter records in Southern Oregon, mostly west of the Cascades.

In winter, they are generally found in dense vegetation, mostly near water. The differences from Lincoln's Sparrow are that the wings on the Swamp Sparrow are generally more reddish than on the Lincoln's, the breast is whitish rather than buffy, and the underparts are only lightly streaked, rather than having the distinct fine streaking of the Lincoln's. Juvenile Swamps and Lincoln's can probably not be told apart in the field.

### Harris's Sparrow (HASP)
*Zonotrichia querula*

The breeding territory of the Harris's Sparrow is in far north central Canada, and their normal wintering ground is from Nebraska to Texas, so it doesn't seem likely they would show up in Oregon. Nevertheless, in the winter we have them somewhere in the state every year, mostly in the northern part, at an average rate of two per year. In Southern Oregon they occasionally make a winter appearance, which could be on either side of the crest.

If they show up at all, it is likely to be with other sparrows at feeders, with some brushy habitat close by. The Harris's is so much bigger than other sparrows that one will immediately stand out from the crowd. In the winter, the cheeks are buff-colored, both in adults and in immatures. There will be a considerable amount of black around the face and throat in the adult, but in an immature the throat will be white, with a variable amount of black across the upper breast. Late in winter, the buffy cheeks will begin to change to gray. The bill is pink, in all plumages.

### White-crowned Sparrow (WCSP)
*Zonotrichia leucophrys*

### White-throated Sparrow (WTSP)
*Zonotrichia albicollis*

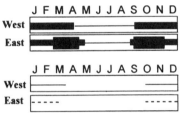

These two birds have some resemblance to each other, which is why they are placed together. The adults of both species have conspicuous black crown stripes and white superciliums. Some adult White-throated Sparrows have tan superciliums, instead of white.

A White-throated Sparrow has a conspicuously white throat that contrasts sharply with the gray on the breast; a White-crowned has a grayish-white throat that blends into the gray. A White-throated Sparrow has a yellow spot in the supercilium next to the eye; White-crowneds lack this spot. The bill on a White-throated is gray; on a White-crowned it is yellowish or pinkish.

White-throated Sparrows breed across Canada almost coast to coast. In our area they are rare winter visitors. Christmas Counts in recent years for Grants Pass and Medford have shown an average of about 2 per year in each location. Then suddenly, in 2001, there were 43 of them on the Medford Christmas Count. The Klamath Falls Christmas Count has had an average of less than one per year.

White-crowneds breed in many places in Oregon. In Southern Oregon, breeding has been confirmed in northern Josephine County and in eastern Klamath County, and there have been many indications of "possible" breeding in the Cascades and Siskiyous. Those that breed west of the Cascades are mostly of the subspecies *pugetensis,* which have white lores. Those that breed east of the Cascades are mostly *oriantha,* which have black lores. Some of these birds move south in winter, but the ones that remain are augmented by others who move down from the mountains, or are moving south from their breeding grounds in British Columbia and Alaska

White-crowned Sparrow

Immature White-crowned Sparrows sometimes cause puzzlement in the minds of those who haven't encountered them before. The pattern of stripes on the head is similar to that of the adult, but in the adult the stripes are a vivid black and white, making the adult White-crowned one of the more beautiful of our sparrows. In the immature White-crowned, these stripes are brown and tan, making the bird look like it belongs to an entirely different species.

White-crowned Sparrows have a variety of songs, that differ from region to region. There are even different "dialects" within regions. One typical song consists of sweet whistled notes, starting with a prolonged note on a sustained pitch, followed by others in an up and down pattern -- *seeeeee seetelee see see see.* In winter they form small flocks, and generally forage in more open habitats than either White-throated or Golden-crowned Sparrows. When frightened, the members of a flock will typically fly up into a tree, making them easy to see, after which they drop back down to the ground one by one, after the danger is gone.

## Golden-crowned Sparrow (GCSP)
*Zonotrichia atricapilla*

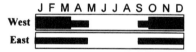

In the winter, in the valleys west of the Cascades, this is our most abundant sparrow. The number counted in the Medford Christmas Count for 2001 was 1,335. On the west side of the Cascades, they far outnumber White-crowned Sparrows, and in the Grants Pass Christmas Counts for recent years have outnumbered White-crowneds by ten to one. In the Medford counts, they outnumbered White-crowneds by five to one. Over the crest, in the Klamath Falls counts, the ratio is reversed, and White-crowneds outnumber Golden-crowneds by more than two to one.

In winter, there are just fewer sparrows on the east side. The average number of Golden-crowneds in the Klamath Falls Christmas Counts of recent years is 75; in the Medford counts, the average is 950. But in summer you won't see Golden-crowneds at all in Southern Oregon, because they breed far to the north in British Columbia and Alaska.

For most of the winter, Golden-crowneds are pretty plain looking, more so with the immature birds than with the adults. In early winter the adults will show a certain amount of gold color on the top of the head, but this changes to a brilliant gold cap as spring approaches, with a crisp broad black border on each side. The immatures show less color on the head in early winter, but still show a bit of yellow or yellow-brown on the forecrown.

Golden-crowneds gather in small flocks in winter, sometimes with other sparrows. Never are they very far from brush, but will come out to the edges to forage, disappearing at the slightest alarm. They might sing at any time during the winter, as is also true of their other *Zonotrichia* cousins. They are usually out of sight as they sing, so all you get is the song, but it has the virtue of being instantly recognizable, and is not likely to be confused with other songs. It typically consists of three plaintive whistles, each at a lower pitch than its predecessor, and has sometimes been represented as saying, "Oh, dear me." Sometimes the bird will cut it short, and say, "Oh dear." And sometimes shorter yet, and just say, "Oh."

## Dark-eyed Junco
*Junco hyemalis*

**"Oregon Junco"** (ORJU)

J F M A M J J A S O N D

**"Slate-colored Junco"** (SCJU)

J F M A M J J A S O N D
|--------          ----|

Like the Yellow-rumped Warbler, this is another case where birds that were previously classified as separate species have been lumped together, but where bird-banders continue to record them separately and give them separate codes. Christmas Counts also keep track of them separately. There are 12 subspecies, separable into five recognizable groups that used to be considered full species. These are listed below. The birds of all the groups have conspicuous white outer tail feathers.

**"Oregon Junco."** This is the familiar bird of the west, recognizable by the dark hood, rusty back, and pinkish flanks. The hoods on females are not as dark as on the males. Overwhelmingly, this is the bird we see in Southern Oregon, both summer and winter.

**"Slate-colored Junco."** For much of the country, this is *the* junco. Most of the body is indeed slate-colored, and the belly is white. Males are darker-colored than females. They breed in northern Canada and Alaska, and winter throughout the Lower 48 states. "Slate-coloreds" appear regularly somewhere in Oregon every year in small numbers in winter, and irregularly in Southern

Oregon. In the Christmas Counts of 2000, there were three of them found on the Medford count, and one on the Grants Pass count. Klamath Falls had one on the 1999 count. Something to look for is the fact that the hood on a "Slate-colored" is concave on the breast in the shape of an inverted "U." In the "Oregon Junco," on the other hand, the hood is convex. "Slate-coloreds" and "Oregons" hybridize on a regular basis in the northern Rockies, producing birds with mixed characteristics.

**"Gray-headed Junco."** (GHJU) This bird breeds in the Great Basin, and winters in the southwest. A pair was found breeding in the extreme southeastern part of Oregon in June 1999, and another pair the following year. There is one record from Douglas County, but none for our area.

**"Pink-sided Junco."** This one breeds in the northern mountain states, and winters as far south as New Mexico and Texas. Individuals of this form are occasionally reported in Oregon, but none from Southern Oregon. First year female "Oregon Juncos" look a lot like female "Pink-sided Juncos." Bird-banders apparently think "Pink-sideds" look so much like "Oregons" that they don't have a separate code for them.

**"White-winged Junco."** (WWJU) The principal breeding range for this bird is in the Black Hills of South Dakota, and the wintering range extends from there down through Colorado. The "white wings" are just white wing-bars, and some "Slate-coloreds" have white wing-bars that are as prominent as in the "White-wingeds." However, there is a good deal more white in the outer tail feathers in this bird than in the other groups. There is only one record in Oregon, near Bend, in February 1987.

Everybody knows and loves the junco. It is one of our most abundant and widespread birds. It is also one of the hardiest, and tends to remain in the mountains late in the season, until driven down by storms. They breed widely in Southern Oregon, and are most often found during breeding season in or near coniferous forests, most commonly at the edges of meadows or clearcuts, sometimes in aspens, junipers, and in suburban areas. Following breeding, there is generally an up-slope dispersal to higher elevations. In winter they form small flocks, and are readily observable.

The song is a sustained trill, a little slower and more musical than that of a Chipping Sparrow. It resembles the song of an Orange-crowned Warbler, except that the trill of the junco is usually held at a steady pitch, whereas that of the Orange-crowned tends to fall off at the end, either in pitch or frequency, or both.

Where did the "Dark-eyed" part of the name come from? All of the subspecies of Dark-eyed Junco do have dark eyes, and there is a separate species in southeast Arizona and Mexico with yellow eyes, called (no surprise) Yellow-eyed Junco.

## Lapland Longspur (LALO)
*Calcarius lapponicus*

|  | J F M A M J J A S O N D |
|---|---|
| West | --- ----- |
| East | ⎯⎯⎯⎯⎯   ⎯⎯⎯ |

## McCown's Longspur (MCLO)
*Calcarius mccownii*

|  | J F M A M J J A S O N D |
|---|---|
| West | Vagrant |
| East | --- -- |

## Chestnut-collared Longspur (CCLO)
*Calcarius ornatus*

Vagrant

These three longspurs are readily told apart in breeding plumage, but we are not likely to see them in that plumage in our area. In their nonbreeding plumages they can be a problem, and are grouped here for that reason. Of the three, only Lapland Longspur is reasonably regular in our area, in the Klamath Basin. Longspurs are given that name because of their long and slender hind claws.

Lapland Longspurs breed around the world in northern regions, including Lapland. In North America, they breed along the edges of the Arctic Ocean, and principally winter in the central and eastern parts of the continent. Smith's Longspur also breeds in the far north, and winters in Oklahoma and Arkansas. It has not been recorded in Oregon. The other two, McCown's and Chestnut-collared, breed on the northern plains and primarily winter in the southwest.

Nonbreeding longspurs not only have plumages that distressingly resemble each other, they also are among the most difficult birds to see well. Their typical behavior is to crouch in short grass, and even to move about in a crouching position. Since they often join with Horned Larks or Pipits in flocks, this behavior is one way to pick them out. Horned Larks and Pipits tend to move around a lot and be highly visible. To find a longspur, look for the bird that barely shows its head or part of its back, and may hold very still, often in a grassy depression.

The best place for longspurs in Southern Oregon is in that part of the Lower Klamath NWR which lies between Stateline Road (CA 161) and Township Road, in Klamath County. There are large fields with gravel or dirt roads on the tops of adjacent dikes (some of which may not be passable in winter). Lapland Longspurs are fairly regular here in winter, and seek out areas with short grass, or burned areas. They are usually in the company of Horned Larks, and have sometimes appeared in large flocks. The largest on record had 500 birds in it. In the Rogue Valley they sometimes show up on edges of reservoirs such as Agate Lake or Lost Creek Lake, when the water is very low and large grassy expanses are exposed.

McCown's Longspurs appear on an irregular basis in the Klamath Basin, almost always in the area between Stateline Road and Township Road. They have not been recorded in the Rogue Valley. There are two records of Chestnut-collared Longspur in the Klamath Basin, and one in the Rogue Valley.

The identification of longspurs in winter, when all of them fall into the classic category of "little brown birds," requires a lot of attention to small details. No attempt will be made here to supply all the details, but a few useful hints can be given. (For more detail, see Kevin Zimmer's excellent book, *Birding in the American West.*)

The easiest longspur to identify in winter is Smith's -- the one that hasn't been recorded in Oregon. At all times of the year, Smith's Longspurs, both male and female, are tan and buffy all over. In what follows, the Smith's will not be mentioned further.

Lapland Longspurs can be separated from McCown's and Chestnut-collareds by the amount of white in their tail feathers, visible in flight. Laplands have the least amount of white -- just the outer tail feathers. Both of the other longspurs have much more extensive white. This can be useful in an initial separation, letting you know either that you are looking at a Lapland, or that it is one of the other two. Also, Laplands have the most distinctive face pattern, in both male and female. The auriculars are conspicuously outlined with a dark frame, and there is a dark malar stripe. There are broad dark streaks on the flanks, lacking in the other two, although the Chestnut-collared may have blurry streaks. The greater coverts are rufous-edged. In the male Lapland, there may be vestiges of the rich chestnut color on the nape that goes with the breeding plumage, but the male Chestnut-collared might show the same.

McCown's Longspur is the palest, with a plain face, a broad pale supercilium, and an unstreaked breast. There is a lot of white in the tail, and field guides sometimes emphasize the fact that the black in the center of the tail forms an inverted "T." In the Chestnut-collared, which also has a lot of white in the tail, the black in the center of the tail forms a black triangle. If you can get a real good look, this is an excellent identification mark, but it is rare when you can get a real good look, at a time when the birds are leaping into the air and flying away. Another mark that can help is that the McCown's has a larger bill than a Chestnut-collared. A male McCown's may show some rufous in the middle part of the wing, and a male Chestnut-collared may have a white spot on the shoulder.

## Snow Bunting (SNBU)
*Plectrophenax nivalis*

|  | J F M A M J J A S O N D |
|---|---|
| West | Vagrant |
| East | ---                          ---- |

This bird is unmistakable in all plumages. In summer it is mostly a small white bird with a dark back. In winter it is a white bird with a brown back, and it has flashing white wing patches in all plumages. It is a breeder of the Arctic shores, around the world, and in North America it winters in the southern Canadian provinces and northern states. In Oregon it is reasonably common in winter in the northeastern part of the state, and is sporadic elsewhere. It appears irregularly in the Klamath Basin, often in the company of longspurs and Horned Larks. There is one record in the Rogue Valley, in May 1994.

# Family CARDINALIDAE: Cardinals, Saltators, and Allies

**Black-headed Grosbeak** (BHGR)
*Pheucticus melanocephalis*

**Rose-breasted Grosbeak** (RBGR)
*Pheucticus ludovicianus*

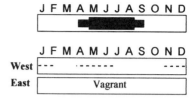

The Black-headed Grosbeak is a western bird and the Rose-breasted Grosbeak is an eastern bird. That ought to make things simple, but individuals of both species wander so frequently to the "wrong" region, that confusion can occur. They hybridize to some degree where their ranges meet in the Great Plains, and some authorities consider them to be one species. Individual variations, plus the existence of hybrids, means that some birds may not be identifiable as to species.

There's no confusion with identifying adult males, which are striking in appearance. The head of the Black-headed is black, the breast is a rich tawny cinnamon color, and the wings are black and white. The Rose-breasted is similarly patterned, except that there is a large rose-red patch on the breast, and the belly is white. The bills of both species are very large, justifying the name "grosbeak."

The trouble comes with the females and the first-year males, which all look disturbingly alike. All of these have boldly striped heads. The females of the two species can generally be told apart by the nature of the streaking on their breasts. In the female Black-headed, the streaking is fine and mostly confined to the sides of the breast; in breeding plumage, the streaks may even disappear. In the female Rose-breasted, the streaking is bold, extends all the way across the breast, and is retained in the breeding plumage.

Some first-year male Rose-breasteds may look much like female Black-headeds, but something that could help is the color of the underwing coverts. The underwings on Black-headed Grosbeaks of both sexes are yellowish. They are also yellowish on female Rose-breasted Grosbeaks, but are pink on male Rose-breasteds, including first-year birds.

Black-headed Grosbeaks breed widely in Southern Oregon on both sides of the Cascades in deciduous and mixed forests, mostly in the valleys, and occasionally up to 5000 feet. They are among our loveliest singers, sounding much like robins, but with more spontaneity and liveliness, and sometimes going on for a long time.

I once came upon a Black-headed Grosbeak nest at eye-level, right next to a trail. It was a skimpy little structure, hardly enough to support the nestlings, but there were three of them in the nest. They would raise their heads and open their mouths at the slightest vibration of the branch they were on, obviously thinking a parent with food had arrived. In spite of the proximity of the nest to a trail, the parents managed to raise the brood successfully.

There are scores of records for Rose-breasted Grosbeak in Oregon, with at least ten in Southern Oregon, on both sides of the crest. Most of these have been in spring, but a surprising number have been in winter. Pairs have been seen a couple of times, but not in Southern Oregon, and there are no cases of confirmed breeding in the state. However, there was a case of an apparent pairing between a Black-headed and a Rose-breasted. They built a nest, but no incubation took place.

## Lazuli Bunting (LAZB)
*Passerina amoena*

Here's another candidate for "most beautiful bird." The male is an azure-blue on the head, throat, and back, has a rich cinnamon color on the breast, a white belly, and white wing-bars. The female is pretty much brown all over, with two faint wing-bars. She is almost a dead ringer for the female Indigo Bunting, which is a vagrant in Oregon. Female Indigos, however, usually have some faint streaking on the underparts, while female Lazulis are usually unstreaked.

Lazuli Bunting is a western bird, and is widely distributed in Oregon during breeding season, including almost all parts of Southern Oregon. In winter they go to Mexico. For nesting purposes, this is a highly adaptable bird, because it breeds in everything from chaparral, to clearcuts, burned areas, and subalpine meadows, but generally not in suburban surroundings. It was once found breeding at 6500 feet in Crater Lake NP.

The song, usually delivered from a high perch, is a fast, somewhat jumbled set of high-pitched notes, and has been put into English words as *see-see sweet sweet zee zeer see-see,* although the pattern is variable. It has been referred to as "vivacious," and "sweet." In relatively open areas, the males often select dead snags for singing, and then they are highly visible with their gaudy colors. But if located in a wooded area, a male in the shadows can fade almost into invisibility, and be hard to locate. One thing that helps is that an individual may sing for a long time from the same perch. Even so, I have spent a lot of time searching for and pinning down Lazuli Buntings singing from leafy perches.

Some people pronounce the name as "lah-ZOO-lee," but my encyclopedia says it should be "LAZZ-you-lie."

## Indigo Bunting (INBU)                                    Vagrant
*Passerina cyanea*

This is an eastern and southwestern bird that is a close relative of the western Lazuli Bunting. In their zone of contact they sometimes hybridize. In Oregon, they have turned up numerous times, mostly in spring, and mostly in the eastern part of the state. In a few cases, male Indigo Buntings have been observed paired up with female Lazuli Buntings. In one such case there were

Lark Sparrow

Savannah Sparrow

Dark-eyed Junco ("Oregon Junco")

White-throated Sparrow (white-striped adult)

Fox Sparrow ("Sooty Fox Sparrow")

Golden-crowned Sparrow

**PLATE XI**

**Evening Grosbreak (male)**

**Yellow-headed Blackbird (female and male)**

**Hooded Oriole (male)**

**Cassin's Finch (male)**

**Gray-crowned Rosy-Finch**

**Brewer's Blackbird (male)**

**PLATE XII**

two fledglings in a nest being attended by a mixed pair. One appeared to be a young bunting, and the other was a young Brown-headed Cowbird.

An adult male Indigo Bunting is deep blue all over. Seen in full sunshine, the bird is a knockout. Seen in deep shade, it just looks black. The female is pretty much brown all over, with faint wing-bars, looking very much like a female Lazuli Bunting. Female Indigos, however, usually have some faint streaking on the underparts, while female Lazulis are usually unstreaked.

The very first verified Oregon record was of a male that was collected near Fort Klamath, in July 1941. There are also a few records from the Rogue Valley, one of them of a singing bird in July 1998, and one from Horse Creek Meadow, in the Siskiyous. The song is a bit more regular than that of the Lazuli Bunting, although it, like the Lazuli's, is variable. One form is a set of whistles -- *see see wheer wheer zeer zeer.*

**Dickcissel** (DICK)                                                       Vagrant
*Spiza americana*

The male Dickcissel in breeding plumage looks like a miniature version of a meadowlark, with his black bib and yellow breast. In fact, in the past he has been called the "little meadowlark." The song, however, is nothing like a meadowlark's, but consists of a more or less repetitive version of the bird's name -- *dick dick dickcissel.* The female looks very much like a female House Sparrow, but she has a yellowish breast.

Since these are birds of the midwest, and generally go to Mexico and South America for the winter, we wouldn't expect to see any in Oregon, but we have -- at least a dozen or so, mostly on the coast. There have been two records in the Rogue Valley, one in October 1993, and one in the winter of 2001-02. The latter bird stayed long enough to molt into adult male plumage.

## Family **ICTERIDAE**: Blackbirds

**Bobolink** (BOBO)                                       J F M A M J J A S O N D
*Dolichonyx oryzivorus*                                         ------

Arthur Cleveland Bent, in his inimitable way, described the song of the Bobolink thus:

> No description of the song of the bobolink is adequate to convey to the reader who has not heard it any appreciation of its beauty and vivacity. It is unique among bird songs, the despair of the recorder or the imitator; even the famed mockingbird cannot reproduce it. It is a bubbling delirium of ecstatic music that flows from the gifted throat of the bird like sparkling champagne.

A less poetic observer has described it as bubbly, but containing so many notes that they seem to stumble over each other as the tempo speeds up. Both descriptions are not bad, and together may convey some feeling for the song.

In earlier times this was apparently mostly a bird of the east and midwest, and who did not care much for the virgin prairies. As settlement proceeded westward, Bobolinks apparently found the cultivated grasslands to their liking, and expanded their range along with settlement. They arrived in Oregon about 1903, and now are reasonably well established breeding birds in many parts of eastern Oregon. The largest population west of the plains states is at Malheur NWR, where 539 males were counted in 1998.

Breeding was confirmed in the Klamath Basin for the first time in 1996, east of Klamath Falls, and spring and summer records in other locations in Southern Oregon indicate the possibility of other breeding pairs. One was seen near Fort Klamath in July 1997, and the grassy habitat in that region should prove attractive to the species. On the west side of the Cascades, the first Oregon record was from Medford, in 1966, and there was a pair seen near Ashland, in June 1978.

Bobolinks are long-range migrants. They spend the winter in South America, and most of them migrate across the Caribbean, hopping to Jamaica, then to Cuba, and then to Florida. The ones that get as far as Oregon appear to use the Caribbean route, and then move westward across the U.S. to get to us. On the return, they mostly use the same route in reverse, although small numbers migrate more directly south, through Mexico.

The male in breeding plumage is striking and unmistakable. The body is all black, except for a straw-colored nape, a white rump, and white scapulars. The female is mostly brown; there are dark stripes on the head, and the underparts are buffy, with streaking on the sides. In fall and winter, the males resemble the females. In all plumages, the birds have sharply pointed tail feathers.

These are ground nesters, and prefer agricultural fields with grassy growth, provided the fields are not mowed too early. The males sing their songs from perches, or while airborne in a flight display. The females mostly remain hidden in the grass, and are hard to see.

In the 19th century, Bent estimates that thousands, perhaps millions, of Bobolinks were killed, partly because they were considered destructive to rice during both spring and fall migration, and partly because they were sought for the market. They were called "Reed-birds" or "Rice-birds" at that time. Bent said they were prized by restaurants and were "luscious morsels" when genuine, although blackbirds and House Sparrows were often included without the patrons detecting the differences.

According to Bent, there were two principal methods for taking them -- shooting during the day, and hunting them at night by torchlight, where the dazzled birds were picked off the reeds, or swept into the boat with branches. It was not uncommon to get 12 to 13 dozen by daylight, and 20 to 30 dozen per night, per person. They were then sold for the market at about 25 cents a dozen. The game warden for South Carolina reported that, in one year, 60,000

"Rice-birds" had been shipped from just one location, but by 1912 the number shipped had fallen off because of "the reduced number of the birds."

## Red-winged Blackbird (RWBL)
*Agelaius phoenicieus*

A friend of mine, who normally paid little attention to birds, once asked me what those blackbirds with the red wings were called. I said, "Red-winged Blackbirds." My friend was certain that I was making fun of him, and that the real name must be something more dignified. Actually, I was impressed, and pleased that my friend was taking note of birds and asking questions about them. I don't know whether he was ever convinced I was telling the truth.

The Red-winged Blackbird is probably the best known and most abundant bird in North America. Any place with water and enough tules or cattails to offer perching places has got them in spring. Their loud *conqueree* is one of the best-known of bird songs, making up in exuberance for what it lacks in melody.

They breed in all parts of the state, and in the marshes of the Klamath Basin may number in the thousands in summer. In mild winters, large numbers may remain in the Klamath Basin and form large flocks, often mixed with starlings and other blackbirds. However, many leave the Basin in winter, and in cold winters they may be uncommon there.

To the west of the Cascades, they are more likely to remain for the winter. In typical winters, 200 or so may be counted on the Grants Pass Christmas Count, with 500 or 600 being typical for Medford. In the five-year period I examined, the number in the Klamath Falls count ranged from 37 to 372.

In the 2001 count in Medford, there were 1044 Red-wings. This may seem like a goodly number until it is compared with the numbers counted at Pine Prairie, Louisiana, which typically has 4 or 5 *million* of them each winter. The record all-time count at Pine Prairie was 53 million, in 1988.

A male Red-wing will typically set up a territory that he dominates, driving out all competitors. This is quite different from the custom of a close relative, the Tricolored Blackbird, which nests in dense colonies. It has been observed that there are typically more female Red-wings in an area than there are males, leading to the conclusion that a male often has multiple mates. It works the other way round, too, with a female sometimes accepting more than one mate.

Arthur Cleveland Bent provides an appealing description of the male's courtship display:

> The male lowers and opens his tail in wide fan shape, spreads and droops his wings until the tips reach to or below his feet, raises his red wing patches outward and forward like a pair of flaming brands, and having swelled out as large as possible, utters his curious throaty song, *long-leur-ee*. Usually this is done while he is perched; less often he mounts into the air and flies slowly over a circling course without departing far from the object of his attention.

The color of the red shoulder patch of the male (the lesser coverts) is usually described as bright vermilion or scarlet, as contrasted to the much darker red of the Tricolored Blackbird. In most of the country, including Oregon, the red patch is bordered below by a buffy or even yellow stripe (the median coverts). In Central California, the buffy stripe is absent or nearly so, and the birds there were once recognized as a separate species, the "Bicolored Blackbird." In fact, Audubon recognized three species of blackbird: the "Red-and-buff-shouldered Blackbird," the "Red-and-white-shouldered Blackbird" (today's Tricolored Blackbird), and the "Red-and-black-shouldered Blackbird." In the last-named case, he meant the "Bicolored Blackbird," because the median coverts are black instead of buffy or white. In later years, it was found that there were all sorts of intergradations between the "Bicolored" and the other blackbirds (except for the Tricolored), so the bicolored form was reduced to subspecies status.

Females are rather cryptically plumaged, are brown above, have a noticeable supercilium, and are black-and-white streaked below. Females in the east have much more pronounced streaking below than do females in the west. A pinkish or salmon tinge may be present on some of the upperparts.

In the 19th and early 20th century, redwings were killed in large numbers and sold on the market as "Rice-birds," along with Bobolinks. They were prized by gourmands as "delicious little morsels." But humans are not the only creatures that want to turn blackbirds or their eggs into meals. Minks, weasels, squirrels, snakes, and almost everybody else, prey on the eggs or the nestlings. Even the cute little Marsh Wren has been observed to make for a blackbird nest when it was unattended, break open an egg, and sip its contents.

The Redwings don't exactly take all this lying down, of course. They are known for pursuing and attacking their enemies. Ravens and magpies are often pursued by small groups of attacking blackbirds, although it is not clear whether contact is actually made. Nevertheless, the larger birds generally seem anxious to escape the attacks by making hasty departures.

## Tricolored Blackbird (TRBL)
*Agelaius tricolor*

When birders from the east come west, a bird that is very high on their "want lists" is the Tricolored Blackbird. They just don't have Tricoloreds in the east. Except for an overlap into Southern Oregon, this bird in the past belonged almost exclusively to California. But it seems to have been expanding its range northward. Not only are there the long-established breeding colonies in the Klamath Basin and the Rogue Valley, there also are about a dozen colonies at other places in Oregon, all the way to the Columbia River. In 1998, a small colony was found in Washington, about 120 miles north of any previously known colonies.

Tricoloreds are known to be somewhat nomadic, both in their selection of breeding colonies and in their winter movements, so it isn't surprising that Christmas Counts show sporadic results. In some years, none at all are recorded on Christmas Counts in either Klamath Falls or Medford. In other years, substantial numbers are reported. The all-time high for Klamath Falls is 810 in 1980, but in the 5 years from 1996 to 2000, the maximum number was 3. Medford had its all-time high of 2067 in 1964, but had 251 in 2001; the year before that there were only six.

Telling a male Red-wing from a male Tricolored mostly is fairly straightforward. The male Red-wing's shoulder patch is a much brighter vermilion color than the Tricolored's, which is a deep red. The stripe below the red patch is buffy or yellow in a Red-wing, and is a brilliant white in the Tricolored. Sometimes, in a sitting bird, the red patch on a Tricolored may be almost covered up and invisible, and only the broad white stripe will be visible. In a winter flock, the flashes of white on the wings of flying Tricoloreds will stand out. One troubling little factor is that first-year males and some adult males in winter may have the white stripe more or less tinged with brownish-buff, making them look a lot like Red-wings.

**Tricolored Blackbird**

The songs of the two are somewhat similar, but there are differences. The song of the Red-wing is a ringing *con-quer-reeeee,* with the last part higher than the other notes, in a buzzy trill. The song of the Tricolored has been described as a "bray." It has the same syllables as a Red-wing, and might be written *on-KEE-yew,* with the *KEE* higher and harsher than the other notes. Arthur Cleveland Bent writes it as *awaay awaay choke.* Females resemble female Red-wings, except the underparts from the breast down will be much darker than on the female Red-wings, almost black.

Tricoloreds are colonial nesters, sometimes with thousands of birds in one colony, usually in a marsh. William Leon Dawson, in the 1920s, described their nests in one marsh as follows:

> The nests, I say, are *everywhere.* . . . Now and again they crowd each other, when two or three birds select the same stems. Here are two nests side by side, and here one above another. Here a bird has lashed her foundation too high, and the top will not go on because of a neighbor's foundation.

Dawson reported that he was able to touch 26 nests when he was standing in a nesting colony, without moving from one location. In the past, the total number of Tricoloreds was estimated in the millions, but by 1995 it was estimated that the entire population in the State of California -- the species' presumed stronghold -- was only 300,000 birds. In the past, hundreds of thousands of them were hunted for market. Also, farmers put out poisoned grain for them, because the birds damaged the farmers' crops. In addition, many of their former marshy habitats have been drained, so the birds more and more have taken to nesting in blackberry tangles, thistles, and even in farmers' fields of cereal crops.

Tricoloreds are noted for abandoning a colony, even after eggs have been laid. Some causes for abandonment have been because of mass invasions by starlings, or perhaps because of failure of a local food supply. If a colony is abandoned, the Tricoloreds may move to a different site and start over again. In nesting season, the staple food for the adults is grain, but the young are fed almost exclusively on insects, such as grasshoppers or locusts. They may wander many miles in search of such prey, and have sometimes been referred to as "locust birds."

## Western Meadowlark (WEME)
*Sturnella neglecta*

I was about 12 years old when I first heard a Western Meadowlark sing. It stopped me in my tracks, and even though kids are often indifferent to such things, I knew I was hearing something special. In fact, it was probably the key event that caused me to become a birder.

Arthur Cleveland Bent apparently was similarly impressed the first time he heard one sing. Bent was an easterner, and was familiar with the song of the Eastern Meadowlark. He said:

> I could hardly believe it was a meadowlark singing, so different were the notes from those we were accustomed to in the east, until I saw the plump bird perched on a telegraph pole, facing the sun, his yellow breast and black cravat gleaming in the clear prairie sunlight. His sweet voice fairly thrilled us and seemed to combine the flutelike quality of the wood thrush with the rich melody of the Baltimore Oriole. I have heard it many times since but have never ceased to marvel at it. It seems to be the very spirit of the boundless prairie.

Another observer quoted by Bent, said:

> It seems to me this westerner is something of a yodeler... To my ear, its song has a very pleasing alto quality which makes the eastern bird's song seem a rather thin falsetto by comparison.

All of this dwelling upon the songs is very much to the point of separating the Western from the Eastern, because the two species are virtually indistinguishable by their visual field marks. It is their songs that identify them. Even though we are not likely to encounter an Eastern Meadowlark in Oregon, it is useful to know the difference in their songs. The Eastern's song is a simple set of high whistles, usually in the pattern *seeeeyou seeh yah,* alternating high, low, higher, and back to high. As to expressing the Western's song in syllables, some have declared any attempt to be useless in giving an adequate idea of it, and I agree.

Meadowlarks nest widely in Oregon, especially in the open country of the eastern part of the state, and are widespread breeders in Southern Oregon, up to 6000 feet. They are found in the state year-round, although many of them leave the colder eastern parts in winter -- some going south, and some apparently moving over to the west side of the Cascades. In fact, the wintering population west of the crest is typically higher than the breeding population, because of the winter influx from other areas

The Rogue Valley has generally had the highest wintering populations of meadowlarks in the state, although the numbers have declined over the years. The number recorded on the Medford Christmas Counts of the past averaged more than 600 birds per count, but in recent years has been less than 400. Speculation regarding the reasons for the decline include loss of habitat, unintentional destruction of their nests by crop mowing machines, and increasing predation by feral and domestic cats.

**Western Meadowlark**

The Western Meadowlark is one of the best-known and most easily recognizable birds in the west It is Oregon's official state bird. Meadowlarks like rangeland and agricultural areas, and place their nests in deep grass, which is why they are at risk from mowing machines. The nests are well concealed, and generally have dome-like canopies over their tops. Typically, two broods are raised per season, with perhaps five young per brood, which is probably why they have managed to maintain their numbers as high as they have, given the risks they face. The young are quite precocious, and scatter from the nest within 4 or 5 days after hatching. After scattering, they hide in the grass, being cared for by the parents until they are old enough to be on their own.

Incidentally, why should such a wonderful bird be named *neglecta*, meaning "neglected"? Well, the name was given by Audubon in 1844, as an indication of his irritation with the ornithologists who had named the eastern bird almost 100 years earlier, and had neglected to recognize the western bird as a separate species for such a long time.

## Yellow-headed Blackbird (YHBL)
*Xanthocephalus xanthocephalus*

A male Yellow-headed Blackbird is not likely to be confused with anything else, with its black body, yellow head, and white wing patches. The female is a little harder to identify but is still distinctive, with a certain amount of yellowish on the throat and breast.

The Klamath Basin is one of their strongholds for breeding. Colonies have been seen at such places as Klamath Marsh NWR, Upper Klamath Lake, Miller Island, and Lower Klamath NWR. Smaller colonies have been found in Jackson County, and, in the Breeding Bird Atlas program, a possible colony was found in Josephine County.

The colonies are not dense ones, as with Tricolored Blackbirds, but are looser, sometimes consisting of scattered groups of nesting birds. The birds prefer to build their nests in tules and cattails over standing water that is fairly deep. There often are far more females tending nests in an area than there are males, indicating polygyny, and it is believed that a male may have 1 to 6 females in his "harem." The "song" of the male Yellow-head is interesting, to say the least. William Leon Dawson put it best, when he said:

> Grasping a reed firmly in both fists, he leans forward, and, after premonitory gulps and gasps, he succeeds in pressing out a wail of despairing agony which would do credit to a dying catamount.

As with all wild creatures, life is risky, and raising young is the riskiest process of all. The enemies are many, including predatory birds such as ravens, snakes, small mammals, and even fish. In one case, a researcher watched a fledgling leave the nest and work its way among the cattail stems, when a large fish rose from the water and swallowed it. But the major enemy is the weather. In one colony that was monitored closely, 443 eggs were laid, 314 were hatched, and 215 fledglings were destroyed before they could leave the nest. All of the dangerous elements listed above were believed to be involved, but the worst was a heavy rainstorm accompanied by high winds. In yet another colony under study, 100 percent of the nestlings disappeared, from an unknown cause.

Yellow-heads do what they can to protect their nests. They regularly gang up on birds such as hawks and crows that enter their neighborhood, and drive them away. An American Bittern that came near a colony was attacked so bitterly that it had to crawl down among the bulrush stems to avoid its tormentors. The Yellow-heads will also attack small birds such as Marsh Wrens, which are known to puncture unguarded eggs.

After nesting, the Yellow-heads form large flocks and forage over great distances, often in company with other blackbirds and starlings. By mid-fall, most of them have left the state and gone south to California and Mexico.

## Brewer's Blackbird (BRBL)
*Euphagus cyanocephalus*

J F M A M J J A S O N D

## Rusty Blackbird (RUBL)
*Euphagus carolinus*

Vagrant

Other birds may come and go, but the Brewer's Blackbird is always with us. It originally was mostly a bird of the west and still is, but expanded its range to the east considerably in the 20th century, as far as the Great Lakes region. In the west it is one of our commonest and most widespread birds, and in winter they form large flocks. In the Christmas Counts for the period 1996-2000, the numbers at Grants Pass and Klamath Falls averaged about 1500 birds at each location, and averaged over 3000 at Medford.

The Rusty Blackbird of the east is a close lookalike, and has appeared in Oregon perhaps a dozen times, usually at inland locations west of the crest, and usually in fall or winter. There are three records for the Rogue Valley. The Oregon Birds Forum has said, "Difficulties in separating this species from the closely-related Brewer's Blackbird make most sight records questionable."

Rusty Blackbirds are rusty-looking in fall and winter, but in summer the male Brewer's and male Rusty are almost identical. The Rusty's rusty feathers in fall and winter are helpful of course, but female Brewer's Blackbirds look pretty brown, and even the male Brewer's can have some rusty-looking feathers on the head and shoulders in the fall. The key is to look at the tertials and wing coverts, which will be rusty in fall and winter in the Rusty, but not in the Brewer's.

Eye color has often been called upon to help in identification, but even this supposedly dependable rule sometimes fails. In the Rusty, both the males and females have pale yellowish eyes, whereas in the Brewer's the male has a yellow eye and the female has a brown one. But female Brewer's sometimes also turn up with pale eyes, often causing consternation among birders, who think they have discovered a Rusty.

Brewer's Blackbirds breed almost everywhere in Oregon, even up to 6000 feet. They nest, often in loose colonies, on the ground and high in trees, in grasses and bushes, in hedges, in ornamental trees, in agricultural areas, in sagebrush, and in mountain meadows. They apparently are often polygamous. In one colony that was carefully monitored, with about 15 to 20 males, it was found that seven males had two mates each, four had three, and one had four.

As always is the case in nature, the birds have many enemies. They are widely known for their willingness to attack hawks, crows, and ravens, and also will attack humans who happen to walk near their nests. I've been hit on the head more than once. There is a row of ornamental shrubs that I can look down on from my deck, and the Brewer's Blackbirds in breeding season are constantly entering and exiting from those shrubs, presumably because they are nesting there. On one occasion I watched a raven slowly waddling along below the shrubs, looking up into them, while a crowd of blackbirds hovered above, shrieking frantically. The raven inspected the whole line of shrubs and apparently never spotted a thing, because it departed empty-handed.

Brewer's Blackbirds have a number of courtship displays. One of them is the "head-up" display, and it can be seen in the photo on Plate XII. However, this is considered to be a "threat" display, and might be used any time of the year in addition to breeding season, perhaps in a dispute over food.

One of the "songs" of the Brewer's that is frequently heard is a loud hoarse whistle with an upward inflection -- *k-ksheee*. The alarm call is a loud *tcheck!* which I have usually heard just before being hit on the head.

Large flocks in winter have a characteristic foraging behavior, in which individuals walk forward in a zigzagging fashion, but all proceeding in the same general direction. Those left in the rear compensate by flying to the front of the flock to continue foraging, giving a sort of "rolling" motion to the flock. Individual birds have also been observed turning objects over with their bills, such as small pieces of wood, clods of earth, and even flipping dried piles of cow manure upside down, searching for food.

## Common Grackle (COGR)  Vagrant
*Quiscalus quiscula*

## Great-tailed Grackle (GTGR)  Vagrant
*Quiscalus mexicanus*

Both of the birds appear to be expanding their ranges into Oregon, the Common Grackle from the east, and the Great-tailed Grackle from the south.

The breeding range for the Common Grackle is mostly east of the Rockies, from Alberta to the east coast, but in recent years it has been found breeding in Idaho and Nevada. The first Oregon record was at Malheur NWR in 1977, and since then there have been a score of so of sightings, mostly east of the crest, but with some on the coast, almost all in the April to October period. There is one record for Jackson County, in October 1994. There are no confirmed breeding records yet for Oregon.

**Great-tailed Grackle**

The breeding range for the Great-tailed Grackle extends from the Gulf Coast through the southwestern states. It entered the Imperial Valley in California in the 1960s, and now breeds there in large numbers. It has been steadily moving northward, reached Oregon in 1980, and was confirmed breeding at Malheur NWR in 1995. There are a dozen or so records in Oregon, mostly at Malheur, with a few records from the Klamath Basin, one in February, two of them in May, and one in July.

Both species have long "keeled" tails, especially in the males. Both sexes of both species have pale eyes, except in the juveniles. The male Great-tailed is 50 percent longer than a Common Grackle of either sex, and in the male, the tail appears enormously exaggerated, constituting about half the length of the body.

Even though Commons are smaller than male Great-taileds, a bird seen by itself may be difficult to judge. Thus, the color of the back can be useful -- greenish-olive, or "bronzed," in the Common Grackle of either sex, and a purple-blue iridescent color on the male Great-tailed. Male and female Common Grackles are similar in appearance, but the female Great-tailed looks so different from the male Great-tailed that she might be taken for a different species. She weighs half as much, is 50 percent shorter than the male, and is brownish all over.

The "songs" of both kinds of grackles are wondrous to hear. The Common's song is a series of grating, raspy notes, interspersed with metallic squeals. That of the Great-tailed might even be classified as outrageous, is very loud, and is a collection of squeaks, clatters, and clacks. Given early in the morning, it is guaranteed to wake you up.

## Brown-headed Cowbird (BHCO)
*Molothrus ater*

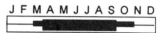

Hardly anyone has a good word to say about the cowbird, because of its habit of parasitizing other birds' nests. Yet it does appear that the birds have developed a remarkable strategy for perpetuating their species, and one that is successful. Think what a marvelous energy-saver it is, not to have to build a nest, and then not to have to run oneself ragged to feed a batch of demanding youngsters.

The strategy appears all the more remarkable when viewed in the light that only about 3 percent of the cowbirds' eggs are successful. But this low rate is offset by the fact that a single female cowbird can produce as many as 80 eggs per season. Since the making of eggs is the most energy-intensive process of all, one wonders if the cowbird's strategy is so clever after all.

It has been determined that about 220 North American species are parasitized by cowbirds. Heading the list as "most-parsitized" are Yellow Warbler and Song Sparrow, followed by others such as Chipping Sparrow, Spotted Towhee, Common Yellowthroat, Yellow-breasted Chat, Red-winged Blackbird, and Willow Flycatcher.

In the breeding season, a male and female will establish a loose territory, but do not defend it against other cowbirds. In fact, other cowbirds may be associated with them in the area, and the species in general is believed to be promiscuous. Female cowbirds are expert nest-hunters. A female may sometimes watch nests as they are under construction, so she knows where they are, and may make trips to a nest several times before laying. In fact, she may remove one of the host's eggs a day before laying her own, usually eating it. Typically, only one cowbird egg is laid in a host's nest, although there are cases of more. Hole-nesting birds, such as wrens and chickadees, seem to be mostly free of the process.

A young cowbird usually hatches a day or more before the young of the foster parents, because it has a shorter incubation period. It is generally larger than the parents of the hosts, and grows faster. Sometimes it is so much bigger than the others that it crowds them out of the nest, although this does not appear to be a regular strategy, as it is with the European Cuckoo. Other times, it just gets more of the food, which may be fatal to the other nest occupants. But, even more often, the young cowbird is raised to fledging right along with the young of the hosts. In rare cases, female cowbirds have been observed to come to nests and feed the young cowbirds (but not the others), showing that the parental instincts are not entirely lost.

Some intended host birds can recognize cowbird eggs, and either remove them or abandon the nest. Yellow Warblers frequently employ an unusual strategy. When they detect a cowbird egg, the response is either to abandon the nest, or to build a new nest over all the eggs, their own included, and lay a new clutch. Nests with as many as six "tiers" have been found, with a cowbird egg in every tier.

The mating song of the male cowbird typically consists of two or three initial notes that are low-pitched and gurgly, and then abruptly shifts to a high squeaky note. It has been represented as *bubble bubble squeak*. The initial gurgly notes are so soft that they are inaudible a short distance away, and the "song" may just sound like the *squeak* part.

After breeding, the cowbirds form flocks, frequently with other blackbirds, and roam about the countryside. They are smaller than their other blackbird cousins, and can usually be picked out of a flock on the basis of their size. Often, they associate with cattle -- whence their name -- and roam about underfoot, picking up insects stirred up by the animals. By October, most of them have migrated south.

In one of the mysteries of nature, young cowbirds seem to recognize that they belong with the flocks of their parents, and join them as soon as they can fly, even though their foster parents looked nothing like a cowbird. The young ones are often blotchy-looking and conspicuous, as they molt from juvenal to adult plumage.

Cowbirds are believed to have originated in South America, moved north through Mexico, and spread out into the Great Plains, where they associated with buffalo herds. Then, as European settlers appeared, creating favorable habitat because of cultivation, the birds spread coast to coast, associating with cattle herds instead of buffalo.

# Hooded Oriole (HOOR)
*Icterus cucullatus*

|      | J F M A M J J A S O N D |
|------|-------------------------|
| West | - - - - - - - - -       |
| East | Vagrant                 |

    Hooded Orioles were originally birds of the southwestern deserts and Mexico. As Europeans began to develop the west, the birds moved northward, and by 1972 had expanded their breeding range to northwestern California. The first Oregon record is from Ashland, in May 1965. Since that time, Hooded Orioles have appeared irregularly in Oregon, mostly on the coast, with records both in the spring and in the winter. Most of the records are of birds visiting hummingbird feeders. There are not many records from eastern Oregon, but there is one from Klamath Falls, in May 1987. There are 7 records from the Rogue Valley, mostly in spring.

    The male is easily told from other orioles by its all-yellow head, broken only by a black face and throat, and all-black tail. Females are more cryptic, but can be told from other female orioles by their drabber colors and longer bills.

    Hooded Orioles don't build the typical hanging nests of the other orioles, but tend to weave them into the twigs of trees until the twigs are essentially parts of the nests. When fan palms are available, they plaster their nests on the undersides of the fans, which not only makes the nests hard to see, but provides excellent shelter. To fasten their nests to the palm leaves, they drill holes through the leaves and weave the nest fibers through the holes. In areas with lots of fan palms they are often known as "palm-leaf orioles," but they also use other trees, such as cottonwoods, if there are no palms available.

# Bullock's Oriole (BUOR)
*Icterus bullockii*

J F M A M J J A S O N D

# Baltimore Oriole (BAOR)
*Icterus galbula*

Vagrant

    Bullock's Oriole is a western bird and Baltimore Oriole is an eastern one. Where the ranges of the two come together there is considerable hybridization, creating confusing looking progeny. In 1973, because of the interbreeding, the AOU decided to classify them as one species, Northern Oriole. Many birders thought this was not a good decision, and mourned. Then, in 1995, the AOU split them apart again, giving as its reasons that there are so many differences between them, in plumages, vocalizations, molt schedules, and other things, that they should best be treated as distinct species. Birders rejoiced.

    Bullock's Orioles are regular breeders in Southern Oregon, on both sides of the crest. They build their nests in open deciduous woods, in riparian areas, oak and madrone woodlands, and occasionally near human habitations. Most migrate south in winter, but a few hang around.

Baltimore Orioles are vagrants. There are about 20 records in Oregon, mostly in eastern Oregon, and mostly in spring. There is a record from a feeder at the refuge headquarters near Tule Lake, in July 1996.

The males of both species are orange and black, but the Bullock's has a huge white wing patch (the Baltimore has two wing-bars, one white and one orange), and the Baltimore has a full black hood (the Bullock's has a black cap and black throat).

The females are muted yellowish, brownish, and gray, and can be hard to tell apart. There are two things to check: One is the brightness on the breast and on the side of the head. In the female Baltimore, the breast is the brightest, and the side of the head is brownish. The female Bullock's is brightest on the side of the head, in the auriculars and malar region. The second thing to check is the upper wing-bar. In the Bullock's, the upper edge of this wing-bar is jagged, almost like saw teeth. In the Baltimore, the upper edge is smooth.

The song of the Bullock's Oriole is a set of lovely muted whistles, somewhat jumbled and erratic. To me, it has a sort of casual quality, as if the bird is singing it as an afterthought. The birds also make a rather loud, characteristic chatter.

The nest of an oriole is a fabled structure. It is a densely woven pouch about 6 inches deep, suspended from twigs in the outer branches of a tree, often in plain view. Frequently, it is placed rather low, perhaps 10 or 15 feet up, but in some cases can be higher. There is an opening toward the top of the pouch.

The female does the brooding, and the male stands by on guard. That the function of being "on guard" is more than just one of routine appearances is attested by the observations of a researcher, quoted in Bent:

> [A magpie] was circling about an oriole's nest as though searching for a breakfast of eggs. The magpie soon alighted in the tree in which the nest was hanging and began to come closer and closer to the beautiful swinging structure. Almost at the instant the magpie settled upon the edge of the nest, the male oriole, which apparently was but a few rods away, was heard to give an abrupt and angry call of warning. A moment later the enraged male came with all his force at the intruder, striking it on the crown of the head. The magpie dropped to the ground, stunned to such an extent that I was able to pick it up, and only after 10 minutes could it regain sufficient strength to fly away.

## Family **FRINGILLIDAE:** Fringilline and Cardueline Finches and Allies

### Gray-crowned Rosy-Finch (GCRF)
*Leucosticte tephrocotis*

I love this bird because it lives in high alpine and subalpine places. Most often, I have encountered them while backpacking over some 10,000-foot pass in the mountains. They like barren, rocky terrain, and often are found along the edges of snowfields. Typically, they don't stick around, but quickly disappear over the next ridge. They forage for frozen insects near the snow fields, but most of their food consists of the seeds of tundra plants. In Southern Oregon, they are to be found in summer around Crater Lake and on Mt. McLaughlin, and may descend to neighboring lowlands in winter. Once in a while they are spotted on other high peaks, such as Soda Mountain in the Cascade-Siskiyou National Monument, and Hamaker Mountain, southeast of Klamath Falls.

Since finding them on Mount McLaughlin involves a lengthy hike over high, rough terrain, I decided to look for them at Crater Lake. However, it took five attempts before I succeeded, since the birds are not abundant and could be hidden at any given time down the cliffs of the caldera.

When I finally succeeded, it was ridiculously easy. I reasoned that Cloudcap (almost 8000 feet elevation) is the highest point reached by the road around the rim of the crater, and since the terrain here is easy and open, with sparsely-vegetated meadows scattered among the whitebark pines and mountain hemlocks, this might be a good place to look. I only had to go about a quarter-mile from the Cloudcap parking lot to find four of them foraging in the grass, associating in a loose flock. In their accustomed fashion, they flew off almost as soon as I came upon them.

Until a few years ago, this bird was considered to be the same species as two closely-related ones, the Black Rosy-Finch and the Brown-capped Rosy Finch. Brown-capped Rosy-Finches are found mostly in central Colorado, while Black Rosy-Finches are located mostly in Wyoming and in the mountains of the Great Basin. Steens Mountain, in southeastern Oregon, has the western-most breeding location for Black Rosy-Finch.

Gray-crowned Rosy Finches are the most widespread, and are found from Alaska to California's Sierra Nevada. There are even some on the Pribilof Islands, far out in the middle of the Bering Sea, but these are so much larger than their relatives that they might even be considered to be a separate species.

All of the rosy-finches have lots of rosy coloration, primarily on the underparts, with the males rosier than the females. The distinguishing feature of the Gray-crowned Rosy-Finch is that it has (surprise) a gray crown. But then, so does the Black Rosy-Finch, but the rest of that particular bird has so much black on it that it is distinctive. The thing that is different about our local Gray-crowned Rosy-Finches is that, in addition to gray crowns, they also have gray cheeks, a characteristic they share with those on the Pribilof Islands. This gray-cheeked subspecies (not including the Pribilof birds), which occurs all down the coast from Alaska and into the Cascade range, is often called "Hepburn's Finch," or sometimes simply "Gray-cheeked Rosy-Finch."

## Pine Grosbeak (PIGR)
*Pinicola enucleator*

J F M A M J J A S O N D

This is an enigmatic bird. It breeds regularly to the north of us in the North Cascades of Washington, and there is a disjunct breeding area to the south of us in the high Sierra Nevada. But in Oregon, midway between those breeding areas, the bird is hard to find. It has bred in the Wallowas, although one investigator said he had traveled hundreds of miles in the Wallowas and only had a dozen sightings. It is suspected of breeding in the Blue Mountains and Cascades, and even in the Siskiyous, but without confirmation.

There are several reports from the southern Cascades and Siskiyous, all in spring or early summer: two from Howard Prairie Lake; one near Mount Ashland; one from the Applegate area; and a few from the Crater Lake area. The birds show a preference for true fir and lodgepole pine forests.

Pine Grosbeaks have large, heavy beaks, as befits their name. The male is suffused with rosy red over most of his body, whereas the female is grayish, usually with yellow on the head, sometimes pinkish. The song is a lovely warble, much like the song of a Purple Finch.

## Purple Finch (PUFI)
*Carpodacus purpureus*

## Cassin's Finch (CAFI)
*Carpodacus cassinii*

## House Finch (HOFI)
*Carpodacus mexicanus*

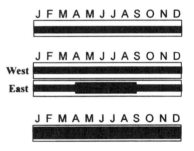

These three common birds are all widespread residents in Southern Oregon, and they can cause trouble in identification. Let's start with the males.

The male House Finch is the familiar red-fronted finch that we are likely to see around our houses, at feeders and the like. It is usually absent from dense forests or from high elevations. Its color can be flaming vermilion, but can also be orange in some birds, and even yellow. There is disagreement about the cause of these different colors -- some say it's diet, some say it's genetics. The cap is brown, but the front of the head is red. The breast is very bright red, and the underparts are heavily streaked; the streaking goes all the way onto the undertail coverts. The tail is not notched, but is squarish -- maybe slightly notched in some cases.

The male Purple Finch is not purple, but is rose-red, looking like it had been dipped into red wine. The rose-red color extends over most of the body. The streaking on the underparts is diffuse, not distinct like it is in the House Finch. The undertail coverts usually are not streaked, and the tail is notched.

The male Cassin's Finch has reddish hues on the throat and breast, but the red cap is by far the brightest element of the plumage, and ends sharply at the brown nape. Many people call them "Red Tops." The bill is the largest of any of the three in this group, and the culmen (top of the bill) is straighter than in the other two. The streaking on the underparts is sharper than on the Purple, and the undertail coverts are streaked. The tail is notched.

All three females are perfect examples of "little brown birds." All are streaked on most of their underparts. If the undertail coverts are not streaked, and there is a conspicuous supercilium, then you've got a Purple Finch. If the undertail coverts are streaked, then you've got either a Cassin's or House Finch. A Cassin's Finch has a much larger bill than a House Finch, and the culmen is straighter in the Cassin's.

**House Finch (female)**

Some probabilities also may be of assistance. In the lowlands, especially around human habitations, the odds are on House Finch. At middle elevations in conifers, if it's breeding season, the odds are on Purple Finch. At high elevations in breeding season, the odds are on Cassin's Finch. In winter, they all may be found at lower elevations.

If the birds are singing, there are some differences in song that can help. All three of them have beautiful warbling songs. The House Finch very often places a harsh *zrriiip* note either in the middle of the song, or at the end, sounding sort of like a Bronx cheer. The presence of that *zrriiip* gives you a good "handle" that it's a House Finch you're listening to.

The other two have songs that resemble each other, although the Cassin's song is a little thinner and less rich than the Purple. Also, the Cassin's is likely to go on longer than the Purple's song. If you are at high elevation, that will give you a pretty good idea that you're listening to a Cassin's. The Purple Finch often gives a rich *cheer-you* call that sounds like a Vireo.

## Red Crossbill (RECR)
*Loxia curvirostra*

J F M A M J J A S O N D

## White-winged Crossbill (WWCR)
*Loxia leucoptera*

Vagrant

Seen up close, a crossbill is unmistakable. The outrageous crossed mandibles clearly mark it. But seen in the very top of a tree, you can't be so sure. And that is where you usually see them -- in the very top of a tree. Either that, or you see them in a flock flying from tree top to tree top, crying out *jip-jip-jip* as they go. To make things worse, some of them aren't even red. The females and immature birds are yellowish, and at any given time they can outnumber the red adult males.

Crossbills live and breed in coniferous forests throughout the state, more so to the east of the Cascades than to the west, and only sporadically in the Siskiyous. They depend for their livelihoods upon the seeds of coniferous trees, and their bills are adapted to prying open the cones to get the seeds. Some of the bills cross to the left and some to the right, and a given bird is either "left-handed" or "right-handed" in the way it twists open the cones. If the seeds in one area are in poor supply, they will often move long distances in search of a better supply. Thus, they are nomadic, and may be present in large numbers in a particular area one year, and absent the next. They possess the unusual ability to nest at any time of the year, provided the days aren't too short in length, and depending upon the food supply.

If things get real bad with the availability of seeds, they may eat the buds of deciduous trees, and have been known to eat juniper berries. They also appear to require a certain amount of minerals in their diet, and will consume charcoal and ash grit to get it. This explains a sighting I had one time of a flock of crossbills energetically foraging in a campground fire pit. I assumed they were after garbage, because people do sometimes throw their garbage in fire pits, but I examined the pit and found none. Evidently, they were after the ashes.

Different subspecies of crossbills specialize in the seeds of certain kinds of conifers, and the development of their bill structures reflects this specialization. Bill lengths range from less than ½ inch to ¾ inch. Those birds with the smallest bills apparently prefer Sitka spruce and western hemlock, and are to be found principally in the Coast Range. Those with the largest bills apparently prefer ponderosa and lodgepole pine cones, and are to be found principally in eastern Oregon.

There has been discussion regarding the possible split of Red Crossbill into as many as 8 separate species, depending upon their bill sizes, seed preferences, and flight calls. But there is an enormous amount of overlap in bill sizes, and the birds may sometimes switch to the "wrong" seed type, depending upon availability. Thus, they cannot be separated in the field, and must be identified by careful analysis of their recorded flight calls. Some birders have declared, if it comes to this, they will just have to give up on crossbills.

White-winged Crossbills resemble Red Crossbills, except they have prominent white wing-bars. (Note: juveniles and some female Red Crossbills may show narrow buffy wing-bars.) White-wingeds are normally year-round residents of Canada, but in some "invasion years," probably caused by seed shortages, they may appear in Oregon. There were invasion years in 1981 and 1985, when White-wingeds were seen in numerous places in the Cascades, including northern Klamath County. Also, one was found on the northern border of Jackson County in 1997, during the breeding bird atlas program   The only confirmed breeding record in Oregon is from the Wallowa Mountains.

## Common Redpoll (CORE)
*Carduelis flammea*

Vagrant

This tiny finch with a red top breeds in the far north, and winters as far south as the northern tier of states in the U.S. They turn up irregularly in winter in northeast Oregon, and once in a while in other parts of the state. They have been seen at the Visitor Center at Tule Lake NWR, and in Klamath Falls. There are a couple of December records in the Rogue Valley.

Hoary Redpoll, a cousin of the Common Redpoll, is even more of a northern bird, and has turned up in northeastern Oregon a couple of times but not in Southern Oregon. Hoary Redpolls resemble Common Redpolls, but are slightly larger, have stubbier bills, and have an overall whiter color that has been termed "frosty-looking."

## Pine Siskin (PISI)
*Carduelis pinus*

## Lesser Goldfinch (LEGO)
*Carduelis psaltria*

## American Goldfinch (AMGO)
*Carduelis tristis*

## Lawrence's Goldfinch (LAGO)
*Carduelis lawrencei*

The goldfinches are grouped here together, because there can be some uncertainty in separating them. The Pine Siskin is included, even though it is not normally considered to be a "goldfinch." This is partly because it is a member of the same genus as goldfinches, and partly because it often mingles with goldfinches and can be mistaken for one.

Southern Oregon, especially the Rogue Valley, is definitely goldfinch country. The Rogue Valley is the stronghold of the Lesser Goldfinch in Oregon, and, except for one case, the only place in Oregon where Lawrence's Goldfinches have occurred.

Lesser Goldfinch is the smallest of goldfinches, as its name implies, and at 4 1/2 inches is only a little larger than a hummingbird. They throng to feeders all year long (at least, they throng to *my* feeder, in Medford), together with American Goldfinches. Often, especially in fall and winter, they are joined by Pine Siskins.

A male Lesser Goldfinch can be spotted fairly easily, because he has a yellow front and a black cap all year long. Most of those in the west have olive-green backs, but the ones in Texas have black backs. These were once considered separate species -- "Green-backed Goldfinch" and "Black-backed Goldfinch." But birds don't follow the rules set up for them by human beings, and a few of the "Texas" birds with black backs show up in Oregon. Male Lessers also have a wonderful little identification badge that they carry with them, because they have conspicuous white patches in the wings, and these white patches show up as little rectangular white spots at the base of the primaries when the wings are folded.

Female Lesser Goldfinches, female American Goldfinches, and male American Goldfinches in winter all look pretty much alike. My field guides inform me that Americans have white undertail coverts and Lessers have yellowish undertail coverts, but this distinction has never proved to be very useful, in my experience. One of the reasons is that these little birds are generally so active that I can't get a good look at the undertail coverts. A better distinction, for me, is the white spot in the wings of the Lesser Goldfinch. This spot is much smaller in the female than on the male, but it still usually shows up as a little white fleck at the base of the primaries.

**American Goldfinch**
**(male in breeding plumage)**

A male American Goldfinch in breeding plumage is a delight -- bright yellow over most of the body, with black wings, and a jaunty little black cap set forward just above the eyes. In this plumage they are often called "wild canaries," and are unmistakable.

Pine Siskins are the same size as goldfinches, and behave much like them in winter when they descend from the usual mountain areas to the lower valleys, and form up into flocks. At first glance, as they join goldfinches at feeders, they might be taken for goldfinches, but a good look at their streaked upperparts and underparts marks them as siskins. The males have bright yellow stripes in their wings, easily observable in flight. When the wings are folded, this stripe shows up as a yellow wing-bar. In females, the stripes are smaller and less yellow.

American Goldfinches nest widely in Southern Oregon, in agricultural areas, deciduous riparian woodlands, and around human habitations. Lesser Goldfinches nest mainly in the Rogue and Umpqua Valleys, and also in the Klamath Basin and southern Willamette Valley. They like open shrublands, oak woodlands, and riparian areas.

Pine Siskins are more birds of the mountains. In winter, they are found in the lowlands, but for breeding they prefer coniferous or mixed woodlands. They tend to be erratic, and may be present in a given area in abundance one year, and in small numbers the next.

The Lawrence's Goldfinch is a vagrant. There is one sighting outside the Rogue Valley, on the coast at Florence. There are 8 sightings in the Rogue Valley, most of them in spring, but a couple of them in winter. A male

Lawrence's is instantly recognizable by its black face and extensive yellow in the wings. A female is less easy to recognize, is brownish above, yellowish on the breast, and has some yellow in the wings. They have not been found breeding in Oregon.

The songs of all the goldfinches, including the siskin, sound very much alike to me -- long, lively, high-pitched twitters and trills. However, there are a few clues to the identities of the singers that either turn up as calls, or as parts of calls included in the songs. The American Goldfinch has a whiny call that is often given alone or as part of a song. To me it sounds like it has three slurred syllables, first falling and then rising: *tseeyoueeee.* To the person who named the American Goldfinch, this call apparently sounded mournful, and the bird was given the scientific name *tristis,* meaning "sad." Many people object to this, and feel instead that the call note sounds "sweet." The American also has a very characteristic rollicking flight call, usually written *per-chick-er-ee, per-chick-er-ee,* that is also sometimes incorporated in the song.

The song of the Lesser Goldfinch often contains some rough burry notes, and also may include elements of its call. Lessers have a couple of whiny calls, one of which sounds much like the American's, but the other of which sounds like it has two syllables, and is downslurred: *tseeeeyew.*

The Pine Siskin's song sounds much like the others, but often includes its special call, a loud, buzzy, rising *zhreeeeeee!* The call frequently is given by itself, and when heard it is a certain sign that there are siskins around.

The song of the Lawrence's Goldfinch is often described as "tinkling," and so it is, but then the songs of the others also often sound "tinkling" to me.

## Evening Grosbeak (EVGR)
*Coccothraustes vespertinus*

I've never succeeded in finding this bird when I deliberately set out to do so. Instead, the bird has found me. If they are in the area, they will just suddenly show up, usually in groups. Sometimes, when they are found, it is because of their loud, continuous calls, sounding something like House Sparrows, but louder.

Evening Grosbeaks are notoriously erratic, being abundant in a given location one time, and completely absent the next. For this reason, some people in early times called them "Wandering Grosbeaks." The name "Evening" was given because someone else at that time mistakenly thought they sang only in the evening. This in itself is something of an oddity, since the "song" is a repetitious rendering of their calls.

They breed widely in Southern Oregon in the Cascades and possibly in the Siskiyous, in conifers, especially firs, and mixed forests. They prefer more or less open areas, and avoid dense deciduous woods, and are more likely to be found in montane forests east of the crest than to the west. They feed largely on the seeds of conifers, but also eat insects, maple seeds, berries and fruit, and tree buds. In the winter, flocks of them may move into the lowlands, sometimes creating mini "invasions."

This is an easy bird to recognize. The large head and huge bill identifies both sexes. The male has a black and yellow body, and huge white wing patches. The female echoes the male's pattern, but is mostly brownish and gray, with white wing patches not as large as the male's.

## Family **PASSERIDAE**: Old World Sparrows

### House Sparrow (HOSP)
*Passer domesticus*

The scientific name has got it exactly right: This is a bird that loves to be around human habitations -- "domesticated" places. It breeds throughout Oregon, asking only that there be some sort of structure nearby with a crevice or cavity in it for nesting. A nest-box intended for swallows or bluebirds will do very nicely, thank you, but so will a space between a couple of shakes on the roof, if that is all there is. If absolutely necessary, they will even build their nests in dense vegetation, such as English ivy.

During breeding season, it is easy to tell there are House Sparrows around -- their loud, incessant chirping tells you so. The chirping, often from some invisible point in a dense bush, comes from the male advertising for a mate, and passes for a song. They are not popular with many people, partly because they are noisy, partly because they are aggressive, and partly because they are an introduced species and therefore alien. A hundred years ago, they were also damned by some for being "immoral," presumably a reference to their ability to produce lots of offspring.

House Sparrows were originally called "English Sparrows," because the first ones in this country were introduced from England. However, they have a wide native range in Europe, Africa, and Asia. The first successful introduction was in the New York area in 1853. This was followed by introductions in many other parts of the country, including San Francisco. The first sparrows found in Oregon were in Portland, in 1889.

The attitude toward the sparrows in their early period is well demonstrated through a story related by Arthur Cleveland Bent. Bent's uncle had built a large cage for the sparrows in his garden, and they bred so industriously that the cages soon became overcrowded. The uncle then ordered the sparrows to be liberated, and had nest boxes built for them. They not only soon filled up the boxes, but also drove away the Purple Martins, Tree Swallows, and House Wrens. Bent says,

> When the neighbors' cats killed a few of the precious sparrows, which were the newest pets and were zealously guarded, my uncle became so angered that he ordered his coachman to "kill every cat in the neighborhood." My uncle drove in that night to find the coachman with nine of the neighbors' cats laid out on the stable floor, a cause for some profanity. It was not long, however, before my uncle began to miss the martins, swallows, and wrens and to realize

that the sparrows were not as desirable as expected; so he ordered the coachman to reduce them. This he did effectively by digging a trench and filling it with grain, so that he could kill large numbers with a single raking shot. But the martins, swallows, and wrens never returned.

In the early years, "English" sparrows were introduced in this country because they were thought to be prodigious consumers of insects. Instead, it was found that they were prodigious consumers of grain, especially the undigested grain found in horse manure.

By the latter part of the 19th century, House Sparrows had spread across the country, and they were declared to be "a nuisance without a redeeming quality." This gave rise to "The Great Sparrow War," in which the sparrows were shot, trapped, and poisoned. Their nests were sought and destroyed. Rewards were offered. But the war failed. By the early part of the 20th century, the House Sparrow was deemed to be the most abundant bird in the country. It was the coming of the automobile which finally caused their numbers to decline, because their principal source of grain -- horse manure -- disappeared from the streets.

A male House Sparrow is readily recognized, by his gray head, chestnut striping on the head and back, and black chin and throat. Females are a little tougher, and it is surprising how many "rare bird" reports turn out to be female House Sparrows. She is indeed a "little brown bird," but there are a few helpful clues, such as the stout, short bill, the unstreaked dingy gray breast, and buffy eyebrow.

# Appendix A - DEFINITIONS, NAMES, and ABBREVIATIONS

**ABA** - American Birding Association

**accidental** - A bird outside its normal range that has turned up only a few times, and is not expected to reoccur.

*Accipiter* - A collective term used for birds in the genus *Accipter,* such as Sharp-shinned Hawk, Cooper's Hawk, and Northern Goshawk.

**albinism** - An absence of pigments in feathers, producing a white color. In **total albinism,** all pigments are absent, including in the iris; in **partial albinism,** only some of the feathers will be white. Compare with **leucistic,** which is a paleness of plumage, rather than the absence of pigment.

**alcid** - Familiar term for a bird in the family *Alcidae,* the murres, guillemots, murrelets, auklets, and puffins.

**allopatric** - Occurs in different breeding regions, generally without overlap, or interbreeding.

**alternate plumage** - For those birds that molt twice a year, this is the plumage worn in breeding season.

**altricial** - Refers to a young bird that is helpless and naked when hatched.

**anterior** - Toward the front. (Compare with **posterior.**)

**AOU** - American Ornithologists' Union.

**arthropods** - Invertebrate animals with jointed limbs and body, such as crustaceans, insects, and spiders.

**assortative mating** - Mating in which individuals select mates of the same species.

**auriculars** - The region around the ears, often outlined in a darker color than the neighboring feathers; also called "ear coverts."

**axillaries** - The feathers in the "armpit."

**backcross** - Mating between a hybrid and one of the parent species.

**baldpate** - A familiar name for the American Wigeon.

**basic plumage** - For those birds that molt twice a year, this is the plumage worn during the winter, and is frequently called the "winter plumage."

**Bendire** - Major Charles E. Bendire (1836-1897). As an officer in the U.S. Army, he was stationed at many locations in the west, and during that time vigorously pursued his ornithological work. He was the original author of *Life Histories of North American Birds,* a work that was later taken up and expanded upon by Arthur Cleveland Bent.

**Bent** - Arthur Cleveland Bent (1865-1954). Author of a remarkable 20-volume series on *Life Histories of North American Birds,* the successor to the work begun by Major Charles Bendire.

**brood parasite** - A bird that lays its eggs in another bird's nest. In some cases, the brood parasite builds no nest of its own, as with cowbirds. In other cases, it sometimes may lay its eggs in its own nest and sometimes in the nest of another.

***Buteo*** - A collective term used for the birds in the genus *Buteo,* such as Red-tailed Hawk, Rough-legged Hawk, and Red-shouldered Hawk.

**buzzard** - The name given to the *Buteos,* especially in Great Britain, often applied mistakenly in the U.S. to vultures.

**carpal** - The "wrist" of the wing.

**casual** - Not regularly occurring, but implies more frequent occurrence than "accidental."

**CBC** - Christmas Bird Count.

**cere** - The area of bare skin at the base of the upper mandible, next to the forehead.

**chaparral** - Dense, shrubby, evergreen thickets.

**cline** - A geographical variation within a species involving such things as appearance and behavior.

**clutch** - The number of eggs laid at one nesting. A bird may lay more than one clutch in a breeding season.

**commissure** - The line where the upper and lower mandibles meet when closed. Compare with **gape.**

**conspecific** - Means that the birds under discussion are the same species.

**corvid** - A member of the *Corvidae* (crow family), including jays and magpies.

**coverts** - On the wing, the small feathers covering the flight feathers, divided into "**upperwing coverts,**" and "**underwing coverts.**" The upperwing coverts are typically divided into the "**lesser**" coverts, which are in the area of the "shoulder," the "**median**" coverts, and the "**greater**" coverts, which cover the primaries and secondaries. In the tail, the coverts are divided into "**uppertail coverts,**" and "**undertail coverts.**"

**crepuscular** - relating to twilight conditions.

**crissum** - The area under the base of the tail surrounding the vent. Also called the **undertail coverts.**

**cryptic** - Concealing, or obscure.

**culmen** - The upper surface of the upper mandible.

**cygnet** - A young swan.

**dabblers** - Ducks who feed by tipping up in shallow water, such as Mallards and pintails. (Compare with **divers**.)

**decurved** - Bent downward, as in the bill of a Whimbrel. (*See* **recurved**.)

**diagnostic** - A distinguishing characteristic.

**dihedral** - The angle formed by the wings when held in a glide. A strong dihedral would be when the wing is 15 degrees or so above the horizontal, while a slight dihedral would be 5 degrees or so.

**distal** - Farther away. (Compare with **proximal**.)

**divers** - Ducks who get their food by diving in deeper water, such as Canvasbacks and scaups. (Compare with **dabblers**.)

**dorsal** - Referring to the back. (Compare with **ventral**.)

**drumming** - The sound made by a grouse or a woodpecker to attract a mate or establish a territory.

**eclipse plumage** - A drab plumage that is acquired by most male ducks after the breeding season, which causes them to resemble the females.

**ecotone** - A zone where two types of habitat come together.

**emergent vegetation** - Vegetation that has its roots under water, but has green growth extending above the surface.

**empid** - Familiar term for the *Empidonax* flycatchers.

**exotic** - Not native; foreign.

**extinct** - Applied to a species that no longer exists.

**extirpated** - Applied to a species that has been eliminated in a certain region.

**fecal sac** - A small sac with fecal material voided by young birds, and which is generally carried away from the nest by the parents.

**flammulated** - Reddish; flame-colored.

**fledgling** - A young bird that has left the nest, but still needs to be looked after by the parents.

**flyway** - A major route used for migration, usually applicable to waterfowl.

**fringillid** - Familiar term for the birds in the family *Fringillidae,* including the finches, Pine Grosbeak, Evening Grosbeak, crossbills, siskins, redpolls, and goldfinches.

**gallinaceous** - Term for members of the family *Phasianidae,* such as the grouse, Wild Turkey, and quail.

**gander** - Adult male goose.

**gape** - The space between the mandibles when the mouth is open.

**genus** - The group name given to a closely related set of birds. (See Page 40, **Scientific names.**

**gonys** - The lower surface of the lower mandible.

**gorget** - The colorful chin and throat, as in a hummingbird.

**gosling** - A young goose.

**Grinnell** - Joseph Grinnell (1877-1939). Director of the Museum of Vertebrate Zoology, University of California. Distinguished ornithologist, especially on California birds.

**grinning line** - The dark line along the lower mandible that makes it look like the bird is grinning, as in the Snow Goose.

**gular** - The patch of throat just below the chin. In a pelican, this becomes the **gular pouch.**

**hovering** - Remaining in place in the air by flapping the wings, as opposed to "kiting," which is remaining in place in the air on motionless wings, supported by the wind.

**icterid** - A familiar term for members of the family *Icteridae,* including the blackbirds, meadowlarks, grackles, orioles, and cowbirds.

**imm.** - Abbreviation for **immature.**

**immature** - A word, often used as a noun, applying to any bird that has not yet achieved adult plumage. Not the same thing as **juvenile,** which applies to a bird that is in the first plumage acquired in the nest, referred to as **juvenal plumage.**

**irruption** - A temporary movement of birds into an area where they are not ordinarily common, sometimes also referred to as an **invasion**. (Note the difference between "irrupt," in which birds come *in* to areas where they are not normally present in large numbers, and "erupt," in which birds go *out* of their normal areas in large numbers.)

**juvenal plumage** - The first plumage acquired after a bird loses its downy feathers, and often held only for a brief time. "Juvenal" is an adjective, and "**juvenile**" is a noun.

**juvenile** - A bird in **juvenal** plumage.

**kiting** - Remaining in place in the air on motionless wings, supported by the wind, as opposed to "**hovering**," which is remaining in place in the air by flapping the wings.

**lek** - A piece of ground where male grouse gather in breeding season to display for females.

**leucistic** - applied to a bird with unusually pale plumage. Not the same thing as partial albinism. (*See* **albinism**.)

**lore** - The small area on the face, between the eye and the base of the bill.

**malar stripe** - A dark stripe on the cheek, leading from the base of the bill, bounded above by the auriculars, and below, by the chin and throat.

**mandible** - In general usage, this term means either the upper or the lower half of a bird's bill. Some say that only the lower half is properly called the "mandible," and that the upper half is the "maxilla."

**mantle** - The back and upper wings.

**mast** - Acorns and other nuts, after they have fallen to the ground.

**melanism** - A condition of unusual amounts of dark pigmentation in the feathers, as in a dark morph. (Contrast with **albinism**. *See*, also, **morph** and **phase**.)

**molt** - The replacement of old, worn feathers with new ones. The process of molting can be complex and variable between different species.

**morph** - Different color forms of a species, as in "light morph" and "dark morph." Replaces the older term, **phase**.

**nail** - A horny tip on the upper mandible.

**nearctic** - North America north of tropical Mexico.

**neotropics** - Tropical Mexico, Central America, the Caribbean, and South America.

**NM** - National Monument.

**NP** - National Park.

**NWR** - National Wildlife Refuge

**OBOL** - Oregon Birders On Line

**OBRC** - Oregon Bird Records Committee

**OFO** - Oregon Field Ornithologists

**olivaceous** - Greenish brown.

**ouzel**, or **water ouzel** - Old name for American Dipper.

**palearctic** - Europe, Asia, and Africa north of the Sahara.

**parulid** - A familiar term for members of the family *Parulidae*, the wood-warblers.

**passerine** - A member of the order *Passeriformes*, which includes all the species from the flycatchers to the House Sparrow, sometimes referred to as the **perching birds.**

**patagial marks** - The marks on the **patagium,** the leading edge of the wing between the "wrist" and the body.

**peep** - An informal name for a small sandpiper.

**pelagic** - The deep waters of the ocean.

**perching birds** - The **passerines.**

**phase** - A term formerly applied to different color forms of a species, now replaced by **morph.** The term "phase" implies a temporary, perhaps seasonal condition, whereas "morph" is applied to a permanent condition.

**philopatry** - A condition wherein birds tend to return to breed in the area where they were hatched, or return to the same area year after year.

**picids** - A familiar name for members of the family *Picidae*, the woodpeckers.

**pileated** - Crested.

**piscivorous** - Fish-eating.

**pishing** - Also called "spishing." A *shhhhh* sound made by the lips to attract birds. Sometimes it works; sometimes it doesn't.

**polyandry** - A situation where a female mates with two or more males during the breeding season.

**polygamy** - Having more than one mate at the same time. Includes both *polyandry* (female with more than one mate) and *polygyny* (male with more than one mate).

**polygyny** - A situation where a male mates with two or more females during the breeding season.

**posterior** - Toward the rear. (Compare with **anterior**.)

**precocial** - Refers to a young bird that is mobile soon after hatching.

**primaries** - The large flight feathers on the outer portion of the wing.

**primary projection** - On the folded wing of a bird, the distance from the tip of the longest primary, to the tips of the longest **tertials.**

**proximal** - Closer in. (Compare with **distal**).

**race** - subspecies.

**raptor** - A bird of prey, usually meaning the hawks, but sometimes including the owls.

**rare** - Present on a regular basis but difficult to see, either because of low numbers, or secretive behavior.

**rectrix** (plural: **rectrices**) - One of the large flight feathers in the tail.

**recurved** - curved upward, as in the bill of a godwit. (*See* **decurved**.)

**reeve** - Female Ruff.

**remiges** - The flight feathers of the wing. Includes the **primaries** and **secondaries.**

**resident** - A nonmigratory bird. Same as **sedentary.**

**Ridgway** - Robert Ridgway (1850-1929). Distinguished ornithologist, and Curator of Birds for the United States National Museum from 1880 to 1929.
**riparian** - The zone, usually with trees and bushes, next to a stream or river.
**rookery** - A nest colony, such as those built by Great Blue Herons.
**sage hen** - An old name for Sage Grouse.
**sawbill** - An old name for the mergansers.
**scapulars** - The feathers between the back and the upperwing coverts.
**secondaries** - The flight feathers on the inner portion of the wing.
**sedentary** - Tends to remain in a certain area. Same as **resident.**
**semipalmated** - Feet with small webs between the toes, as opposed to the fully webbed feet of the ducks.
**Seton** - Ernest Thompson Seton (1860-1946). Seton was one of the foremost naturalists of the 19th and 20th centuries. His serious works consisted of *Mammals of Manitoba* (1886), *Birds of Manitoba* (1891), and *Lives of North American Game Mammals* (1926). His popular works, which were best-sellers in their time, included *Wild Animals I Have Known* (1898), *The Biography of a Grizzly* (1900), and *Two Little Savages* (1911). He wrote the first handbook for the Boy Scouts of America, and many people look upon him as the founder of the American Boy Scouts. He was the originator of the method for identifying birds from a distance by employing certain key field marks, which was later expanded by Roger Tory Peterson in his popular field guides.
**shorebirds** - Generally used to mean plovers, sandpipers, and their relatives. See also, **waders.**
**songbird** - Generally, includes all the passerines, which means that a crow is a "songbird." In some cases, people may use the term to apply only to those passerines who actually sing.
**speckle-belly** - A familiar name for Greater White-fronted Goose.
**SP** - State Park.
**sp.** - Abbreviation for species. When written after a name, as in "gull sp.?", it means that the bird can be identified as a gull, but the exact species is uncertain. Many birders will pronounce the foregoing as "gull, *spuh.*"
**speculum** - A brightly colored patch on the secondaries.
**spoonbill** - A familiar name for the Northern Shoveler, not to be confused with a bird of the Gulf Coast called Roseate Spoonbill, which resembles a flamingo.
**sprig** - A familiar name for the Northern Pintail.
**subspecies** - A subset of a species inhabiting a certain area that shows distinctive characteristics, and is capable of interbreeding with members of other subsets of that species.
**stiff-tail** - A familiar name for the Ruddy Duck.
**stint** - A collective term for small sandpipers, used in Great Britain.

**supercilium** - A contrasting line, usually paler than the surrounding feathers, above the eye, sometimes called the "eyebrow." Also known as **superciliary line.**

**superspecies** - A group of two or more similar species, but not enough alike to be classified as subspecies.

**supraloral** - Above the **lores.**

**sympatric** - Species occurring in the same region, but do not interbreed.

**syrinx** - The vocal organ of a bird.

**taiga** - The region south of the tundra but north of the temperate zone.

**tarsus** - The portion of the leg, usually bare, from the toes to the next joint above.

**tertials** - The innermost secondaries, next to the body. Usually, these are short, but in some birds, such as shorebirds, may be long.

**troupials** - The blackbirds and orioles.

**undertail coverts** - *See* **crissum.**

**vagrant** - A bird outside its normal range that has occurred a few times, but might occur again.

**ventral** - The underparts. (Compare with **dorsal**.)

**vermiculate** - Marked with wriggly fine lines.

**WA** - Wildlife Area.

**waders** - Generally used for long-legged water-oriented birds such as egrets, herons, ibises, and storks. In Europe, the term "waders" also includes the **shorebirds.**

**waterfowl** - Collective term for ducks, swans, and geese.

**whiskey-jack** - Old name for Gray Jay.

**wing coverts** - See **coverts.**

## Appendix B - ORGANIZATIONS

**ABA -** American Birding Association
P.O. Box 6599
Colorado Springs, CO 80934-6599
Phone: (800) 850-2473        Web: www.americanbirding.org

**AOU -** American Orthithologists' Union
Suite 402
1313 Dolley Madison Blvd.
McLean, VA 22101        Web: www.aou.org

**OFO -** Oregon Field Ornithologists
P.O. Box 10373
Eugene, OR 97440        Web: www.oregonbirds.org

National Audubon Society
700 Broadway
New York, NY 10003
Phone: (212) 979-3000        Web: www.audubon.org

Klamath Basin Audubon Society
P.O. Box 354
Klamath Falls, OR 97601
Phone: (541) 883-7671        Web: eaglecon.org/kbas.html

Rogue Valley Audubon Society
P.O. Box 8597
Medford, OR 97504        Web: www.grrtech.com/rvas

Siskiyou Audubon Society
P.O. Box 2223
Grants Pass, OR 97528        Web: www.siskiyouaudubon.org

Klamath Basin National Wildlife Refuges
4009 Hill Rd.
Tulelake, CA 96134
Phone: (530) 667-2231        Web: www.klamathnwr.org

Crater Lake National Park
P.O. Box 7
Crater Lake, OR 97604
Phone: (541) 594-3100        Web: www.nps.gov/crla

Fremont National Forest
1301 South G St.
Lakeview, OR 97630
Phone: (541) 947-2151        Web: www.fs.fed.us/r6/fremont

Klamath National Forest
1312 Fairlane Rd.
Yreka, CA 96097-9549
Phone: (530) 842-6131                Web: www.r5.fs.fed.us/klamath

Modoc National Forest
800 West 12th St.
Alturas, CA 96101
Phone: (530) 233-5811                Web: www.r5.fs.fed.us/modoc

Rogue River National Forest
333 W. 8th St./P.O. Box 520
Medford, OR 97501-0209
Phone: (541) 858-2200                Web: www.fs.fed.us/r6/rogue

Siskiyou National Forest
333 W. 8th St.
Medford, OR 97503
Phone: (541) 858-2200                Web: www.fs.fed.us/r6/siskiyou

Winema National Forest
2819 Dahlia St.
Klamath Falls, OR 97601
Phone: (541) 883-6714                Web: www.fs.fed.us/r6/winema

Oregon Caves National Monument
19000 Caves Highway
Cave Junction, OR 97523
Phone: (541) 592-2100                Web: www.nps.gov/orca

Cascade-Siskiyou National Monument
3040 Biddle Road
Medford, OR 97504
Phone: (541) 618-2200                Web: www.or.blm.gov/csnm

Bureau of Land Management
Medford District
3040 Biddle Road
Medford, OR 97504
Phone: (541) 618-2200                Web: www.or.blm.gov/Medford

Bureau of Land Management
Klamath Falls Resource Area
2795 Anderson Ave., Bldg. #25
Klamath Falls, OR 97603
Phone: (541) 883-6916                Web: www.or.blm.gov/Lakeview/kfra

# Appendix C - REFERENCES

Adamus, P.R., et al. 2001. *Oregon Breeding Bird Atlas.* Oregon Field Ornithologists, Eugene, OR. (CD-ROM)

American Ornithologists' Union. 1998. *Check-list of North American Birds* (7th ed.). American Ornithologists' Union, Lawrence, Kans.

American Ornithologists' Union. 2000. "Forty-second supplement to the American Ornithologists' Union Check-list of North American Birds." *The Auk,* vol. 117, no. 3, p. 547.

Beedy, Edward C., and Hamilton, Willliam J. 1996. *Tricolored Blackbird Status Update and Management Guidelines.* U.S. Fish and Wildlife Service, Portland, OR.

Bent, Arthur Cleveland. 1919. *Life Histories of North American Diving Birds.* Smithsonian Institution United States National Museum.

Bent, Arthur Cleveland. 1921. *Life Histories of North American Gulls and Terns.* Smithsonian Institution United States National Museum.

Bent, Arthur Cleveland. 1922. *Life Histories of North American Petrels and Pelicans and Their Allies.* Smithsonian Institution United States National Museum.

Bent, Arthur Cleveland. 1923. *Life Histories of North American Wild Fowl.* Smithsonian Institution United States National Museum.

Bent, Arthur Cleveland. 1926. *Life Histories of North American Marsh Birds.* Smithsonian Institution United States National Museum.

Bent, Arthur Cleveland. 1927. *Life Histories of North American Shore Birds, Part One.* Smithsonian Institution United States National Museum.

Bent, Arthur Cleveland. 1929. *Life Histories of North American Shore Birds, Part Two.* Smithsonian Institution United States National Museum.

Bent, Arthur Cleveland. 1932. *Life Histories of North American Gallinaceous Birds.* Smithsonian Institution United States National Museum.

Bent, Arthur Cleveland. 1937. *Life Histories of North American Birds of Prey, Part One.* Smithsonian Institution United States National Museum.

Bent, Arthur Cleveland. 1938. *Life Histories of North American Birds of Prey, Part Two.* Smithsonian Institution United States National Museum.

Bent, Arthur Cleveland. 1939. *Life Histories of North American Woodpeckers.* Smithsonian Institution United States National Museum.

Bent, Arthur Cleveland. 1940. *Life Histories of North American Cuckoos, Goatsuckers, Hummingbirds, and their Allies.* Smithsonian Institution United States National Museum.

Bent, Arthur Cleveland. 1942. *Life Histories of North American Flycatchers, Larks, Swallows, and their Allies.* Smithsonian Institution United States National Museum.

Bent, Arthur Cleveland. 1946. *Life Histories of North American Jays, Crows, and Titmice.* Smithsonian Institution United States National Museum.

Bent, Arthur Cleveland. 1949. *Life Histories of North American Thrushes, Kinglets, and their Allies.* Smithsonian Institution United States National Museum.

Bent, Arthur Cleveland. 1950. *Life Histories of North American Wagtails, Shrikes, Vireos, and their Allies.* Smithsonian Institution United States National Museum.

Bent, Arthur Cleveland. 1958. *Life Histories of North American Blackbirds, Orioles, Tanagers, and Allies.* Smithsonian Institution United States National Museum.

Bent, Arthur Cleveland. 1963. *Life Histories of North American Wood Warblers, Part I.* Smithsonian Institution United States National Museum.

Bent, Arthur Cleveland. 1963. *Life Histories of North American Wood Warblers, Part II.* Smithsonian Institution United States National Museum.

Choate, Ernest A. 1985. *The Dictionary of American Bird Names.* (Rev. by Raymond A. Paynter, Jr.) The Harvard Common Press, Boston, MA.

Cicero, Carla. 1996. *Sibling Species of Titmice in the* Parus inornatus *Complex (Aves: Paridae),* University of California Publications in Zoology, vol. 128, University of California Press, Berkeley, CA.

Clark, Richard J. 1975. *A Field Study of the Short-eared Owl* Asio flammeus (Pontoppidan) *in North America.* Nov. 1975, No. 46, The Wildlife Society.

Clark, William S., and Wheeler, Brian K. (2nd ed.). 2001. *A Field Guide to Hawks, North America.* Houghton Mifflin, New York, NY.

Claypole, Bob. 1996. *Birds of the Klamath River California, Irongate Dam to Weitchpec* (checklist). The State of California - The Resources Agency - Department of Fish and Game, Sacramento, CA.

Cox, Randall T. *Birder's Dictionary.* 1996. Falcon Press Publishing, Helena, MT.

Dawson, William Leon. 1923. *The Birds of California.* South Moulton Co., San Diego, CA

Debenedictis, Paul A. 1999. "Complex Titmice." *Birding,* vol. 29, no. 3, pp. 238-241.

Dickson, James G. (ed.). 1992. *The Wild Turkey: Biology and Management.* Stackpole Books, Harrisburg, PA.

Dunn, Jon L. (Chief Consultant). 1999. *National Geographic - Field Guide to the Birds of North America* (Third Edition). National Geographic Society, Washington, D.C.

Dunn, Jon L., and Garrett, Kimball L. 1997. *A Field Guide to Warblers of North America.* Houghton Mifflin Co., New York, NY.

Elphick, Chris, Dunning, John B., Jr., and Sibley, David Allen, (eds.). 2001. *National Audubon Society - The Sibley Guide to Bird Life and Behavior.* Alfred A. Knopf, New York.

Ehrlich, Paul R., Dobin, Davis S., and Wheye, Darryl. 1988. *The Birder's Handbook.* Simon and Schuster, New York, NY.

Franklin, Jerry F., and Dyrness, C.T. 1988. *Natural Vegetation of Oregon and Washington.* Oregon State University Press, Corvallis, OR.

Gilligan, Jeff, et al. (eds). 1994. *Birds of Oregon - Status and Distribution.* Cinclus Publications, McMinnville, OR.

Grant, P.J. 1997. *Gulls, A Guide to Identification* (Second Edition). Academic Press, San Diego, CA.

Green, Gregory A., and Anthony, Robert G. 1989. "Nesting success and habitat relationships of Burrowing Owls in the Columbia Basin, Oregon." *The Condor,* vol. 91, pp. 347-354.

Harris, Stanley W. 1996. *Northwestern California Birds.* Humboldt State University Press, Arcata, CA.

Henny, Charles J., and Herron, Gary B. 1989. "DDE, Selenium, Mercury, and White-faced Ibis Reproduction at Carson Lake, Nevada." *J. Wildlife Management,* vol. 53, no. 4, pp. 1032-1045.

Janes, Stewart, et al. 2001. *Birds of Jackson County, Oregon* (checklist). Rogue Valley Audubon Society, Medford, OR.

Janes, S.W., Swisher, O.D., and Cross, S.P. 1996. *Birds of Southern Oregon* (checklist). Southern Oregon University, Ashland, OR.

Johnson, Daniel M., et al. 1985. *Atlas of Oregon Lakes.* Oregon State University Press, Corvallis, OR.

Jonsson, Lars. 1993. *Birds of Europe, with North Africa and the Middle East.* Princeton University Press, Princeton, NJ.

Kemper, John. 1999. *Birding Northern California.* Falcon Press Publishing, Helena, MT.

Kemper, John. 1996. *Discovering Yolo County Wildlife.* Yolo Audubon Society and Yolo Basin Foundation, Davis, CA.

Lane, Daniel and Jaramillo, Alvaro. "Identification of *Hylochichla/Catharus* Thrushes." *Birding,* April 2000, pp. 120-135, and June 2000, pp. 242-254.)

Lanner, Ronald M. 1996. *Made for Each Other: A Symbiosis of Birds and Pines.* Oxford University Press, New York, NY.

Oregon Bird Records Committee. July 2001. *Official Checklist of Oregon Birds.* Oregon Field Ornithologists, Eugene, OR.

Oregon Bird Records Committee. May 2001. *The Records of the Oregon Bird Records Committee.* Oregon Field Ornithologists, Eugene, OR.

*The Oregon Birds Forum,* found at following web location: osu.orst.edu/pubs/birds/bogr/accounts.htm

Page, G.W., et al. 1995. *Snowy Plover.* The Birds of North America, No. 154. The Academy of Natural Sciences, Philadelphia, PA, and The American Ornithologists' Union, Washington, DC.

Paulson, Dennis. 1993. *Shorebirds of the Pacific Northwest.* UBC Press, Vancouver, BC.

Pyle, Peter. 1997. *Identification Guide to North American Birds, Part I.* Slate Creek Press, Bolinas, CA.

Reyes, Chris. 1994. *The Table Rocks of Jackson County: Islands in the Sky.* Last Minute Publications, Ashland, OR.

Rising, James D. 1996. *A Guide to the Identification and Natural History of the Sparrows of the United States and Canada.* Academic Press, San Diego, CA.

Roberson, Don. 1985. *Monterey Birds.* Monterey Peninsula Audubon Society, Carmel, CA.

Roberson, Don. 1980. *Rare Birds of the West Coast.* Woodcock Publications, Pacific Grove, CA.

Roberson, Don. 2000. *Titmice at Lava Beds N.M., Siskiyou Co., California.* Web page at http://monterey bay.com/creagrus/titmouse_id.html

Root, Terry. 1988. *Atlas of Wintering North American Birds -- An Analysis of Christmas Bird Count Data.* The University of Chicago Press, Chicago IL.

Ryser, Fred A., Jr. 1985. *Birds of the Great Basin: A Natural History.* University of Nevada Press, Reno, NV.

Schaffer, Jeffrey P. 1983. *Crater Lake National Park and Vicinity.* Wilderness Press, Berkeley, CA.

Shuford, Dave. 1996. "Ibis Roam the West." *Point Reyes Bird Observatory Newsletter,* Summer 1996, p. 9.

Sibley, David Allen. 2000. *National Audubon Society - The Sibley Guide to Birds.* Alfred A. Knopf, New York.

Summers, Steven D. 1993. *A Birder's Guide to the Klamath Basin.* Klamath Basin Audubon Society, Klamath Falls, OR.

Teale, Edwin Way. 1954. *The Wilderness World of John Muir.* Houghton Mifflin Co., Boston, MA.

Terres, John K. 1991. *The Audubon Society Encyclopedia of North American Birds.* Wings Books, New York.

Terres, John K. 1996. "Crow Talk." *Birder's World.* August 1996, pp. 30-34.

Thomsen, Lise. 1971. "Behavior and ecology of Burrowing Owls on the Oakland Municipal Airport." *The Condor,* vol. 73, pp. 177-192.

Tyler, Hamilton A., and Phillips, Don. 1978. *Owls by Day and Night.* Naturegraph Publishers, Happy Camp, CA.

U.S. Fish and Wildlife Service. 1995. *Wildlife of the Klamath Basin National Wildlife Refuges.* U.S. Department of the Interior, Fish and Wildlife Service, Washington, D.C.

U.S. Fish and Wildlife Service. 1999. *Klamath Basin National Wildlife Refuges - California/Oregon.* U.S. Department of the Interior, Fish and Wildlife Service, Washington, D.C.

Walton, R.K., and Lawson, R.W. 1989. *Eastern/Central Birding by Ear.* Houghton Mifflin Co., Boston, MA.

Walton, R.K., and Lawson, R.W. 1990. *Western Birding by Ear.* Houghton Mifflin Co., Boston, MA.

Walton, R.K., and Lawson, R.W. 1994. *Eastern/Central More Birding by Ear.* Houghton Mifflin Co., Boston, MA.

*Webster's Ninth New Collegiate Dictionary.* 1984. Meriam-Webster Inc., Springfield, MA.

Wheeler, Brian K., and Clark, William S. 1995. *A Phtographic Guide to North American Raptors.* Academic Press, San Diego, CA.

Zeiner, David C., et al. 1990. *California's Wildlife, Volume II: Birds.* The State of California - The Resources Agency - Department of Fish and Game, Sacramento, CA.

Zimmer, Kevin J. 2000. *Birding in the American West.* Cornell University Press, Ithaca, N.Y.

Zimmerman, Paul. 1998. "Snowbirds? Phainopeplas descend on the Southwest en mass each winter -- not to escape blustery weather but to feed their craving for mistletoe berries," *Living Bird,* Summer 1998. pp. 30-35.

# INDEX

Names of birds and page numbers shown in **bold face** refer to accounts of bird species that have occurred in Southern Oregon.

Quotation marks are used for informal birds' names, former names, color morphs, or subspecies.

## A
Agate Lake 29
Aleutian Goose Festival 64
American Birding Association 5
Ashland Pond 28
**Avocet, American 118, Pl. V**

## B
Bald Eagle Conference 87
Bear Creek Greenway 28
**Bittern, American 54**
  **Least 55**
"Blackbird, Bicolored" 286
  **Brewer's 291, Pl. XII**
  **Red-winged 285**
  **Rusty 291**
  **Tricolored 59, 286**
  **Yellow-headed 289, Pl. XII**
"bluebill" 77
**Bluebird, Mountain 230, Pl. X**
  **Western 230**
**Bobolink 283**
Bolan Lake 24
Bonanza 36
Boyle Reservoir 35
**Brant 64**
  "Atlantic" 65
  " Black" 65
**Bufflehead 78**
**Bunting, Indigo 282**
  **Lark 270**
  **Lazuli 282**
  **Snow 280**
**Bushtit 217**
Butte Valley 38
"buzzard" 62

## C
**Canvasback 75**
Cantrall-Buckley County Park 30
Cascade-Sisikiyou NM 30
**Catbird, Gray 237**

Chat, Yellow-breasted 260
Chickadee, Black-capped 215
  **Chestnut-backed 216**
  **Mountain 215**
Christmas Count 13
**Chukar 101**
Clear Lake NWR 37
Cloudcap 30
**Coot, American 110**
Collier Memorial SP 32
Cormorant, Brandt's 53
  **Double-crested 53, Pl. II**
  Pelagic 53
**Cowbird, Brown-headed 293**
**Crane, Sandhill 112, Pl. III**
Crater Lake NP 30
**Creeper, Brown 221**
**Crossbill, Red 299**
  **White-winged 299**
**Crow, American 206**
Crystal Springs Rest Area 33
Cuckoo, European 294
  **Yellow-billed 149**
**Curlew, Long-billed 122, Pl. VI**

## D
Denman WA 26
Devils Garden 38
**Dickcissel 283**
**Dipper, American 227, Pl. VIII**
**Duck, American Black 69**
  **Harlequin 77**
  **Long-tailed 78**
  Masked 83
  **Ring-necked 75, Pl. III**
  **Ruddy 83, Pl. I**
  **Tufted 76**
  **Wood 67, 81, Pl. II**
**Dunlin 128**
**Dove, Mourning 148**
  **Rock 146**
**Dowitcher, Long-billed 130, Pl. VI**
  **Short-billed 130**

322

## E

**Eagle, Bald** 86, Pl. IV
  **Golden** 86
Eagle Ridge Park 34
**Egret, Cattle** 56, Pl. I
  **Great** 56, Pl. I
  **Snowy** 56
Emigrant Lake 28
Ethics, ABA Code of 14

## F

**Falcon, Peregrine** 79, 99
  **Prairie** 99, Pl. IV
Fall Creek Park 38
**Finch, Cassin's** 298, Pl. XII
  " Hepburn's" 297
  **House** 298
  **Purple** 298
Fish Hatchery Park 22
Fish Lake 29
**Flicker, Northern** 181
  "Red-shafted" 181
  "Yellow-shafted" 181
Flycatcher, Alder 186
  **Ash-throated** 191
  **Cordilleran** 189
  **Dusky** 187
  Dusky-capped 191
  **Gray** 188
  **Hammond's** 187
  **Least** 187
  **Olive-sided** 184
  **Pacific-slope** 189
  **Scissor-tailed** 193
  " Traill's" 186
  **Vermilion** 184
  " Western" 189
  **Willow** 185, **186**
  "Wright's" 188
  Yellow-bellied 189
Forest Road 37 29
Fort Klamath 32
Fourmile Lake 33

## G

**Gadwall** 68
**Garganey** 73
**Gnatcatcher, Blue-gray** 230
Godwit Days 123

**Godwit, Hudsonian** 123
  **Marbled** 123
Golden Coyote Wetlands 21
**Goldeneye, Barrow's** 79
  **Common** 79
**Golden-Plover, American** 113
  " Lesser" 114
  **Pacific** 113
**Goldfinch, American** 301
  "Black-backed" 301
  "Green-backed" 301
  **Lawrence's** 301
  **Lesser** 301
"Goose, Aleutian" 64
  "Blue" 63
  "Cackling" 64
  **Canada** 64, Pl. II
  **Emperor** 63
  **Greater White-fronted** 62
  Graylag 62
  **Ross's** 63
  **Snow** 63, Pl. II
  "Tule" 62
**Goshawk, Northern** 89
**Grackle, Common** 292
  **Great-tailed** 292
Grayback Campground 24
**Grebe, Clark's** 50
  **Eared** 48
  **Horned** 48
  **Pied-billed** 47
  **Red-necked** 49
  **Western** 50, Pl. II
Grizzly Creek Campground 29
**Grosbeak, Black-headed** 281, Pl. X
  **Evening** 303, Pl. XII
  **Pine** 298
  **Rose-breasted** 281
**Grouse, Blue** 105, Pl. IV
  **Ruffed** 103
**Gull, Bonaparte's** 137
  **California** 138
  **Common** 138
  **Franklin's** 136
  **Glaucous** 141
  **Glaucous-winged** 141
  **Heermann's** 137
  **Herring** 140
  Iceland 140

Gull (cont.)
**Laughing** 136
**Little** 136
**Mew** 237
**Ring-billed** 138
**Sabine's** 142
**Thayer's** 140
**Western** 141
**Gyrfalcon** 99

# H
habitats 17
Hamaker Mountain 35
**Harrier, Northern** 87
"hawk, chicken" 90
**Hawk, Cooper's** 89, Pl. IV
"Duck" 100
**Ferruginous** 95
"Fish" 84
"Harlan's" 94
"Krider's" 94
"Marsh" 88
"Pigeon" 98
**Red-shouldered** 91
**Red-tailed** 93
**Rough-legged** 96, Pl. IV
**Sharp-shinned** 89
"Sparrow" 97
**Swainson's** 92
Henley 38
Henzel County Park 33
**Heron, Great Blue** 55
**Green** 58
**Little Blue** 58
"Holy Water" 26
Horse Creek Meadow 21
Howard Bay 34
Howard Prairie Lake 29
**Hummingbird, Allen's** 170
**Anna's** 167
Bee 168
**Black-chinned** 166, Pl. VIII
**Broad-tailed** 169
**Calliope** 168
**Costa's** 168
Ruby-throated 165
**Rufous** 170
Hyatt Lake 29

# I
Ibis, Glossy 61
Scarlet 61
White 61
**White-faced** 59
Illinois River Forks SP 24
Indian Mary Park 22
Iron Gate Reservoir 38

# J
Jack Spring 33
**Jaeger, Parasitic** 135
**Long-tailed** 135
**Jay, Blue** 198, **200**
"California" 201
"Canada" 199
"Florida" 201
**Gray** 199
"Oregon" 199
**Pinyon** 203
Scrub (see Scrub-jay)
**Steller's** 200
"Woodhouse's" 202
Juanita Lake 38
**Junco, Dark-eyed** 277, Pl. XI
"Gray-headed" 278
"Pink-sided" 278
"Oregon" 277
"Slate-colored" 277
"White-winged" 278
Yellow-eyed 278

# K
Keno 35
**Kestrel, American** 97
**Killdeer** 116, Pl. V
Kimball SP 32
**Kingbird, Eastern** 192
Tropical 192
**Western** 192, Pl. VIII
**Kingfisher, Belted** 171
**Kinglet, Golden-crowned** 228
**Ruby-crowned** 196, **229**, Pl. IX
King Mountain Rock Garden 21
Kirtland Sewer Ponds 25
Kite, Black-shouldered 85
**White-tailed** 85
**Kittiwake, Black-legged** 142

Klamath Marsh NWR  32
Klamath Refuges Visitor Center  37
Klamath River Canyon  35
**Knot, Red  124**

## L

Lake Euwana  34
Lake of the Woods  33
Lake Selmac  24
Lakeshore Drive  34
Langell Valley  36
**Lark, Horned  208**
Lava Beds NM  37
Link River  34
Lithia Park  28
**Longspur, Chestnut-collared  279**
  Lapland  279
  McCown's  279
  Smith's  279
**Loon, Common  45**
  Pacific  45
  Red-throated  45
  Yellow-billed  46
Lost Creek Lake  26
Lower Klamath NWR  37
Lynn Newbry Park  28

## M

"Magpie, American"  204
  **Black-billed  204**
  Yellow-billed  205
**Mallard  70, Pl. III**
Malone Springs  33
Mares Egg Spring  33
**Martin, Purple  209**
  Sand  212
McGregor Park  26
Meadowlark, Eastern  288
  **Western  242, 288**
Meiss Lake  38
**Merganser, Common  81**
  Hooded  80
  Red-breasted  81, 234
**Merlin  98**
Miller Island  35
Millican Lek  104
Mockingbird, Blue  238
  "Mountain"  238
  **Northern  238**

Moore Park  34
**Moorhen, Common  110**
Mount Ashland  30
"mudhen"  111
**Murrelet, Ancient  145**

## N

**Nighthawk, Common  162**
**Night-Heron, Black-crowned  58, Pl. I**
Nightjar, English  162
**Nutcracker, Clark's  203, Pl. IX**
**Nuthatch, Pygmy  220, Pl. IX**
  Red-breasted  218
  White-breasted  218

## O

Odessa Creek Campground  34
"Oldsquaw"  78
Oregon Bird Records Committee  43
Oregon Caves NM  24
**Oriole, Baltimore  295**
  Bullock's  295
  Hooded  295, Pl. XII
  "Northern"  295
**Osprey  84**
"Ouzel, Water"  227
**Ovenbird  256**
**Owl, Barn  149**
  Barred  157
  Boreal  160
  Burrowing  156
  Flammulated  150
  Great Gray  159, Pl. VII
  Great Horned  152
  Long-eared  152
  Northern Saw-whet  161, Pl. VII
  Short-eared  160
  Snowy  154
  Spotted  157

## P

"partridge"  103
**Parula, Northern  248**
Pearce Riffle Park  22
**Pelican, American White  1, Pl. I**
  Brown  53

Petric Park 33
Petroglyphs Section 37
**Phainopepla 244**
**Phalarope, Red 133**
  Red-necked 133
  Wilson's 133, Pl. V
**Pheasant, Ring-necked 102**
**Phoebe, Black 190**
  Eastern 191
  Say's 191
**Pigeon, Band-tailed 146**
  "Feral" 146
  Passenger 146
**Pintail, Northern 73**
**Pipit, American 241**
  Water 241, 242
**Plover, Black-bellied 113**
  Gray 114
  Kentish 115
  Mountain 117
  **Semipalmated 115, Pl. VI**
  **Snowy 115**
Poe Valley 31
**Poorwill, Common 163**
Provolt 27
**Pygmy-Owl, Northern 155, Pl. VII**

## Q

**Quail, California 106**
  **Mountain 106**

## R

Rail, Black 110
  Clapper 109
  **Virginia 108, Pl. VII**
  **Yellow 108**
**Raven, Common 206**
**Redhead 75, Pl. II**
**Redpoll, Common 301**
**Redstart, American 255**
"reeve" 130
Rivers Edge Park 26
**Robin, American 234, Pl. X**
Rocky Point 33
Rosy-Finch, Black 297
  Brown-capped 297
  "Gray-cheeked" 297
  **Gray-crowned 296, Pl. XII**
Roxy Ann Peak 27
**Ruff 130**

## S

**Sage-Grouse, Greater 104**
  Gunnison 104
  "sage-hen" 104
**Sanderling 124, Pl. V**
**Sandpiper, Baird's 126**
  Buff-breasted 129
  Curlew 128
  Least 124
  Pectoral 127
  Semipalmated 124
  Sharp-tailed 127
  Solitary 120
  Spotted 121, Pl. VI
  Stilt 129
  Upland 122
  Western 124
  White-rumped 126
**Sapsucker, Red-breasted 177**
  **Red-naped 176, Pl. VIII**
  **Williamson's 175**
  Yellow-bellied 176, 177
"sawbill" 82
**Scaup, Greater 76**
  **Lesser 76, Pl. III**
**Scoter, Black 78**
  **Surf 78**
  **White-winged 78**
**Screech-Owl, Western 151, Pl. VII**
Scrub-jay, Island 201
  Florida 201
  **Western 201, Pl. VIII**
Shaffer Lek 104
Sheepy Ridge 37
**Shoveler, Northern 72**
**Shrike, Loggerhead 193**
  Northern 193
**Siskin, Pine 301**
Silver Lake Road 32
Siskiyou Crest 30
**Snipe, Common 132**
**Solitaire, Townsend's 232**
Soda Mountain 30
**Sora 109**
**Sparrow, American Tree 264**
  "Belding's Savannah" 271
  "Bell's" 269
  **Black-chinned 267**
  **Black-throated 268**

326

Sparrow (cont.)
- **Brewer's** 265
- **Chipping** 265
- **Clay-colored** 265
- "English" 304
- **Fox** 272
- **Golden-crowned** 276, Pl. XI
- **Grasshopper** 271
- **Harris's** 275
- **House** 304
- "Ipswich" 271
- "Large-billed Savannah" 271
- **Lark** 268, Pl. XI
- **Lincoln's** 274
- "Red Fox" 272
- **Sage** 269
- **Savannah** 270, Pl. XI
- "Slate-colored Fox" 272
- **Song** 273
- "Sooty Fox" 272
- **Swamp** 274
- "Thick-billed Fox" 272
- "Timberline" 266
- **Vesper** 267
- **White-crowned** 275, Pl. X
- **White-throated** 275, Pl. XI

"speckle-belly" 62
"spoonbill" 72
Sprague River 36
"sprig" 73
**Starling, European** 240
"stiff-tails" 83
**Stilt, Black-necked** 117, Pl. V
Stint, Long-toed 126
  Red-necked 124
Stork, Wood 52, 55
**Storm-Petrel, Leach's** 51
Straits Drain 35
Stukel Mountain 36
**Swallow, Bank** 212, Pl. VIII
- **Barn** 214
- **Cliff** 212
- **Northern Rough-winged** 211
- **Tree** 210
- **Violet-Green** 210

"Swan, Bewick's" 66
- Mute 67
- **Trumpeter** 65, 111
- **Tundra** 65
- "Whistling" 66
- **Whooper** 65

**Swift, Black** 164
- Chimney 164
- Vaux's 164
- **White-throated** 164

## T

Table Rock, Lower 25
  Upper 25
Takilma 23
"Tanager, Louisiana" 262
  **Western** 261
**Tattler, Wandering** 121
**Teal, Baikal** 74
  **Blue-winged** 71, Pl. III
  **Cinnamon** 71, Pl. III
  "Common" 74
  **Green-winged** 74
**Tern, Arctic** 143
  **Black** 145
  **Caspian** 142
  **Common** 143
  **Forster's** 143, Pl. VI
**Thrasher, Brown** 239
  **California** 239
  **Sage** 238
**Thrush, Hermit** 233
  **Swainson's** 233
  **Varied** 234
**Titmouse, Juniper** 216
  **Oak** 216
  "Plain" 216
Tom Pearce Park 22
Topsy Campground 35
Tou Velle SP 25
"Towhee, Brown" 264
  **California** 264
  Canyon 264
  Eastern 234, 263
  **Green-tailed** 262
  **Spotted** 263
  "Rufous-sided" 263
Township Road 35
Trees of Heaven 38
Tule Lake NWR 37
**Turkey, Wild** 105
**Turnstone, Black** 123
  **Ruddy** 123

## U
Upper Klamath Lake 34

## V
Valley of the Rogue SP 25
**Veery 233**
Veterans Memorial Park 35
**Vireo, Bell's 195**
  Blue-headed 195
  **Cassin's 195**
  **Hutton's 196,** 229
  **Plumbeous 195**
  **Red-eyed 198**
  "Solitary" 195
  **Warbling 197**
**Vulture, Turkey 61**

## W
Wagtail, Yellow 242
Warbler, "Audubon's" 250
  **Bay-breasted 254**
  **Black-and-white 252**
  **Black-throated Blue 250**
  **Black-throated Green 253**
  **Black-throated Gray 252**
  Blackpoll 255
  **Canada 260**
  **Chestnut-sided 249**
  "Golden Pileolated" 259
  **Hermit 254**
  **Hooded 259**
  **Lucy's 248**
  **MacGillivray's 257**
  Mourning 257
  "Myrtle" 250
  **Nashville 247, Pl. X**
  "Nuthatch" 252
  **Orange-crowned 246**
  **Prothonotary 256**
  Tennessee 245
  "Tolmie" 257
  **Townsend's 253**
  **Virginia's 247**
  **Wilson's 259**
  **Yellow 248**
  **Yellow-rumped 250, Pl. X**
**Waterthrush, Northern 256**
**Waxwing, Bohemian 243**
  **Cedar 243, Pl. IX**
Westside Road 33

Whetstone Pond 26
**Whimbrel 122**
"whiskey-jack" 199
Whiskey Spring 29
White Horse Park 22
White Lake 37
**Wigeon, American 69, Pl. I**
  **Eurasian 69**
**Willet 120, Pl. VI**
Wocus Bay Road 32
Wolf Creek 23
Wood River Day Use Area 32
Wood River Valley 32
Wood River Wetlands 33
**Woodpecker, Acorn 174**
  **Black-backed** 172, **180**
  **Downy 178**
  **Hairy 178**
  **Lewis's** 172, **173**
  Ladder-backed 178
  **Nuttall's 178**
  **Pileated 183**
  Red-headed 177
  **Three-toed** 172, **178, 180**
  **White-headed 179**
Wood-Pewee, Eastern 185
  **Western 185**
**Wren, Bewick's 223, Pl. IX**
  **Canyon 222**
  **House** 197, **224**
  "Long-billed Marsh" 226
  **Marsh 226**
  **Rock 222**
  Sedge 226
  "Short-billed Marsh" 226
  **Winter 225**
**Wrentit 236**

## Y
**Yellowlegs, Greater 119, Pl. V**
  **Lesser 119**
**Yellowthroat, Common 258**